CATS GALORE

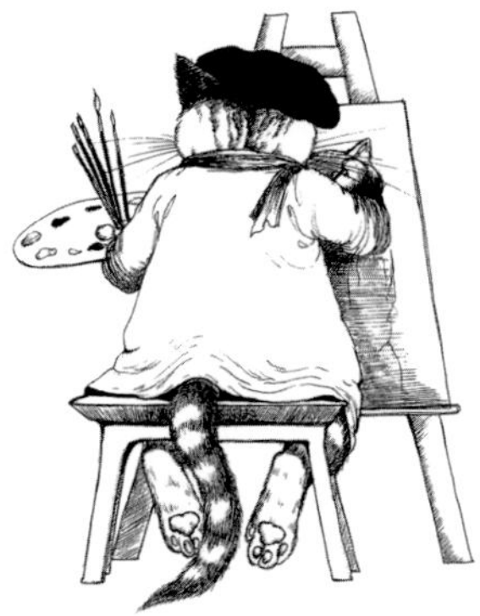

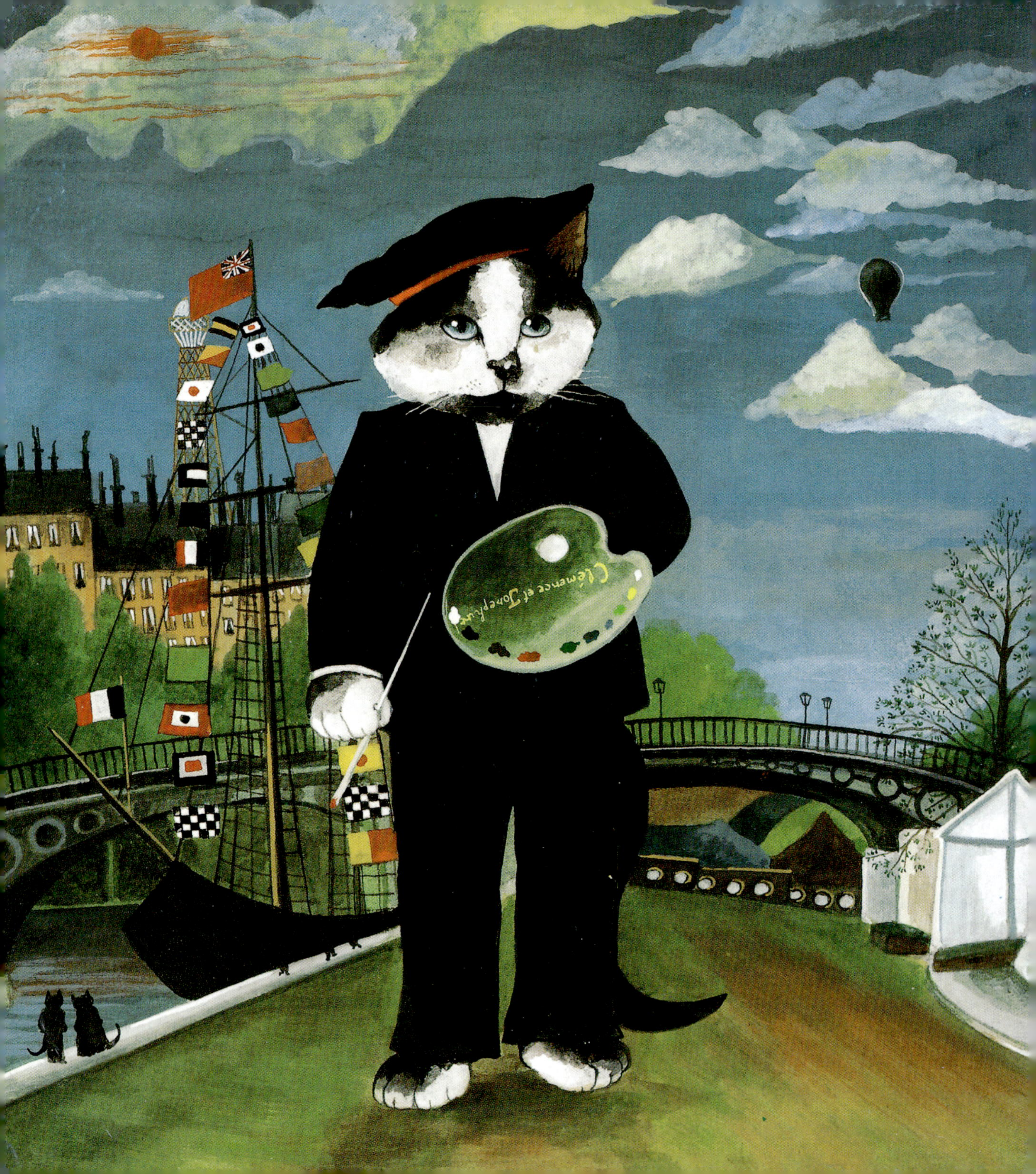
Clémence et Josephine

CATS GALORE

A Compendium of Cultured Cats

SUSAN HERBERT

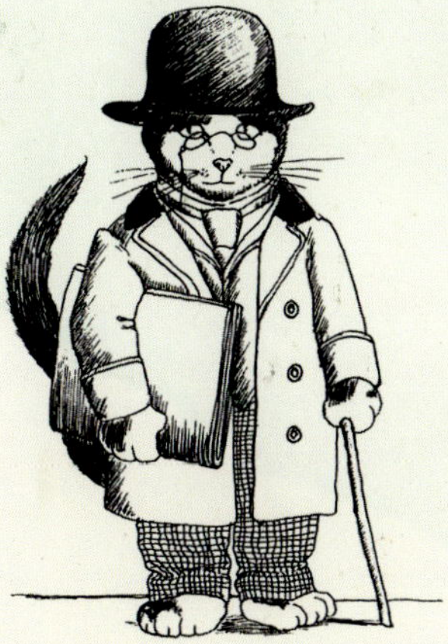

Thames & Hudson

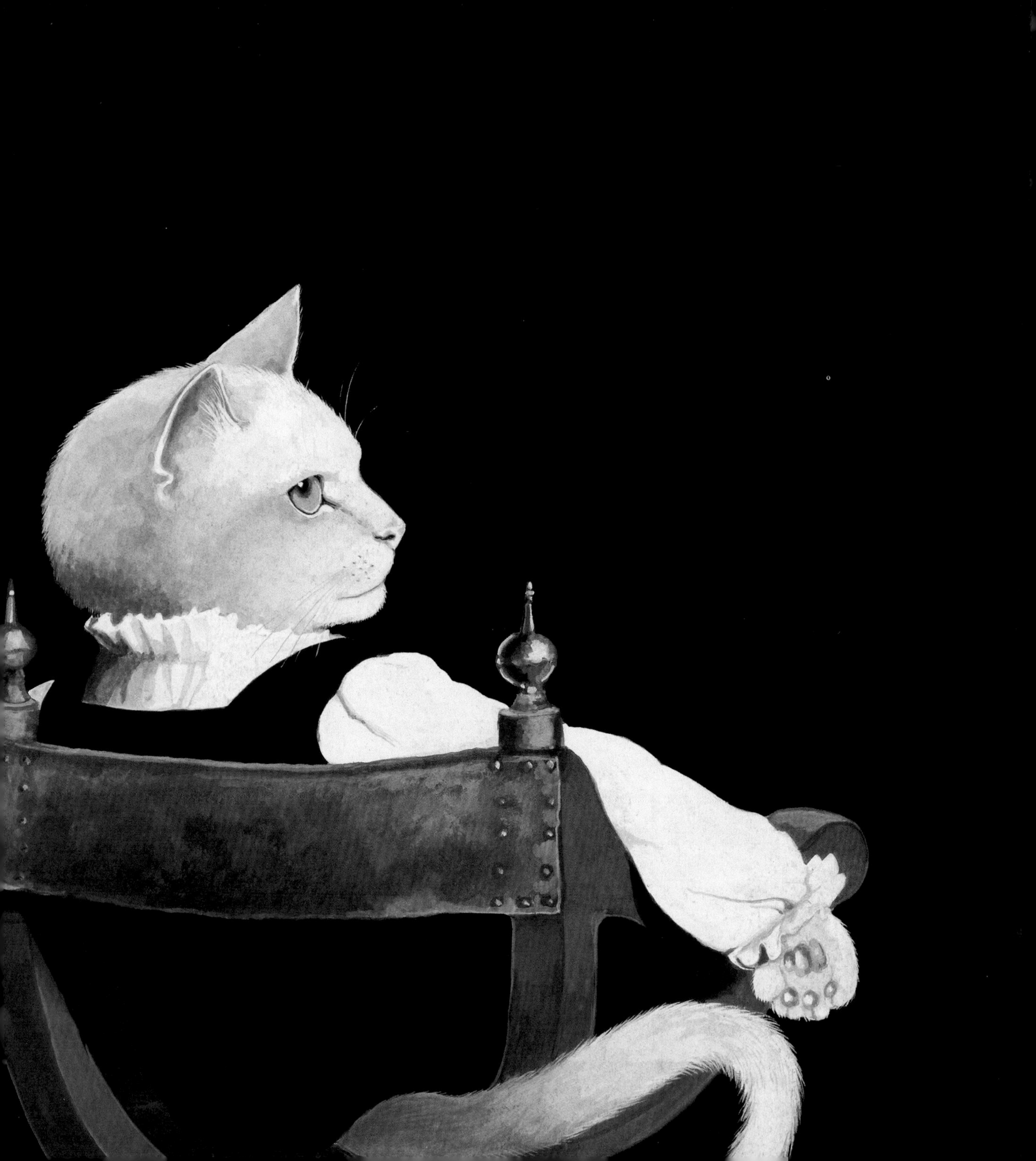

CONTENTS

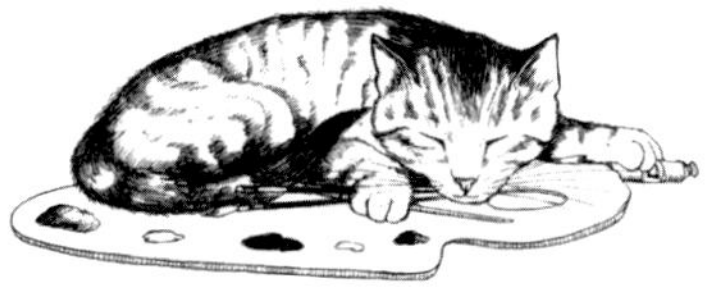

SUSAN HERBERT'S delightful and witty watercolours recreate famous scenes from art, theatre, opera and film with a charming cast of cat characters.

Our first stop will be the world of art, where furry faces and pussycat tails peep out from some of the masterpieces of painting. Cats then take to the stage in Shakespeare's best-loved plays and a selection of lavishly staged operas. Finally we visit Hollywood, where cats are cast in everything from big-budget epics to cult classics, emulating the glamour of the golden age of cinema.

Susan Herbert's feline fantasies have already won over a generation of fervent fans. This compilation of the best of her life's work will surely win them many more.

CATS IN ART

Cover of the Coffin of Tutankhamun

(C. 1340 BC)

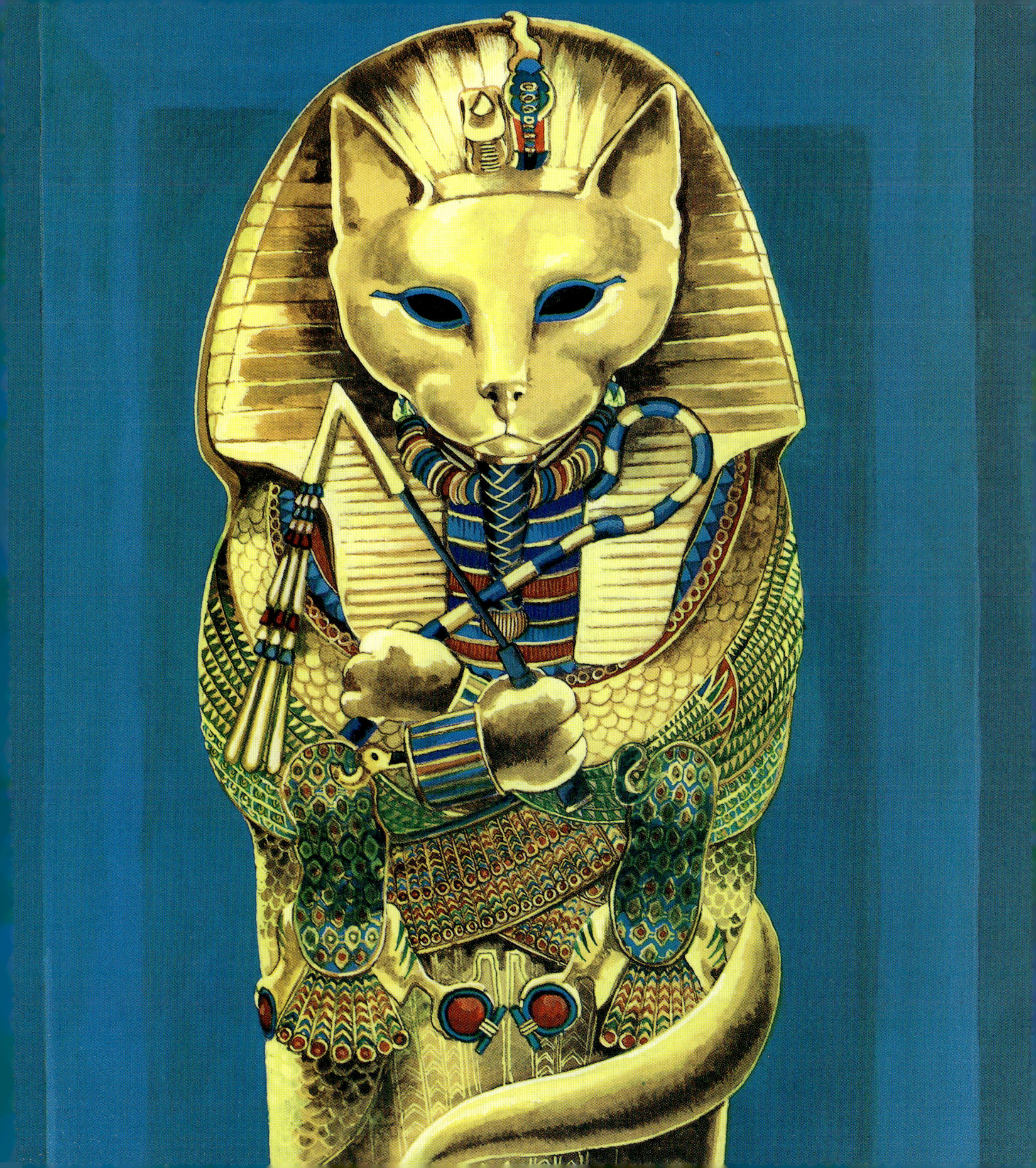

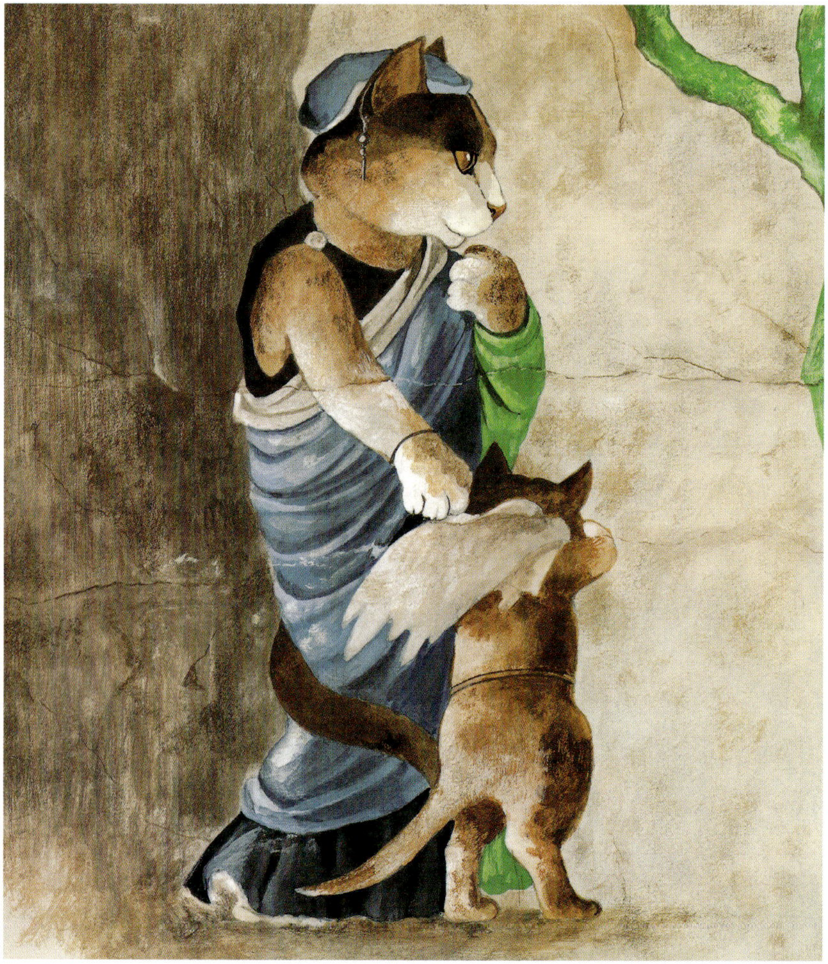

Above ROMAN FRESCO, *Venus Chastising Cupid* (c. 1st century AD)
Opposite EXEKIAS, *Achilles Slays Penthesilea* (c. 540–530 BC)

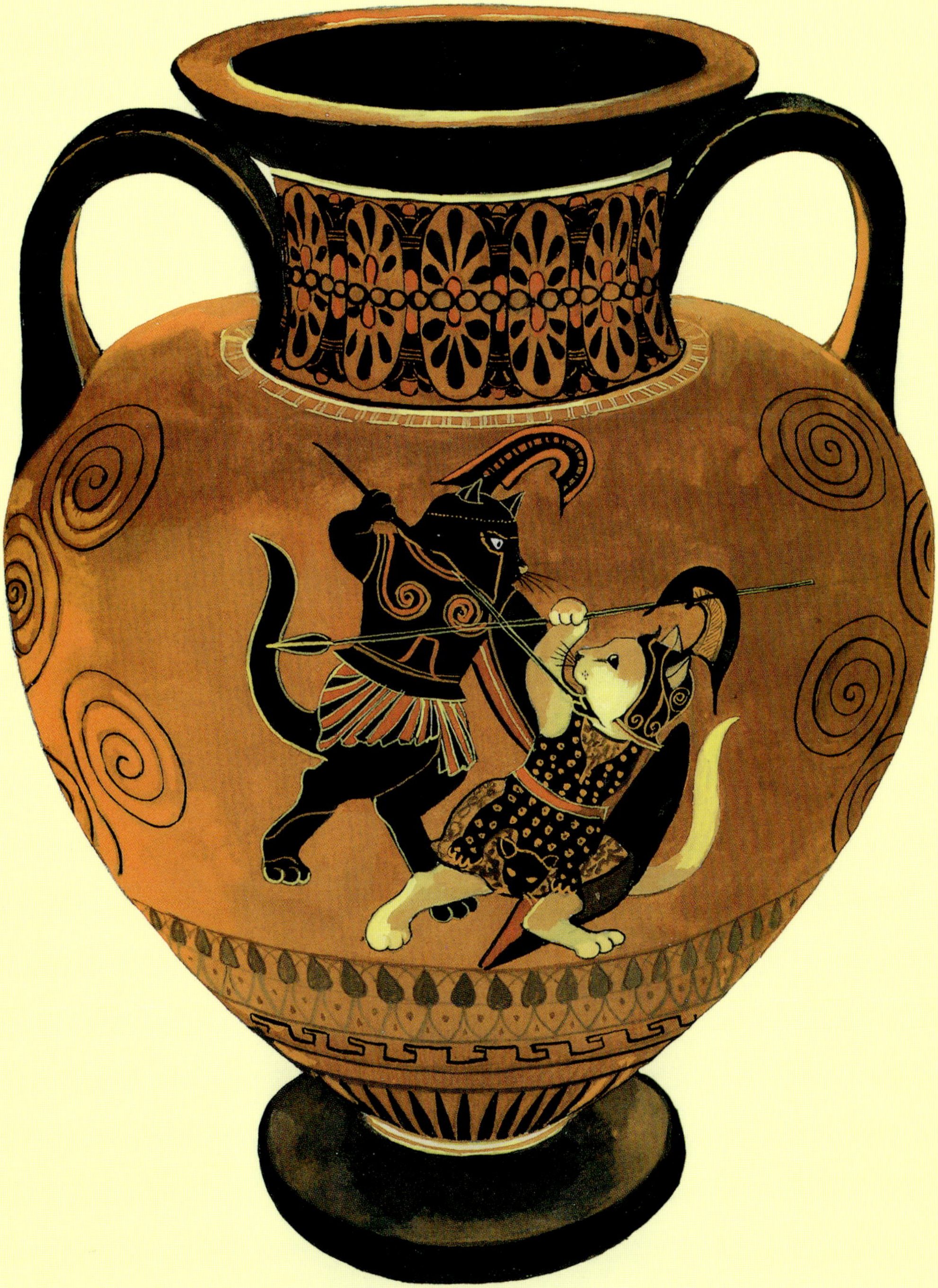

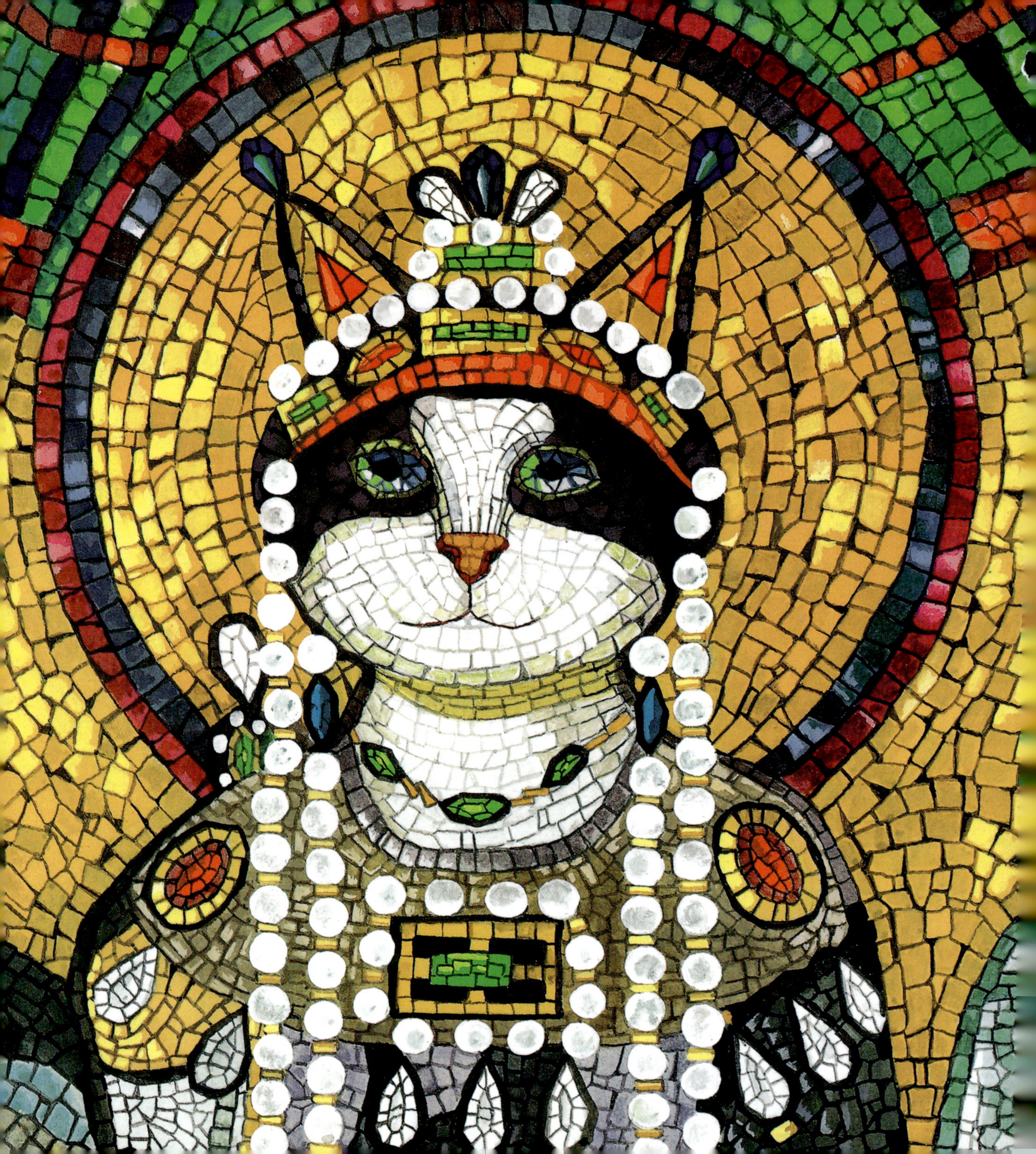

MOSAIC FROM THE CHURCH OF SAN VITALE, RAVENNA

Empress Theodora (6TH CENTURY)

BREVIARY OF QUEEN ISABELLA OF CASTILE

St John on Patmos (c. 1497)

Following pages:

THE HOURS OF PETER II, *Peter II in Prayer* (1455-57)

THE HASTINGS HOURS, *St Catherine of Alexandria* (1475–83)

LES HEURES DE CHARLES D'ANGOULÊME, *Peasants Dancing* (c. 1485)

OVID, LES EPÎTRES ELÉGIAQUES, *Penelope* (1496)

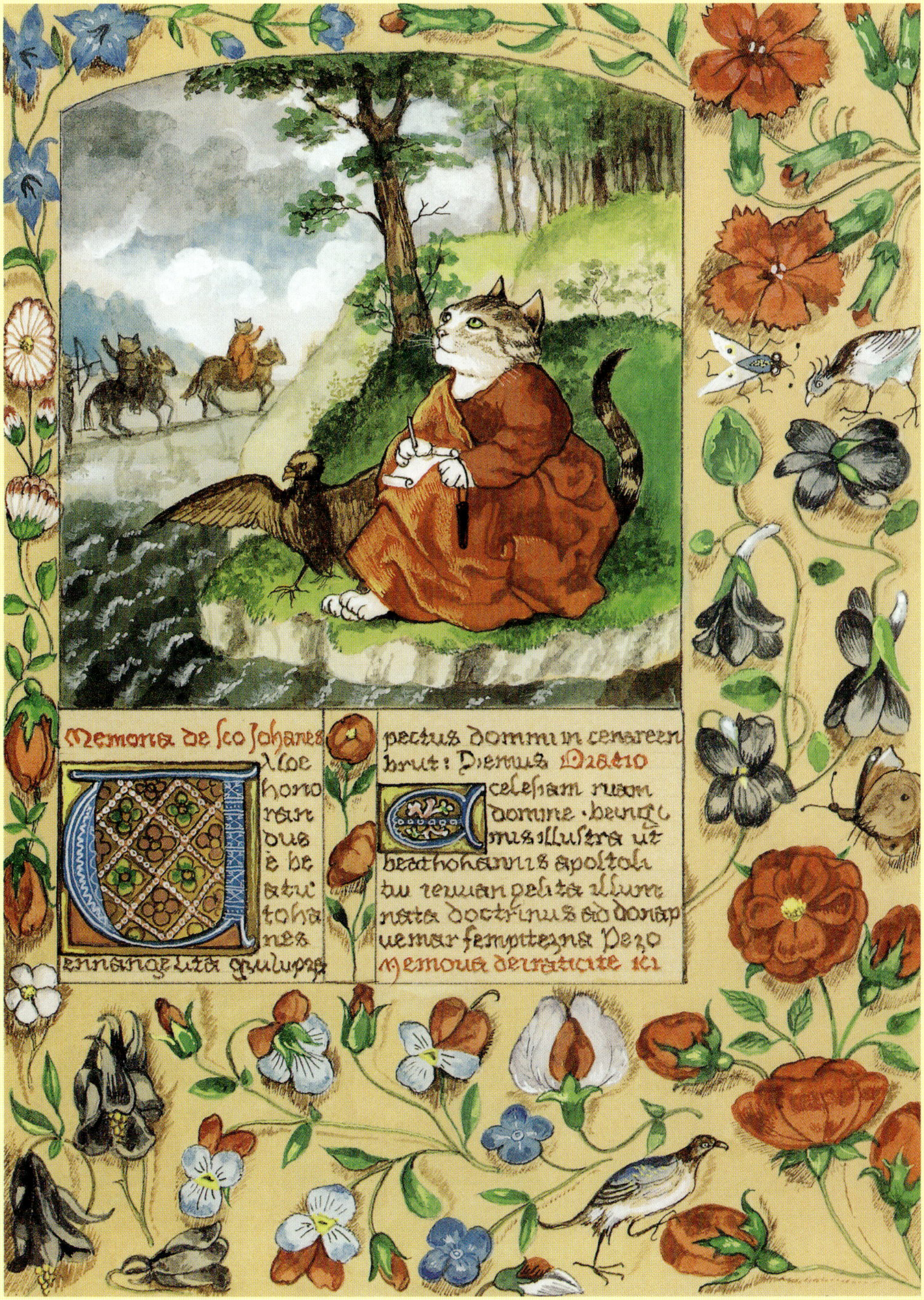

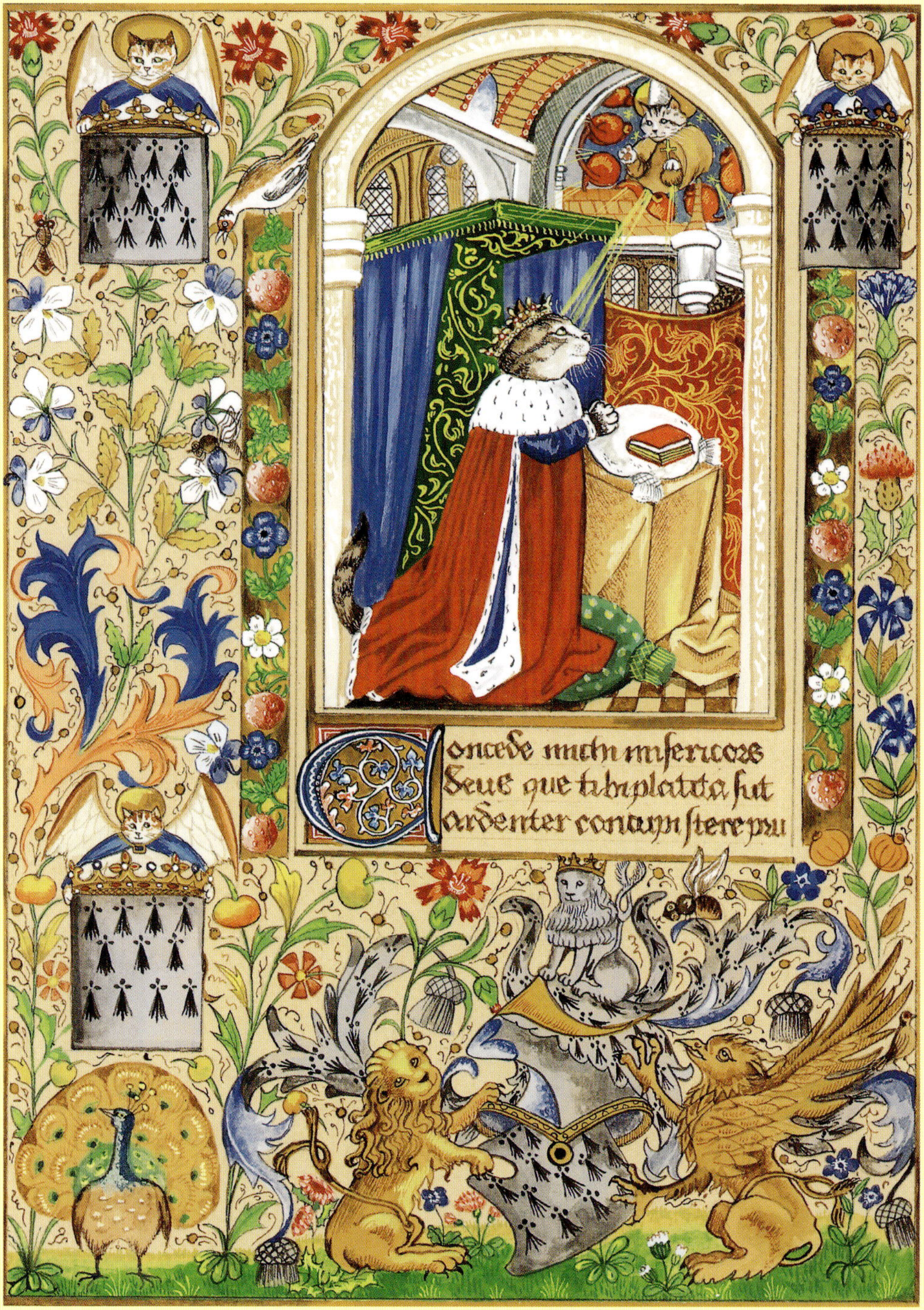
Concede michi misericors
Deus que tibi placita sunt
ardenter concupiscere pru

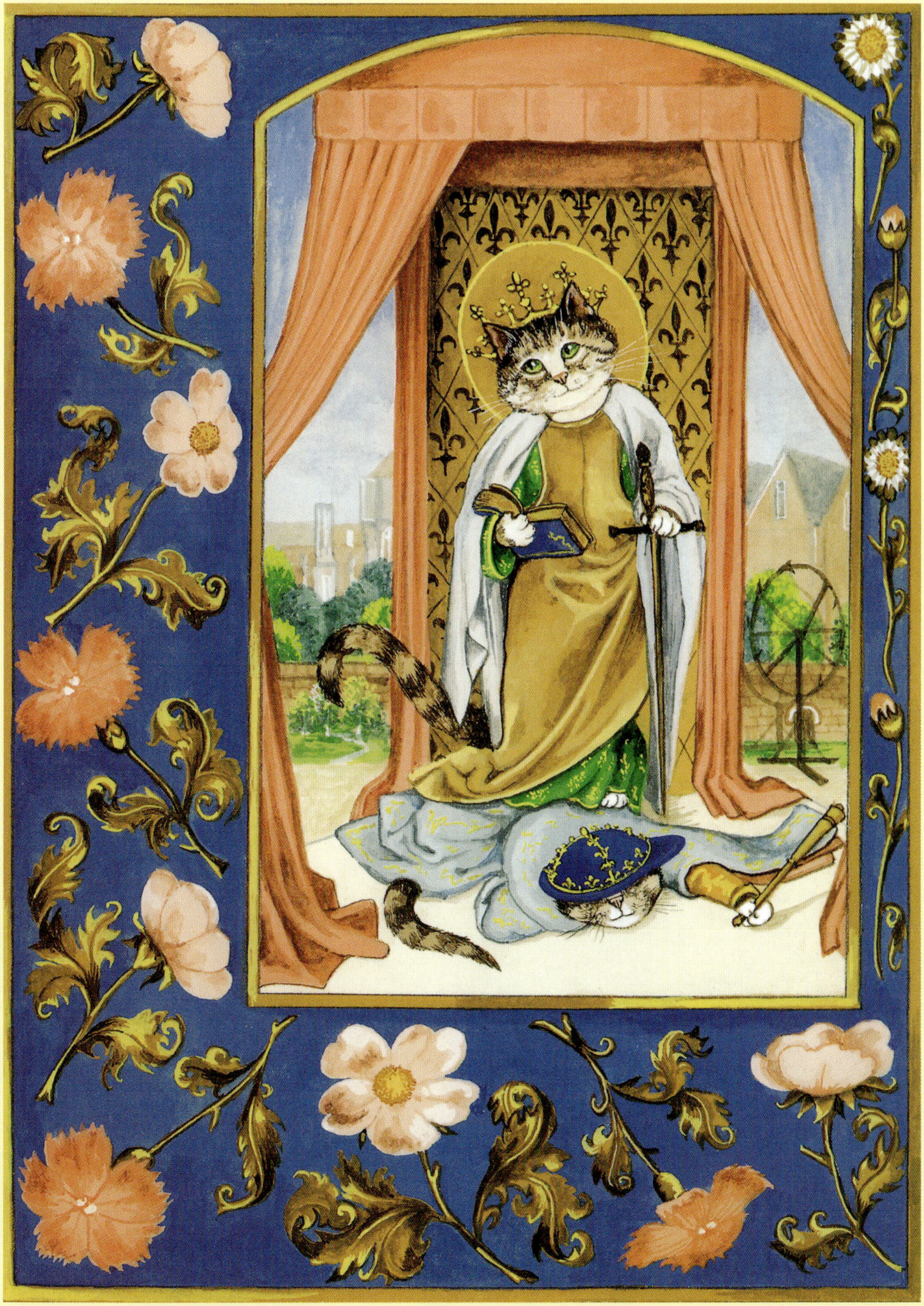

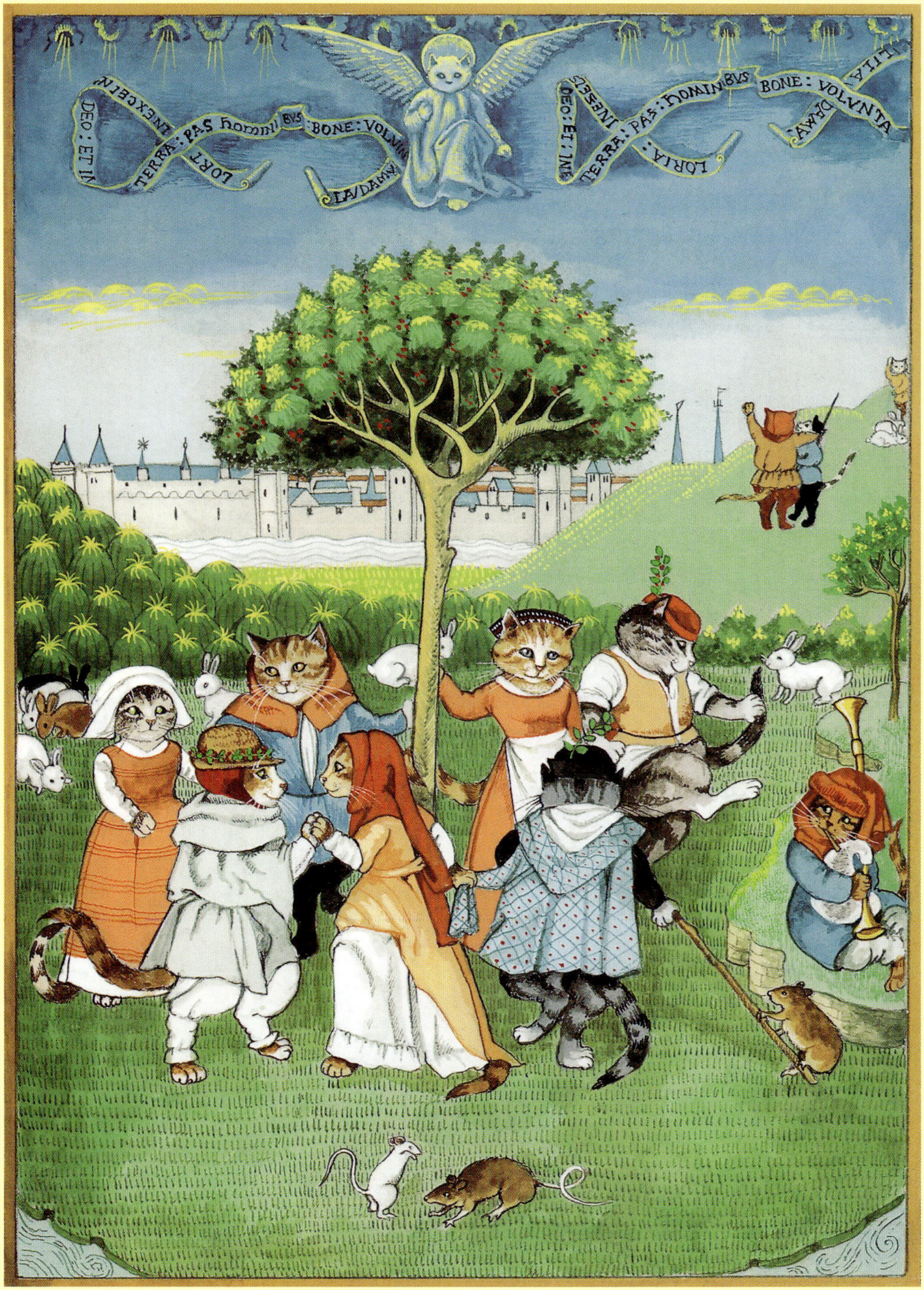

TERRA: PAS homini BVS BONE: VOLVN
LAVDAMV
TERRA: PAS: HOMINI BVS BONE: VOLVNTA

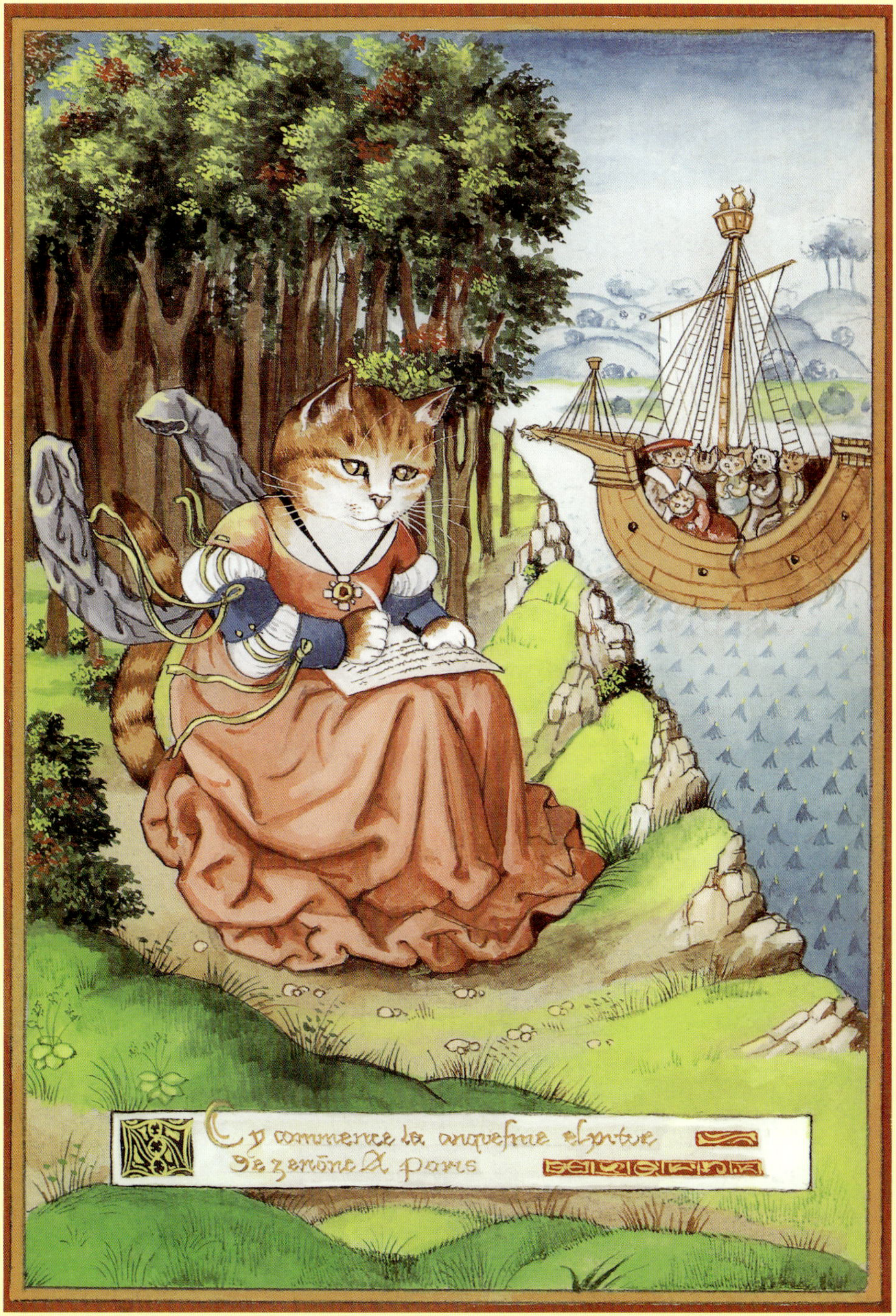
Cy commence la cinquesme epistre
de zenone A paris

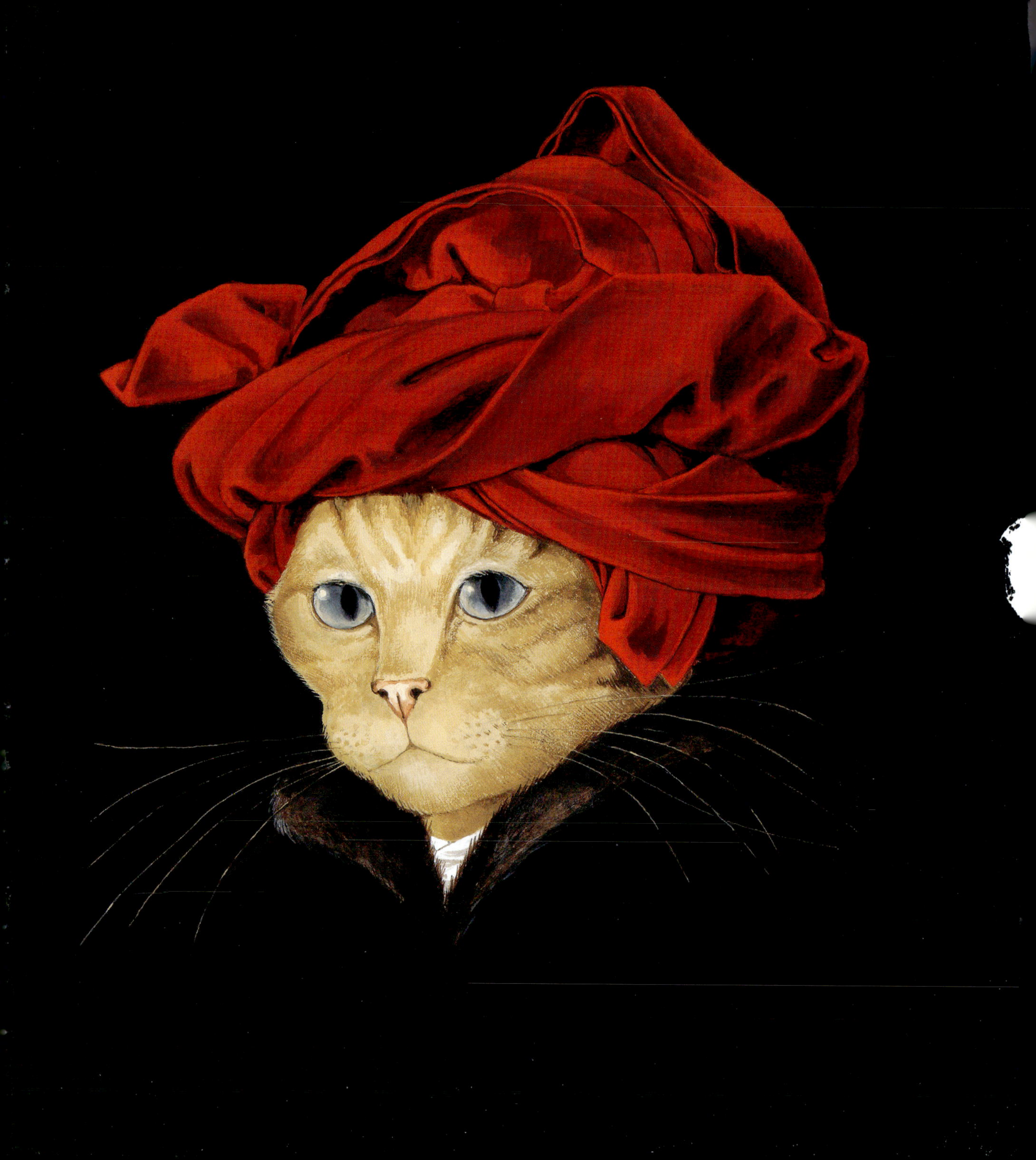

JAN VAN EYCK

Man in a Turban (1433)

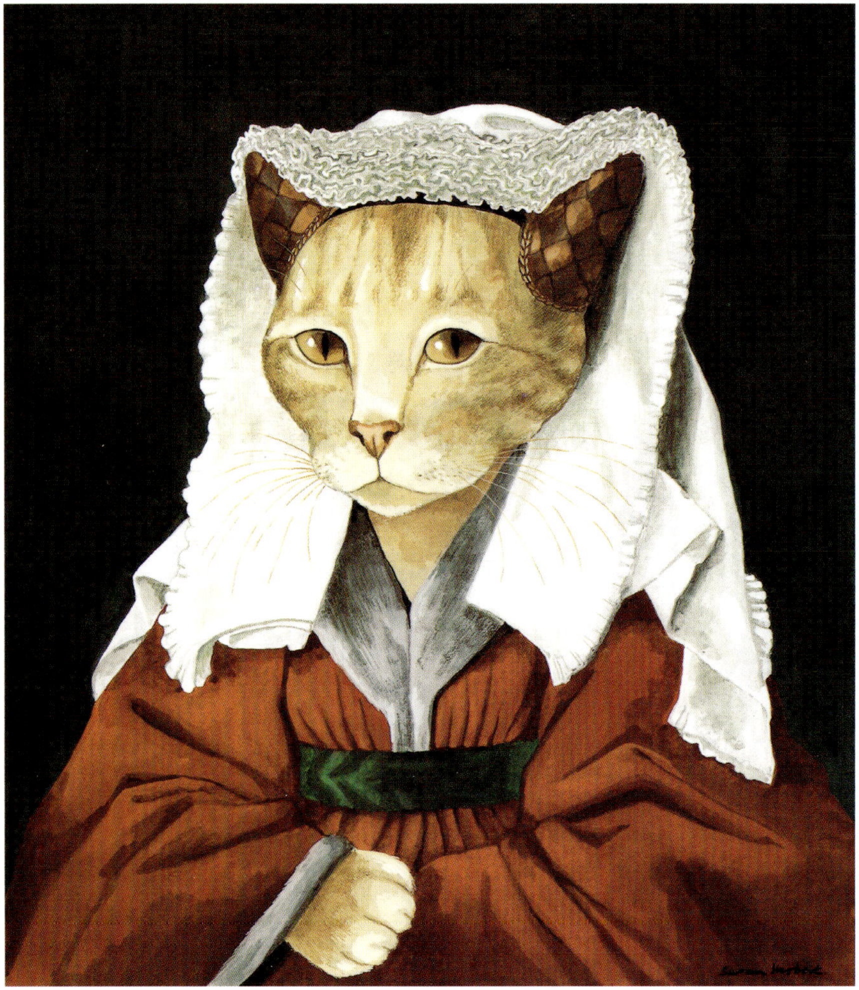

Above JAN VAN EYCK, *Portrait of the Artist's Wife* (1439)
Opposite JAN VAN EYCK, *The Arnolfini Marriage* (1434)

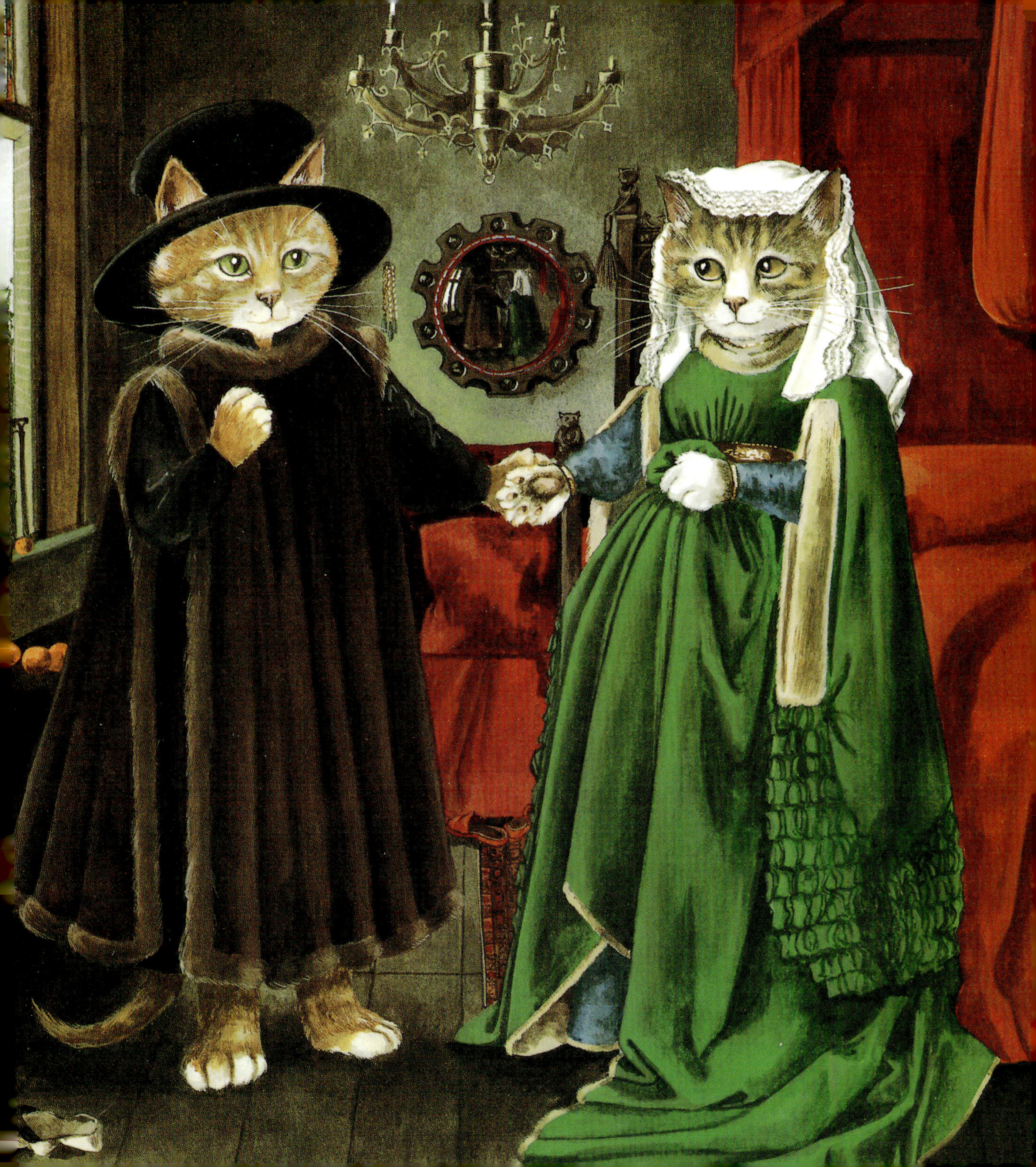

ROGIER VAN DER WEYDEN

Mary Magdalene (1464)

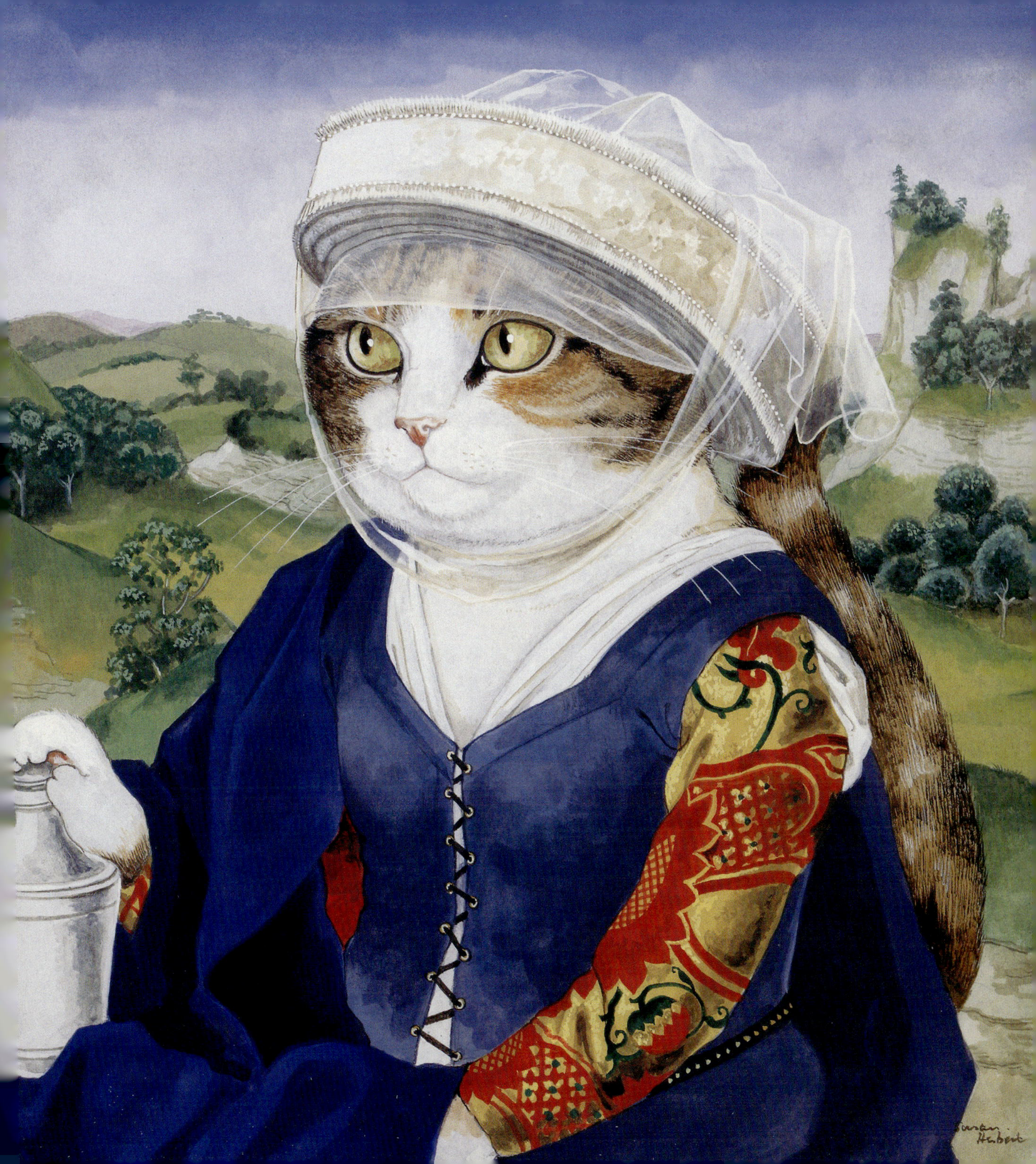
Susan Herbert

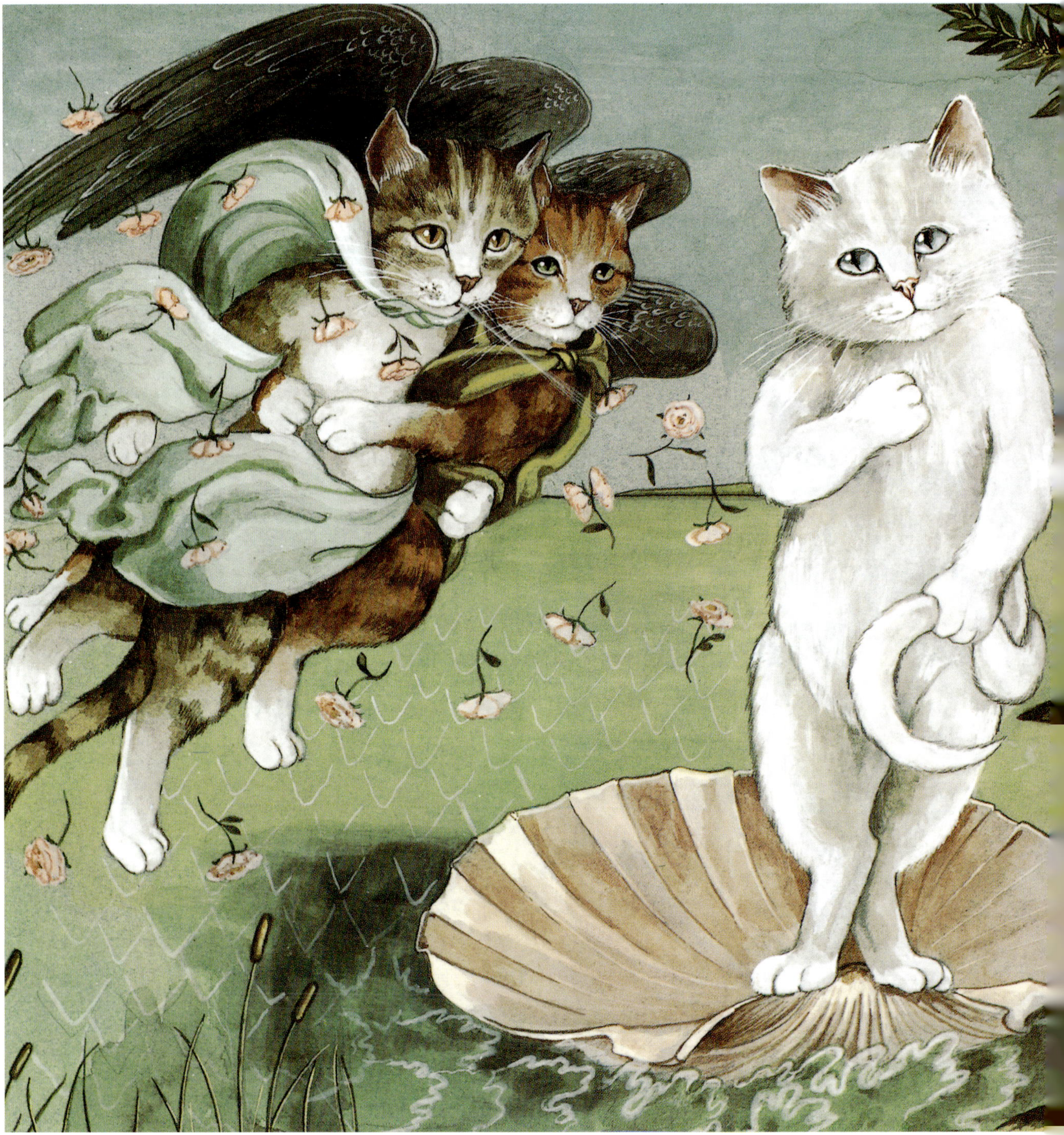

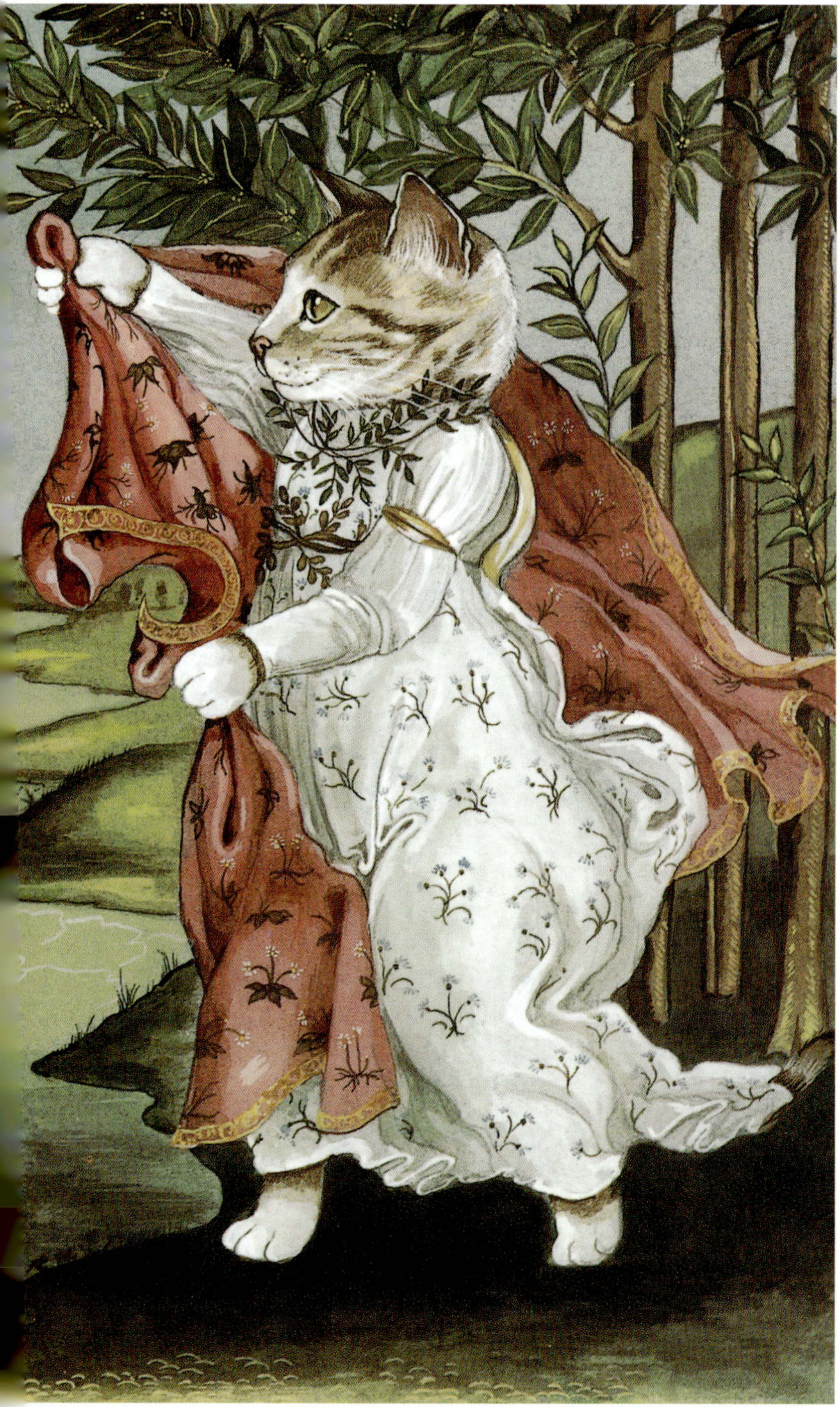

SANDRO BOTTICELLI

The Birth of Venus (1486)

RAPHAEL

St Sebastian (1501–2)

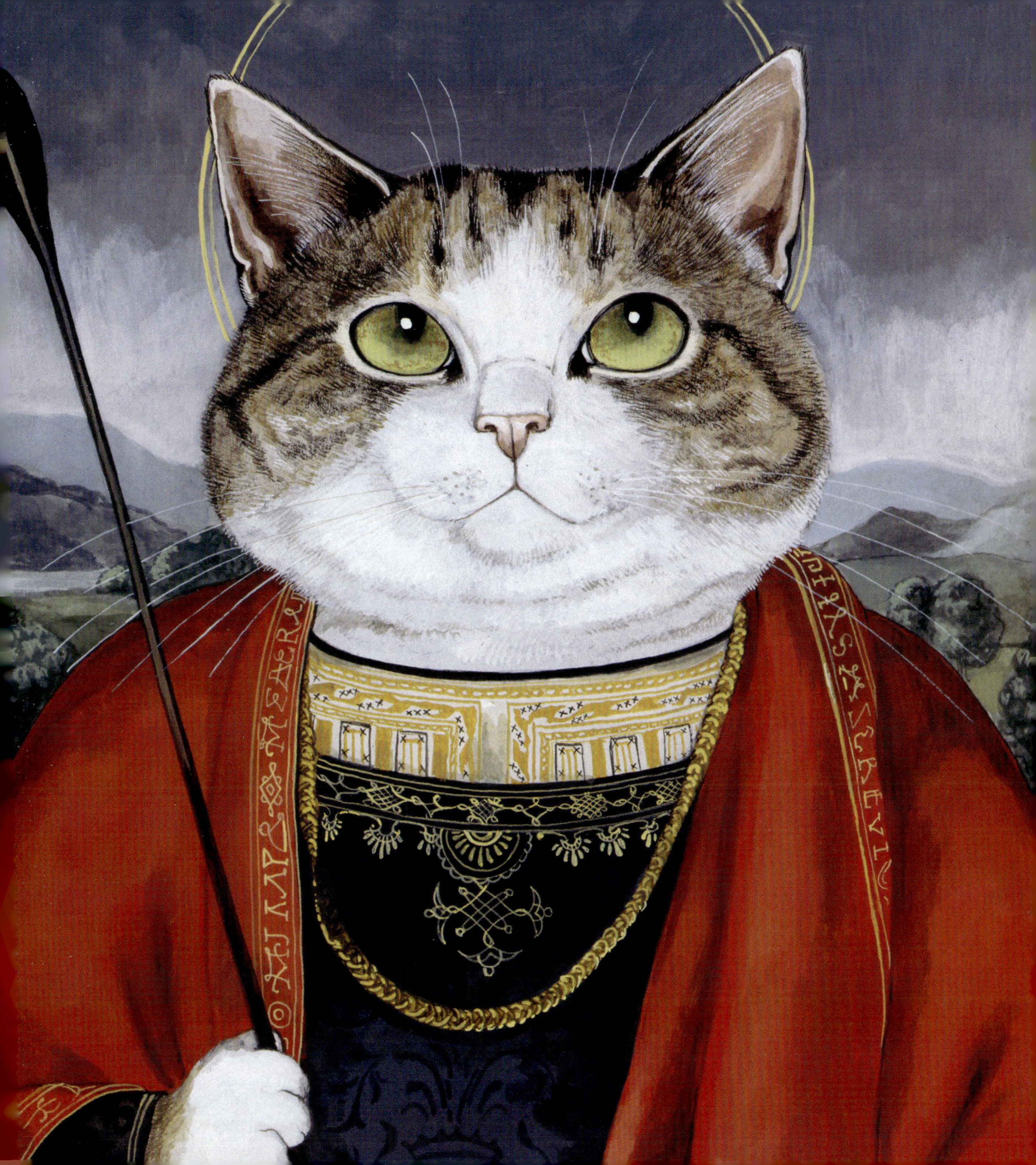

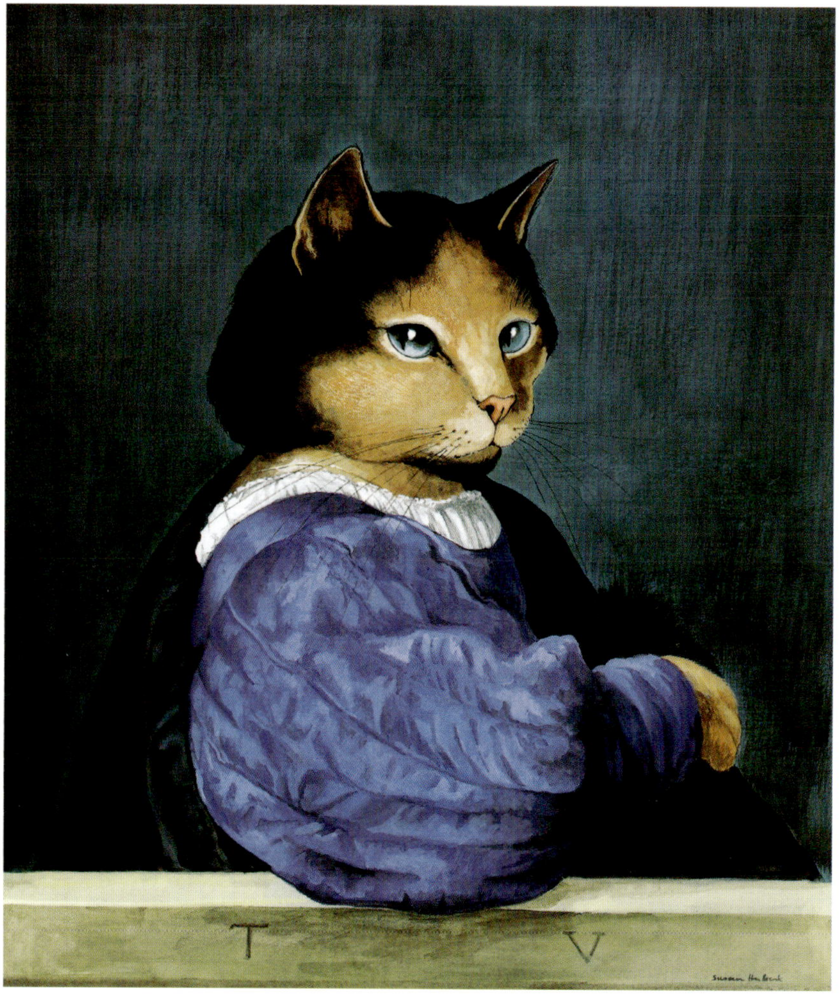

Above TITIAN, *Portrait of a Young Man* (1512)
Opposite LEONARDO DA VINCI, *Lady with an Ermine* (1489–90)

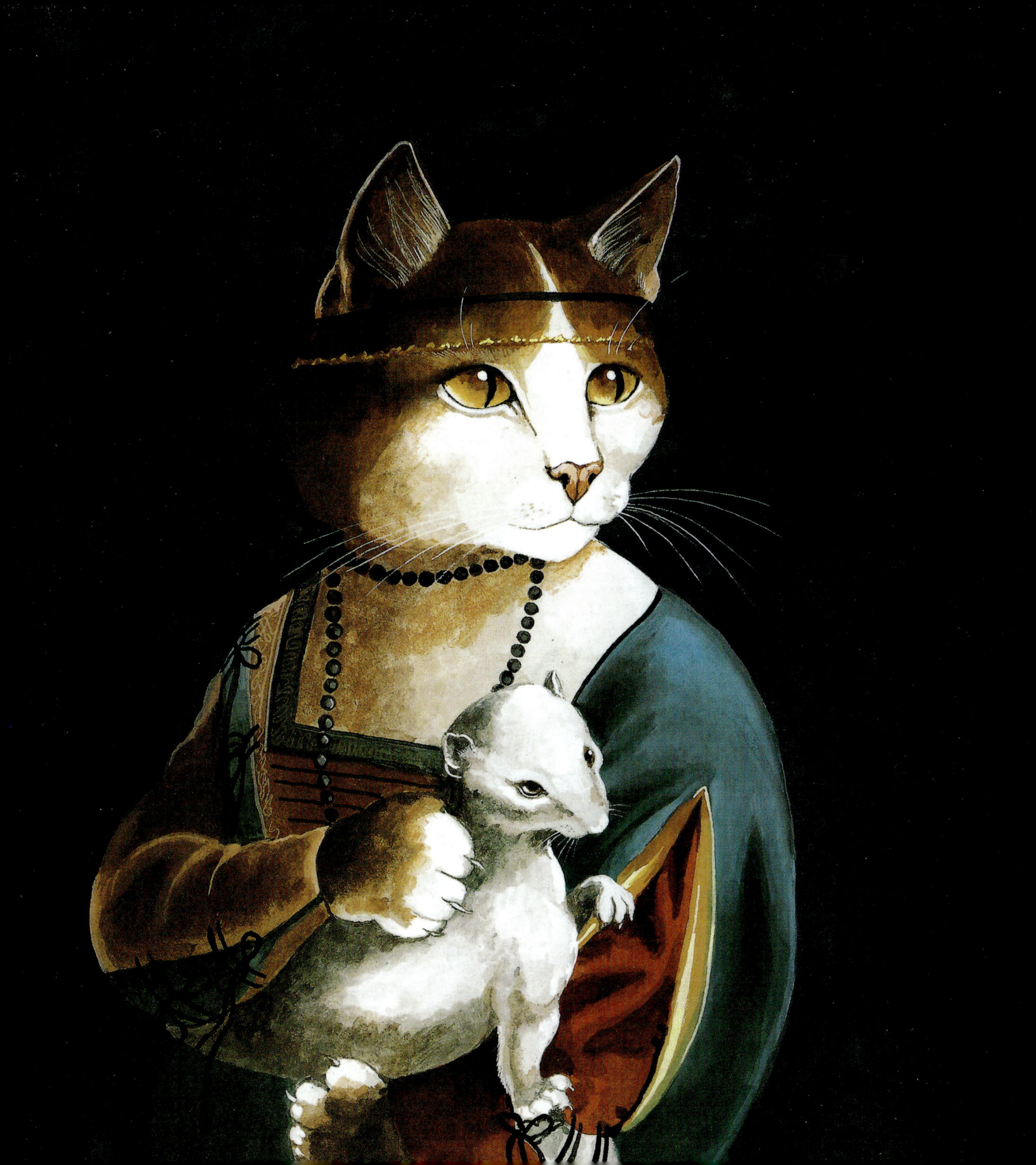

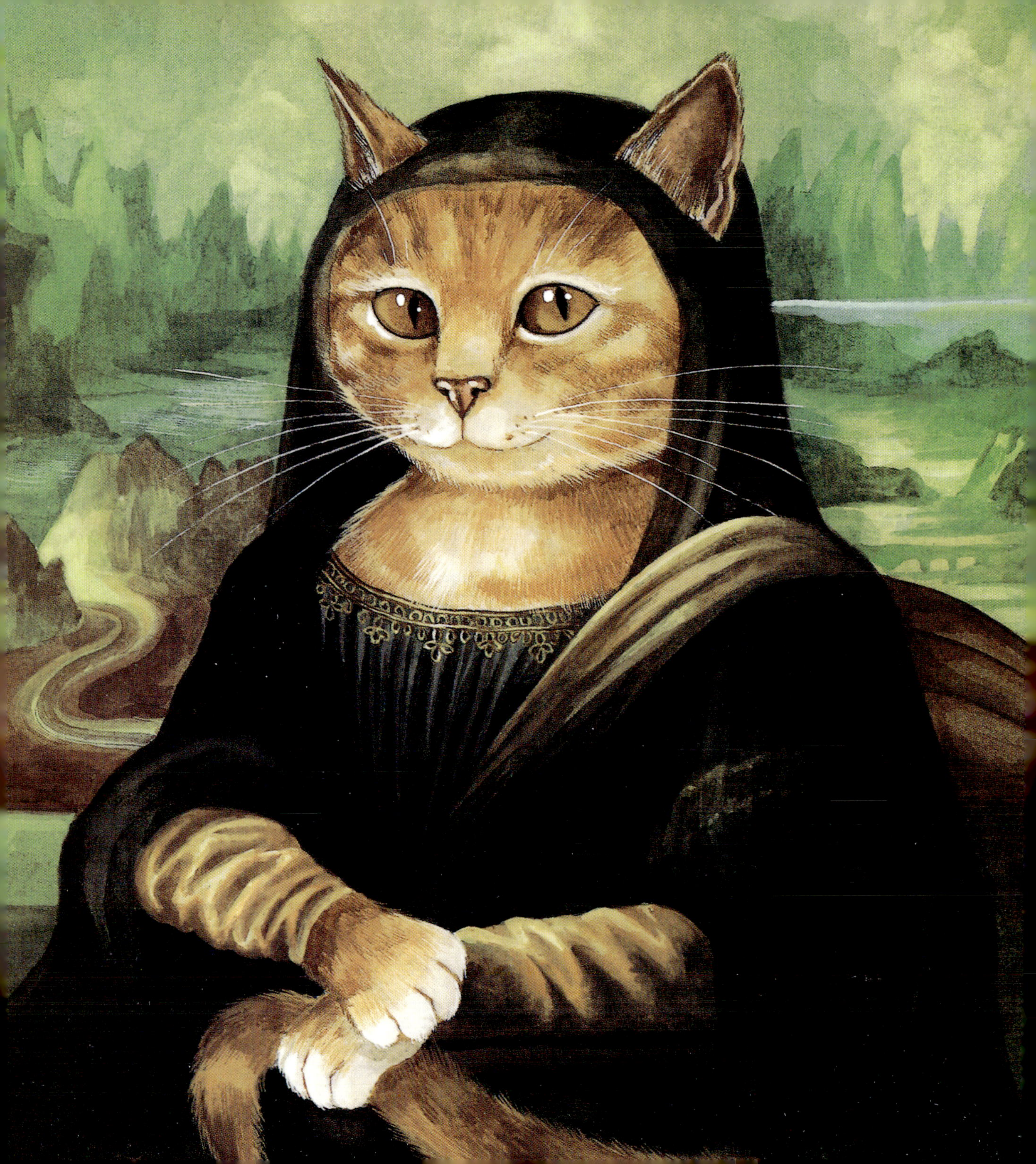

LEONARDO DA VINCI

Mona Lisa (1503–6)

Following pages

MICHELANGELO, *The Creation of Adam* (1511–12)

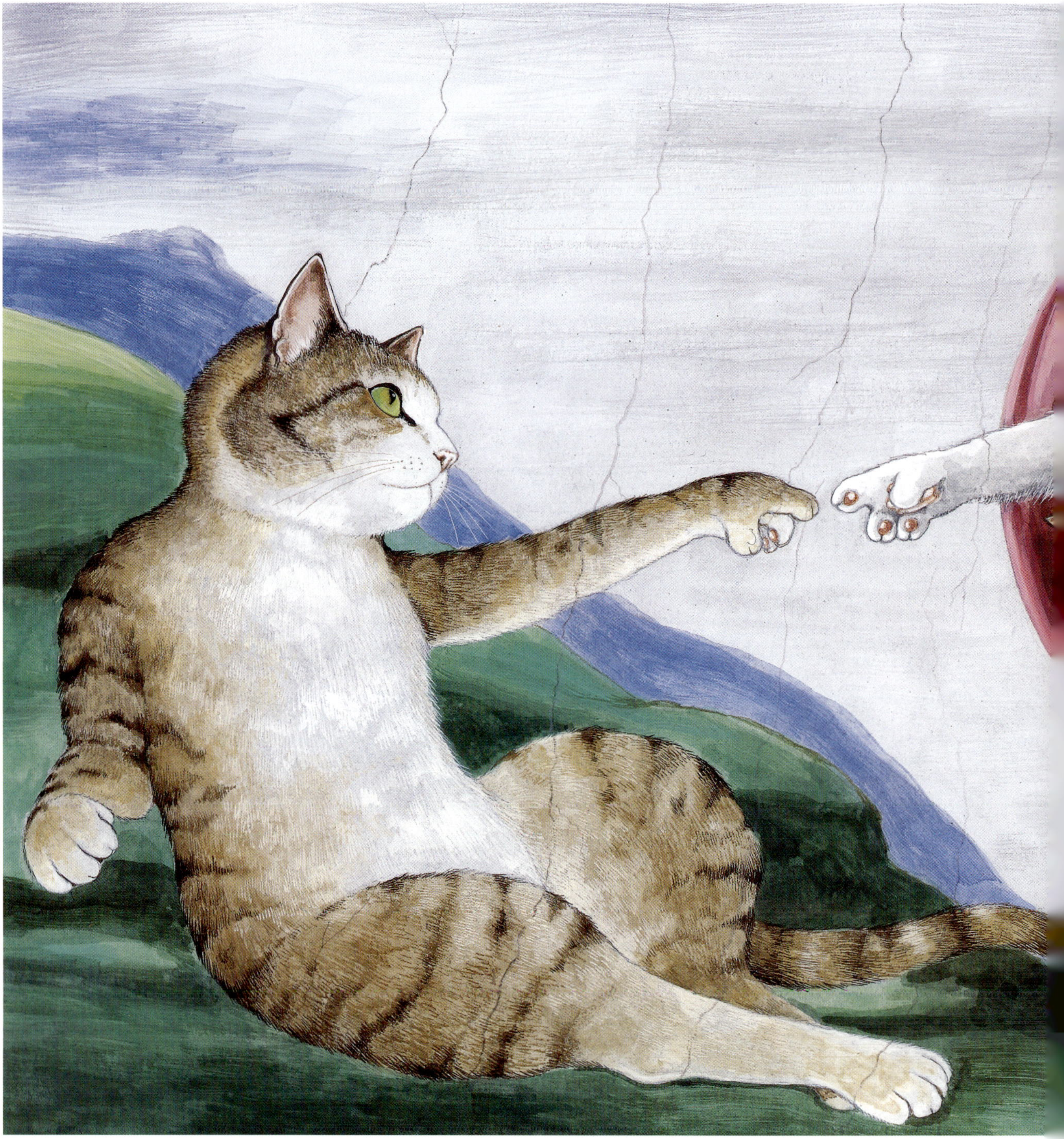

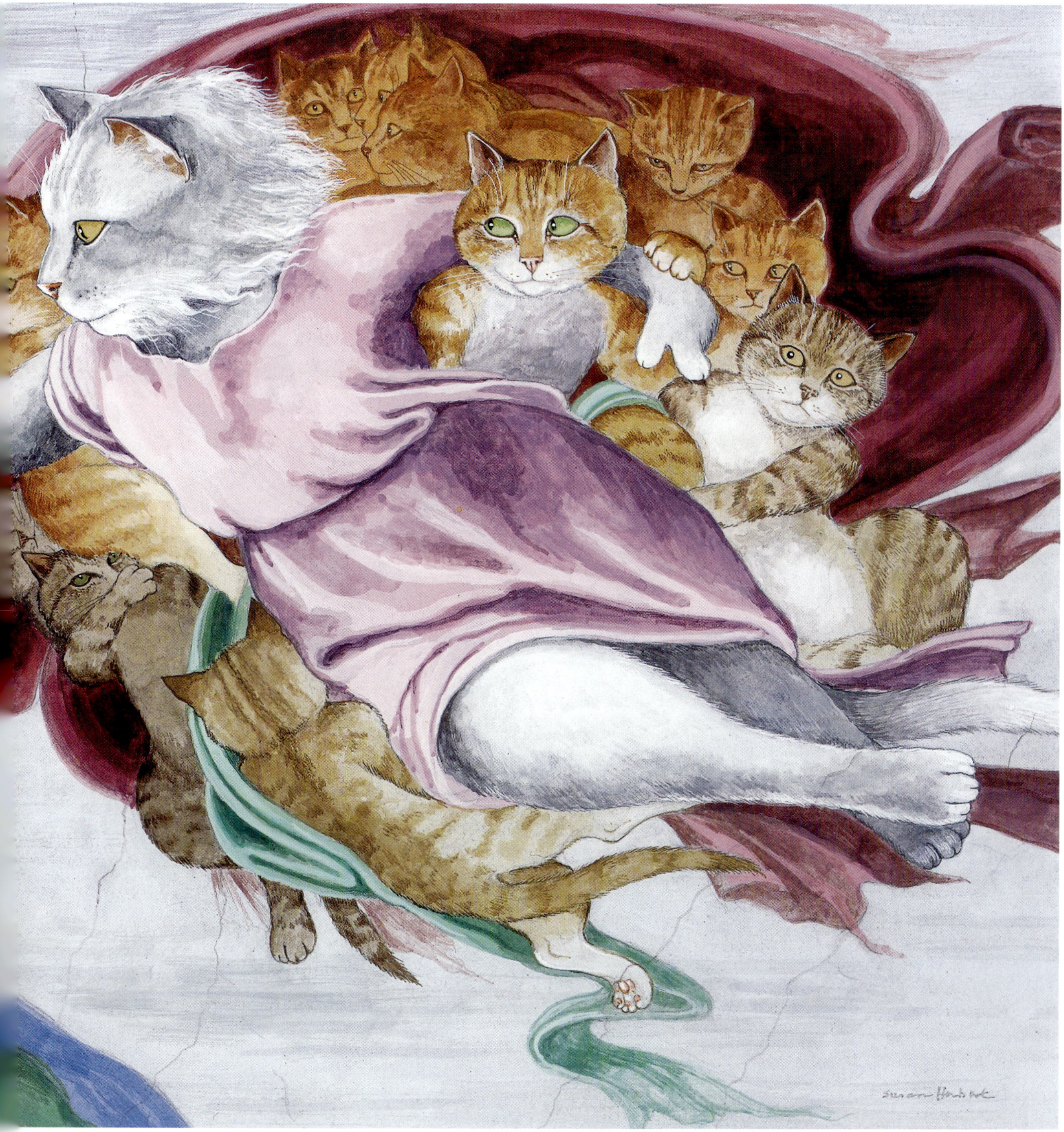

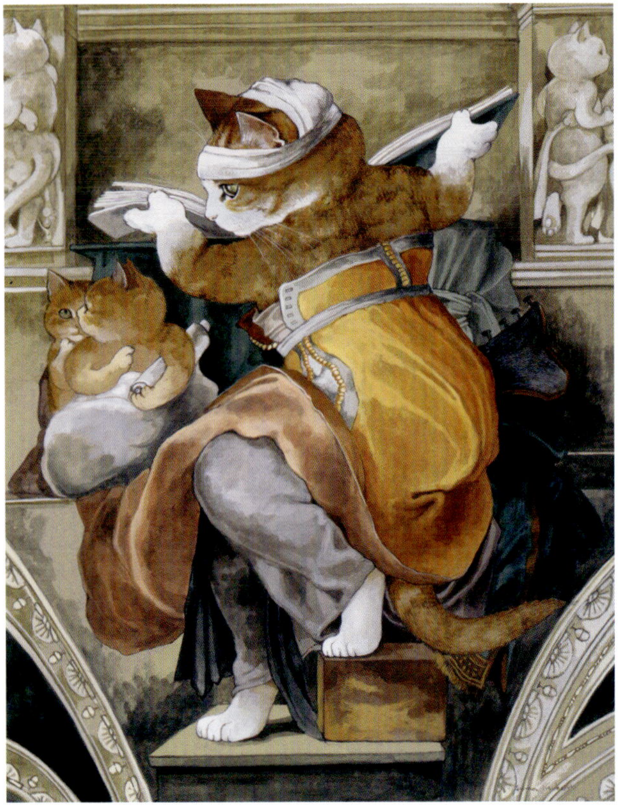

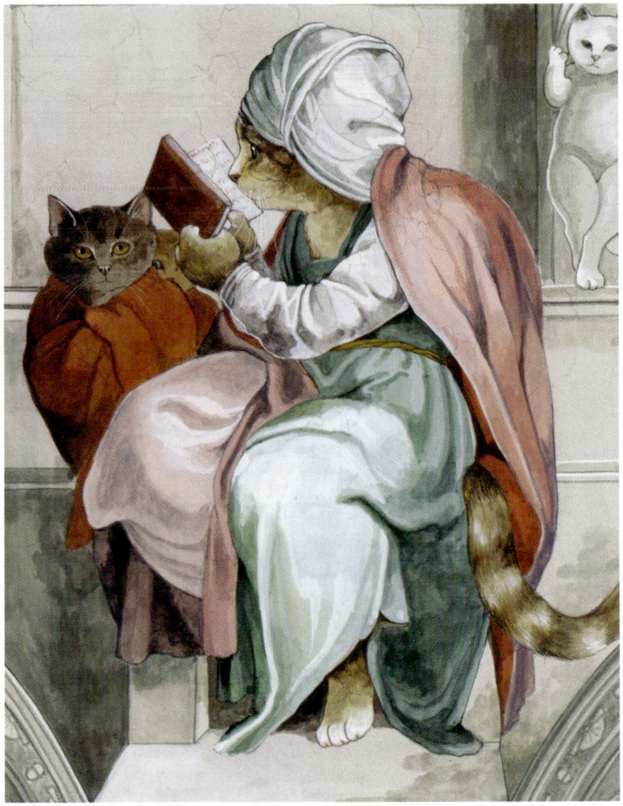

MICHELANGELO

Details from the Sistine Chapel

Above left *Libyan Sibyl* (1508–12)

Above right *Persian Sibyl* (1508–12)

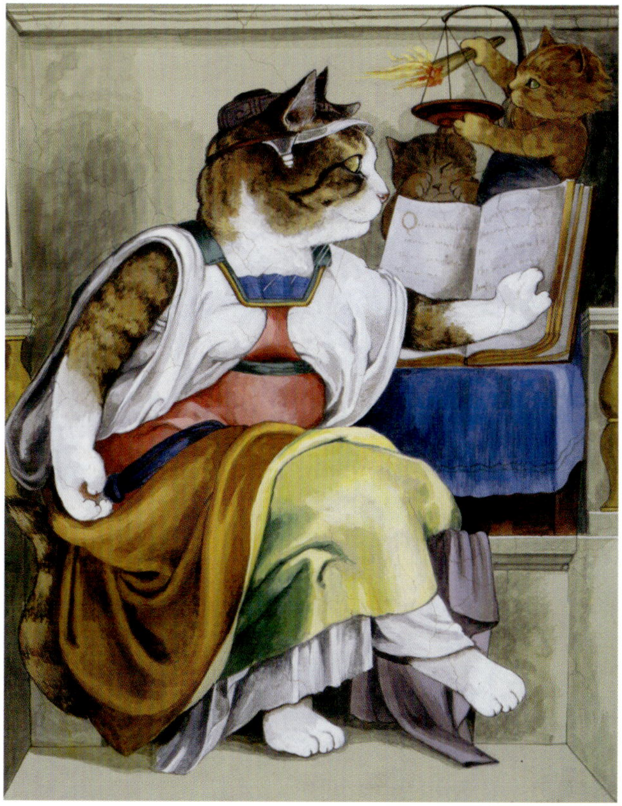

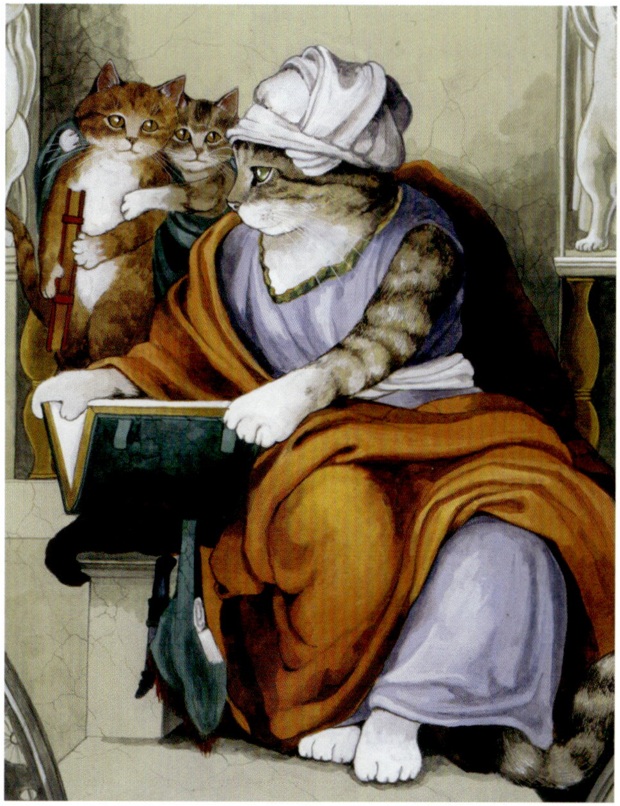

Above left *Erythraean Sibyl* (1508–12)

Above right *Cumaean Sibyl* (1508–12)

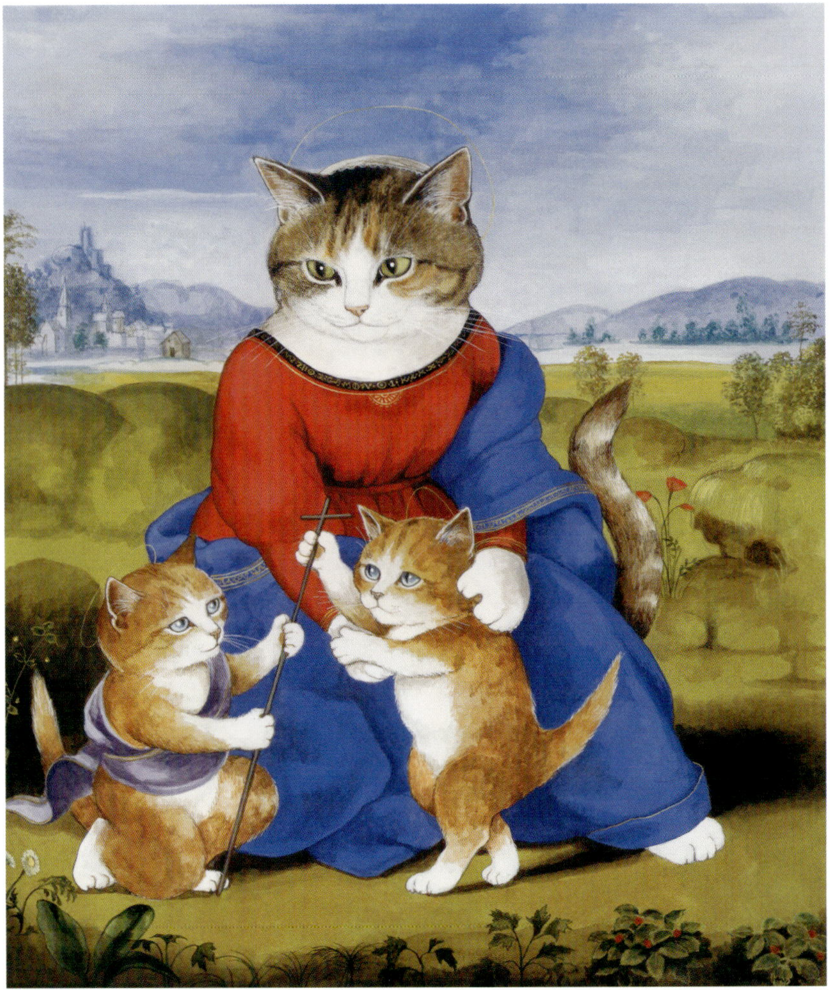

Above RAPHAEL, *Madonna of the Meadows* (1506)

Opposite RAPHAEL, *Pope Leo X* (c. 1517)

Overleaf PAOLO VERONESE, *The Family of Darius Before Alexander* (1565–70)

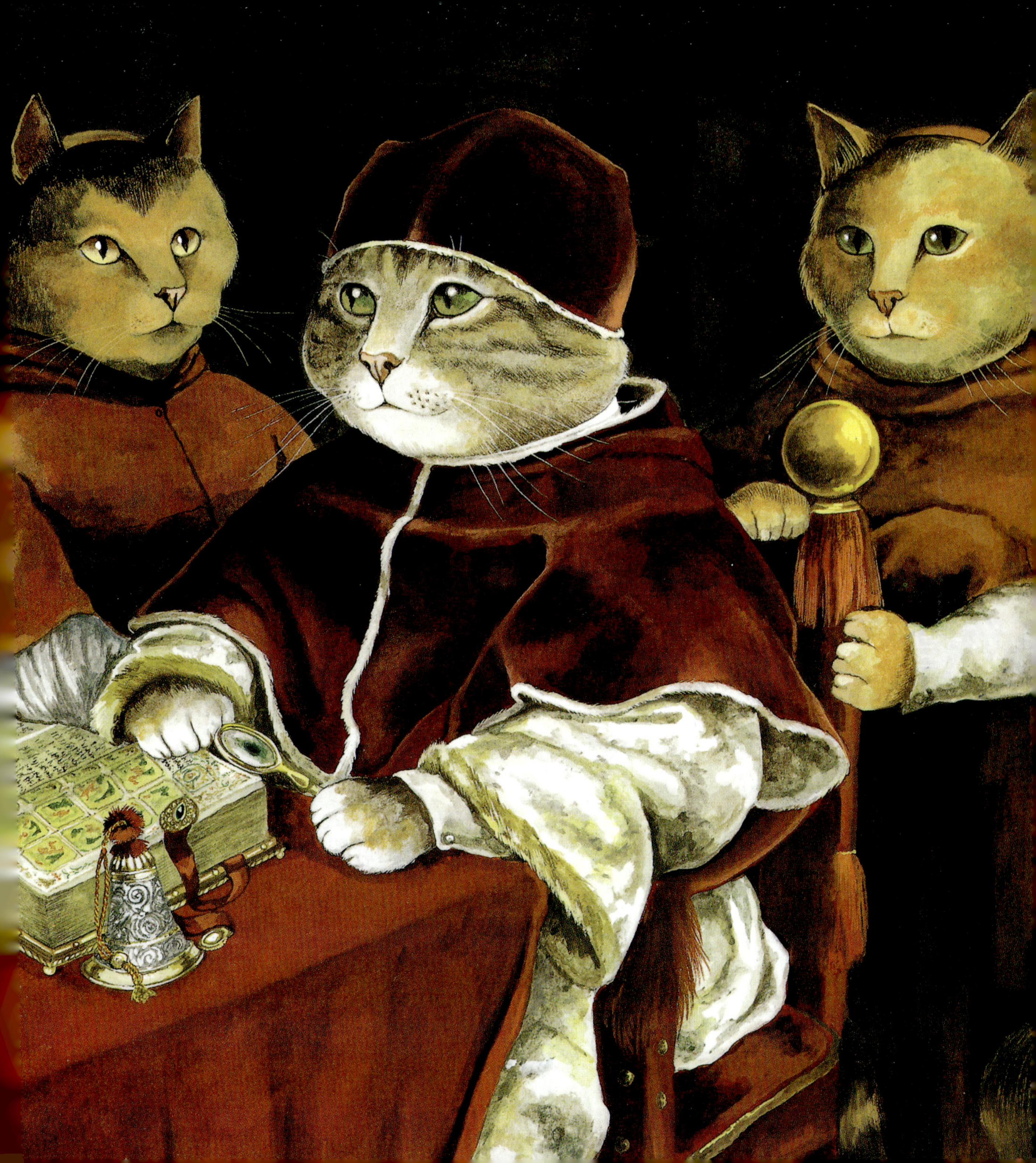

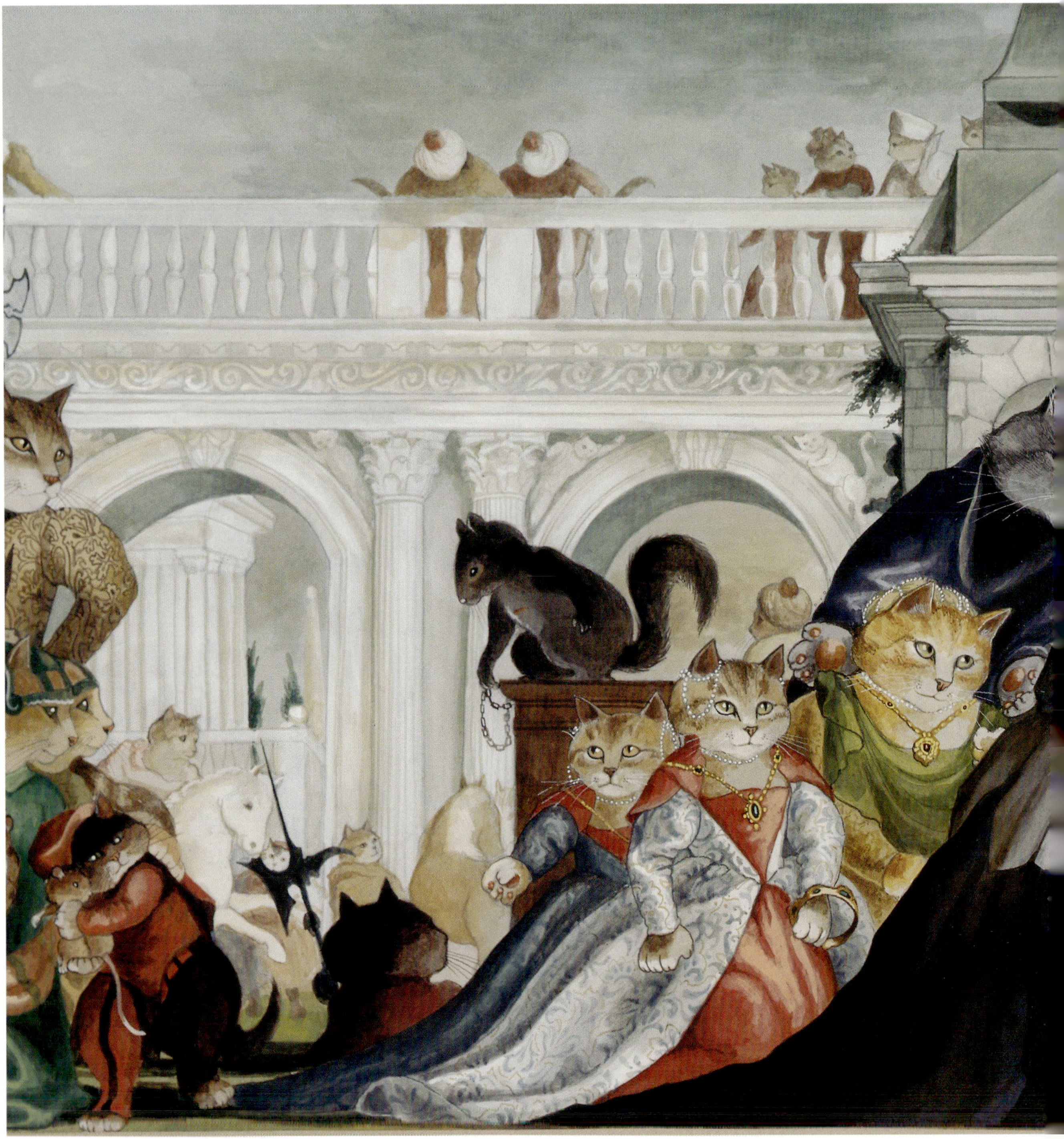

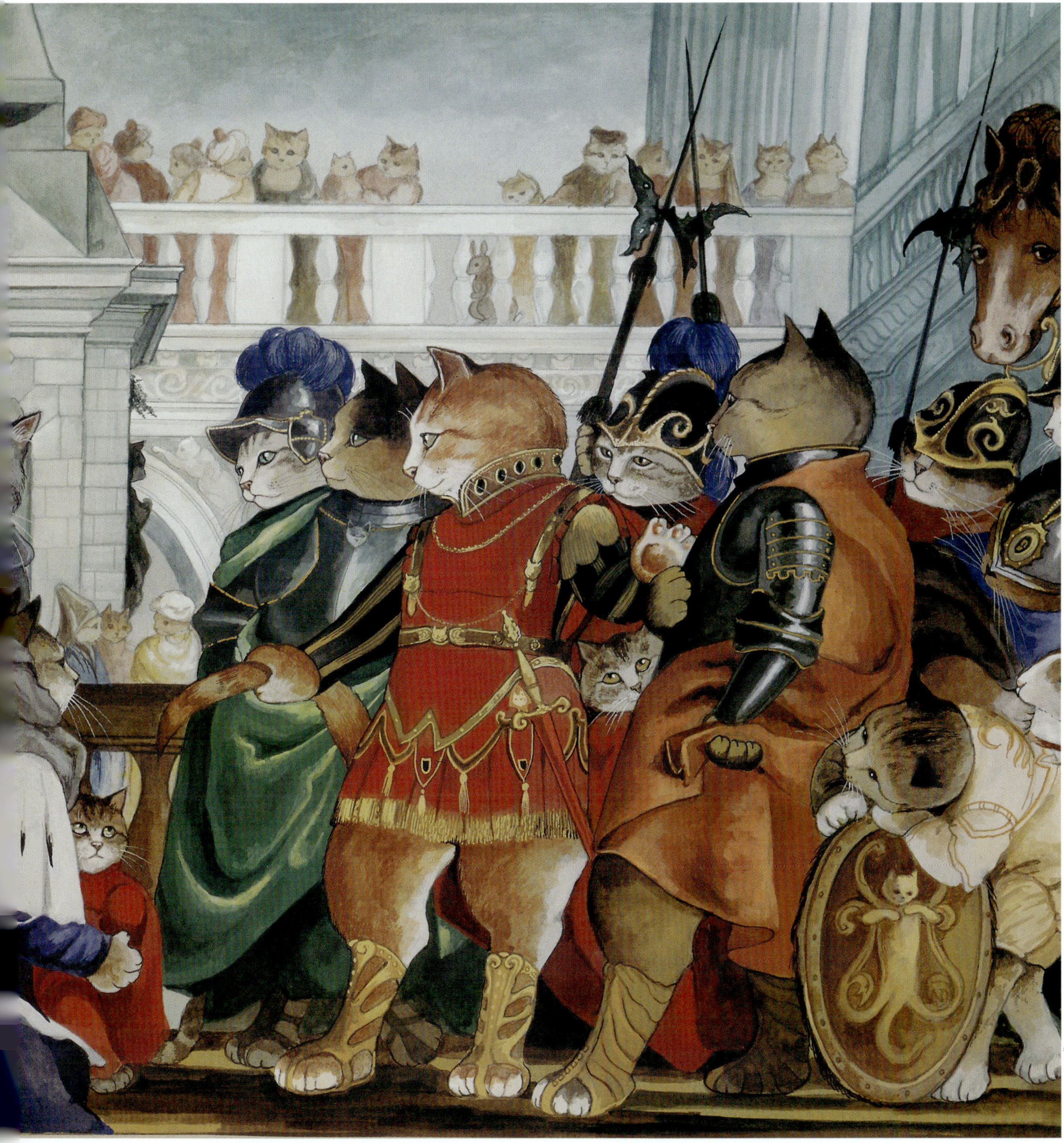

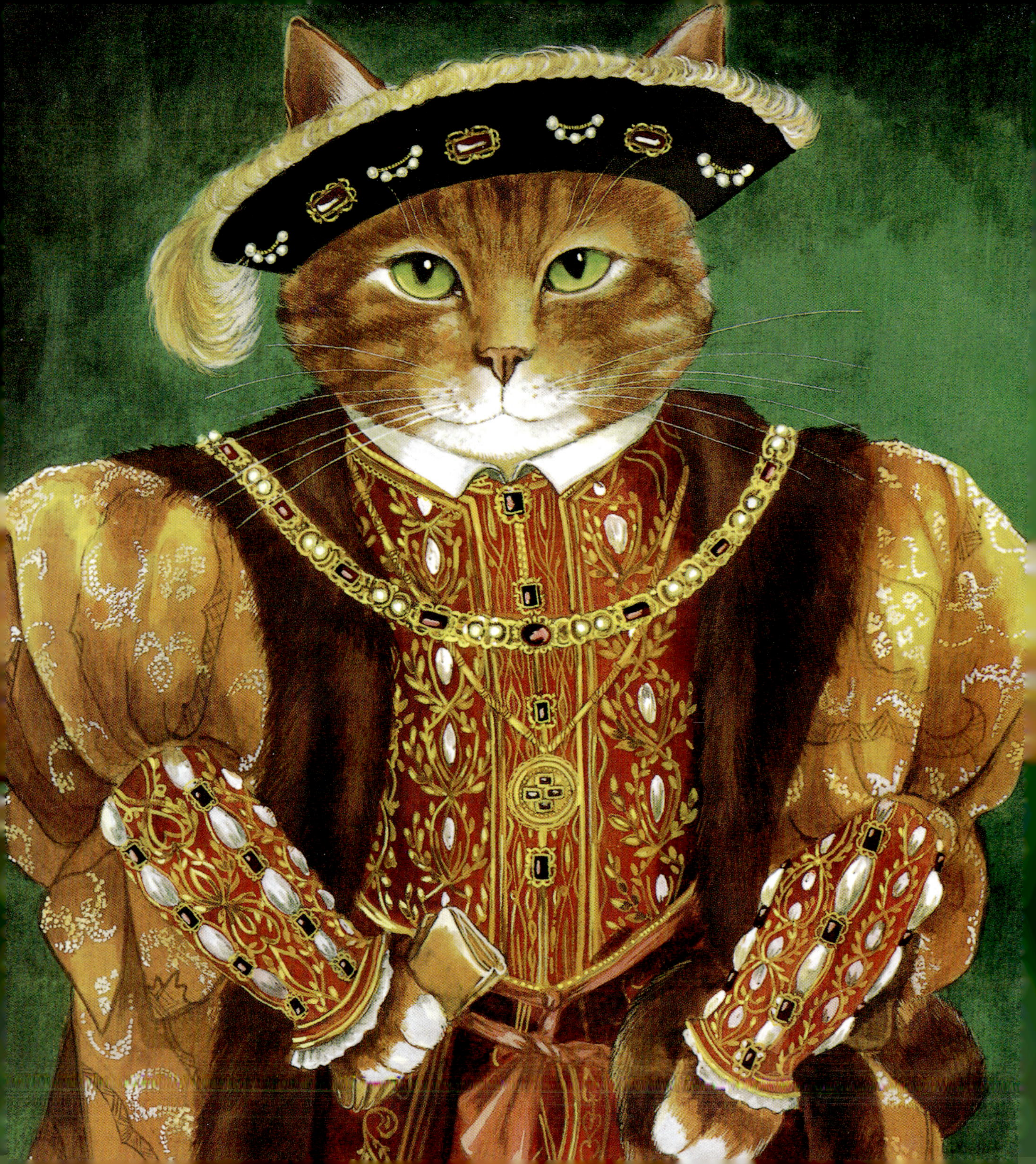

HANS HOLBEIN THE YOUNGER

Portrait of Henry VIII (1540)

PIETER BRUEGHEL THE ELDER

The Peasant Wedding (1566–69)

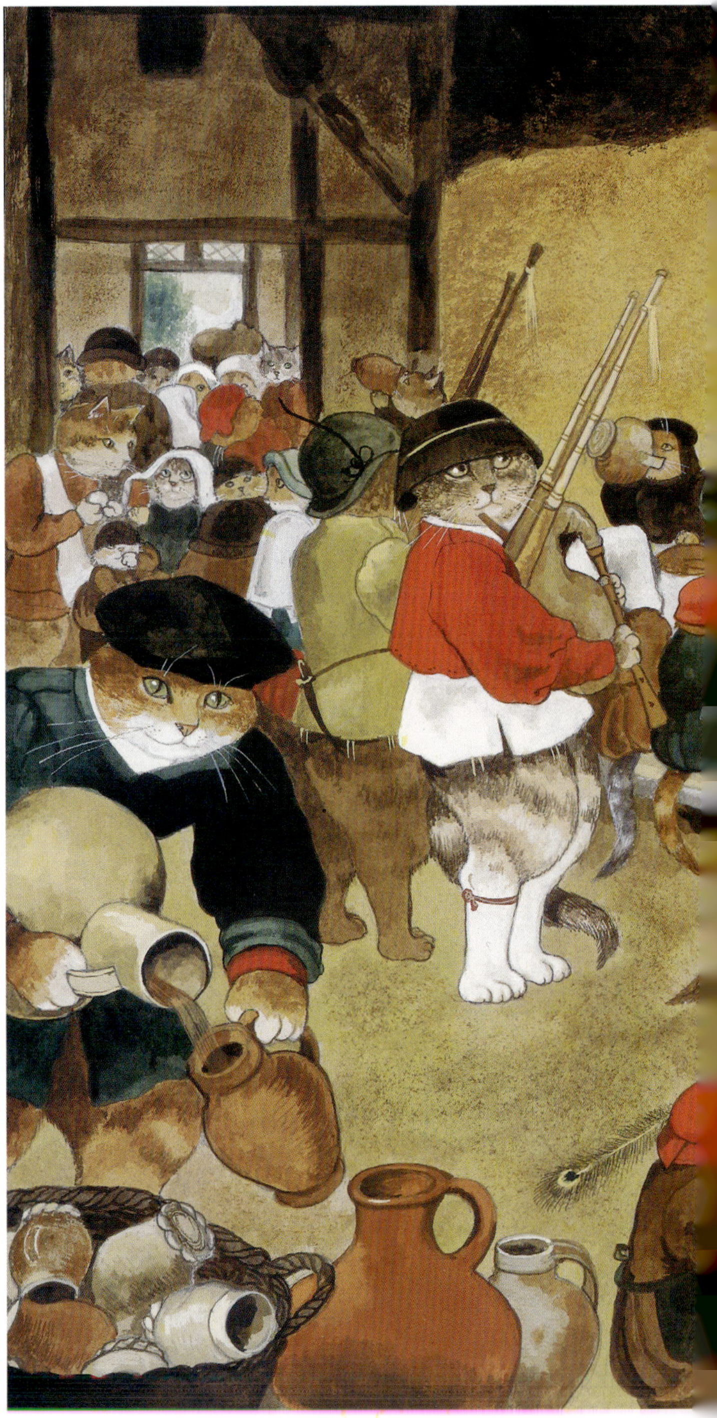

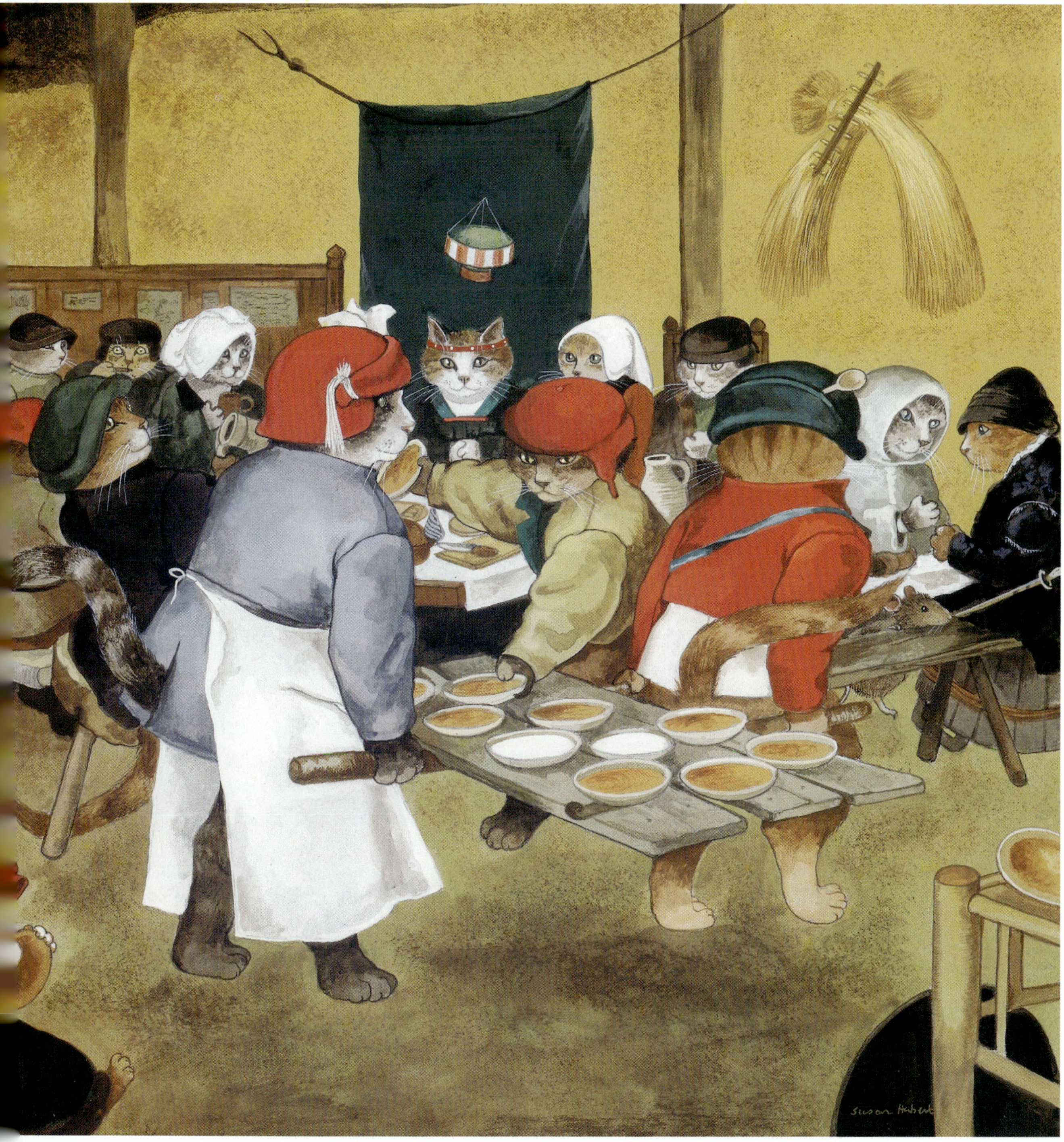
Susan Herbert

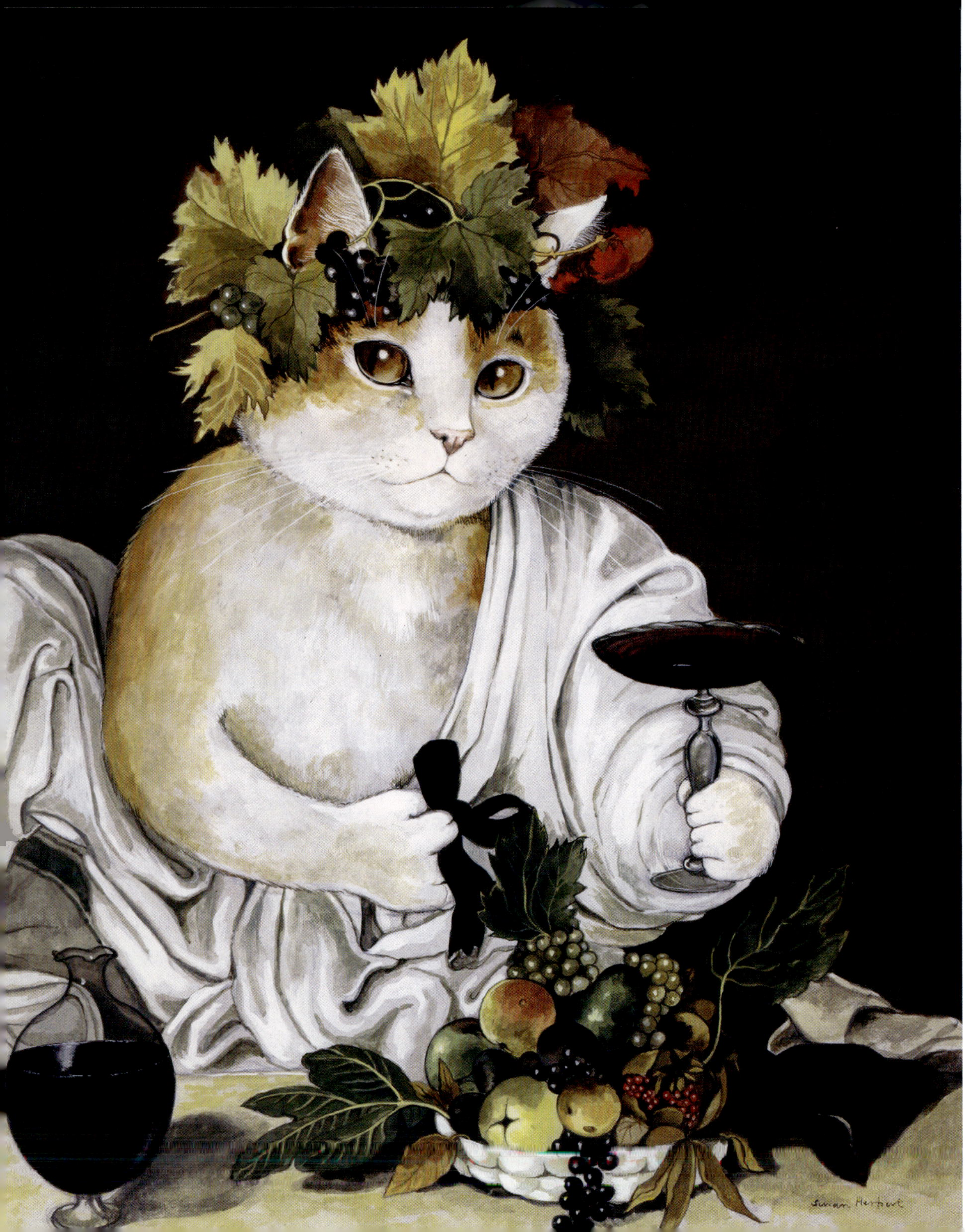
Susan Herbert

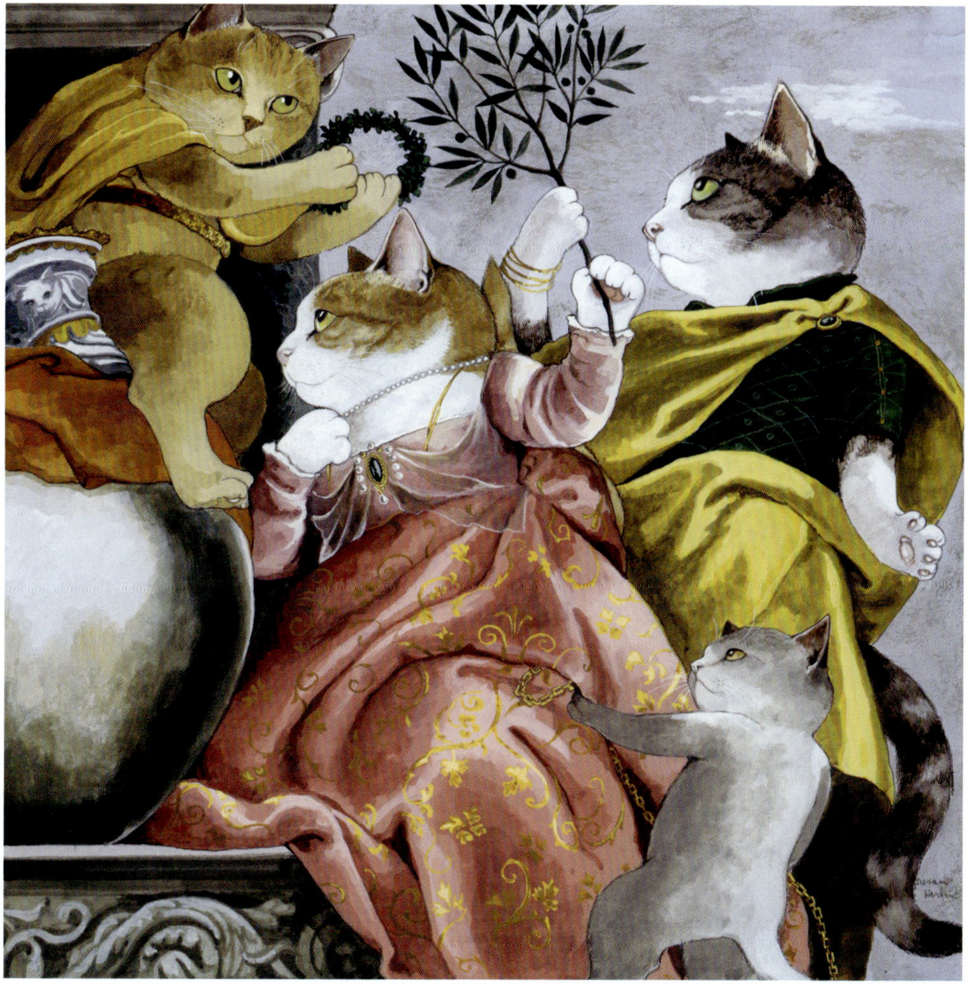

Above PAOLO VERONESE, *Allegory of Love – Happy Union* (c. 1570)
Opposite CARAVAGGIO, *Bacchus* (c. 1595)

CARAVAGGIO

The Supper at Emmaus (1601)

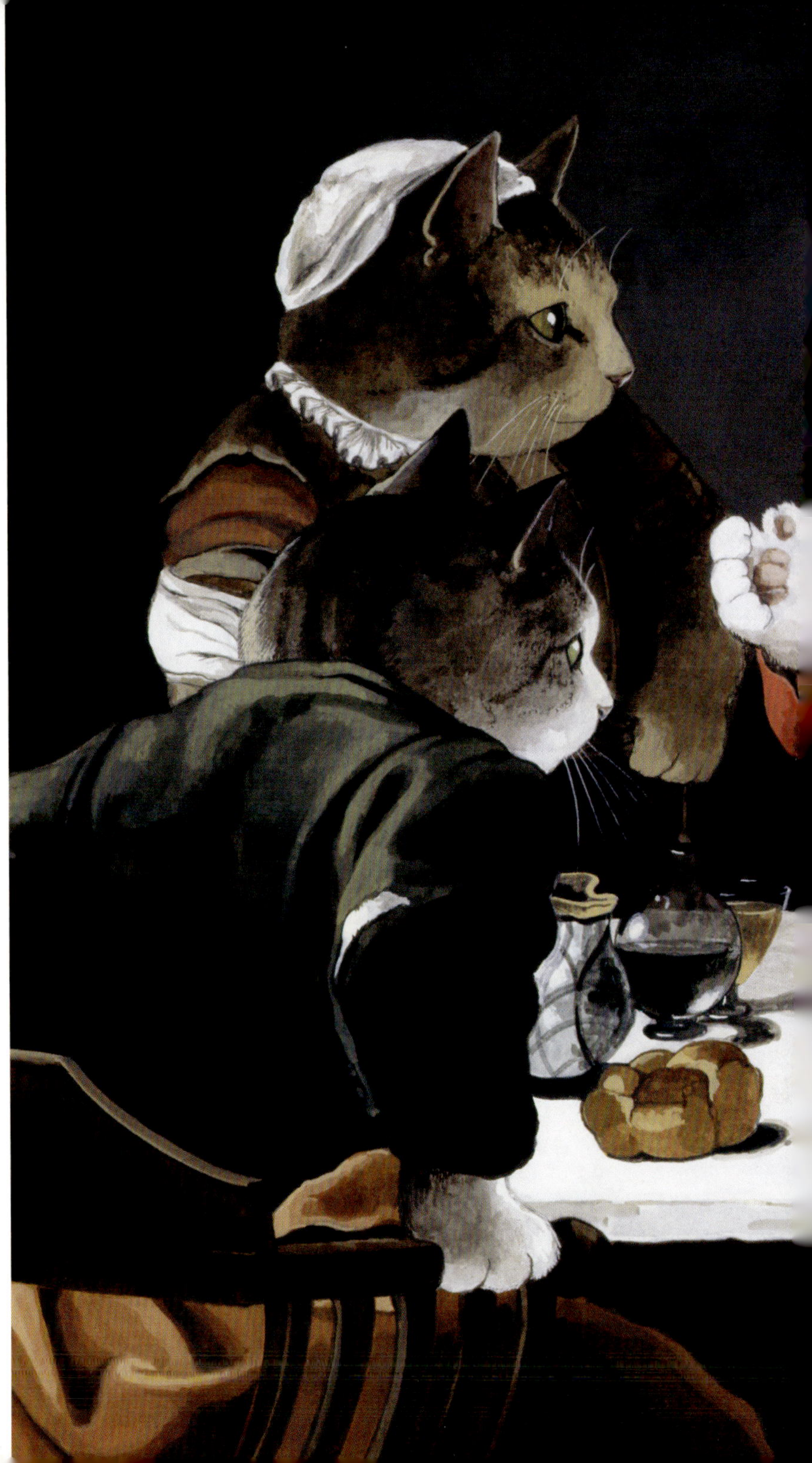

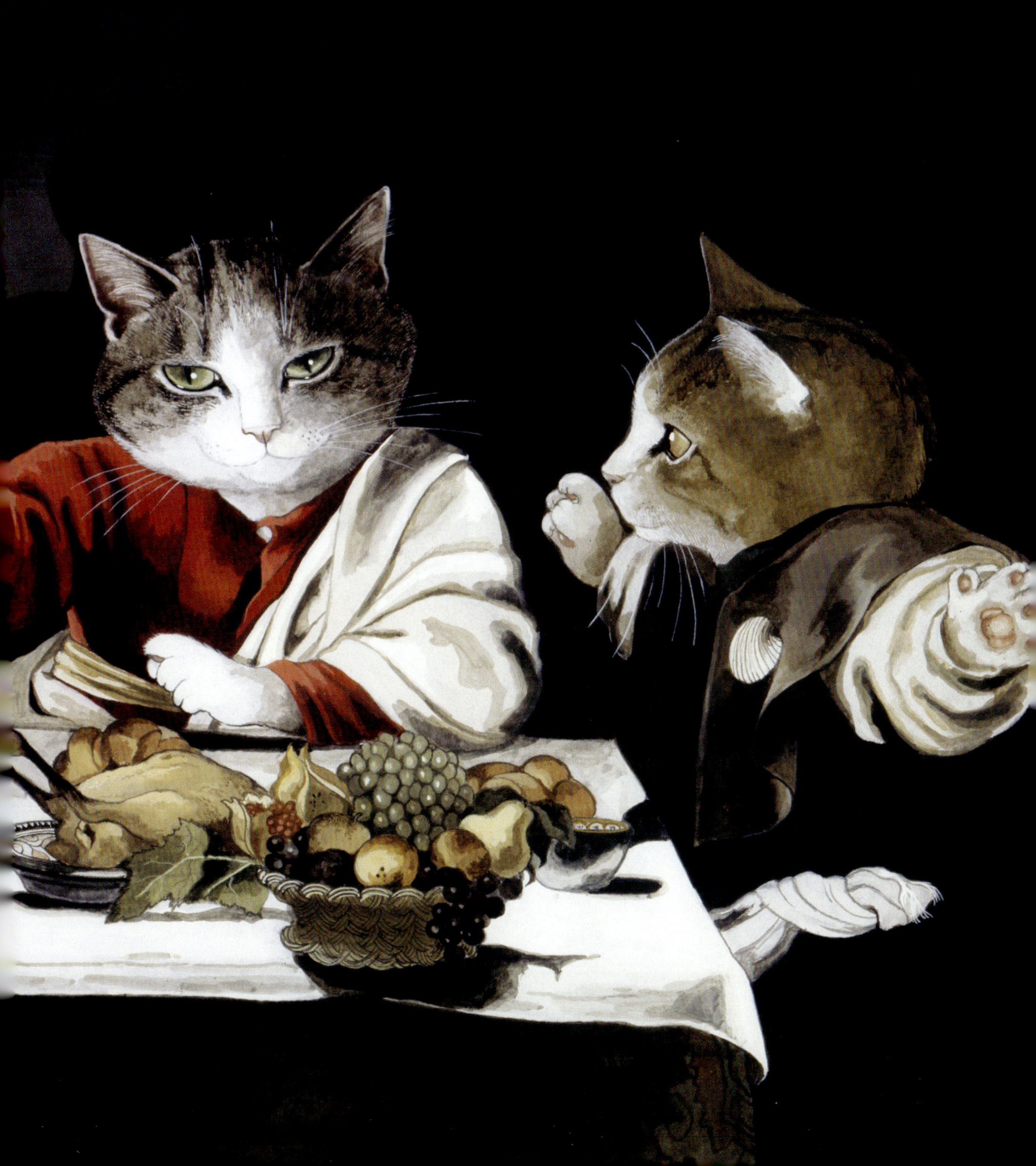

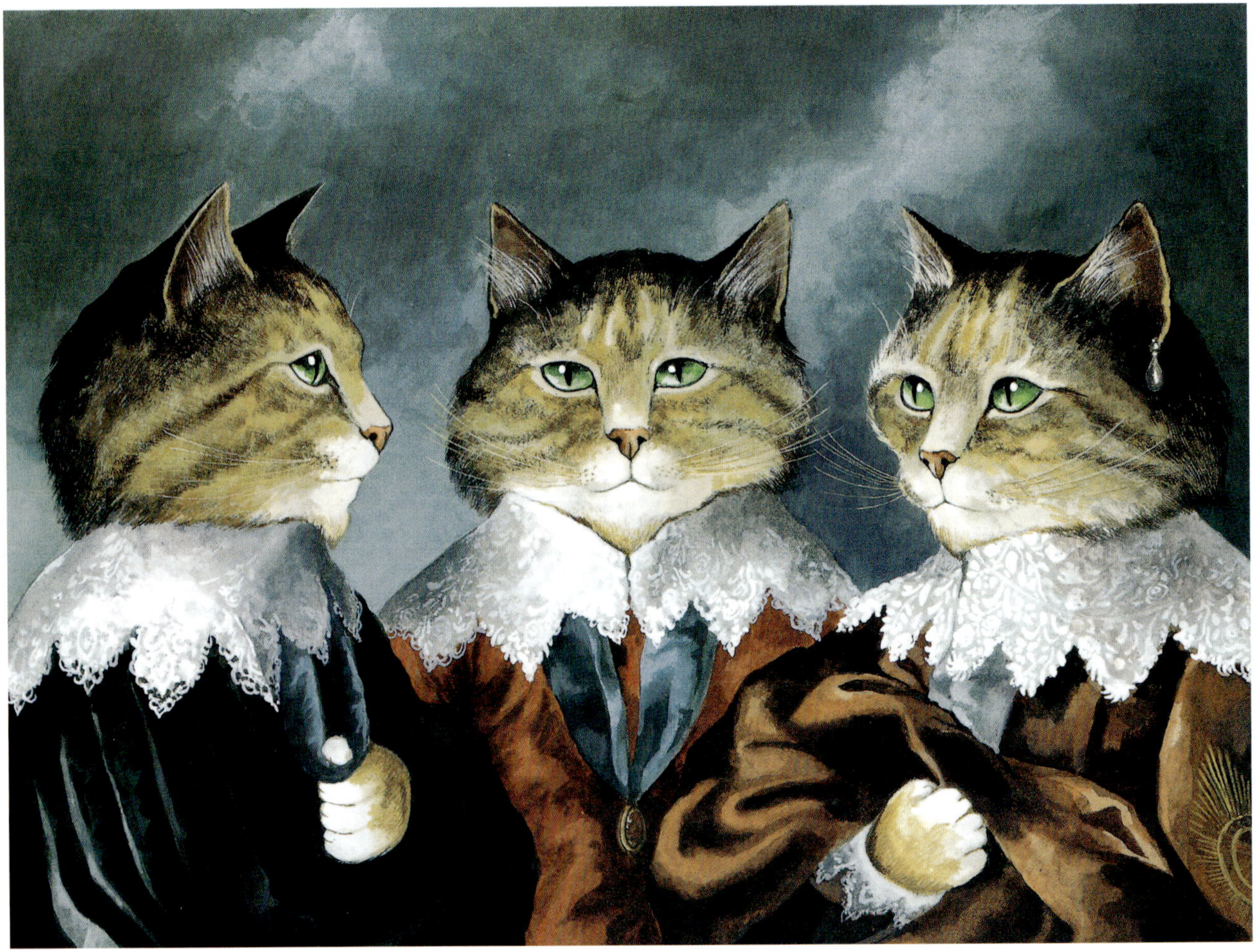

Above SIR ANTHONY VAN DYCK, *King Charles I in Three Positions* (1635 or 1636)

Opposite FRANS HALS, *The Laughing Cavalier* (1624)

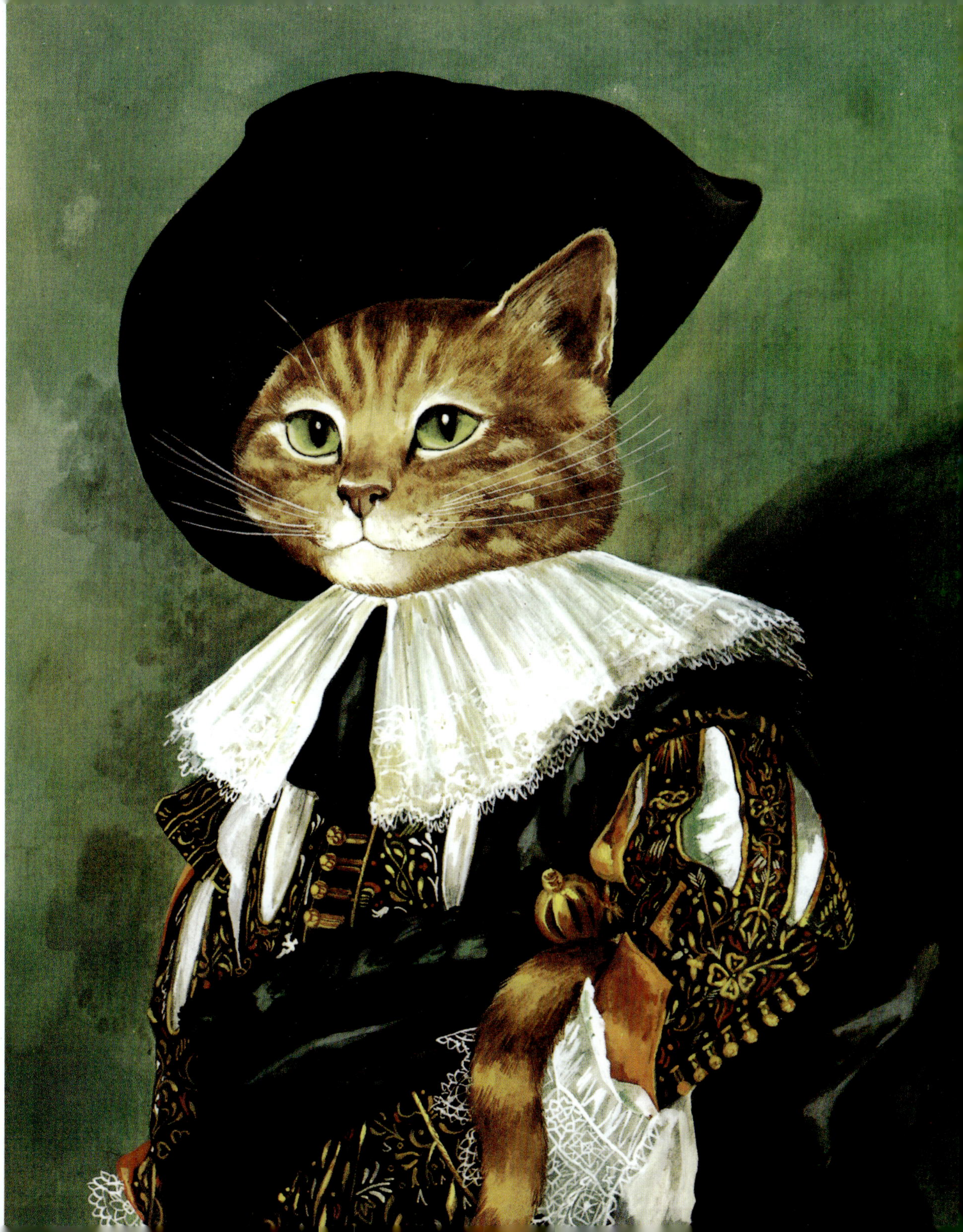

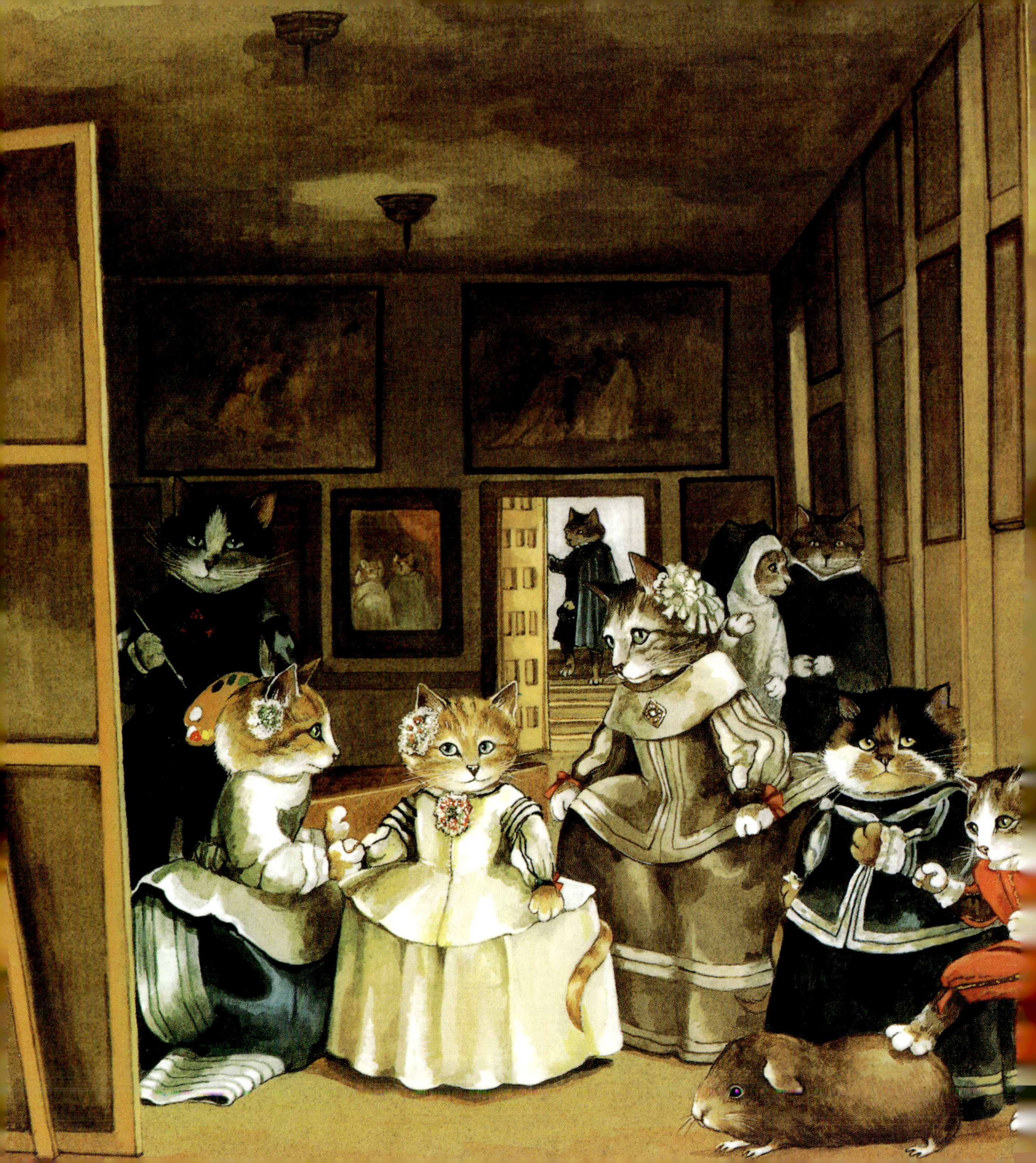

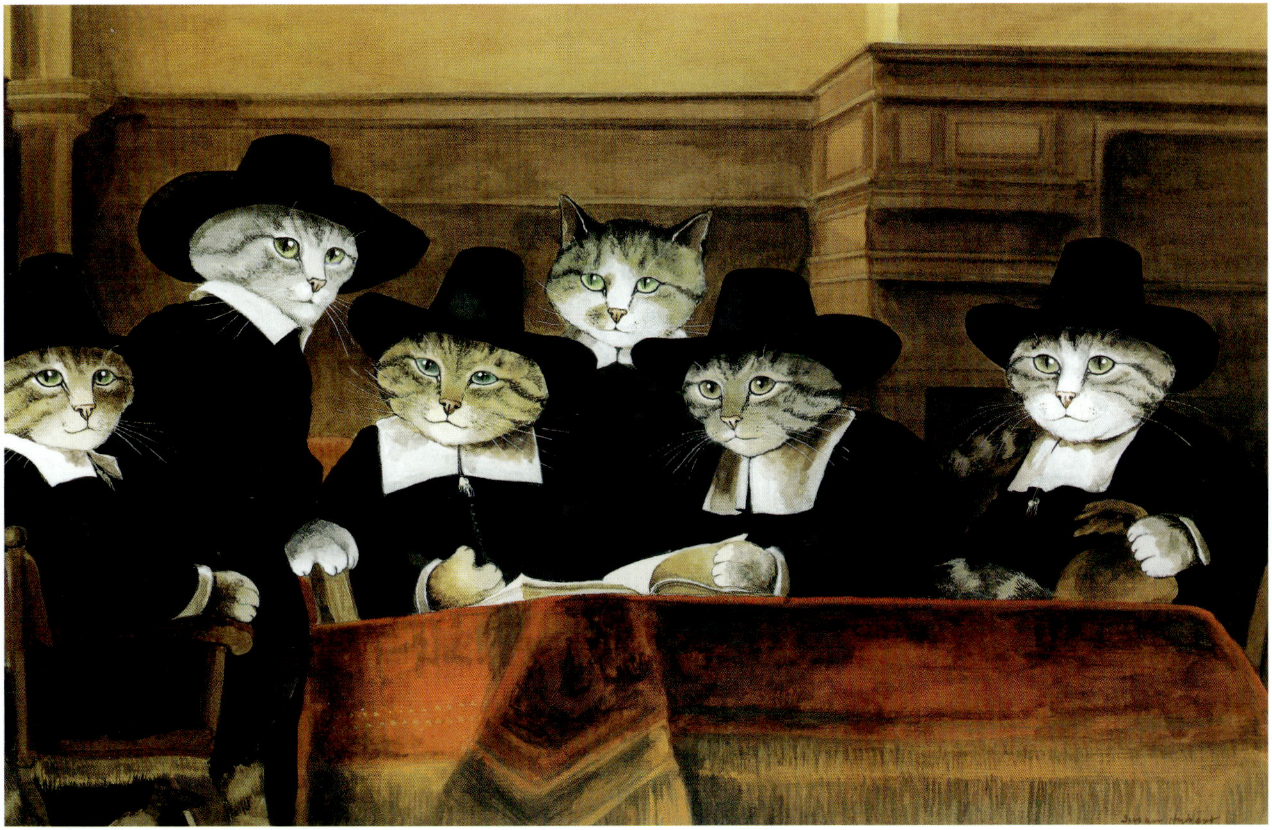

Above REMBRANDT, *The Syndics of the Drapers' Guild* (1662)
Opposite DIEGO VELÁZQUEZ, *Las Meninas* (1656)

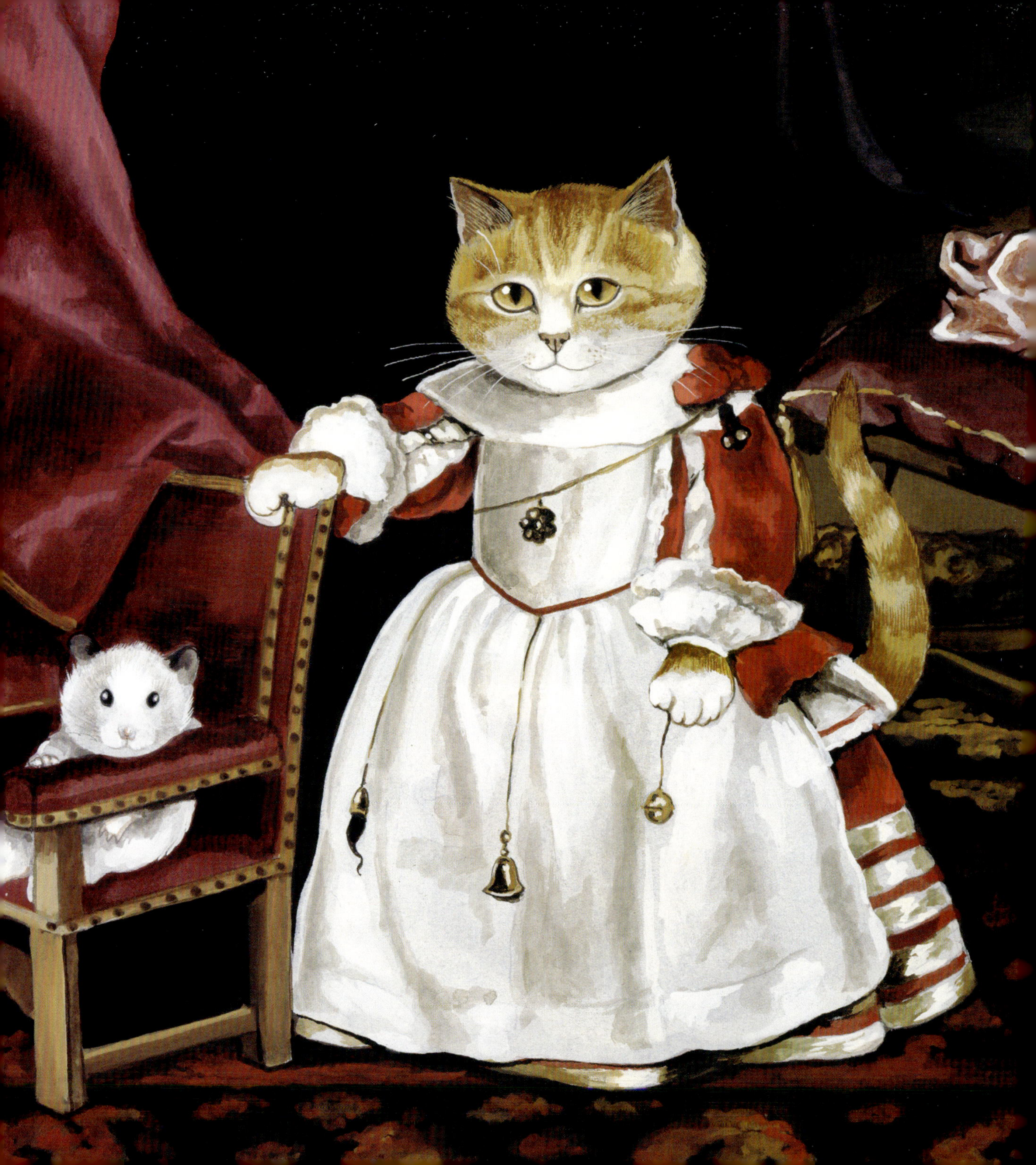

DIEGO VELÁZQUEZ

Portrait of Prince Philip Prospero (1659)

JAN VERMEER

Girl with a Pearl Earring (c. 1665)

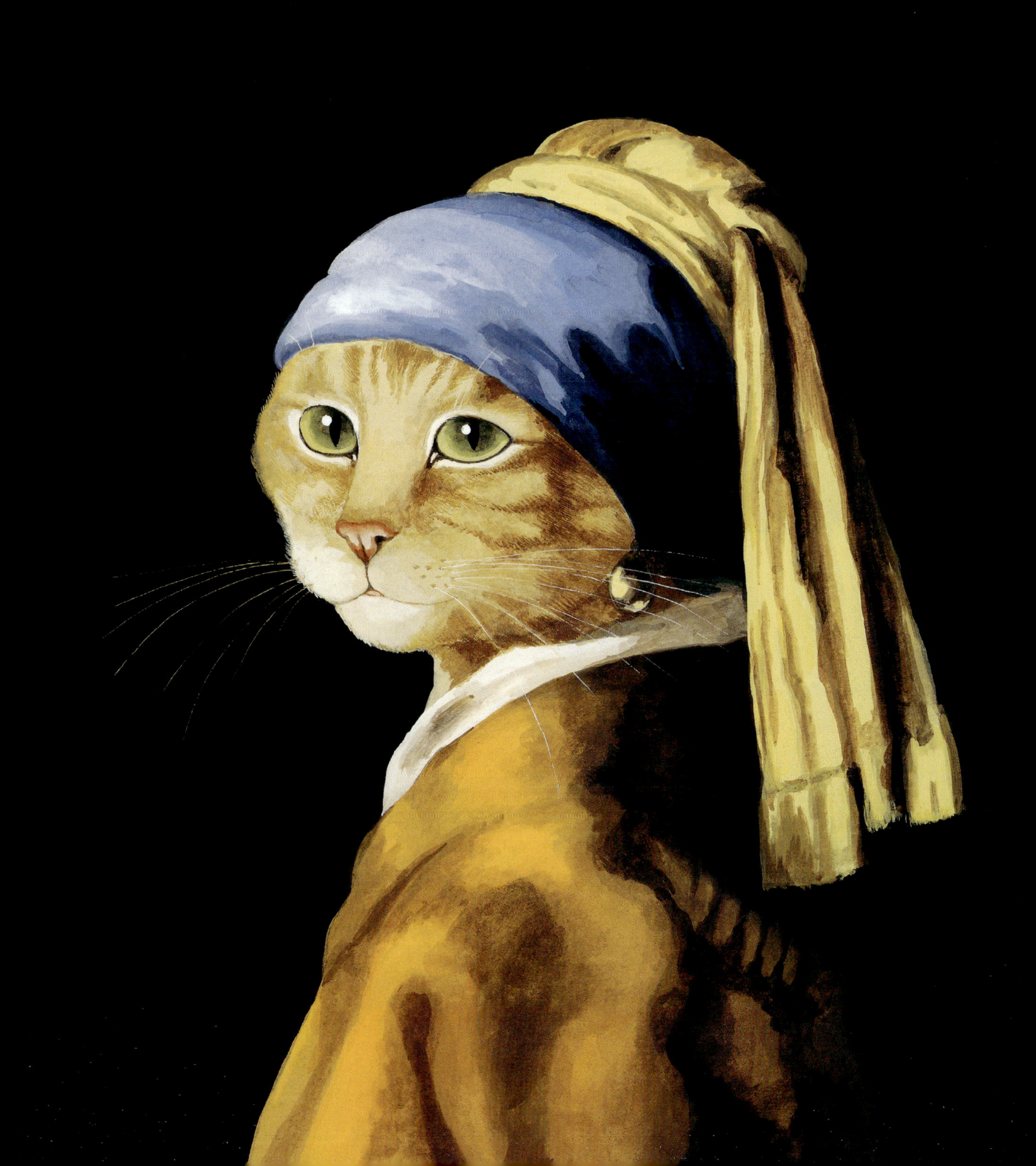

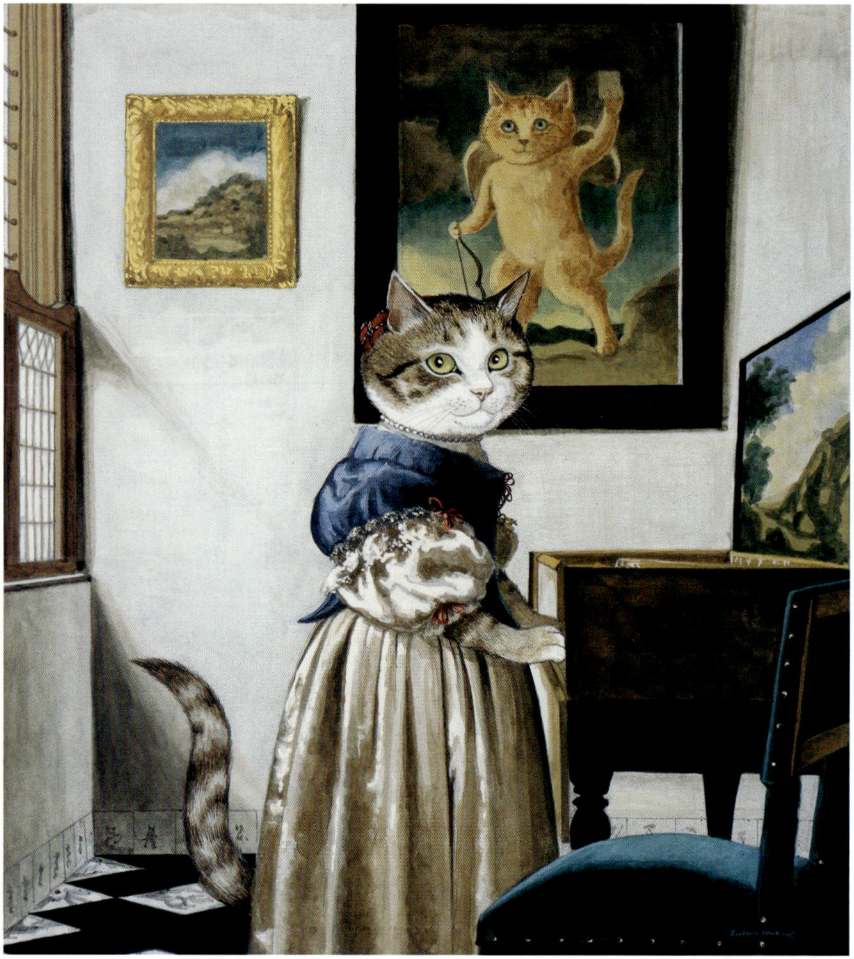

Above JAN VERMEER, *Lady Standing at a Virginal* (1670–72)
Opposite JAN VERMEER, *The Artist in his Studio* (1665–68)

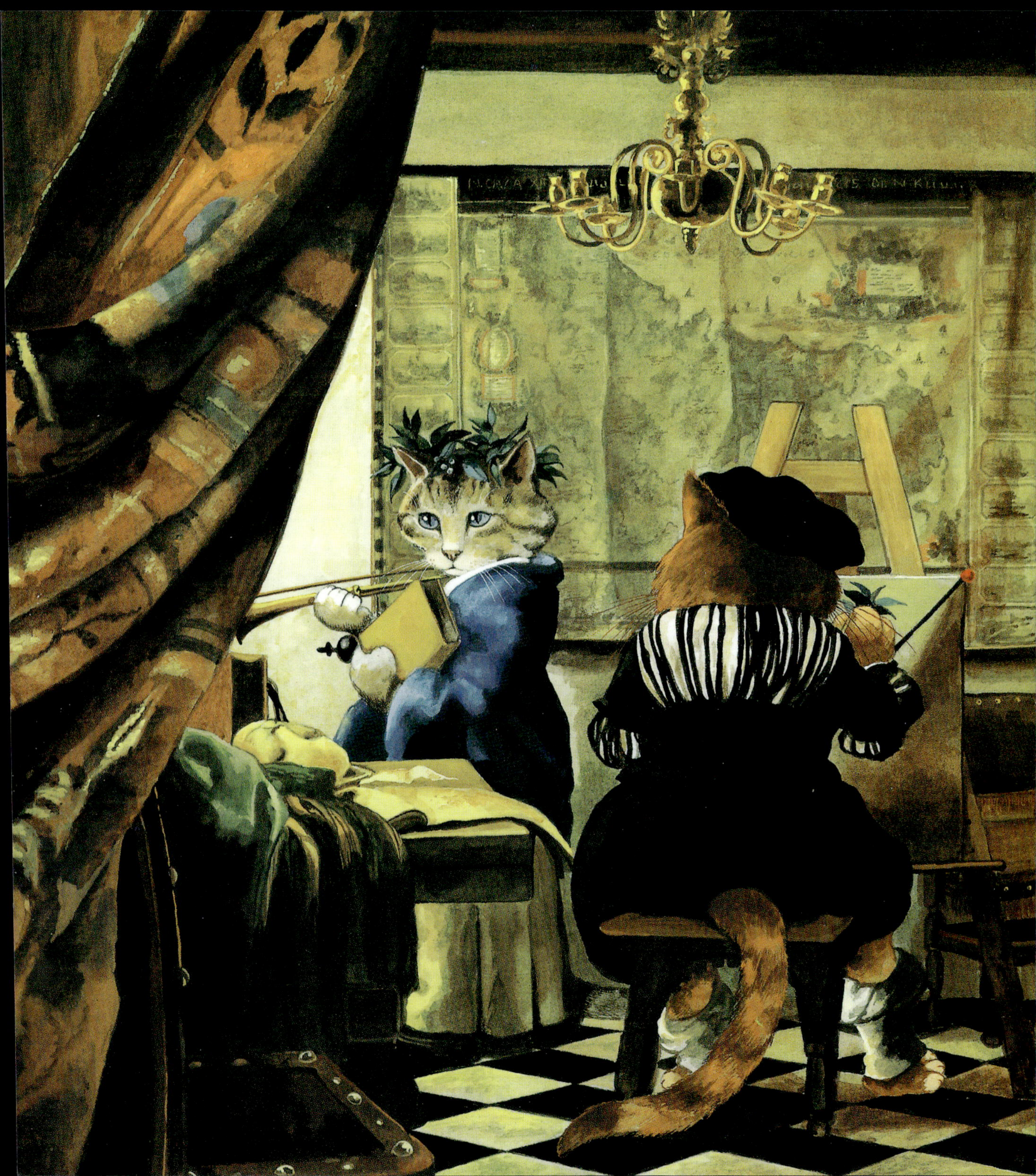

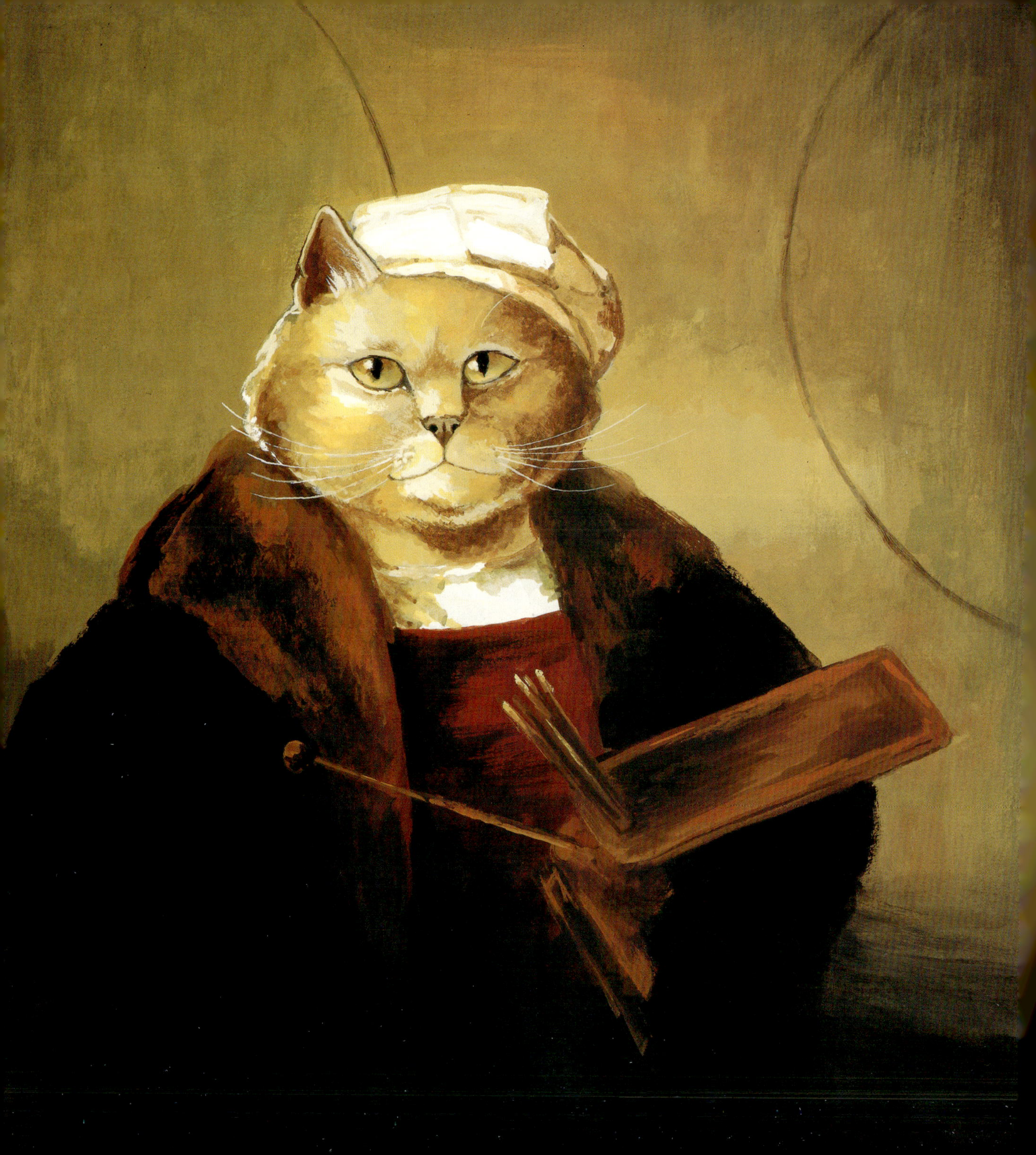

REMBRANDT

Self-Portrait with Two Circles (1665–69)

REMBRANDT

A Man in Armour (c. 1655)

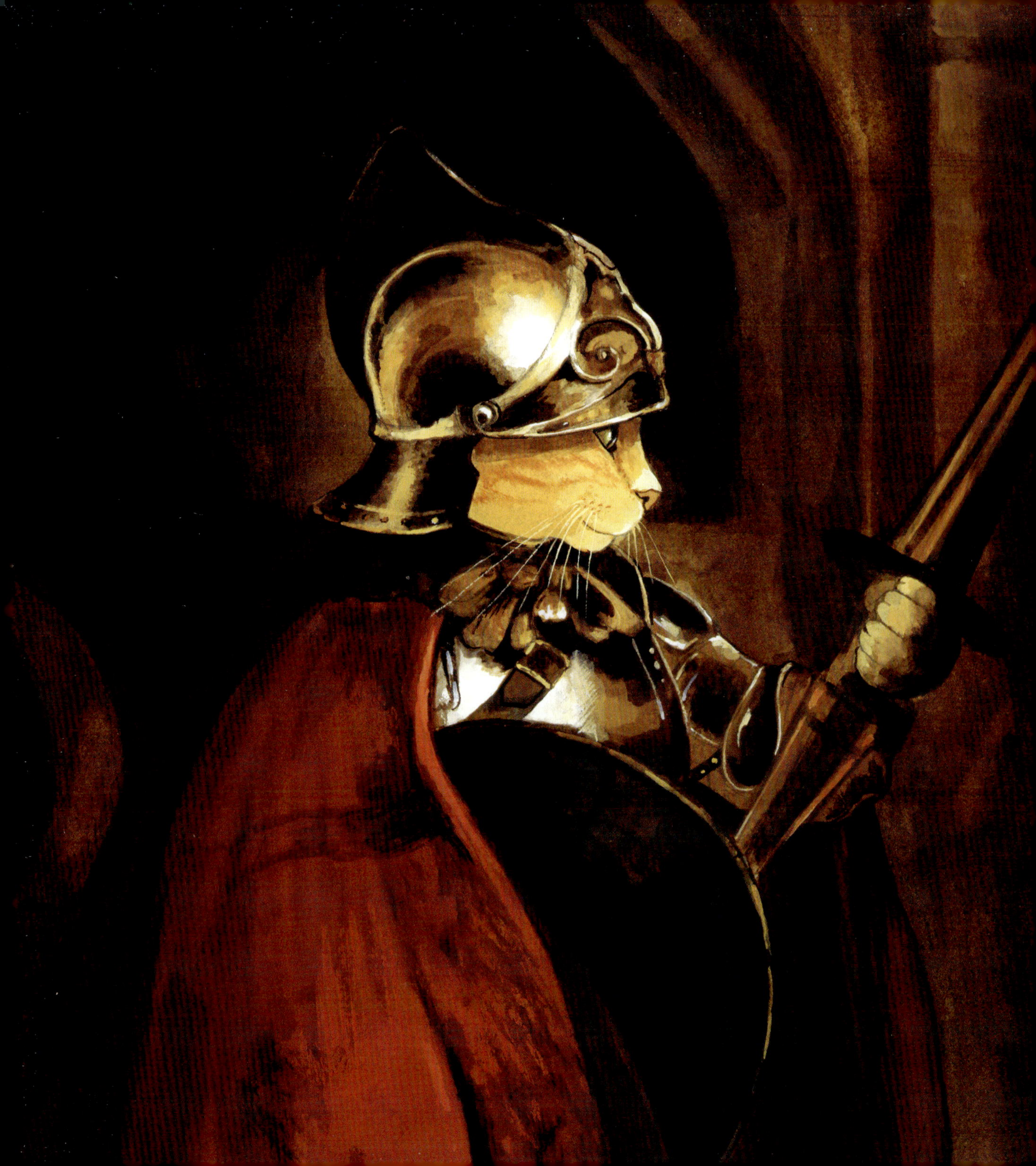

WILLIAM HOGARTH

An Election Entertainment (1754–55)

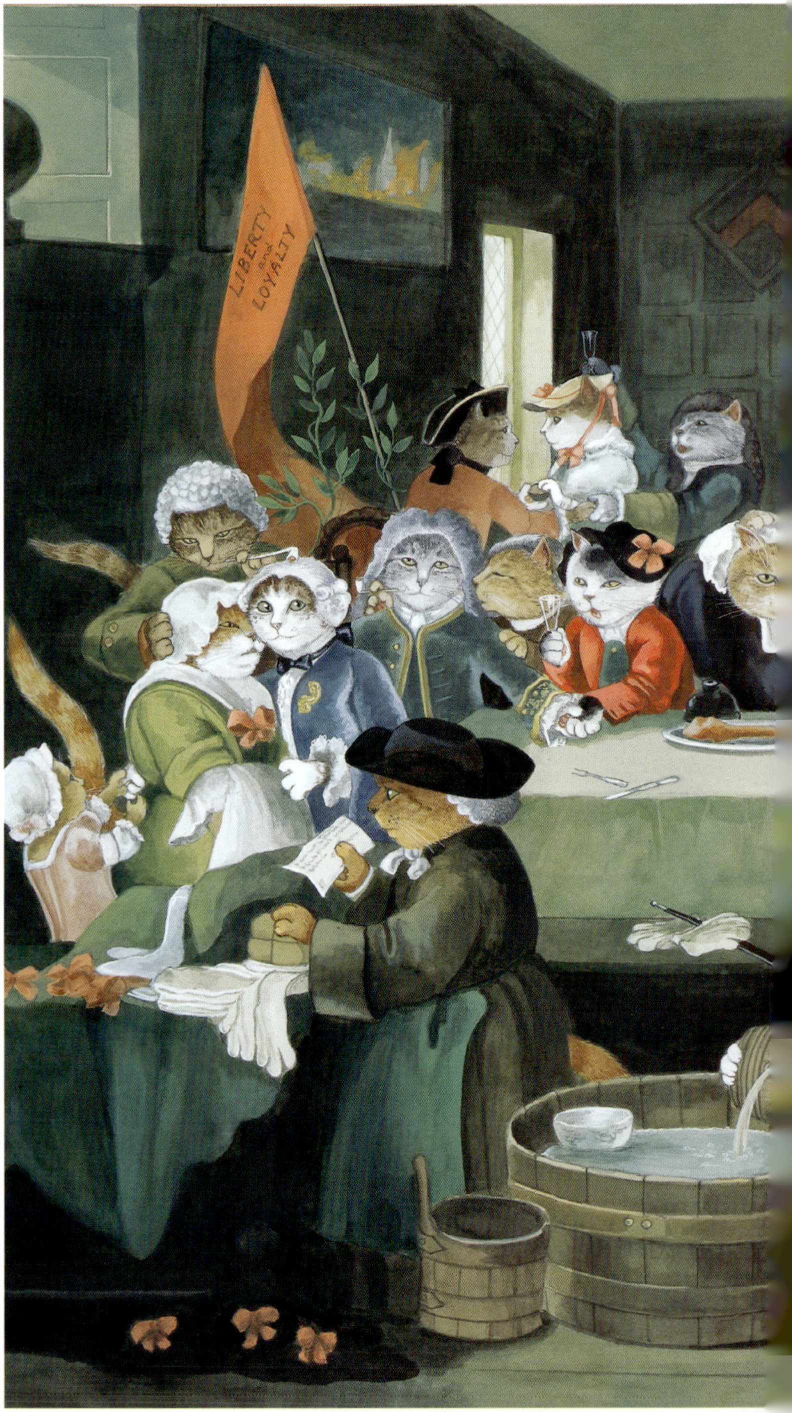

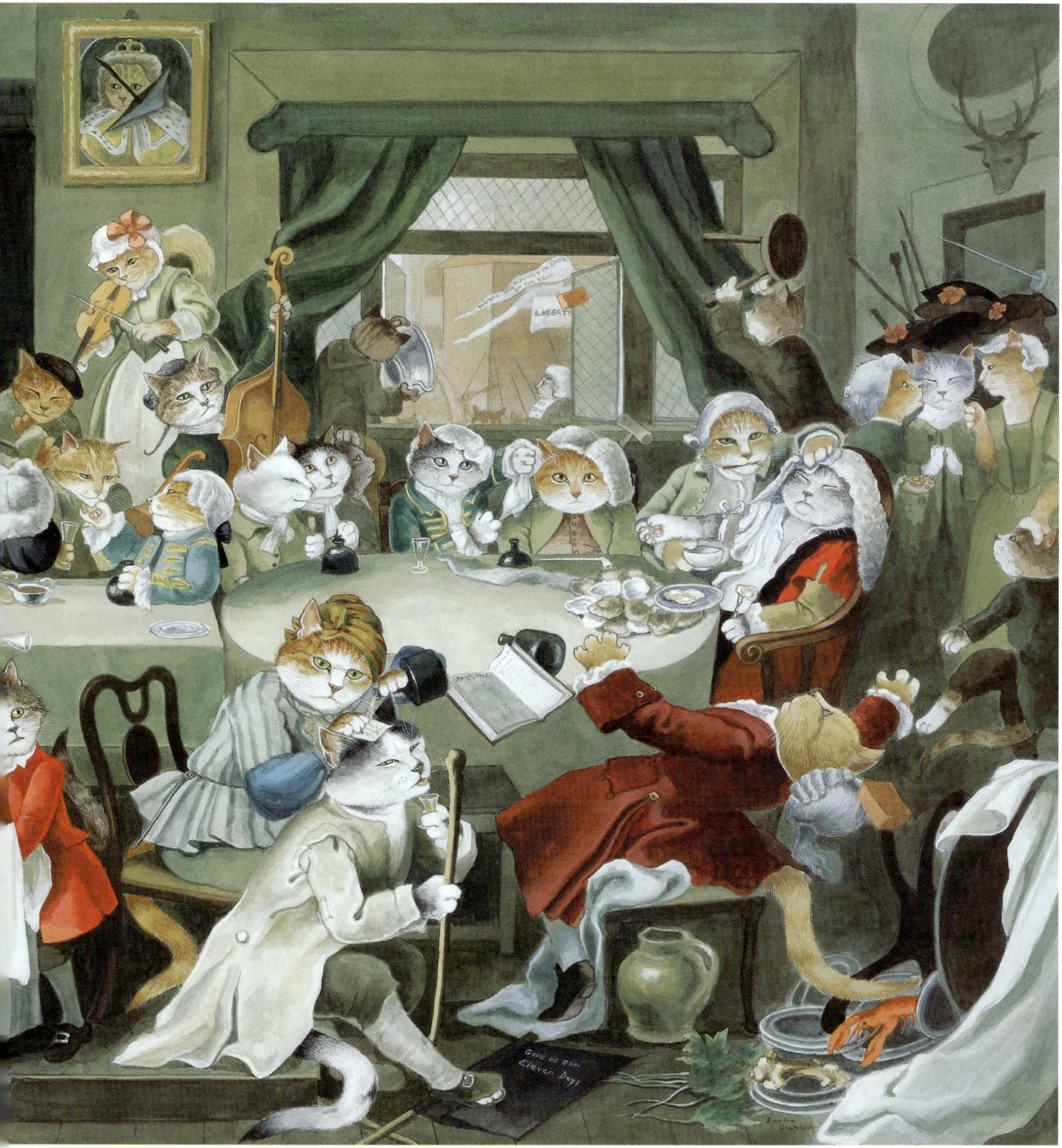
LIBERTY
Give us our
Eleven Days

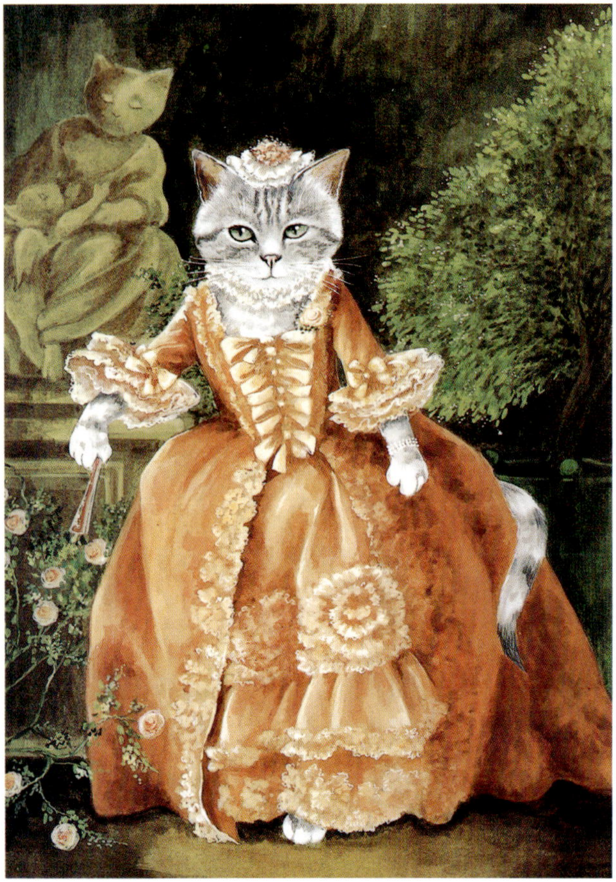 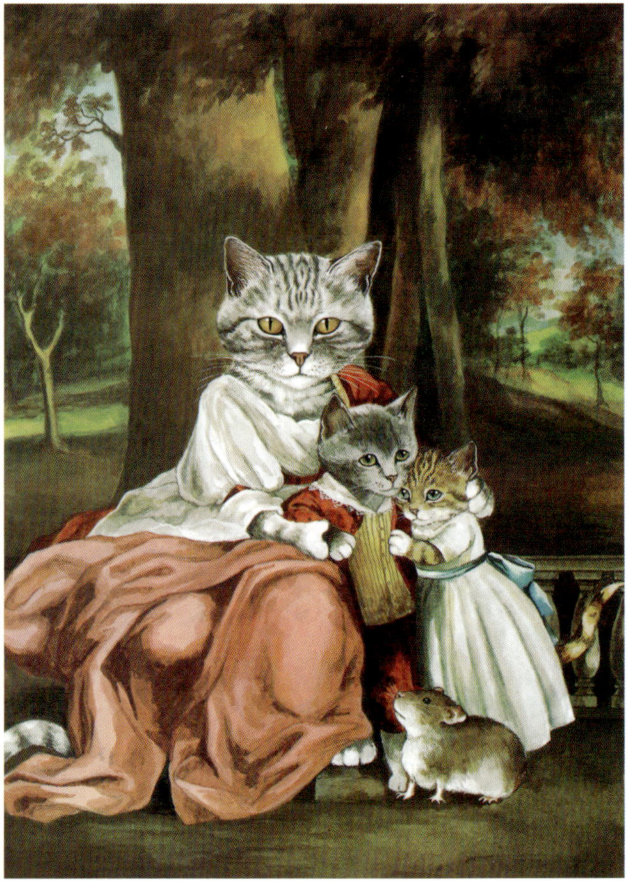

Above left FRANÇOIS BOUCHER, *Madame de Pompadour* (1759)

Above right SIR JOSHUA REYNOLDS, *Lady Elizabeth Delmé and Her Children* (1779)

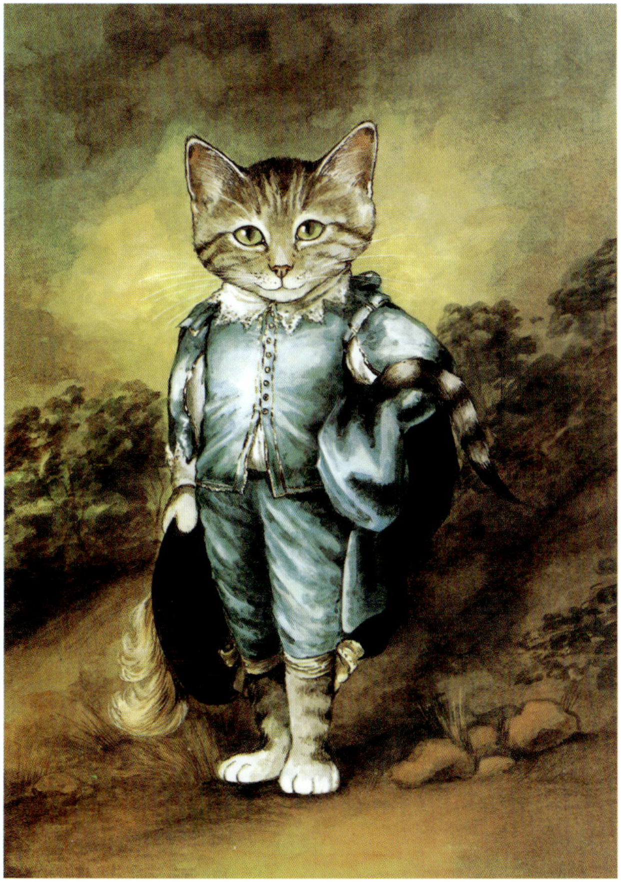

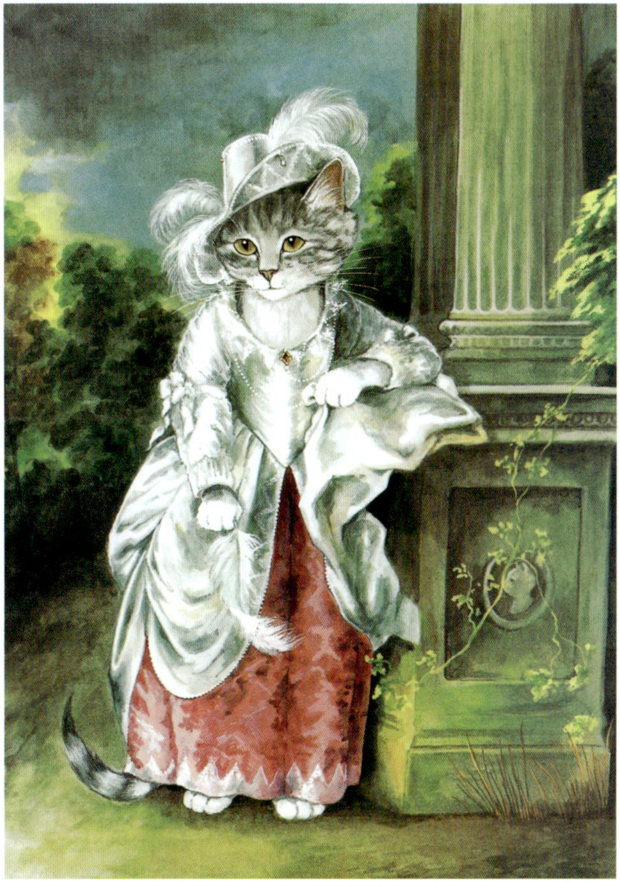

Above left THOMAS GAINSBOROUGH, *The Blue Boy* (c. 1770)

Above right THOMAS GAINSBOROUGH, *The Honourable Mrs Graham* (1775–77)

JEAN-HONORÉ FRAGONARD

The Swing (c. 1767)

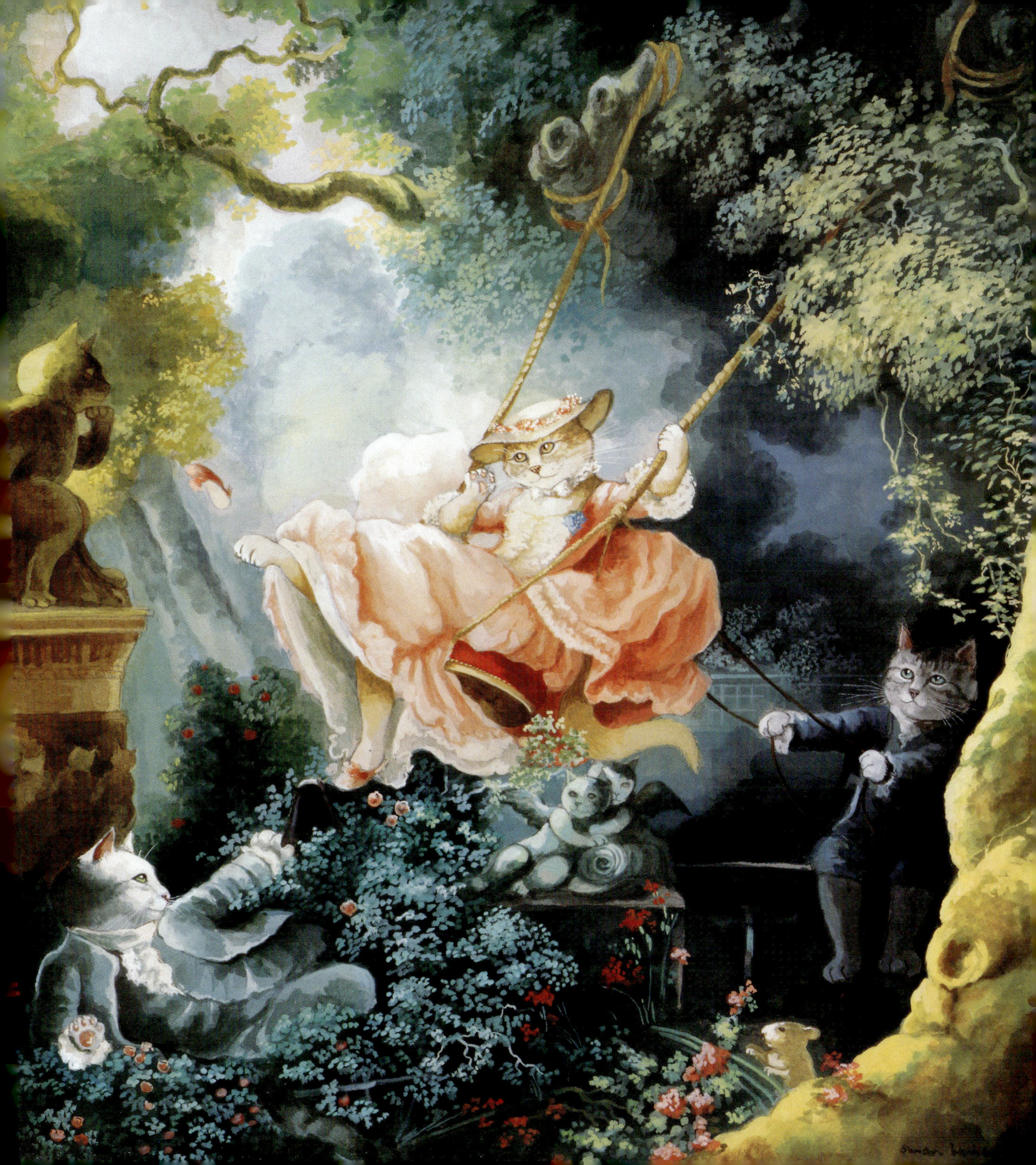

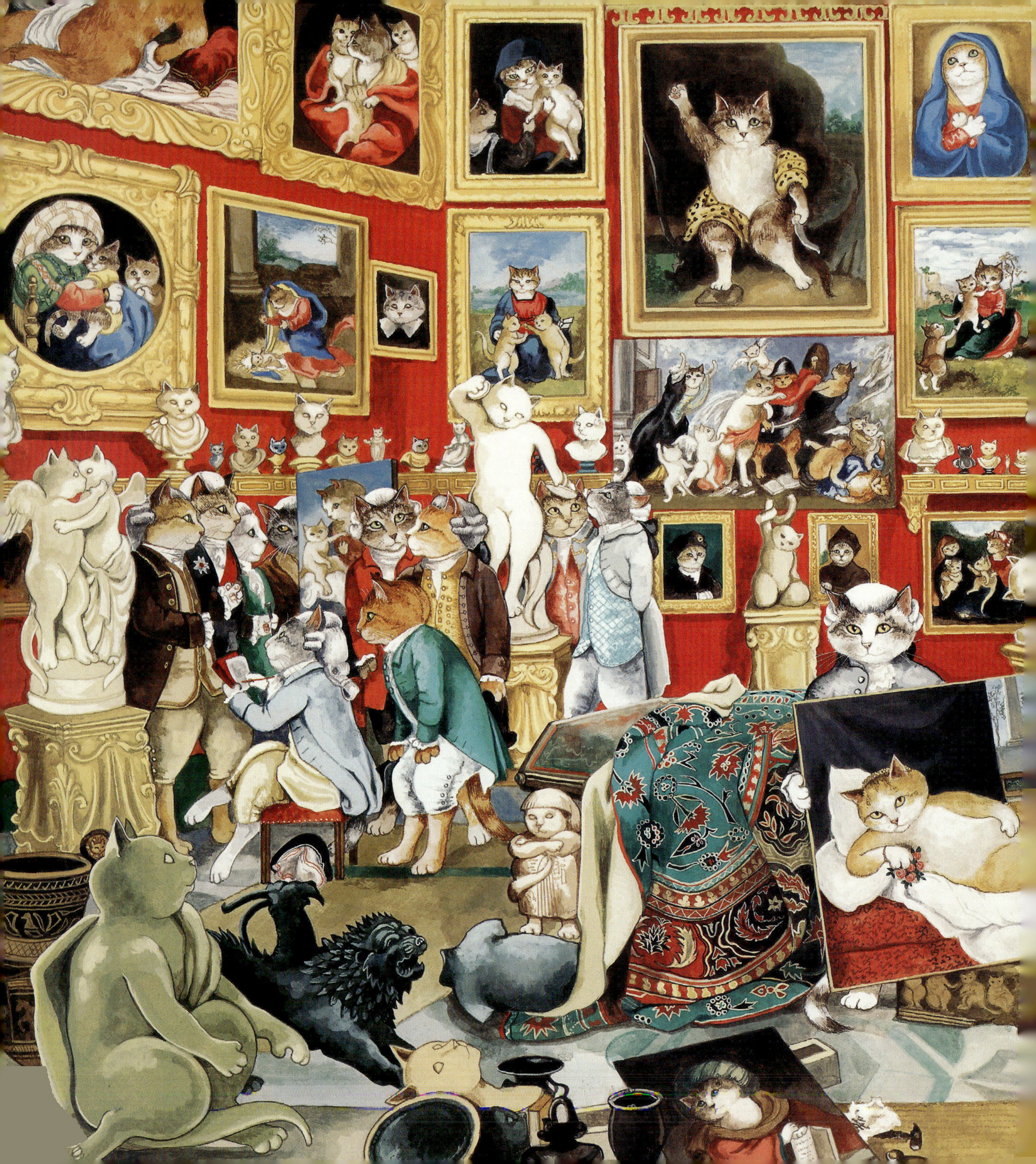

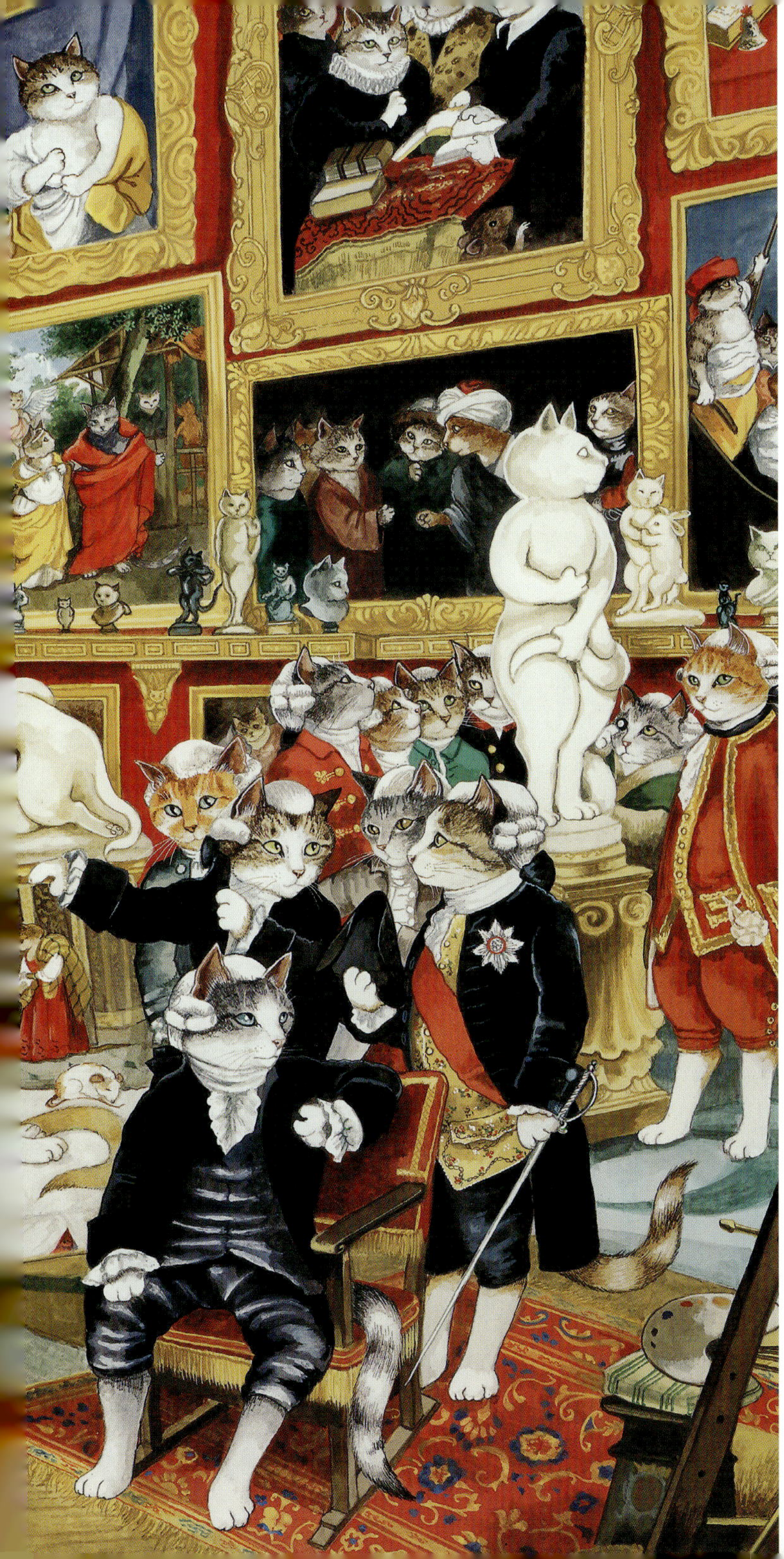

JOHAN ZOFFANY

The Tribuna of the Uffizi (1772–77)

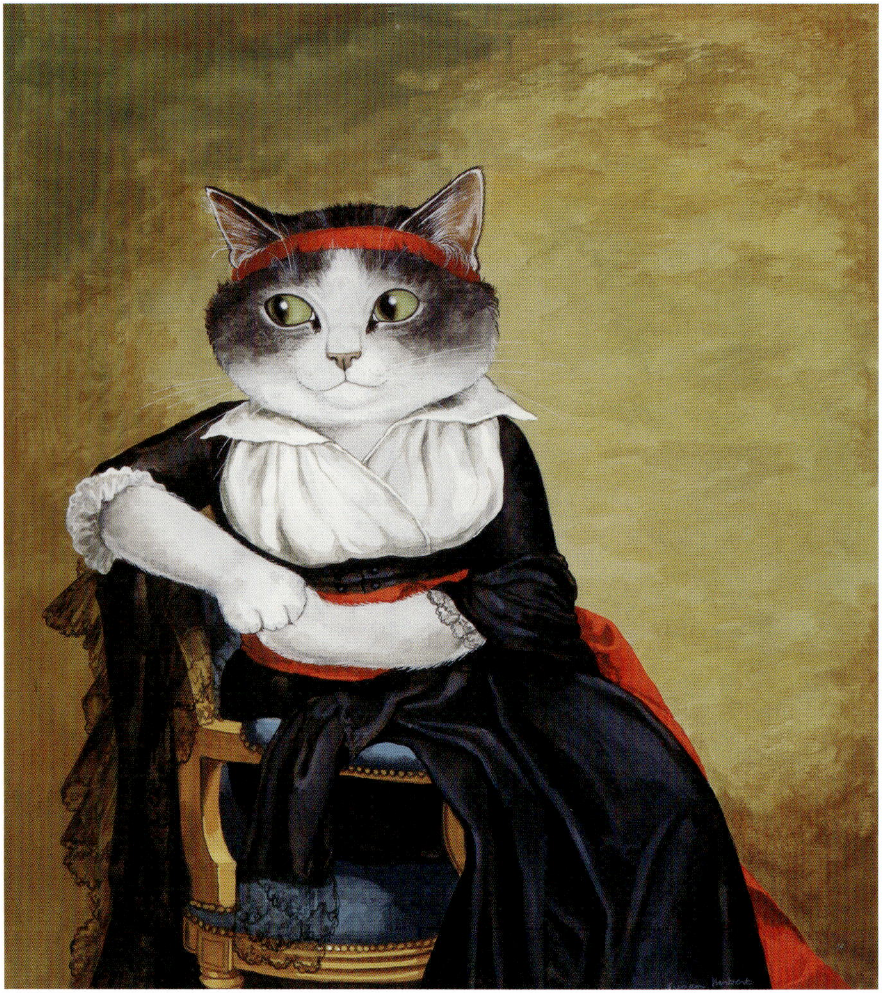

Above JACQUES-LOUIS DAVID, *Portrait of the Marquise d'Orvilliers* (1790)
Opposite JACQUES-LOUIS DAVID, *Portrait of Charles-Pierre Pécoul* (1784)

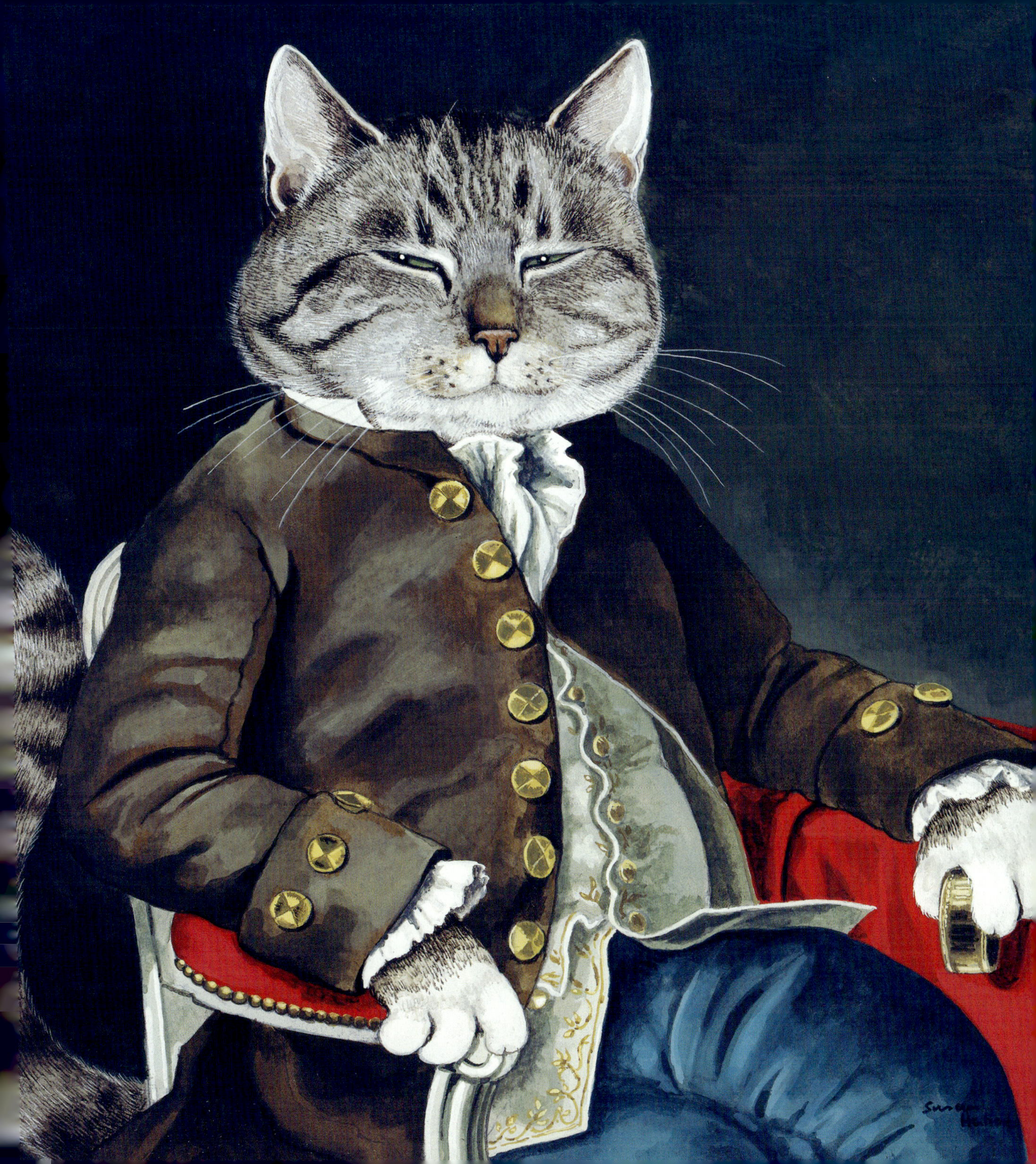

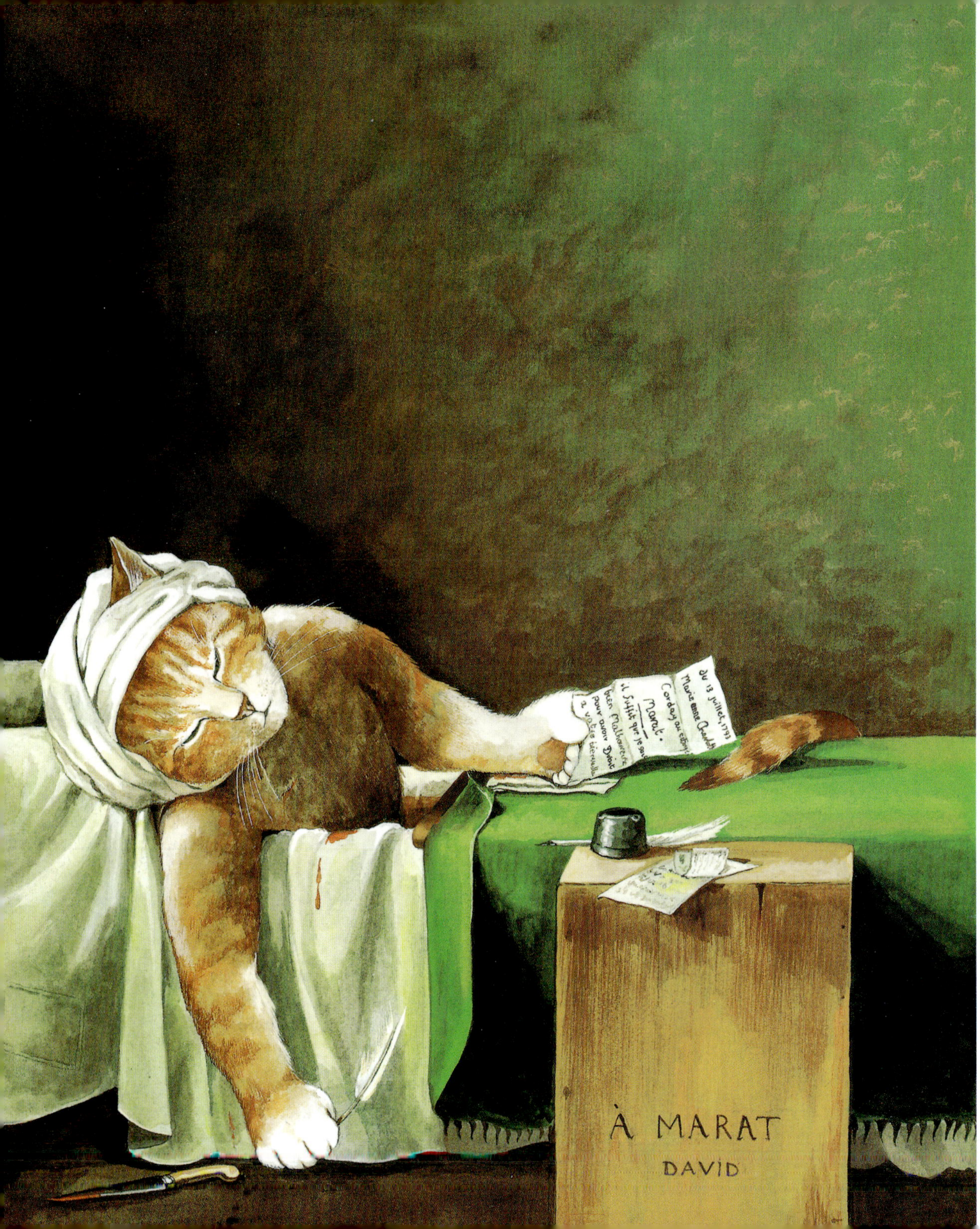
À MARAT
DAVID

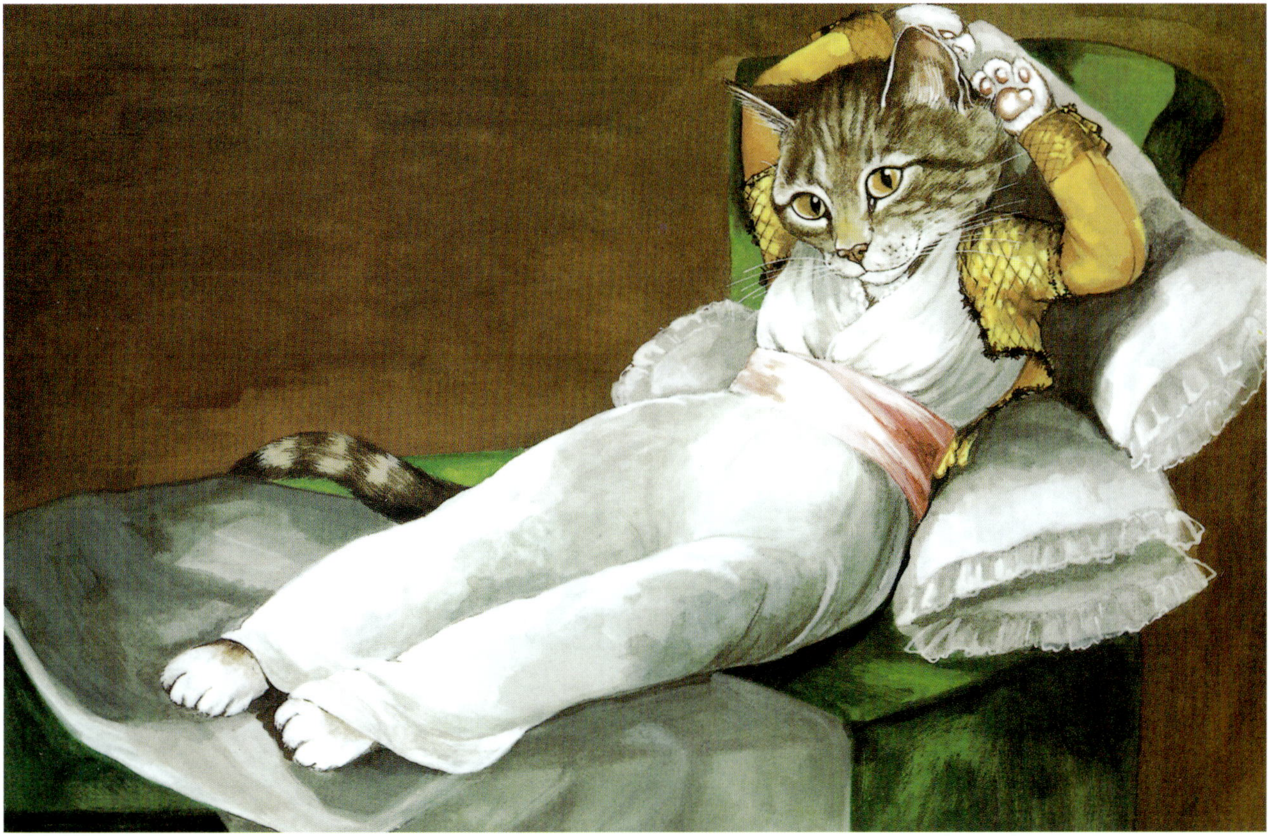

Above FRANCISCO GOYA, *The Clothed Maja* (1800–5)

Opposite JACQUES-LOUIS DAVID, *The Death of Marat* (1793)

WILLIAM BLAKE

The Ancient of Days (1794)

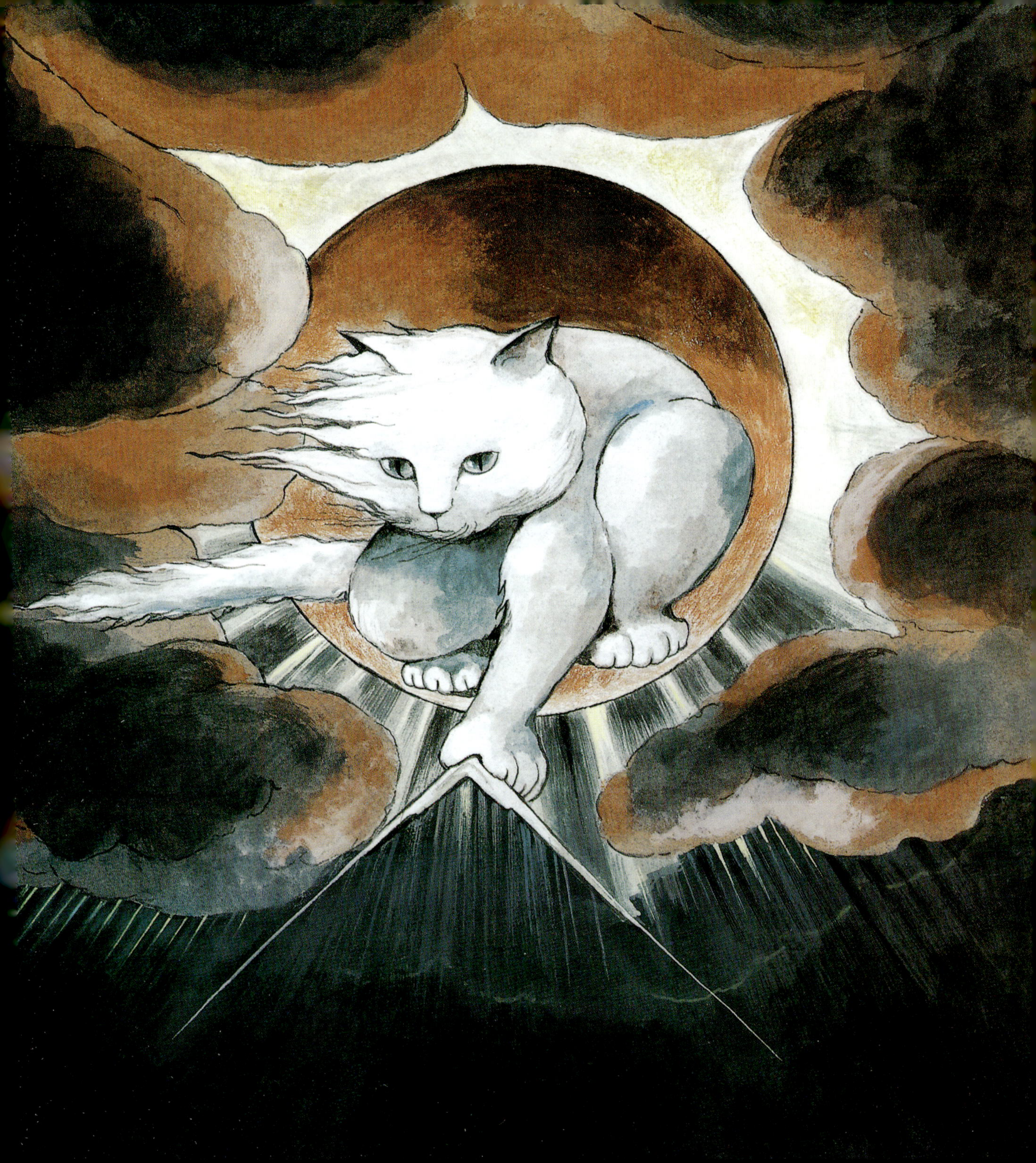

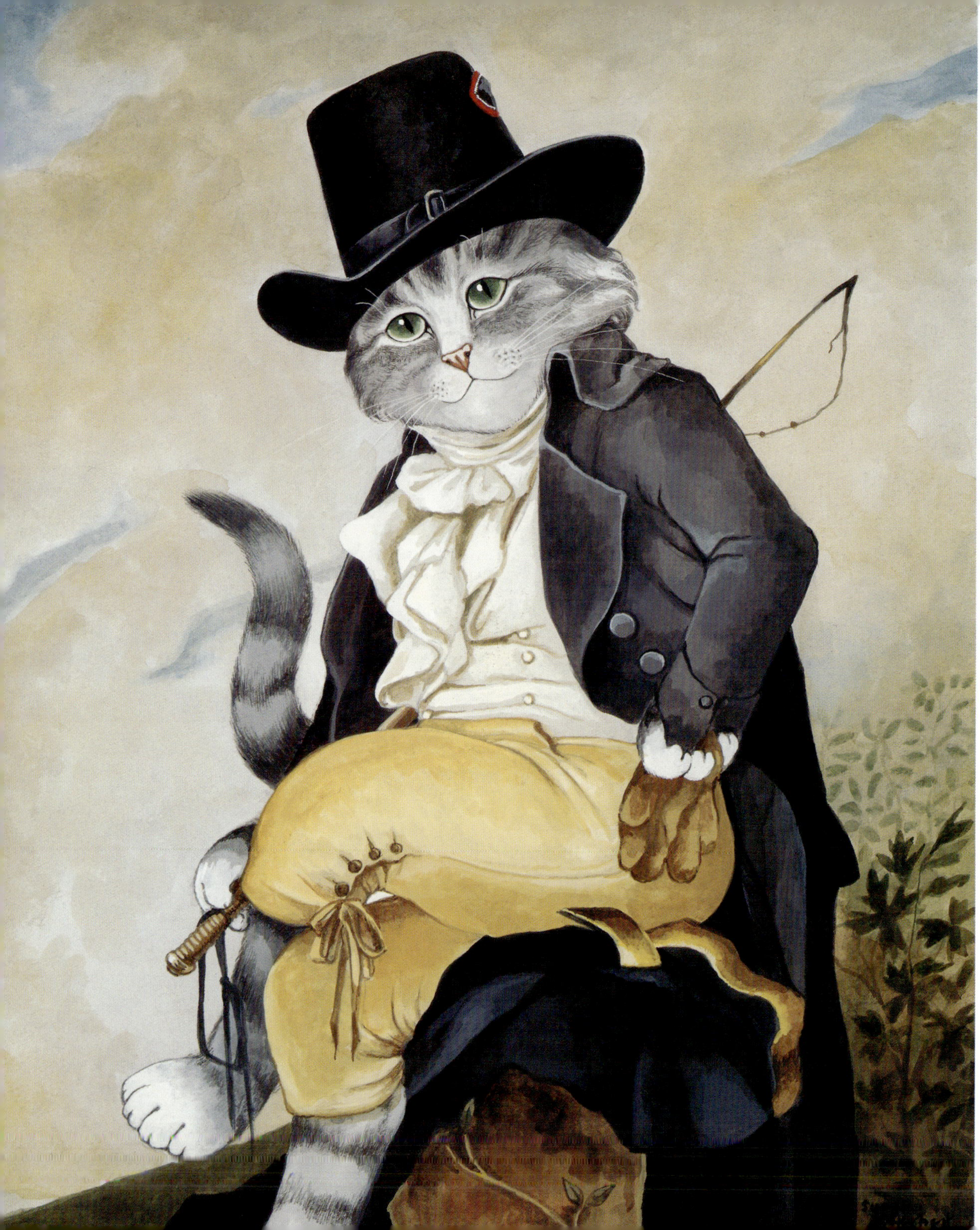

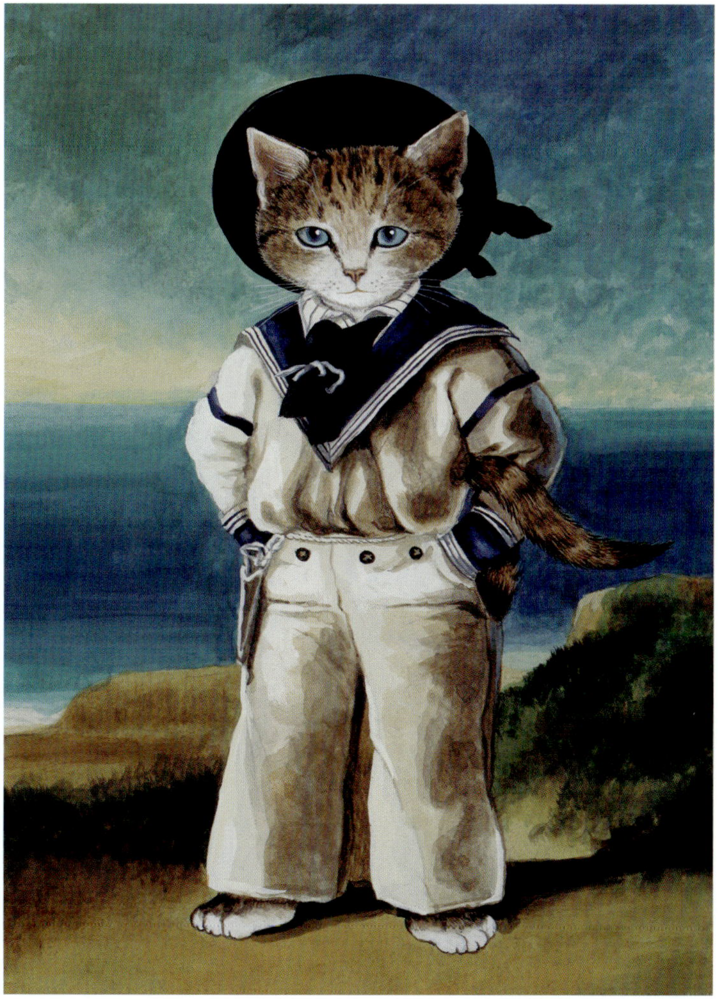

Above FRANZ XAVER WINTERHALTER, *Portrait of Prince Albert Edward* (1846)
Opposite JACQUES-LOUIS DAVID, *Monsieur Seriziat* (1795)

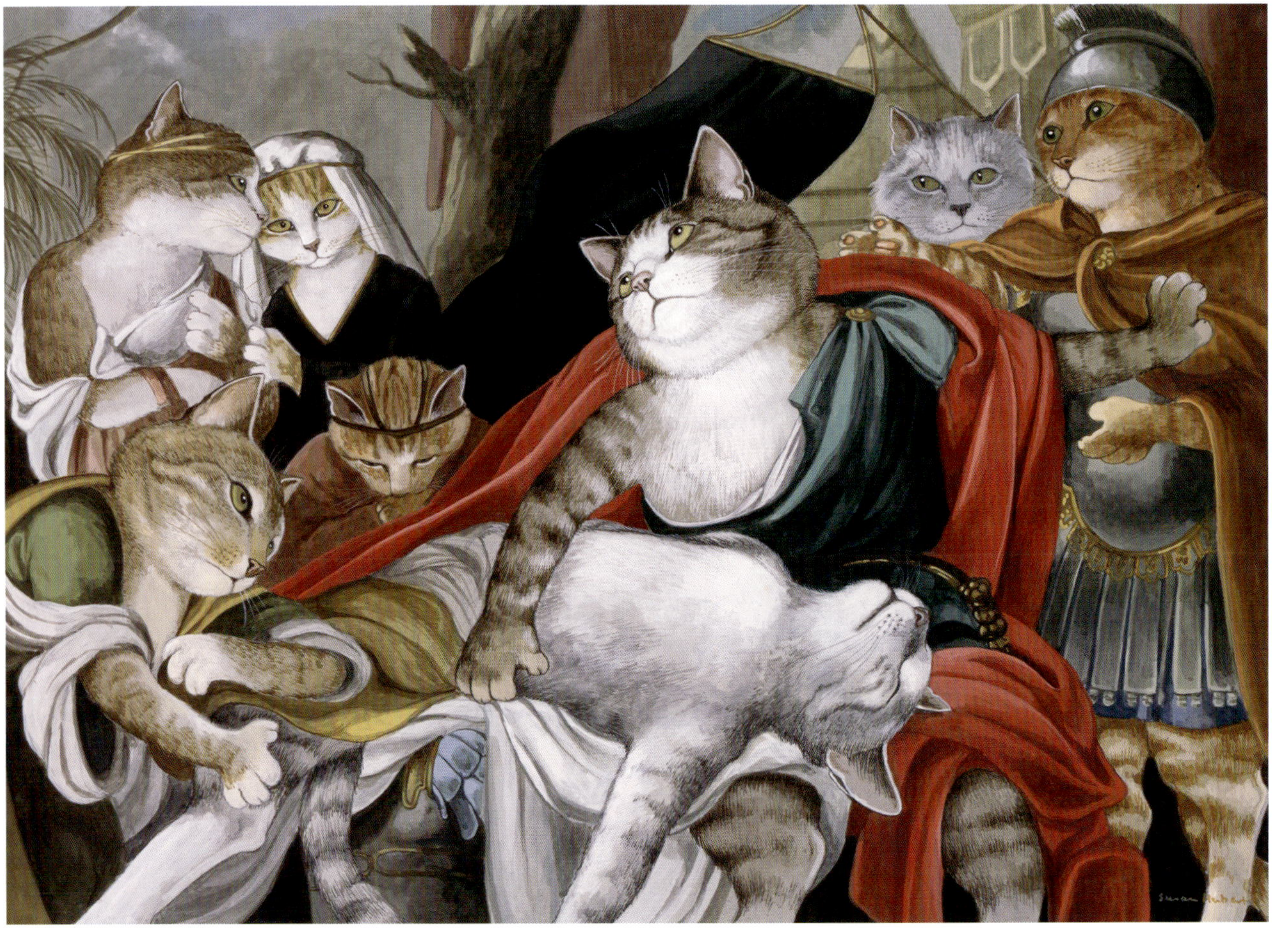

Above GAVIN HAMILTON, *Achilles Lamenting the Death of Patroclus* (1760–63)
Opposite JEAN-AUGUSTE-DOMINIQUE INGRES, *The Valpinçon Bather* (1808)

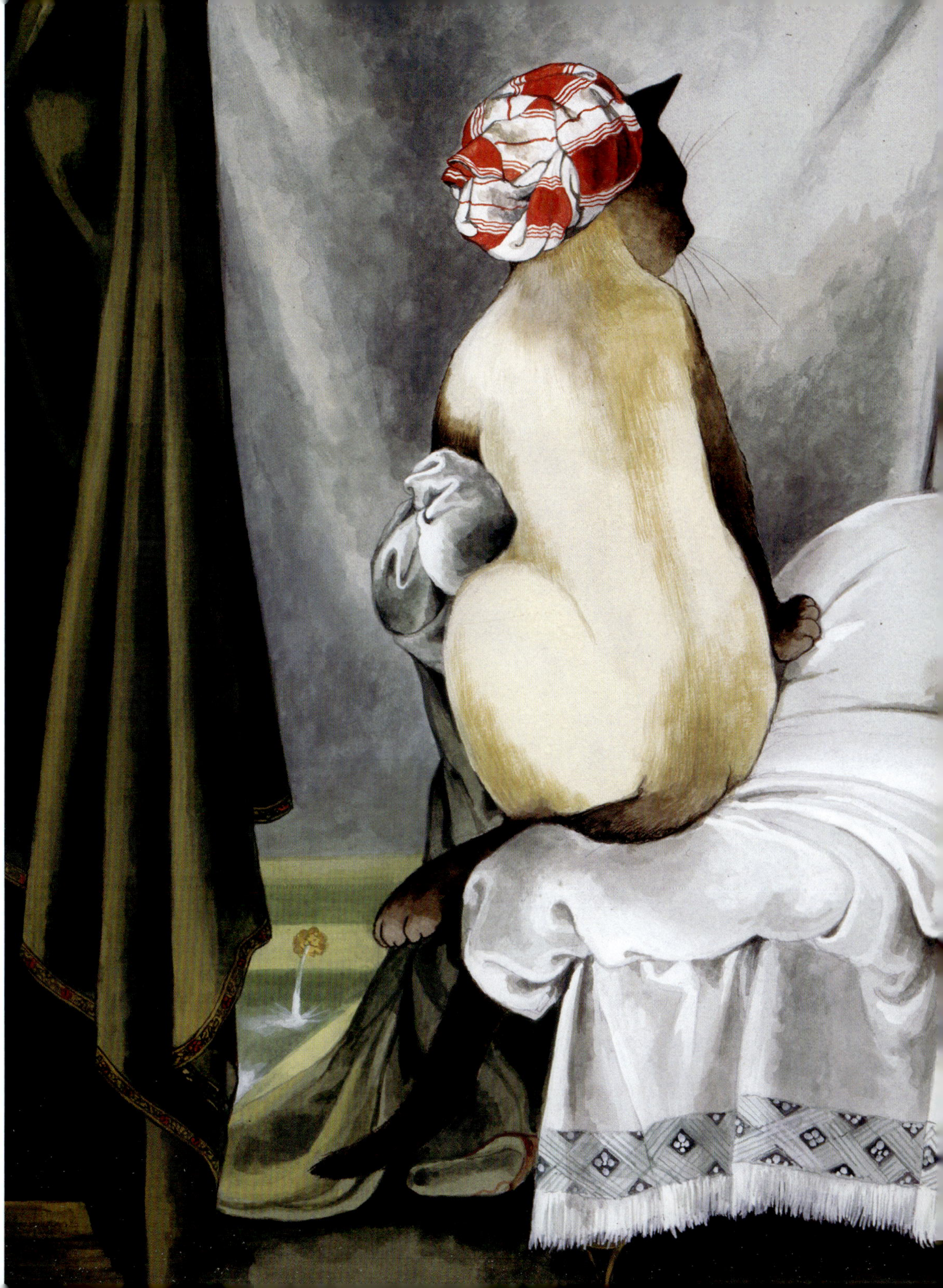

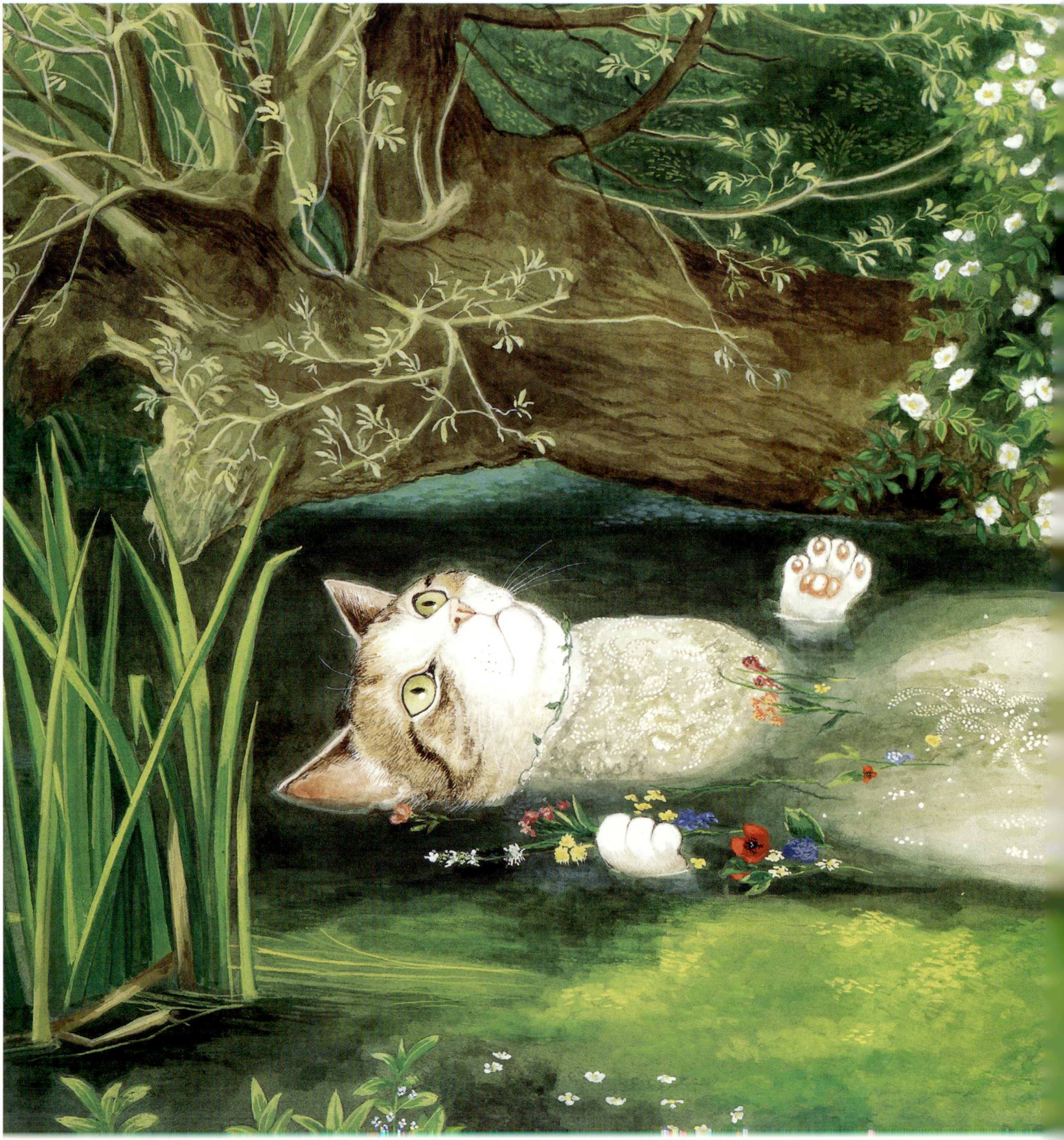

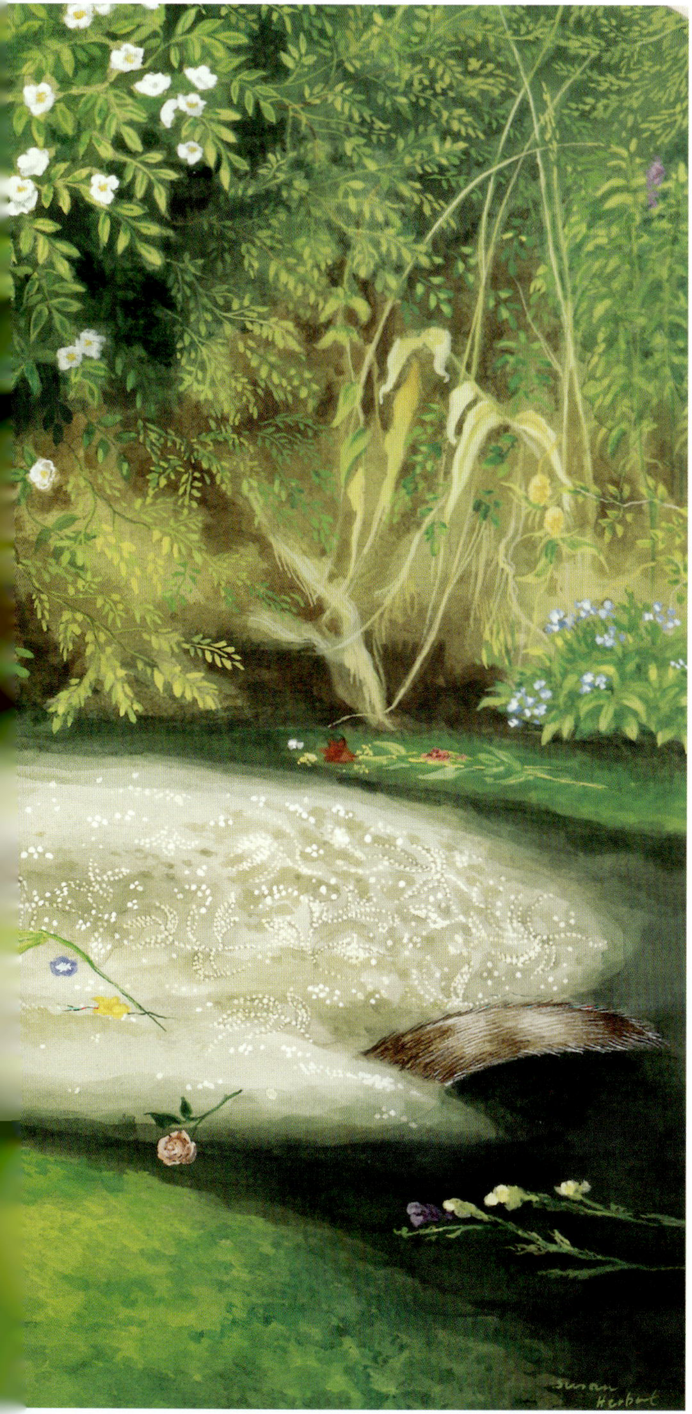

SIR JOHN EVERETT MILLAIS

Ophelia (1850–51)

DANTE GABRIEL ROSETTI

Regina Cordium (1866)

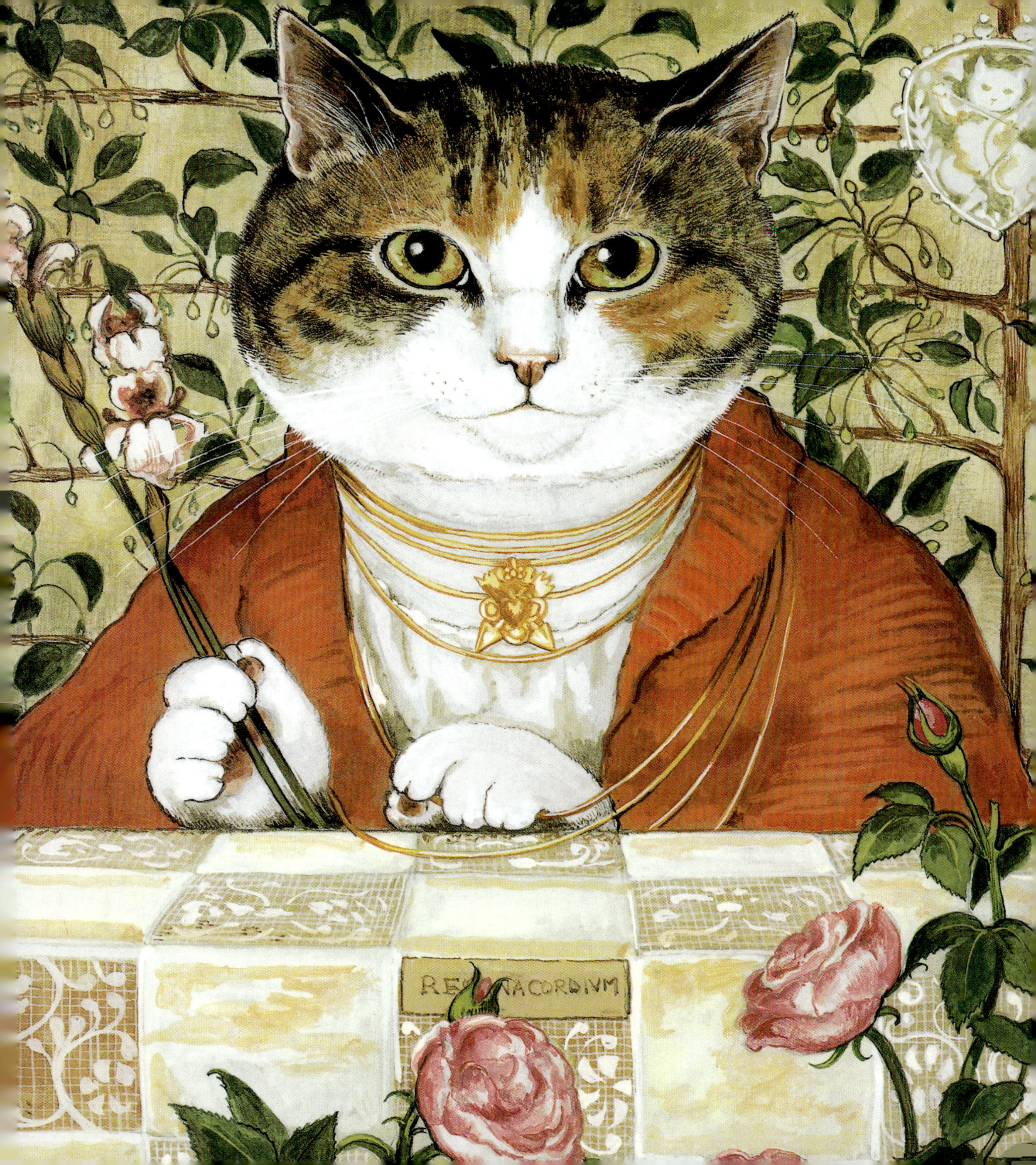
RE NACORDIVM

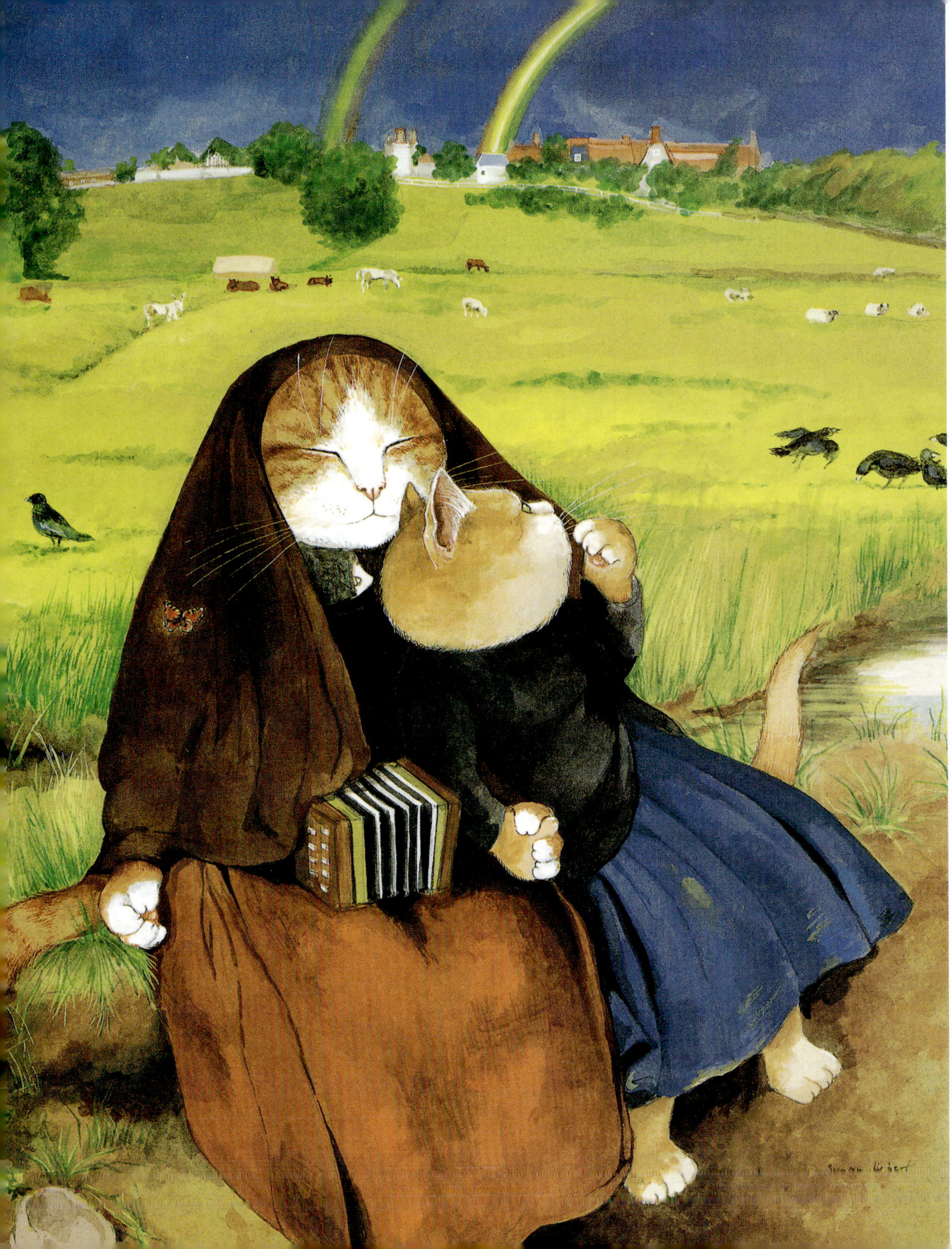

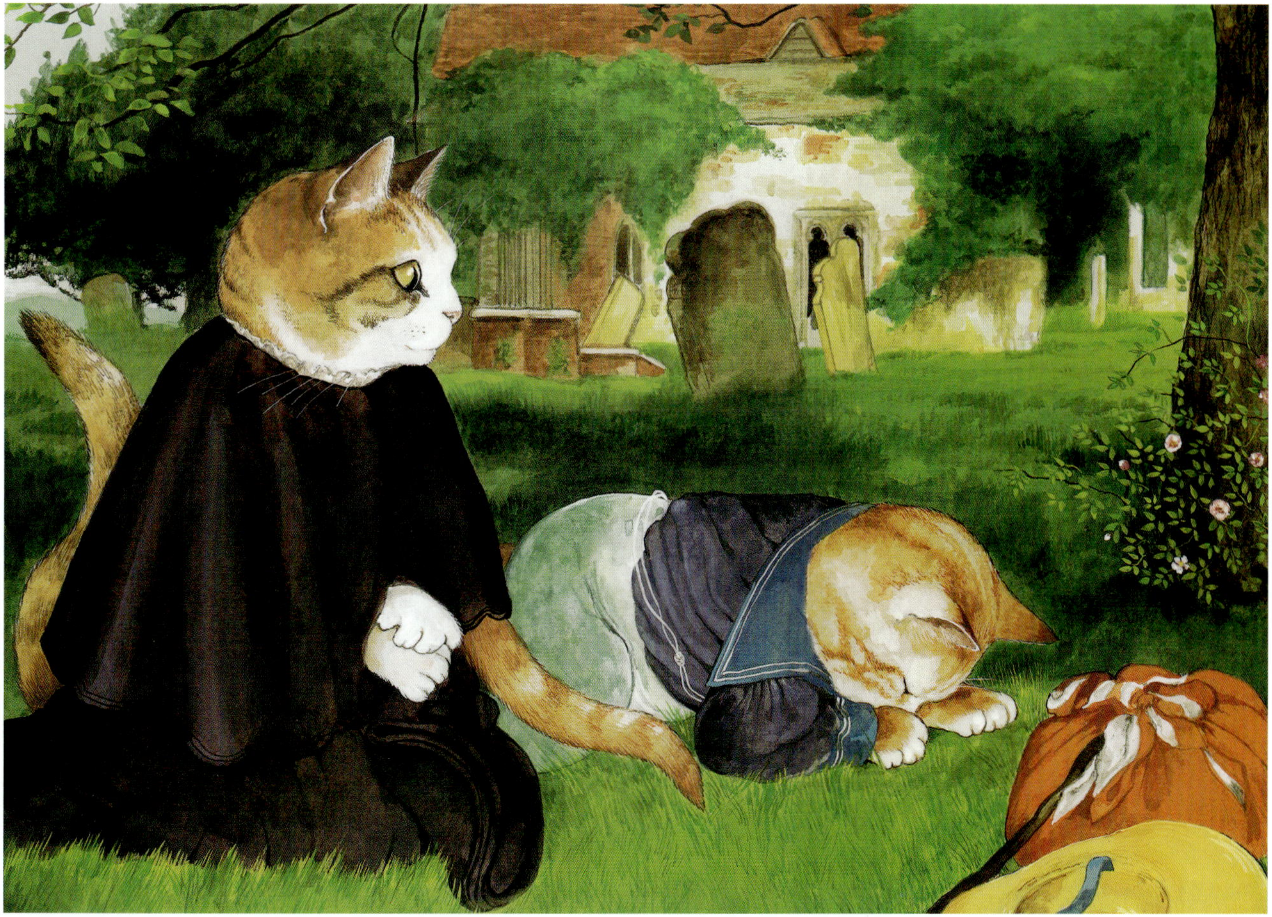

Above ARTHUR HUGHES, *Home from Sea* (1862)

Opposite SIR JOHN EVERETT MILLAIS, *The Blind Girl* (1856)

GUSTAVE COURBET

The Meeting (1854)

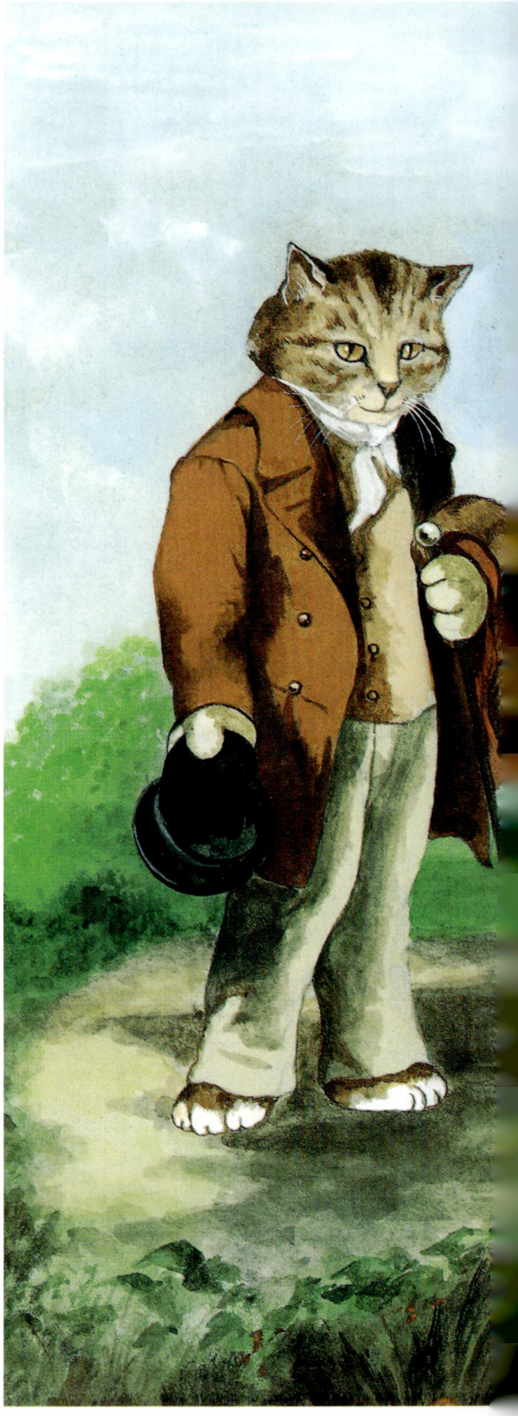

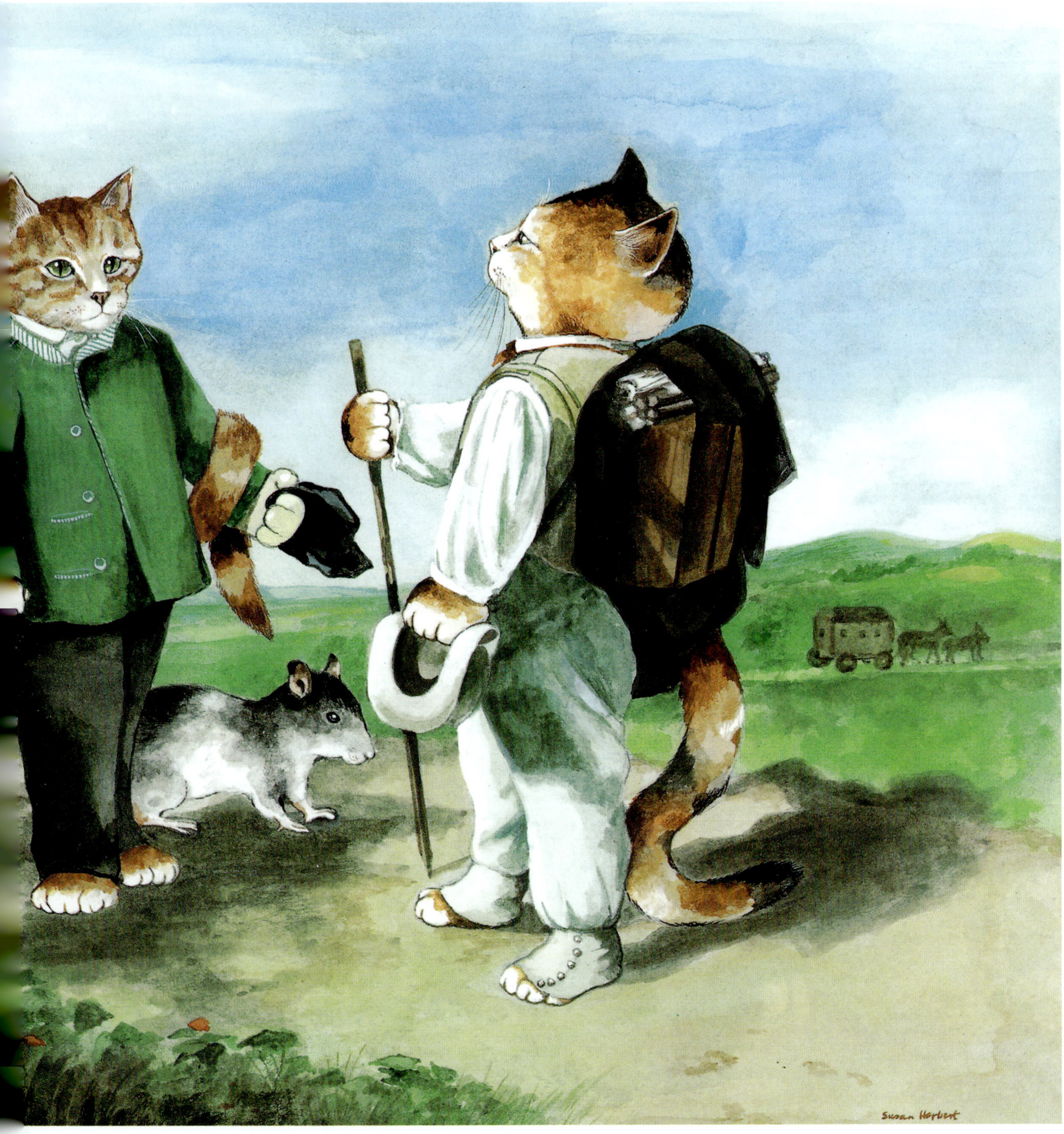
Susan Herbert

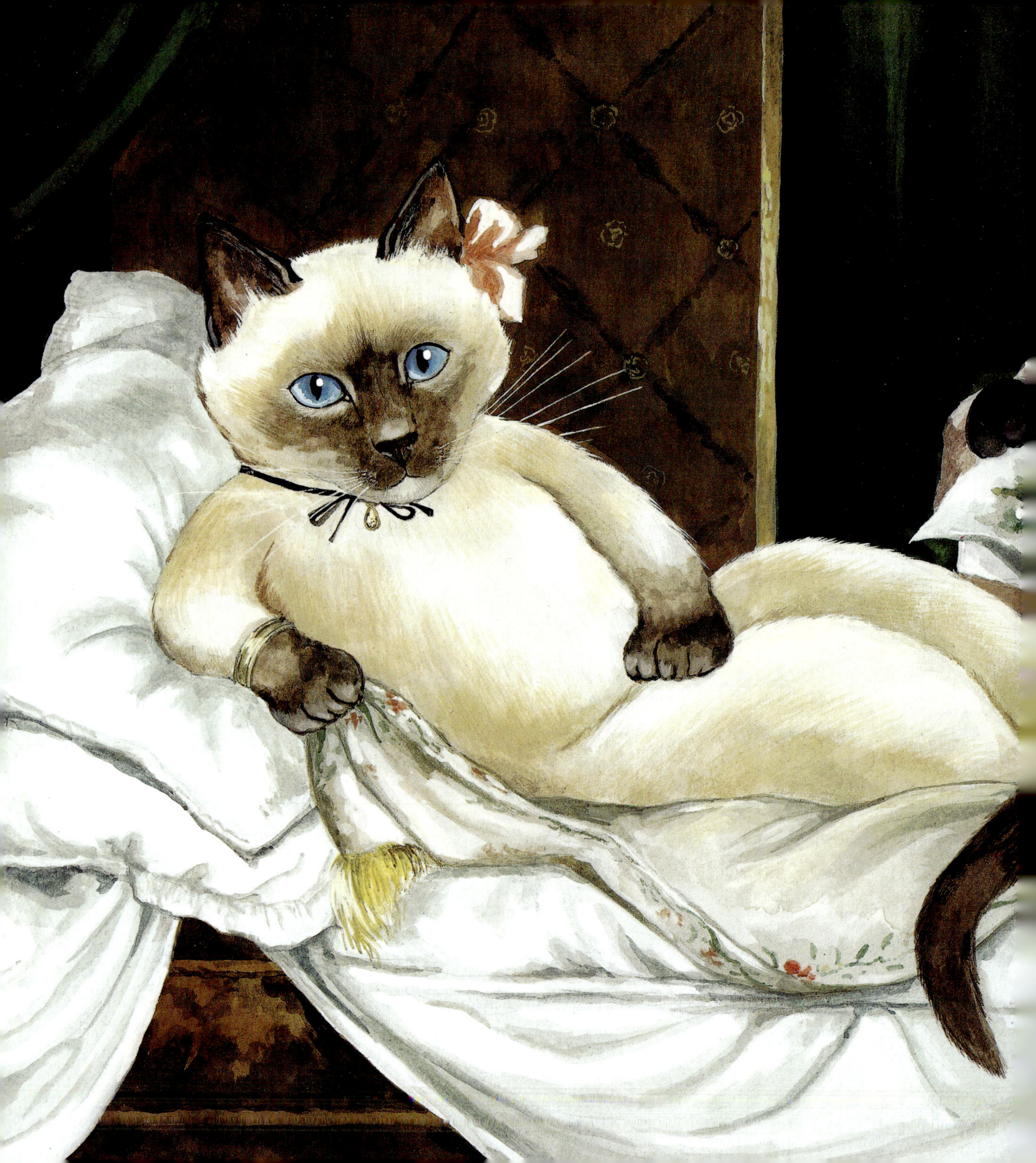

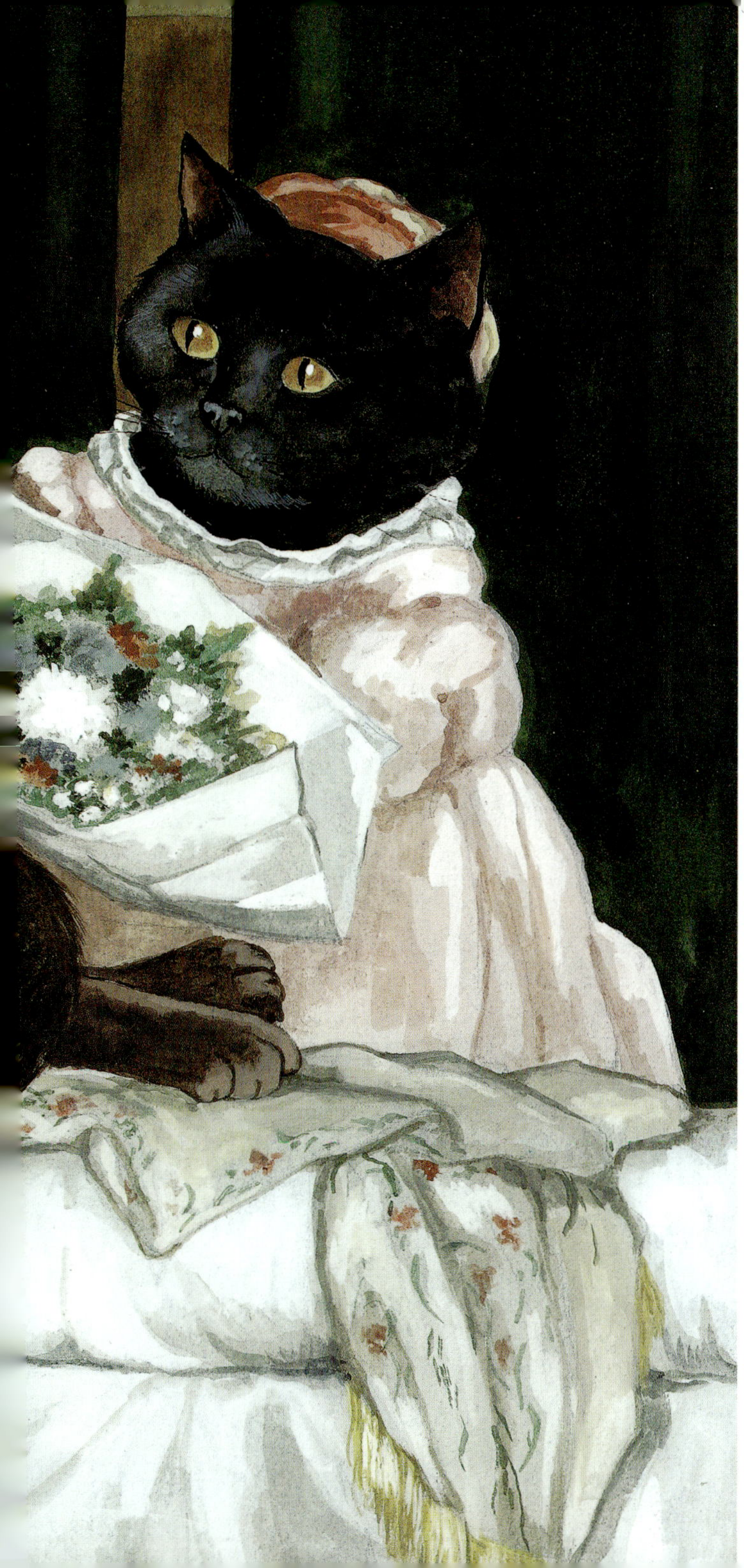

ÉDOUARD MANET

Olympia (1863)

SIR JOHN EVERETT MILLAIS

Leisure Hours (1864)

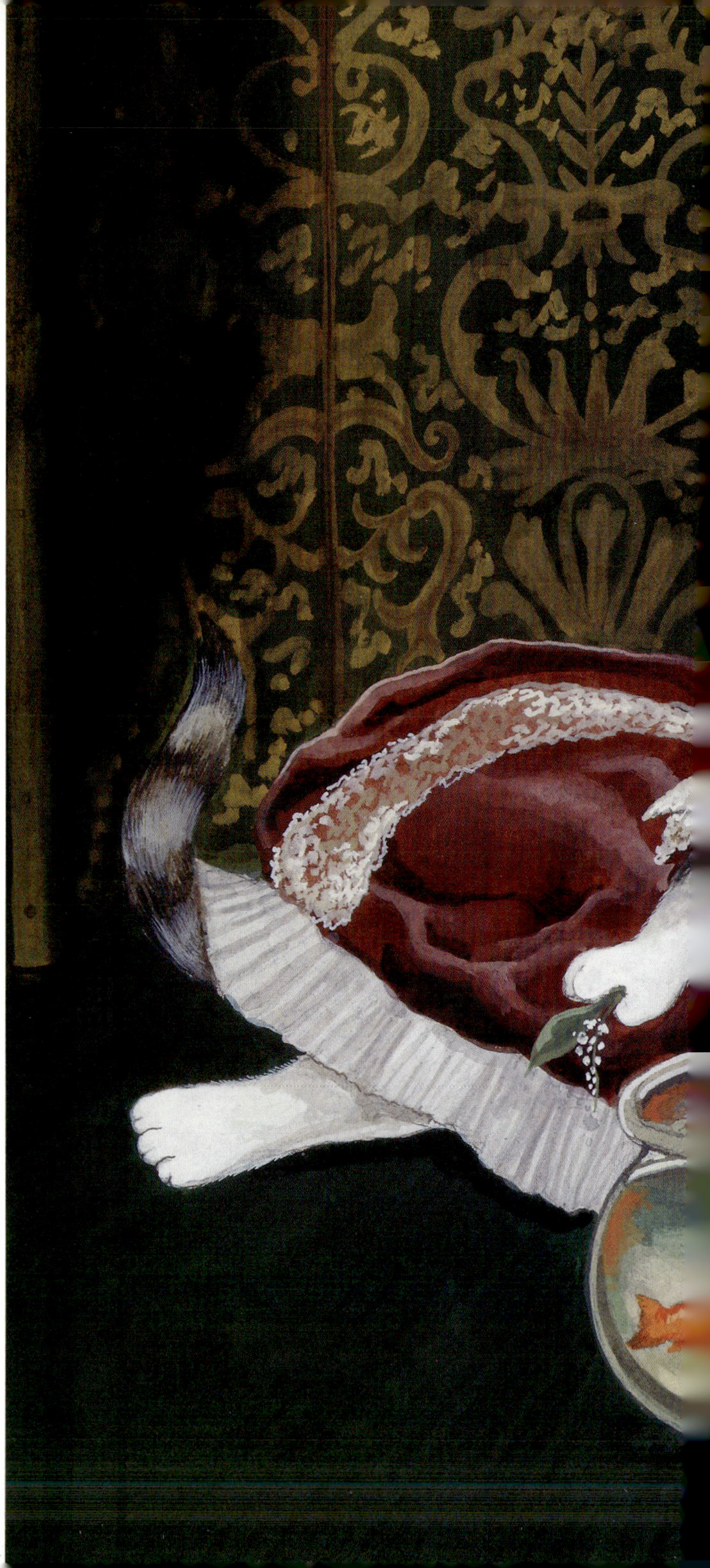

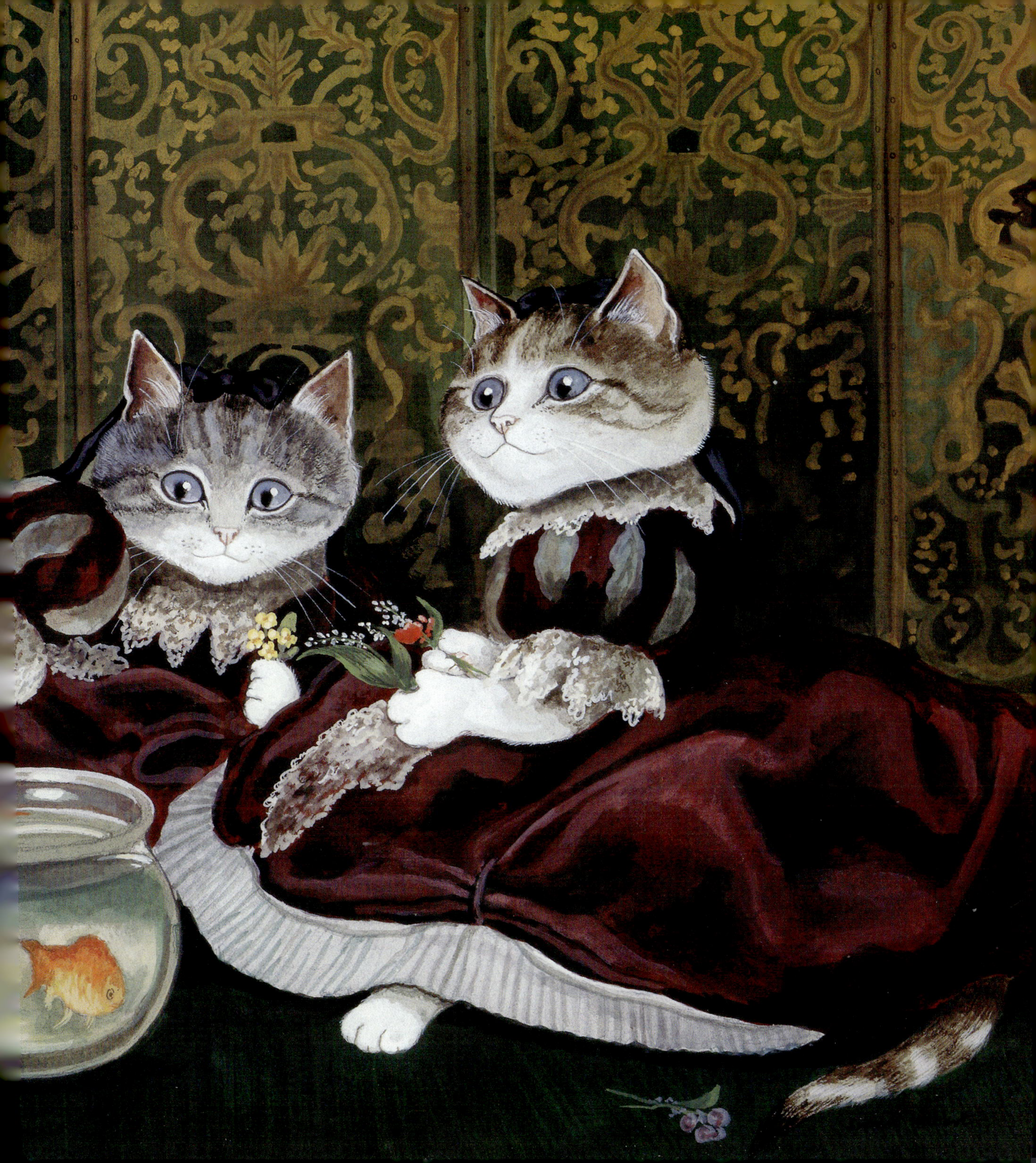

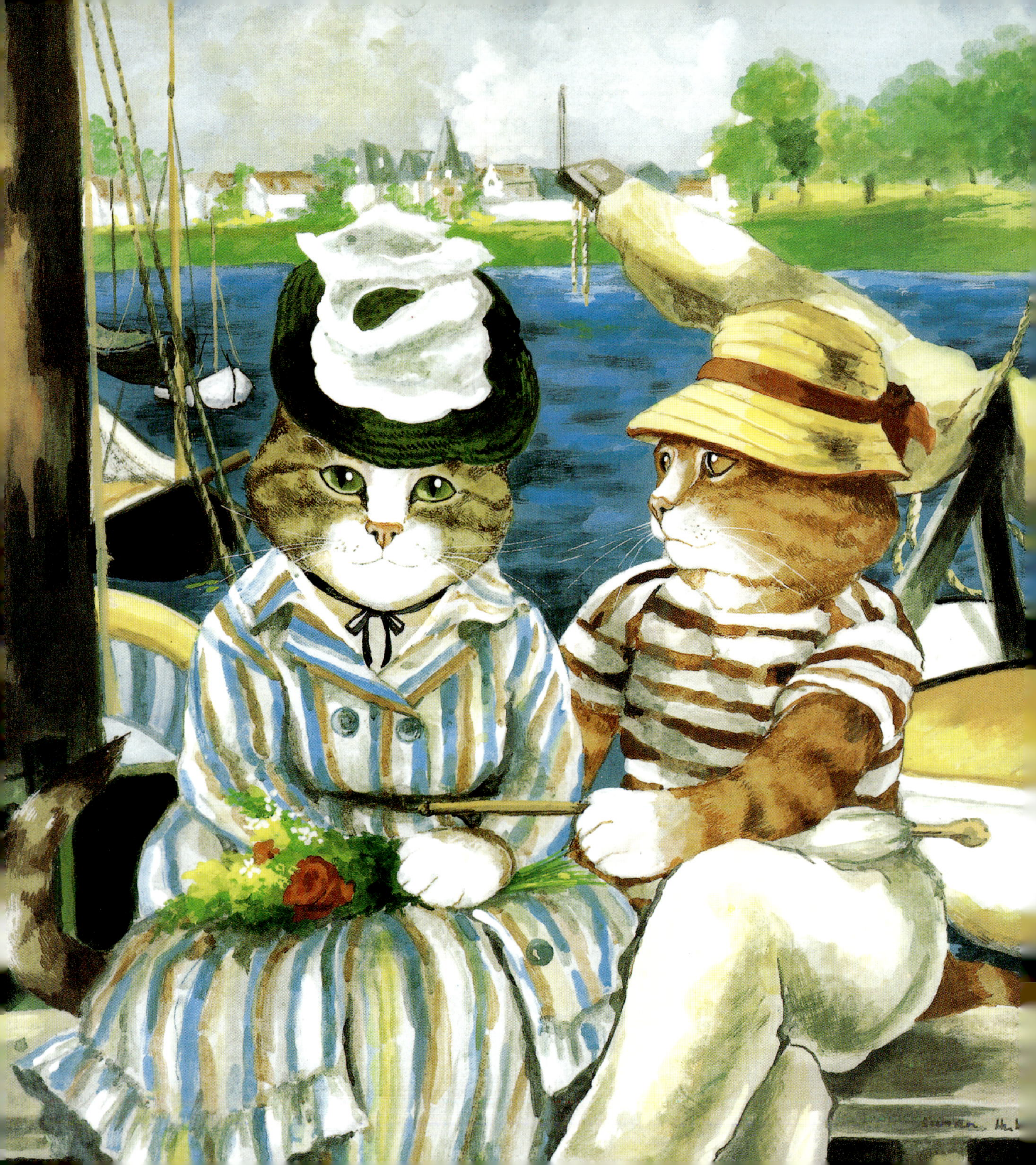

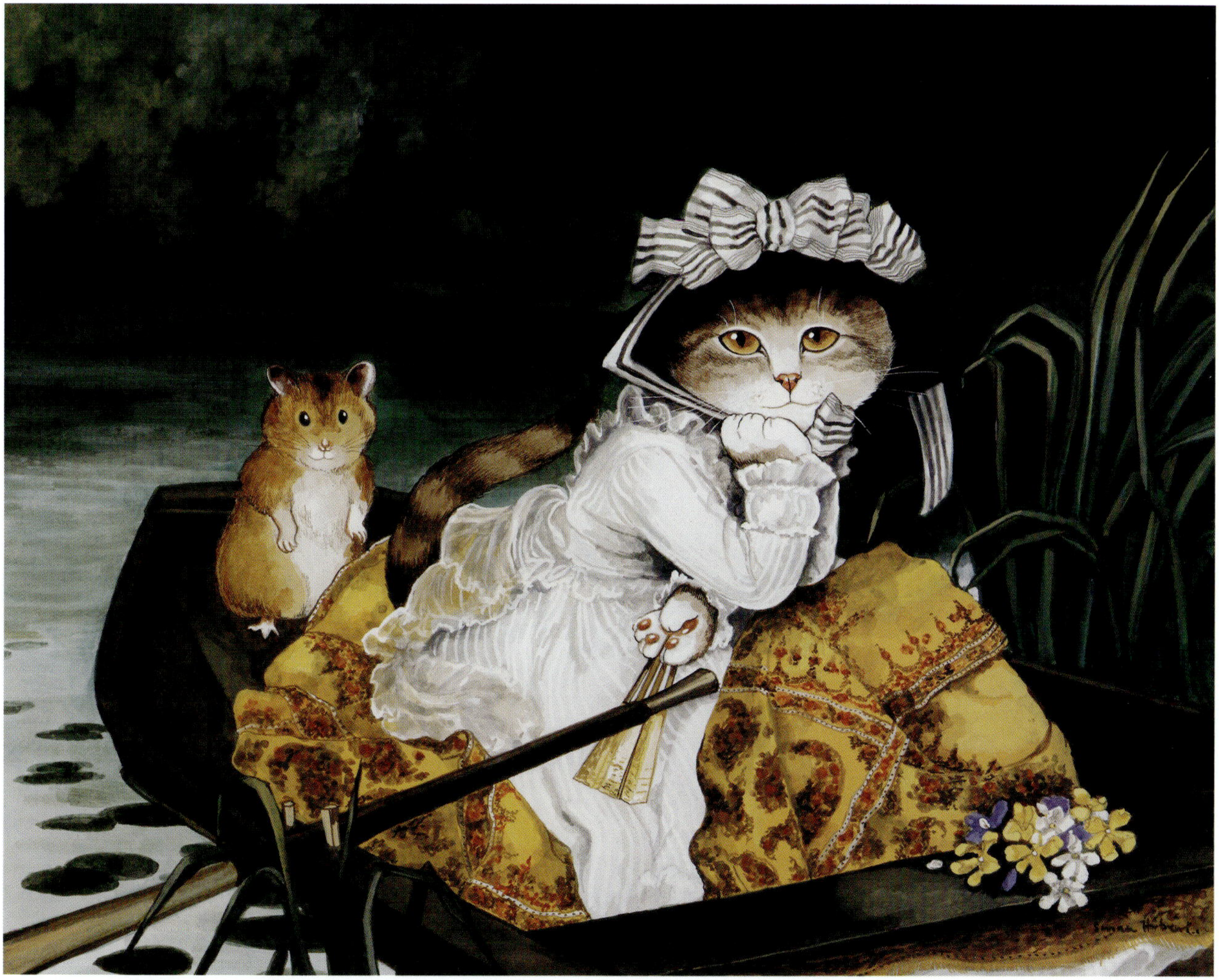

Above JAMES TISSOT, *Young Lady in a Boat* (1870)
Opposite ÉDOUARD MANET, *Argenteuil* (1874)

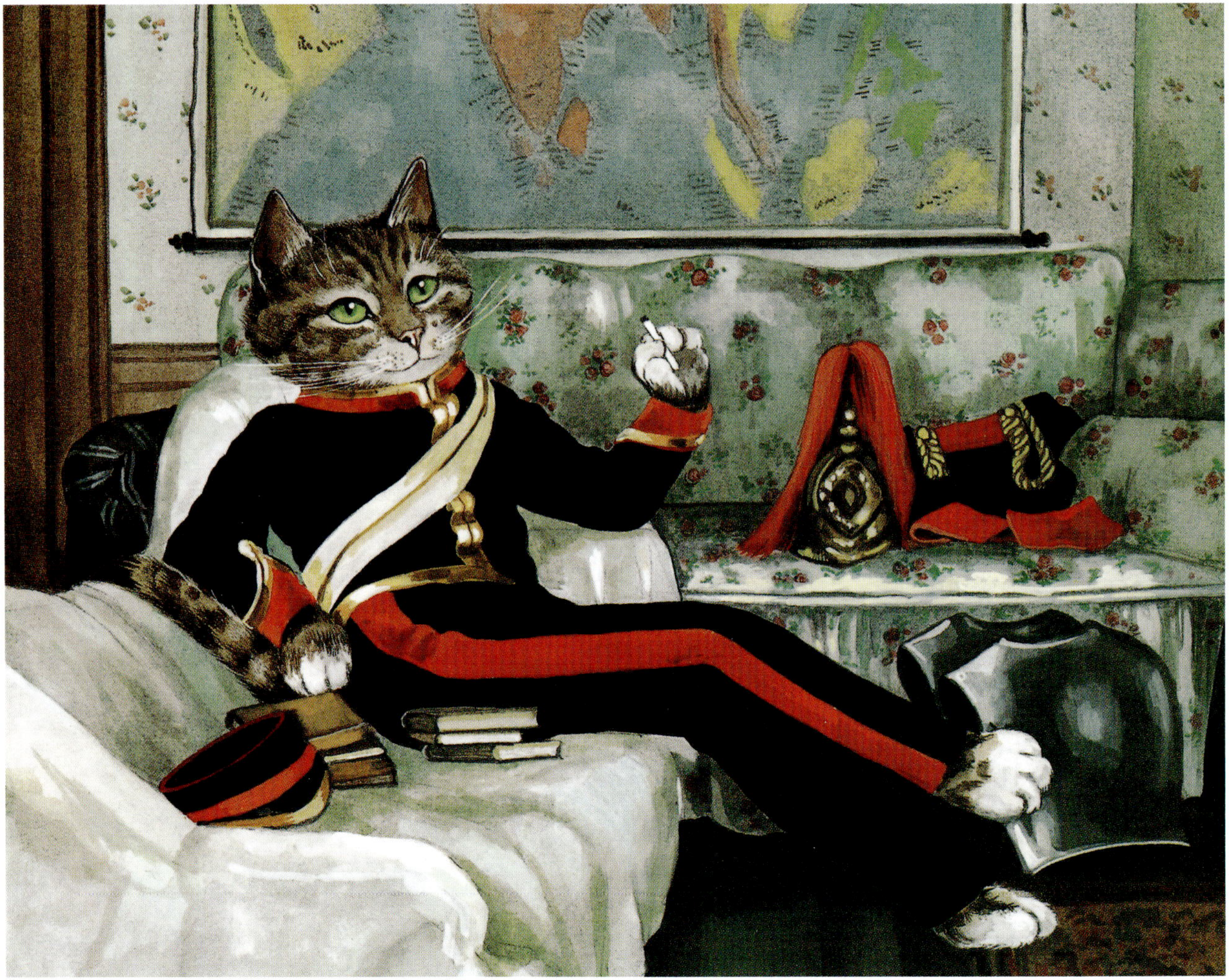

JAMES TISSOT, *Frederick Burnaby* (1870)

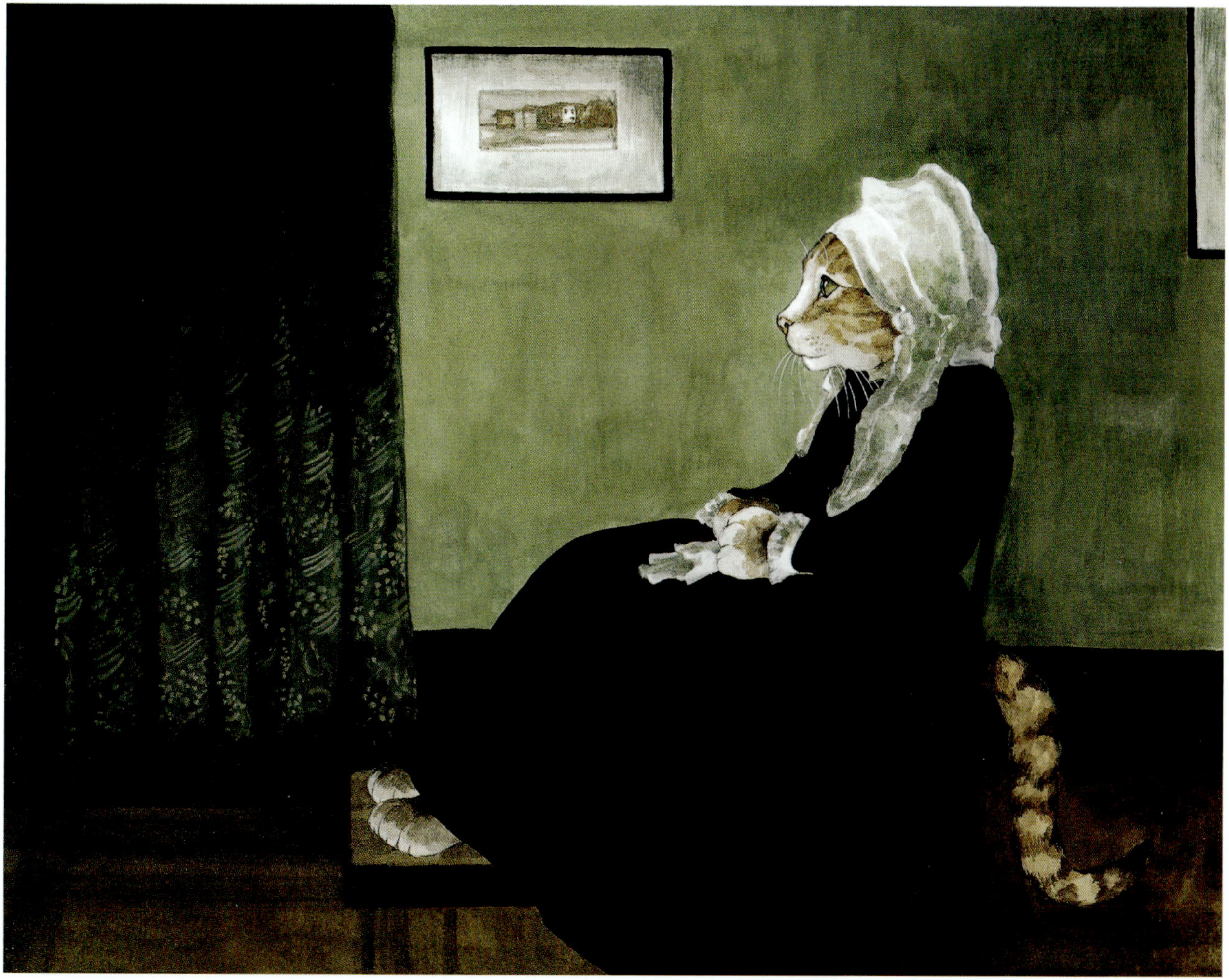

JAMES ABBOTT McNEILL WHISTLER, *Arrangement in Grey and Black No. 1*, also called *Portrait of the Artist's Mother* (1871)

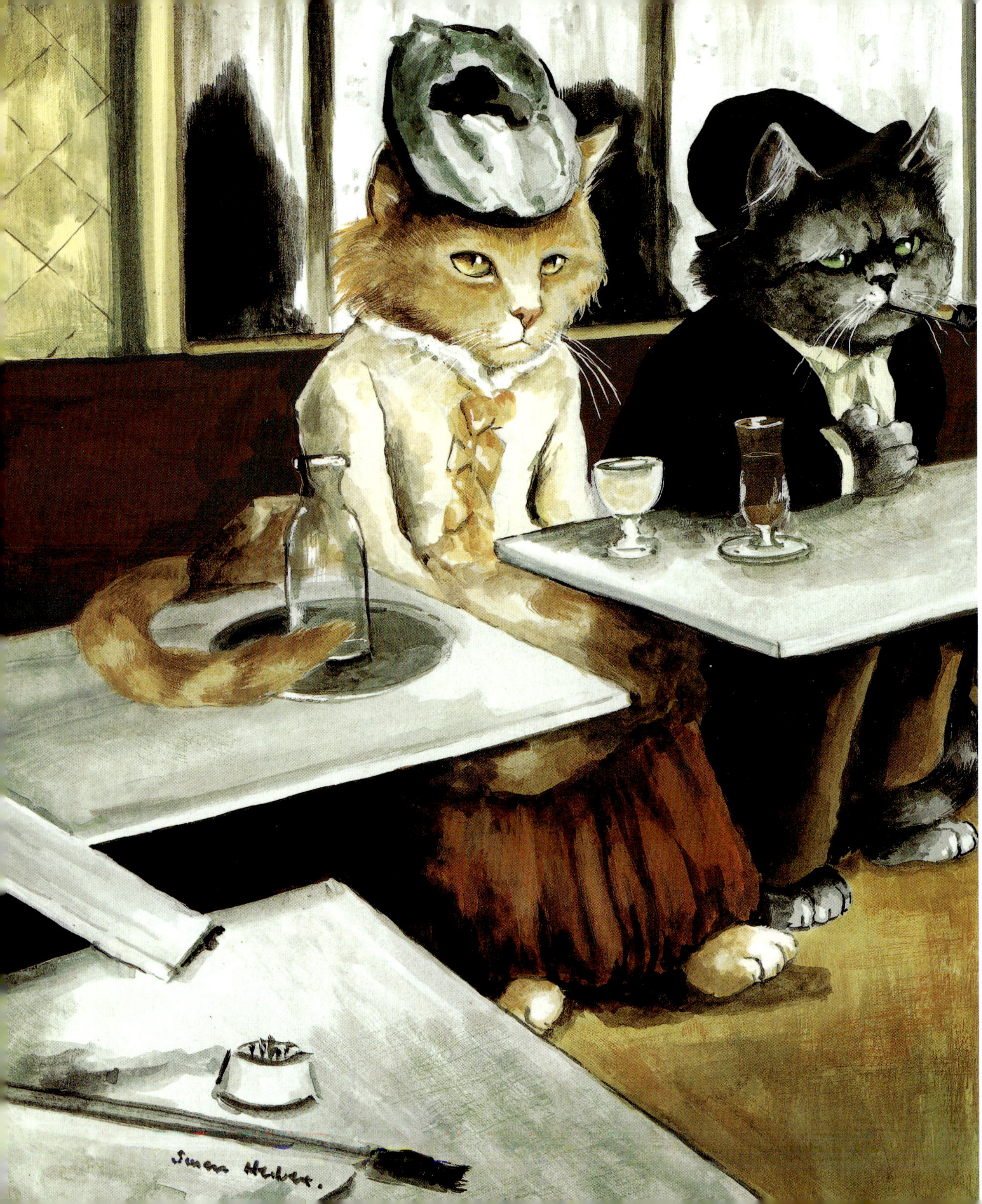
Susan Herbert.

EDGAR DEGAS

Absinthe (1876)

EDGAR DEGAS

The Orchestra at the Opera (c. 1870)

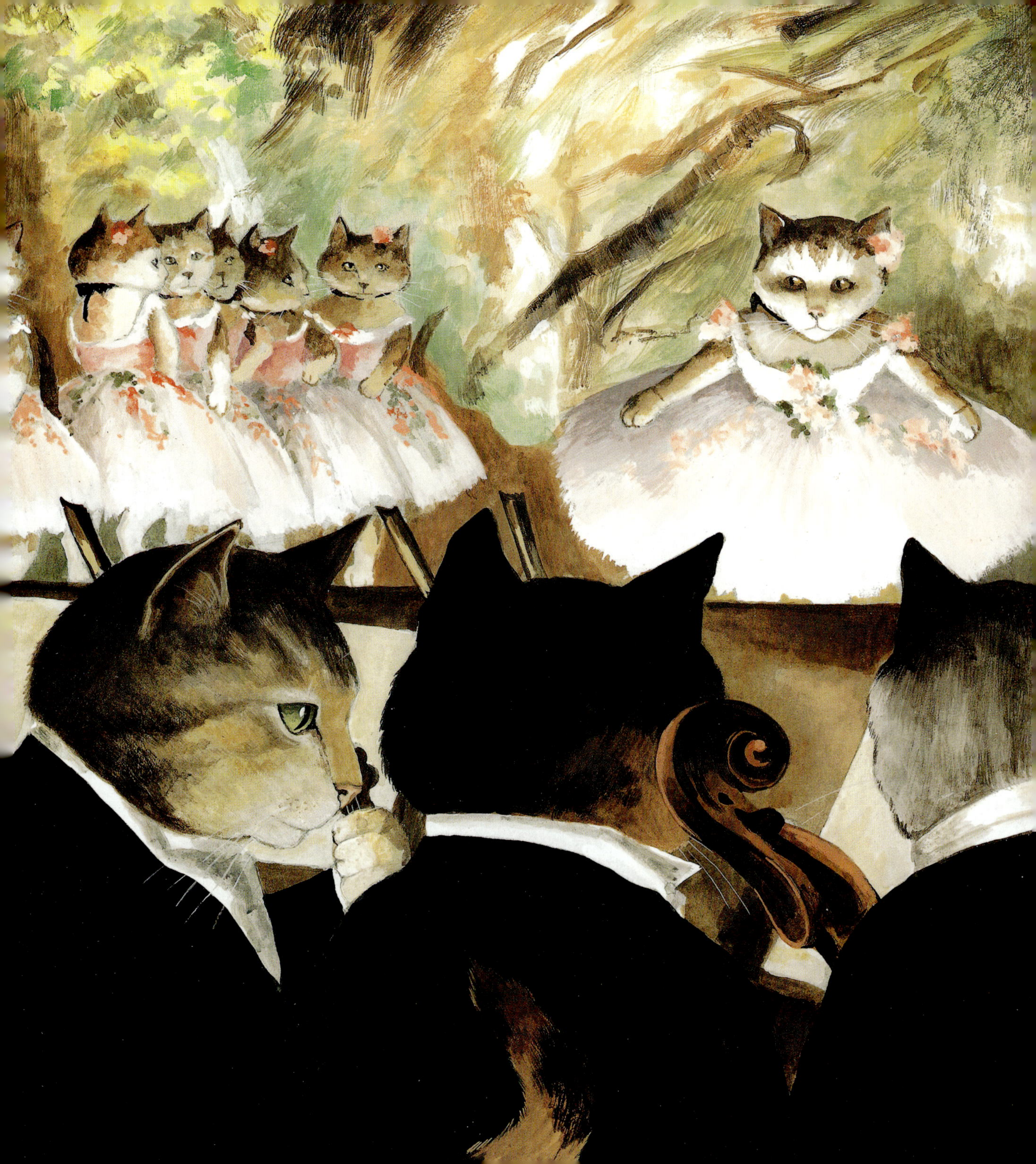

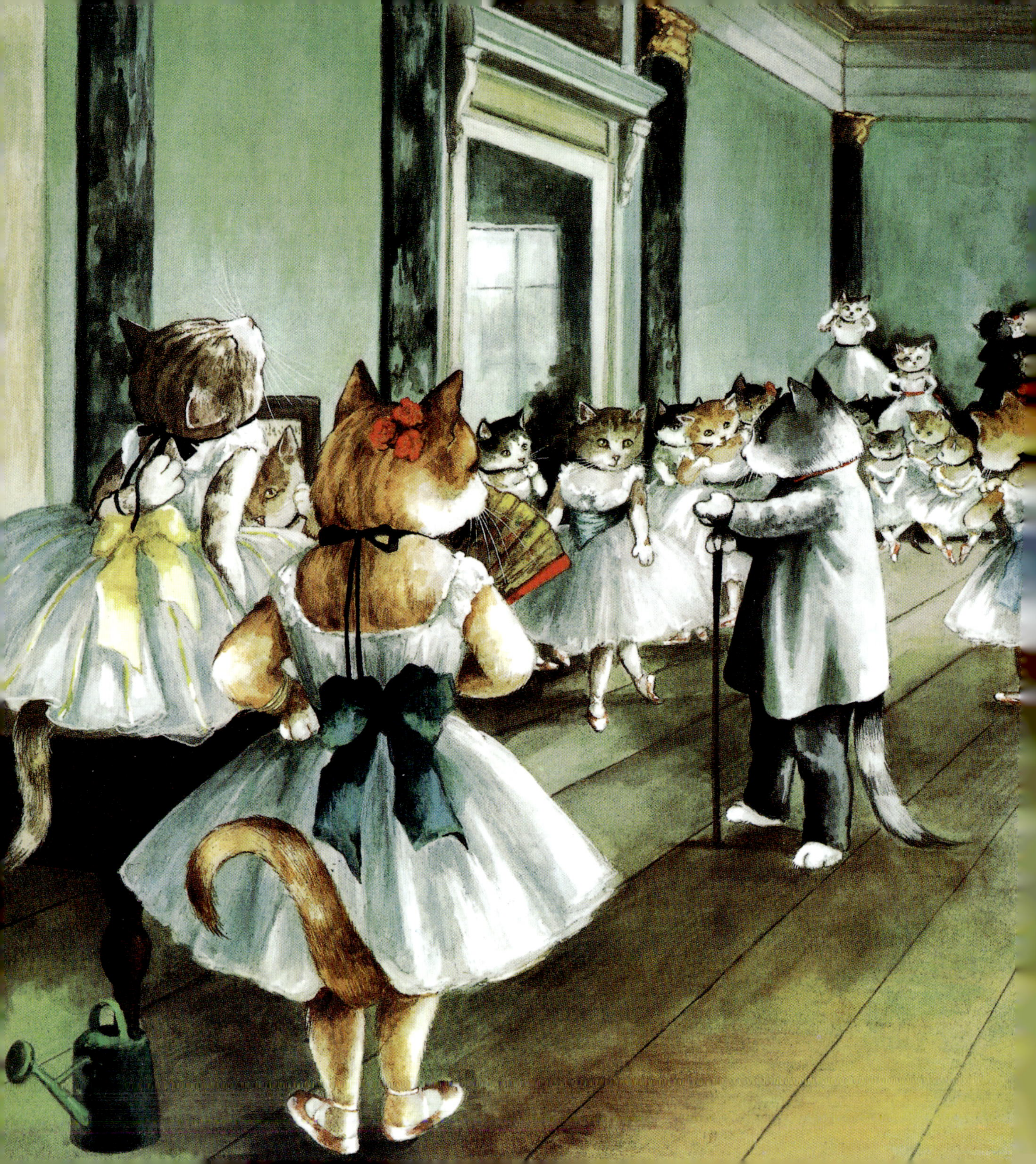

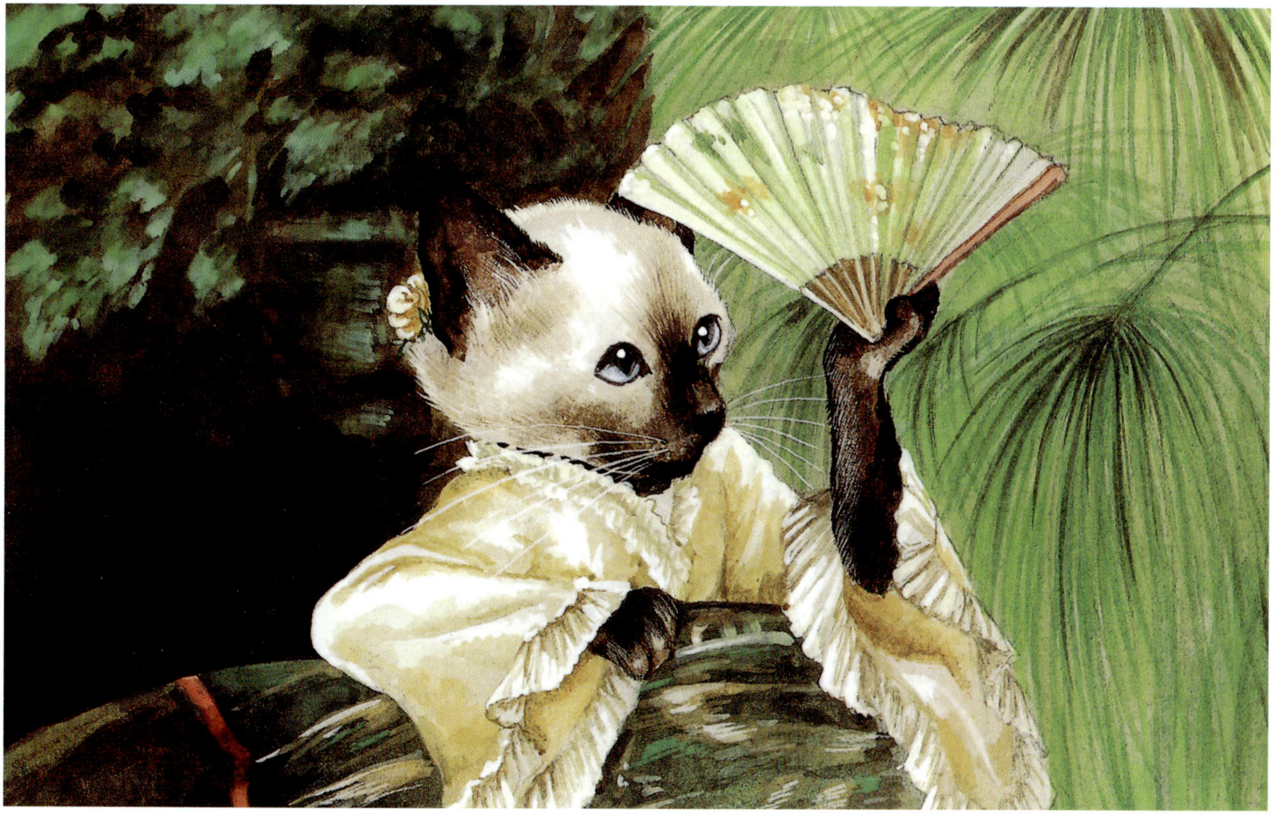

Above JAMES TISSOT, *The Fan* (c. 1875)
Opposite EDGAR DEGAS, *The Ballet Class* (1871)

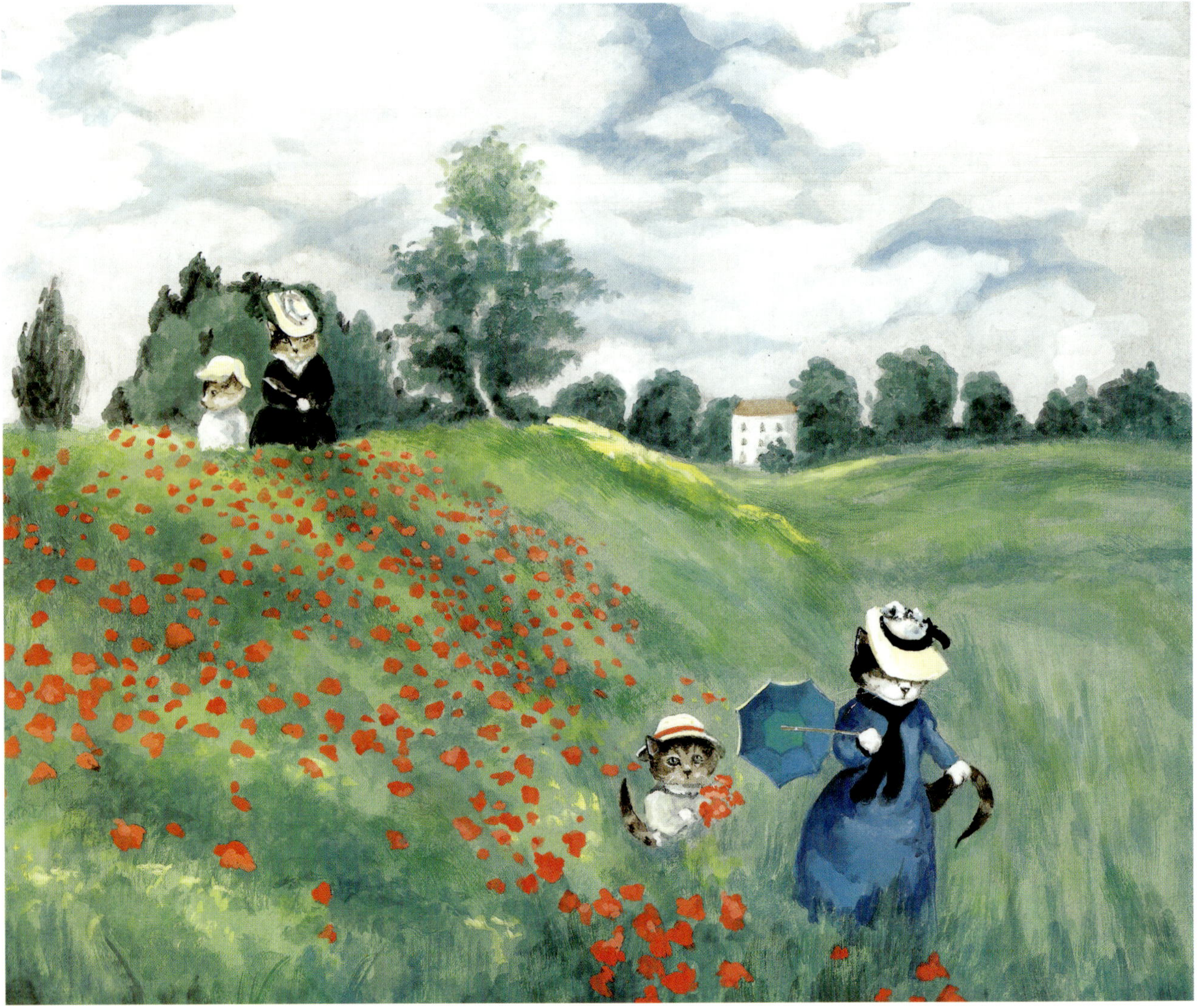

Above CLAUDE MONET, *Poppy Field* (1873)

Opposite CLAUDE MONET, *Woman with a Parasol – Madame Monet and Her Son* (1875)

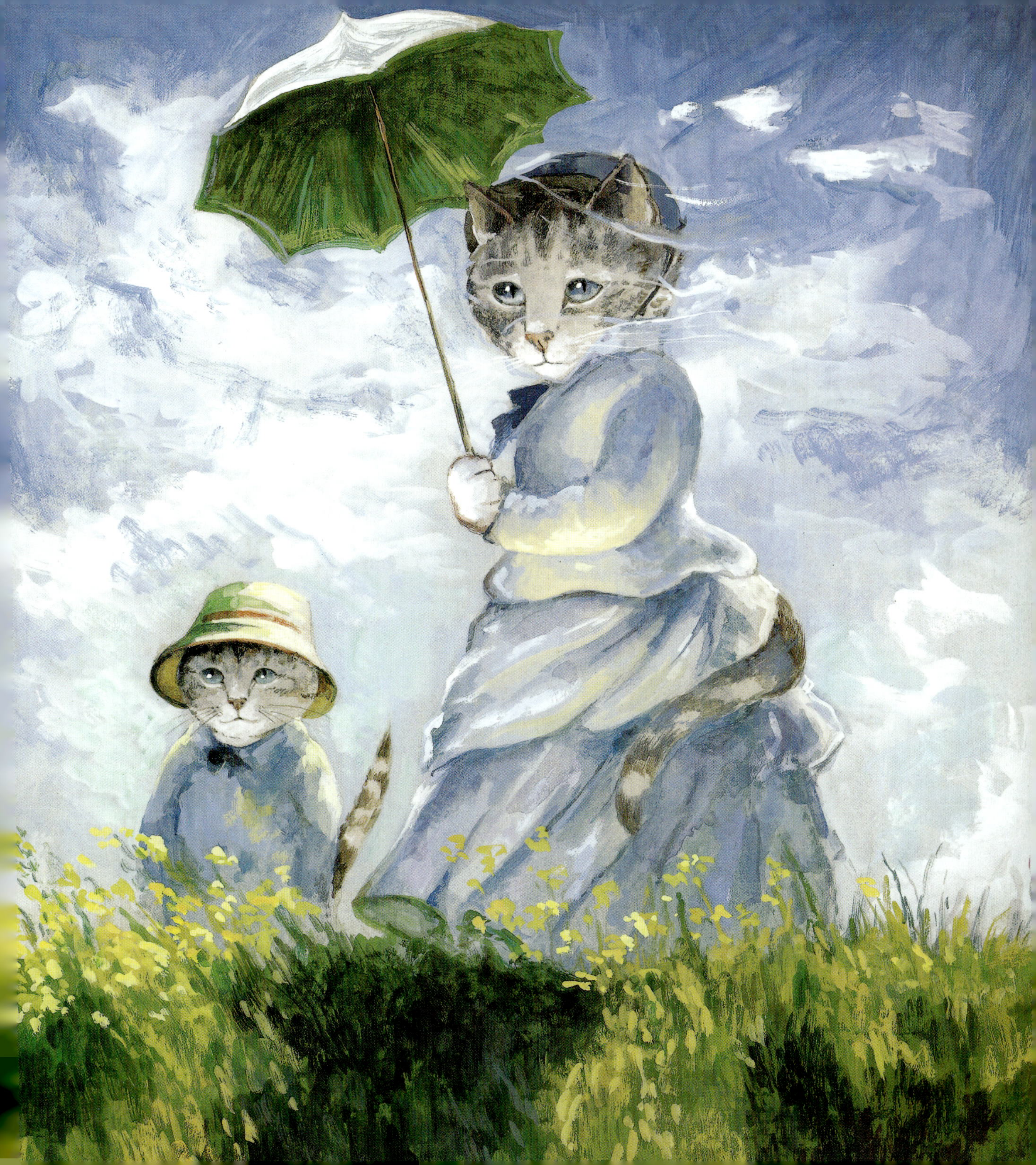

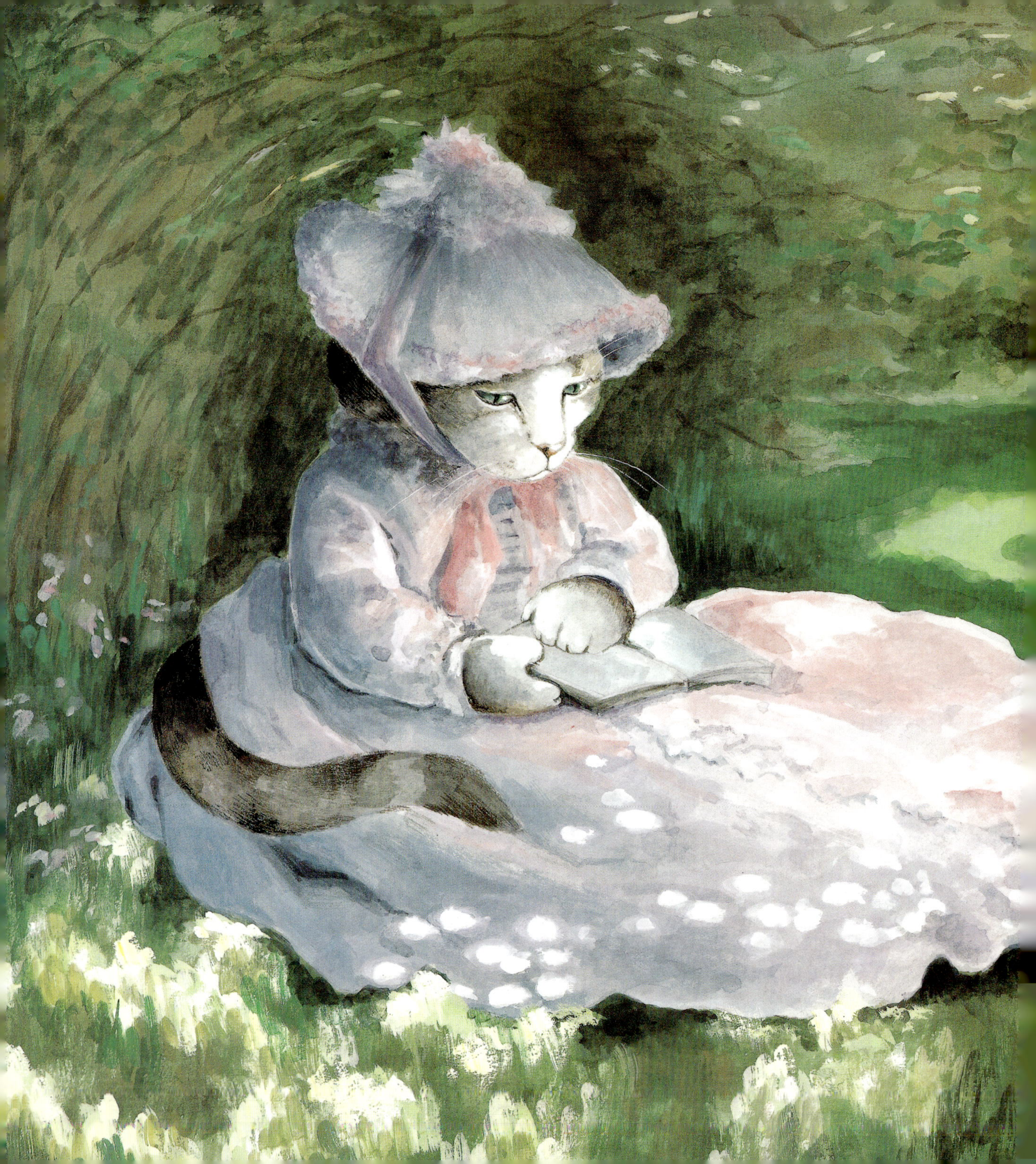

CLAUDE MONET

Springtime (1872)

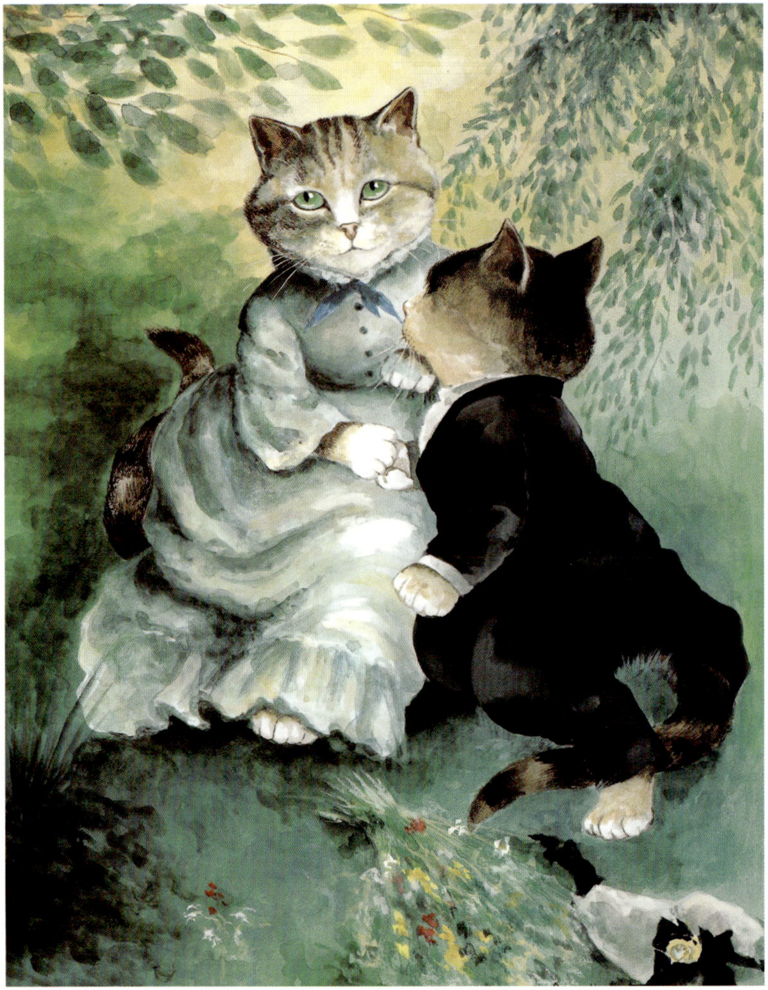

Above PIERRE-AUGUSTE RENOIR, *The Lovers* (c. 1875)
Opposite PIERRE-AUGUSTE RENOIR, *Umbrellas* (c. 1881–85)

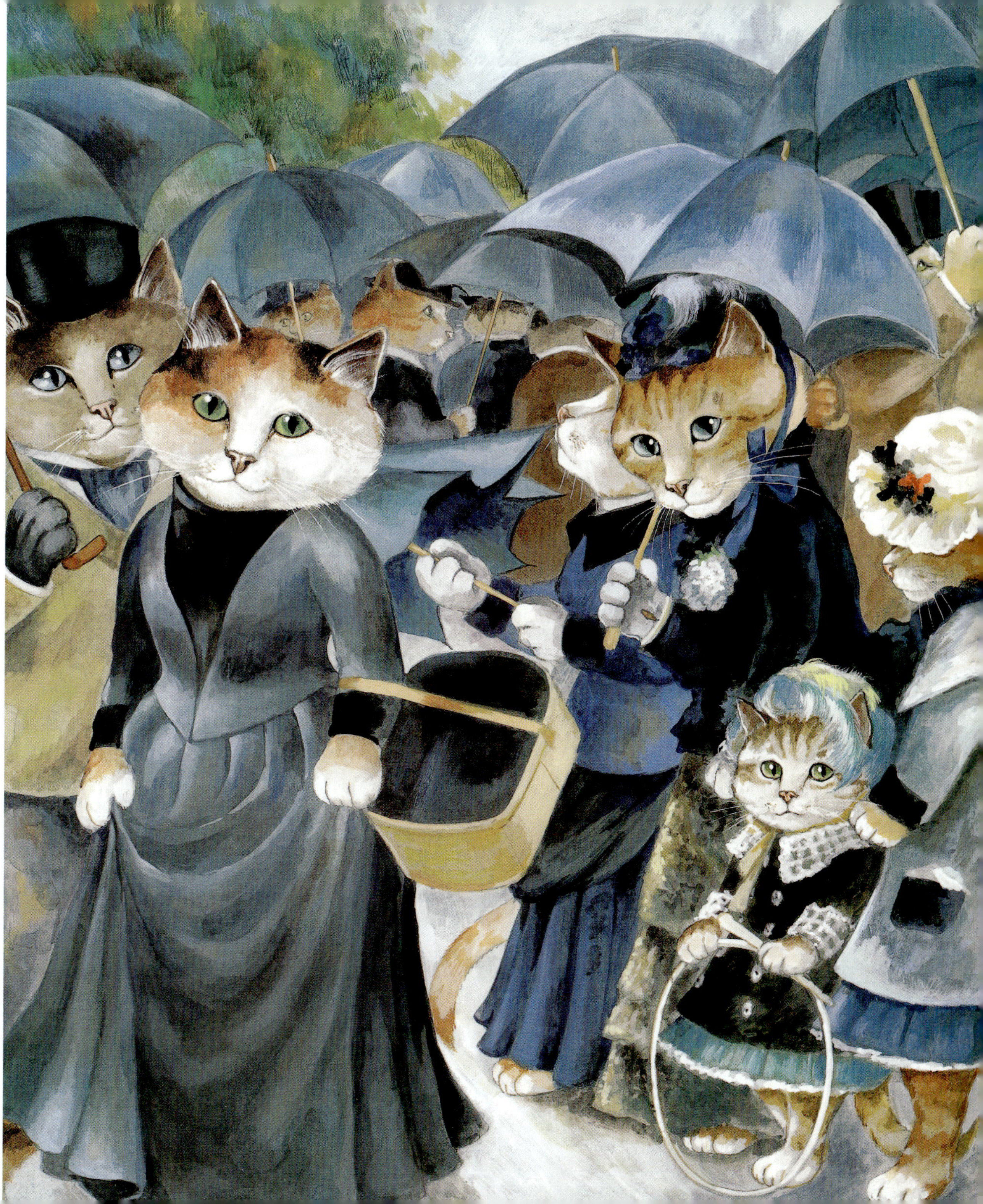

PIERRE-AUGUSTE RENOIR

Luncheon of the Boating Party (1881)

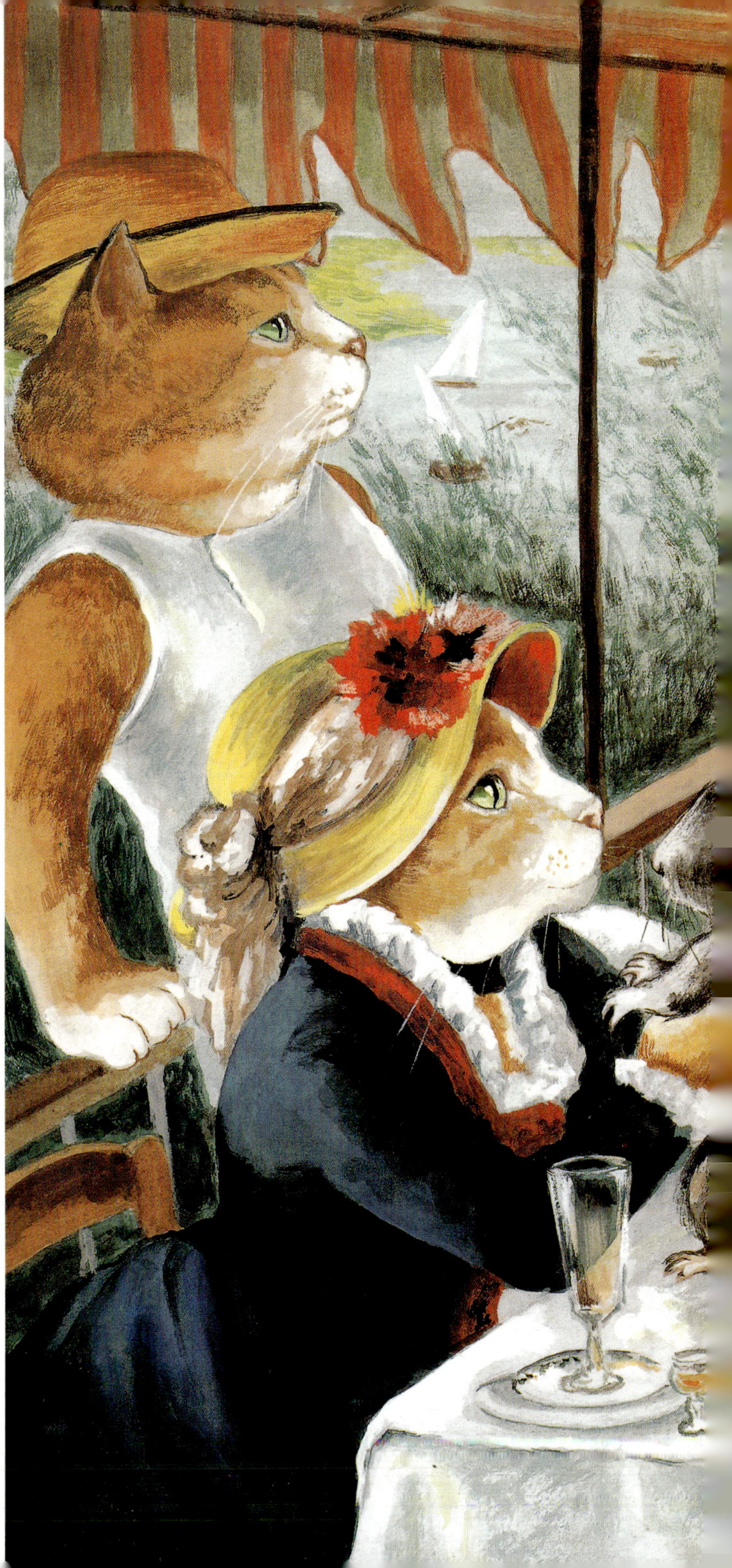

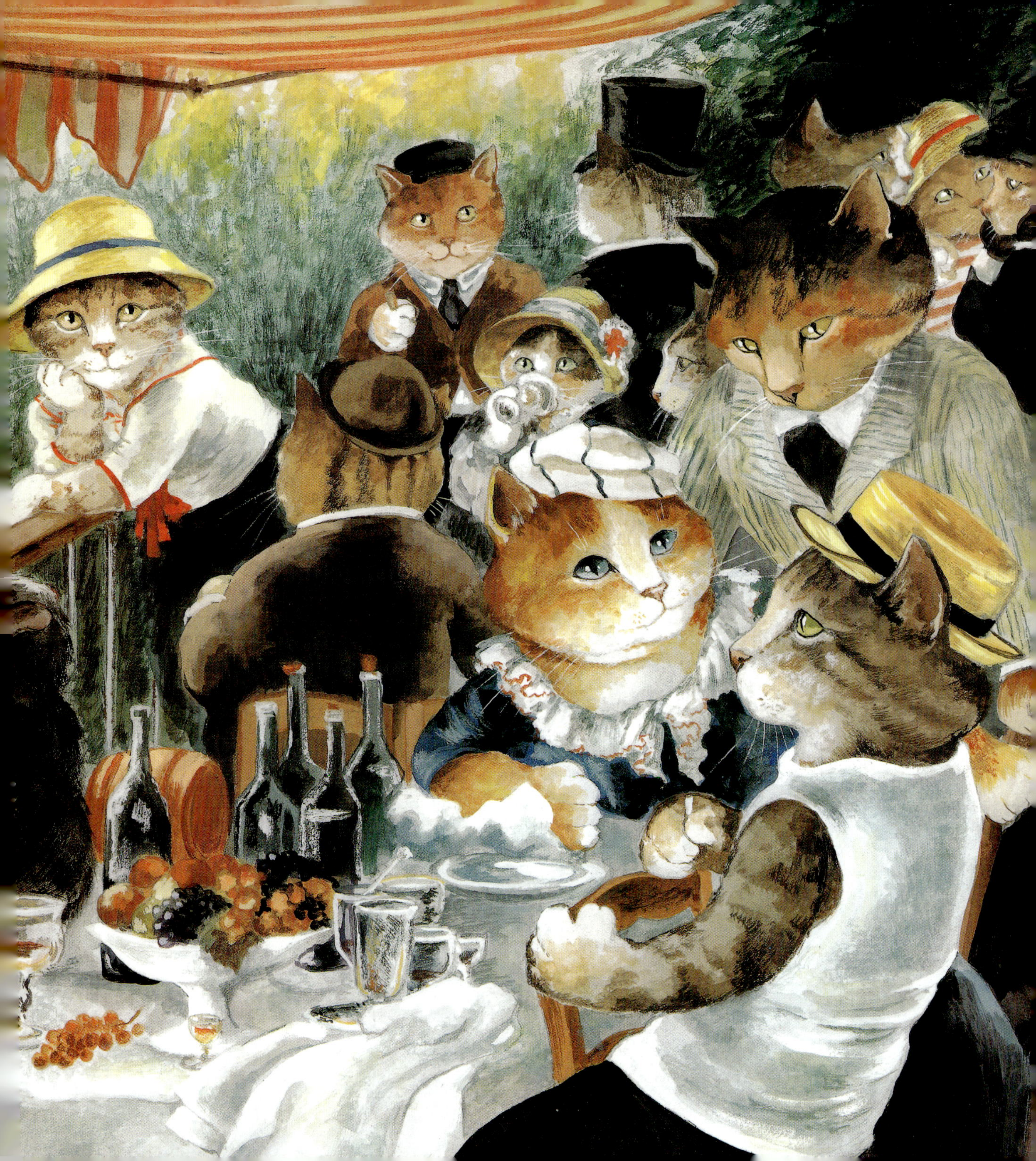

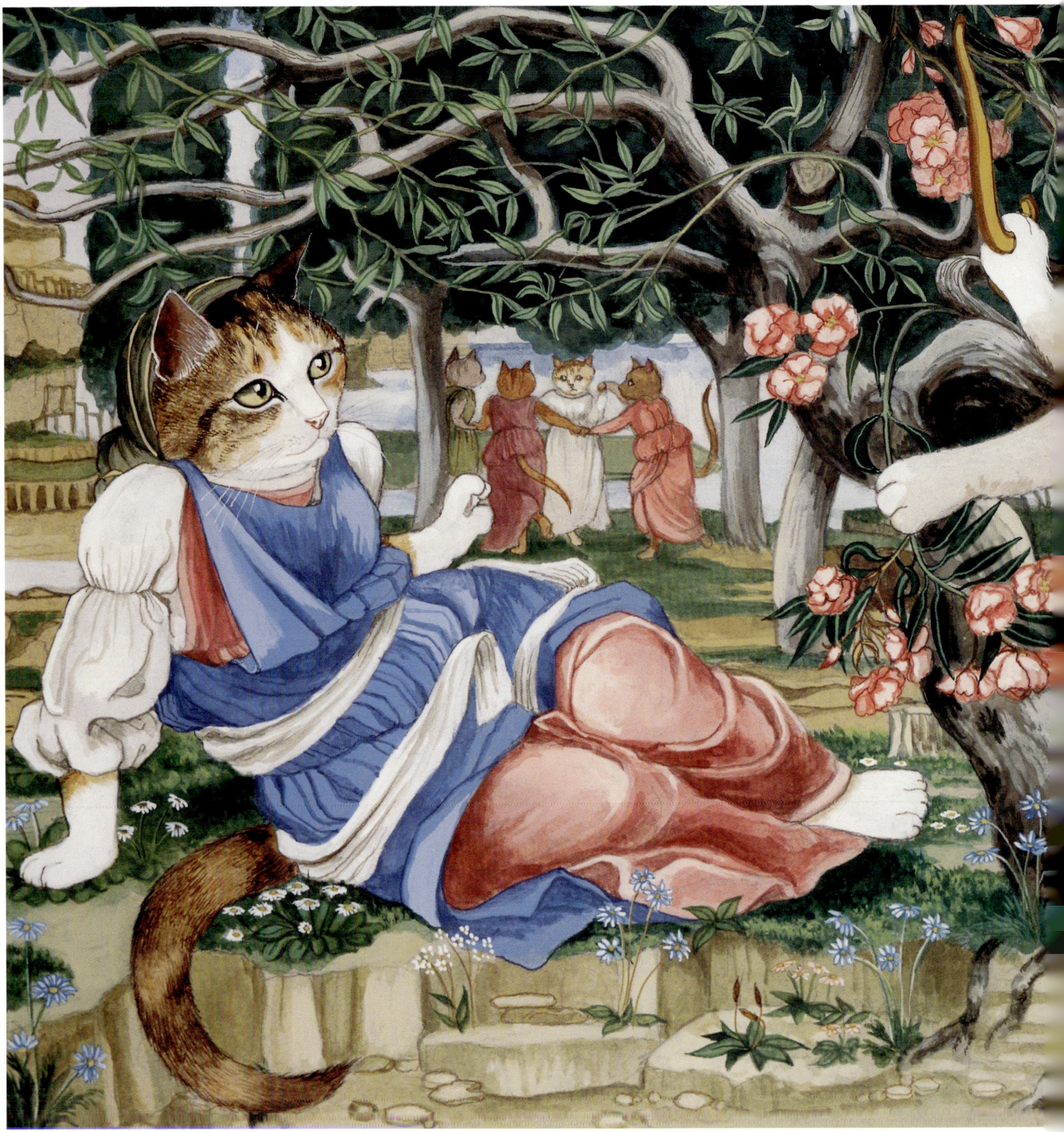

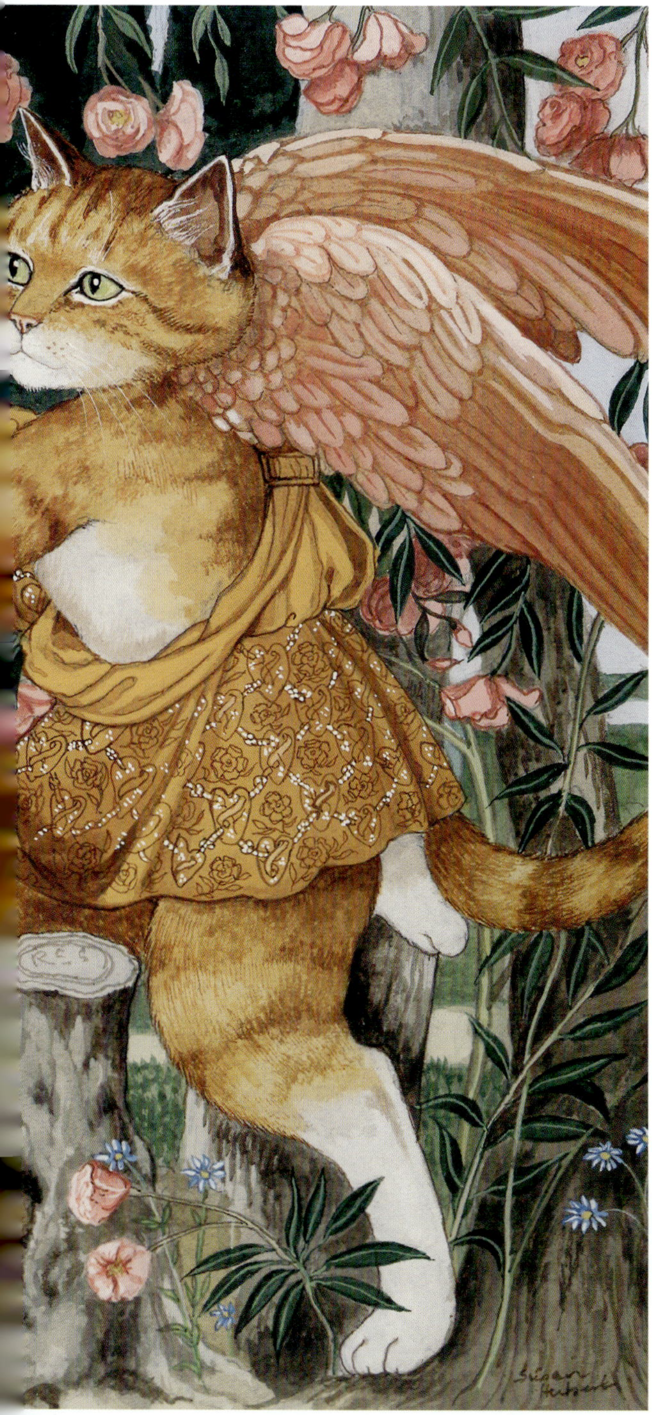

JOHN RODDAM SPENCER STANHOPE

Love and the Maiden (1877)

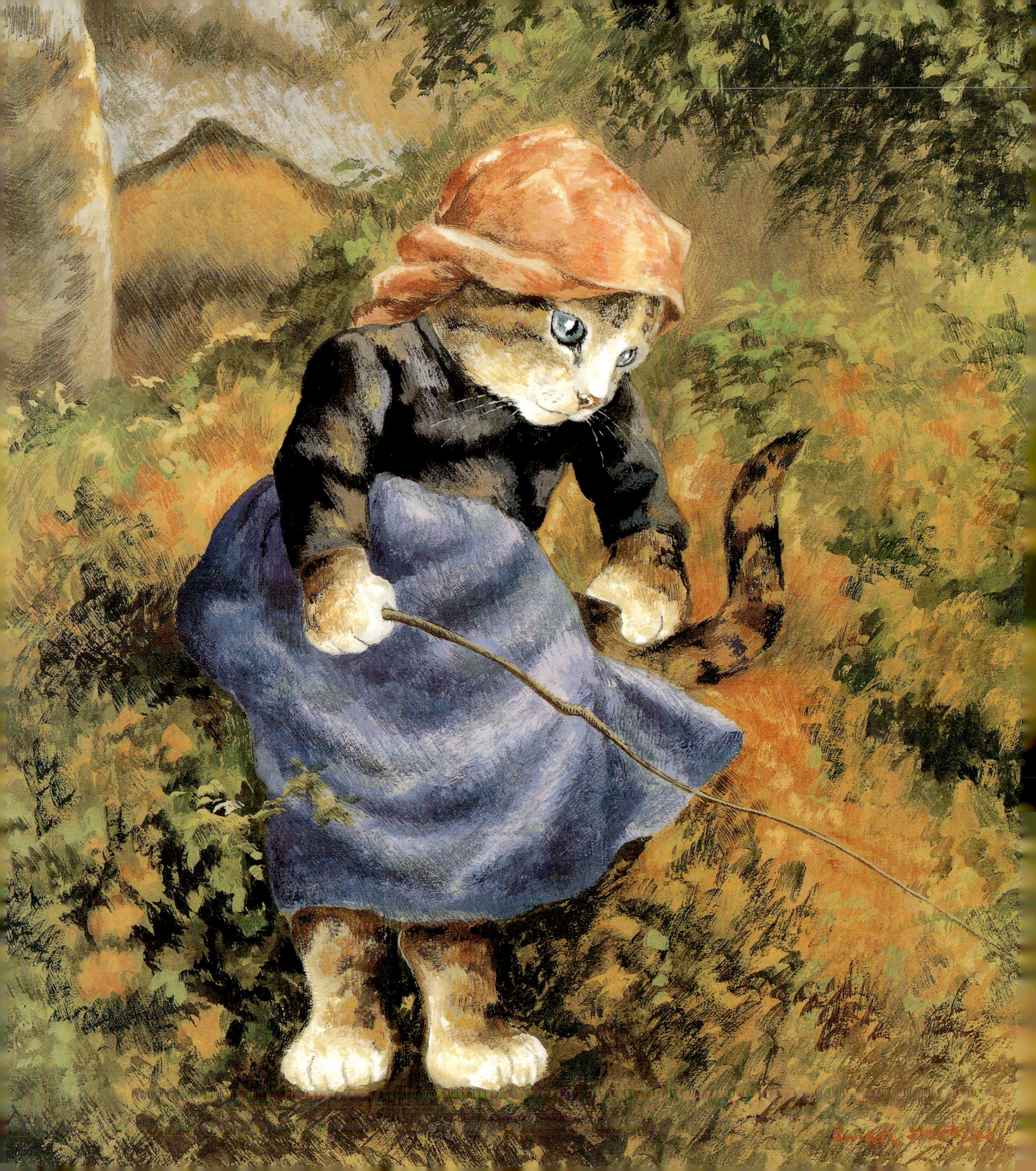

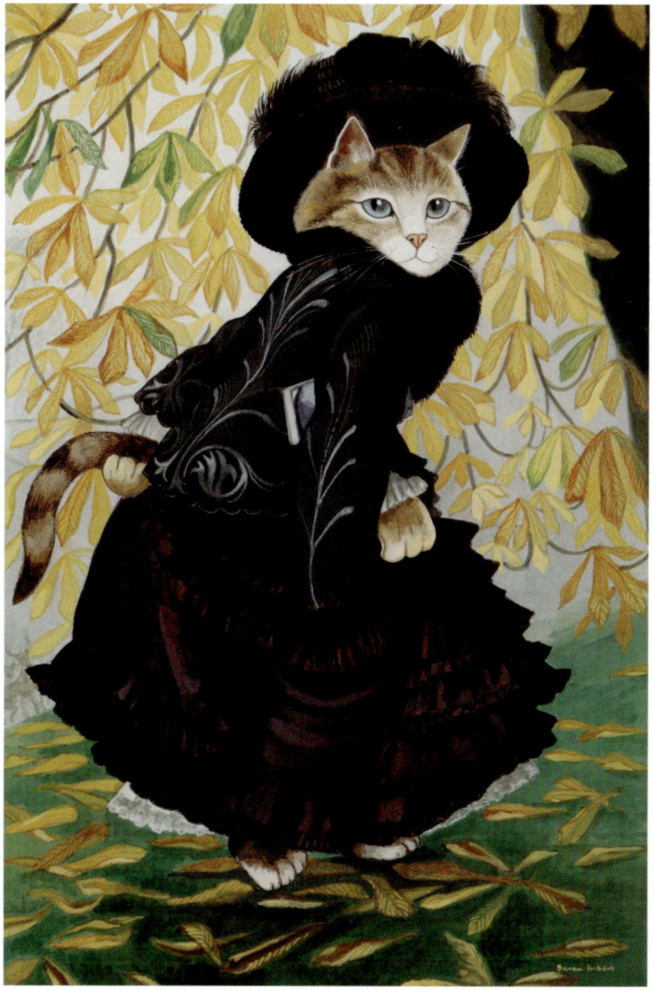

Above JAMES TISSOT, *October* (c. 1878)
Opposite CAMILLE PISSARRO, *Girl with a Stick* (1881)

ÉDOUARD MANET

Bar at the Folies-Bergère (1882)

Overleaf JOHN HENRY HENSHALL

Behind the Bar (1882)

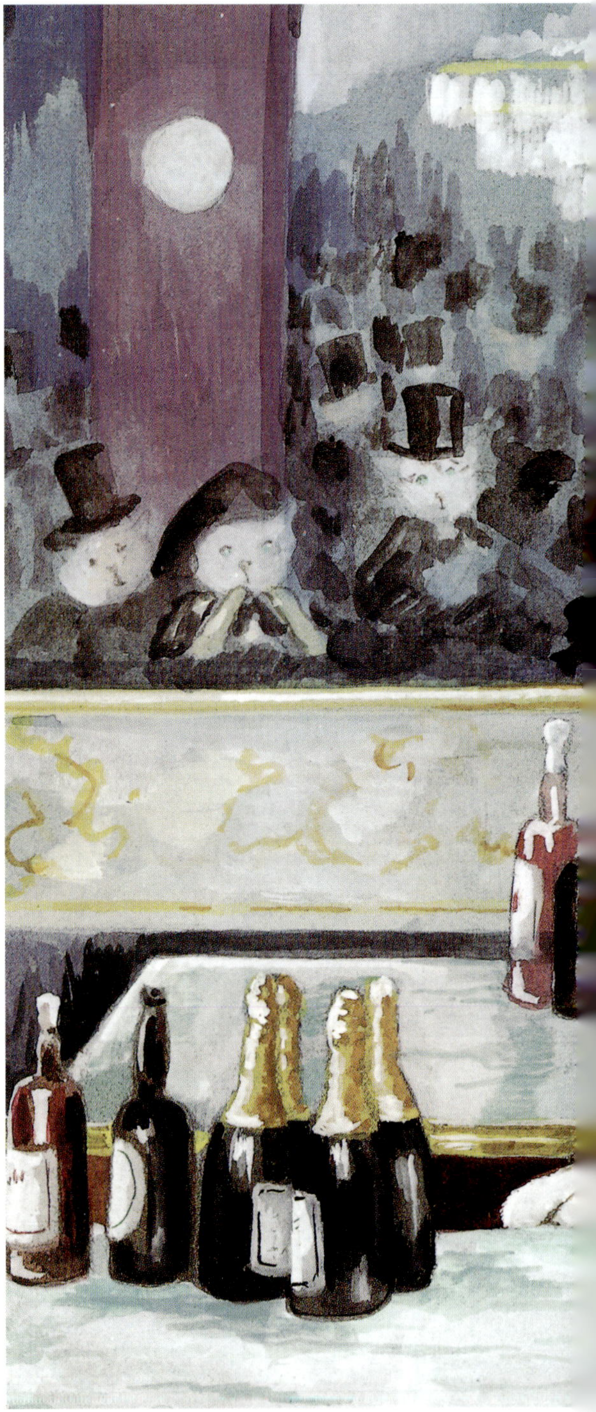

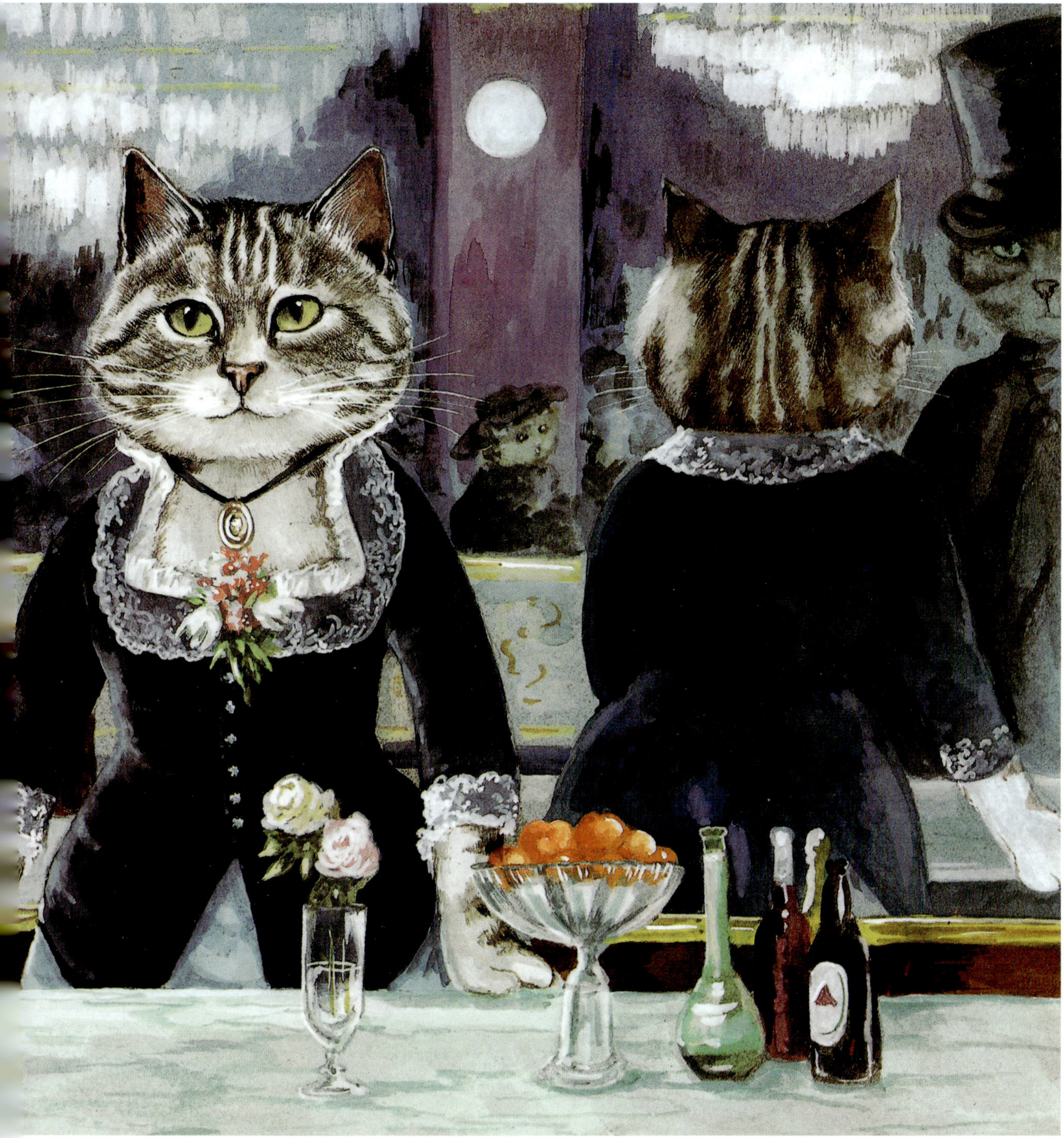

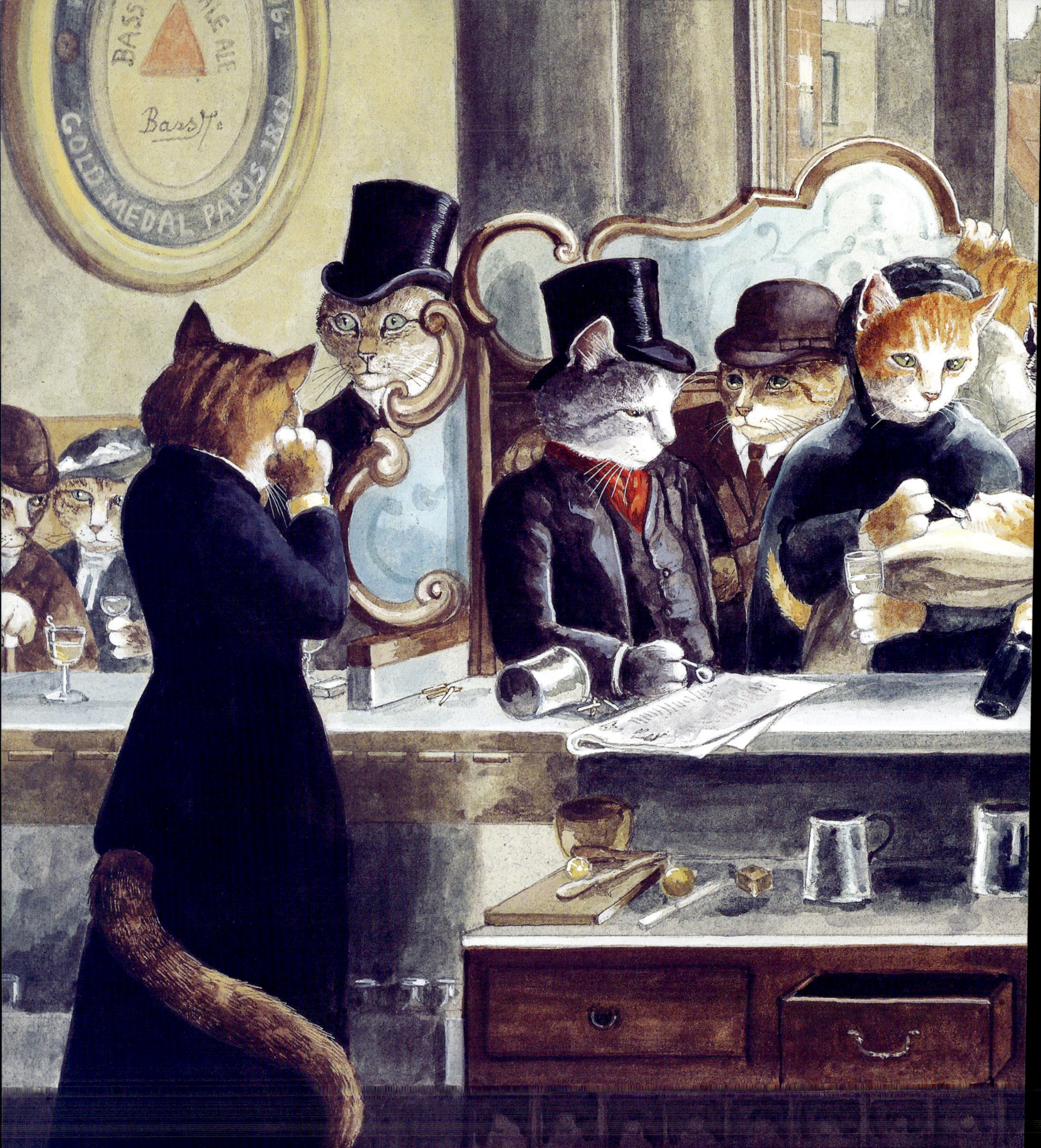
BASS
GOLD MEDAL PARIS 1867

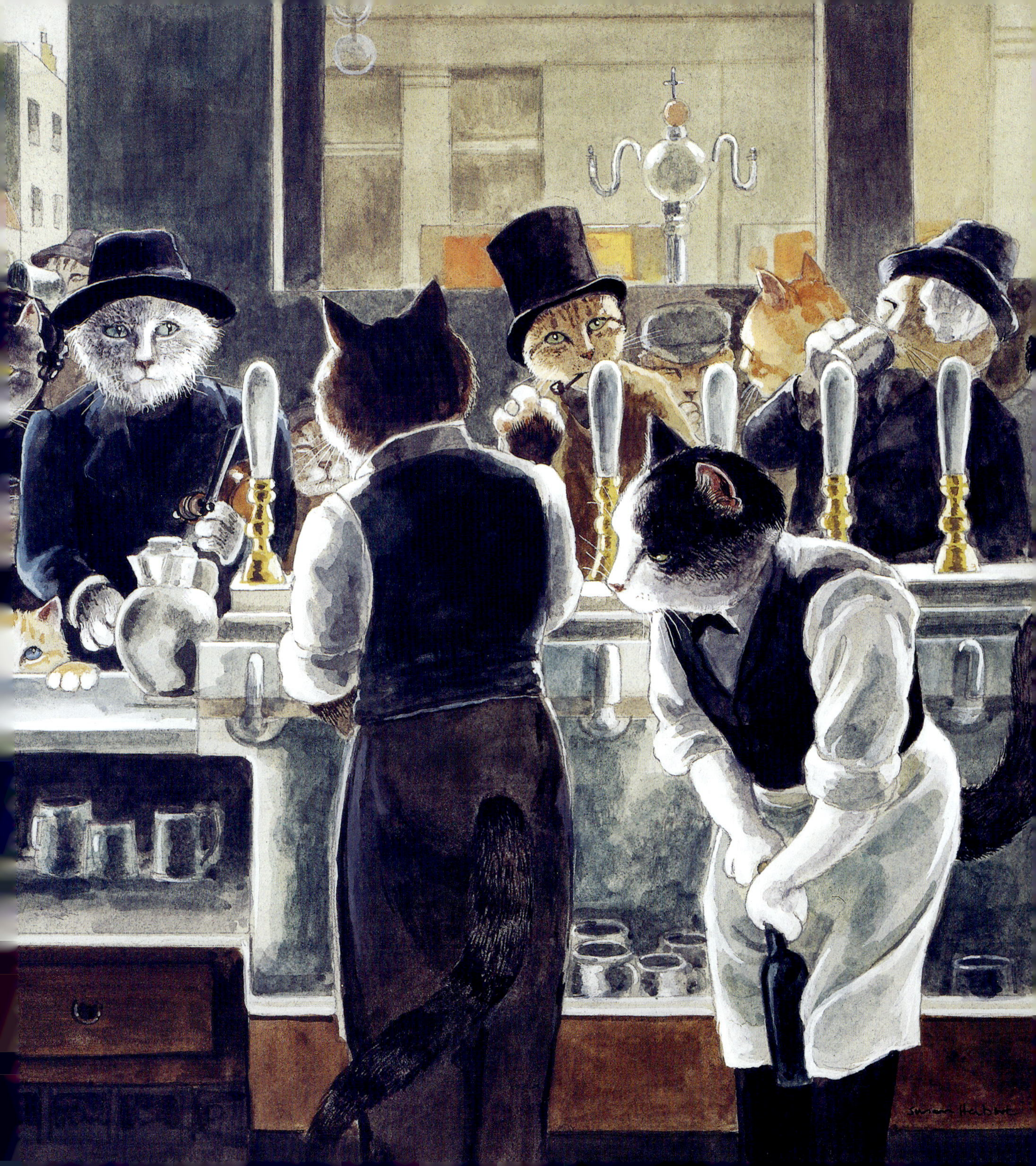

JAMES TISSOT

Women of Paris: The Circus Lover (1885)

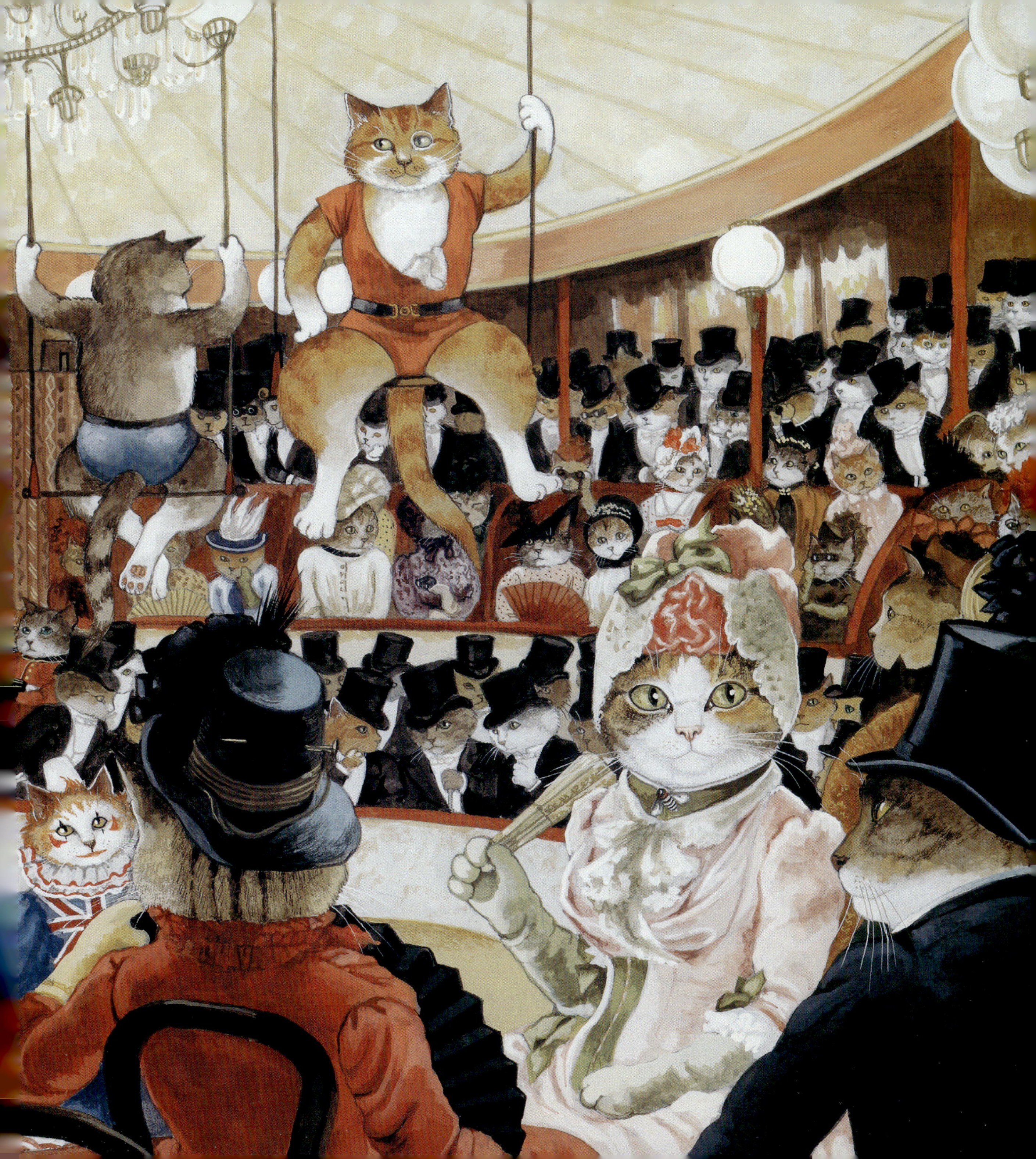

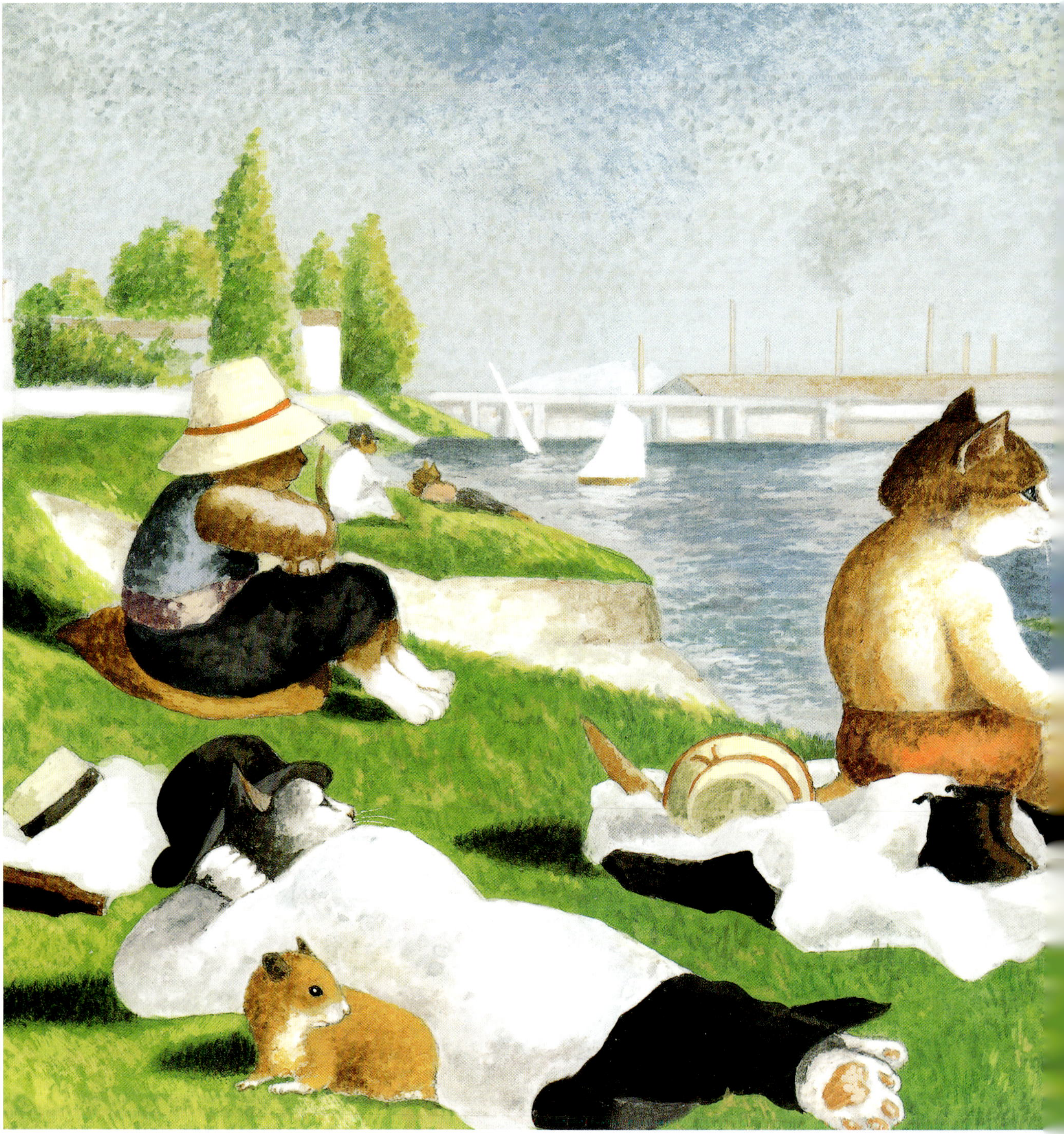

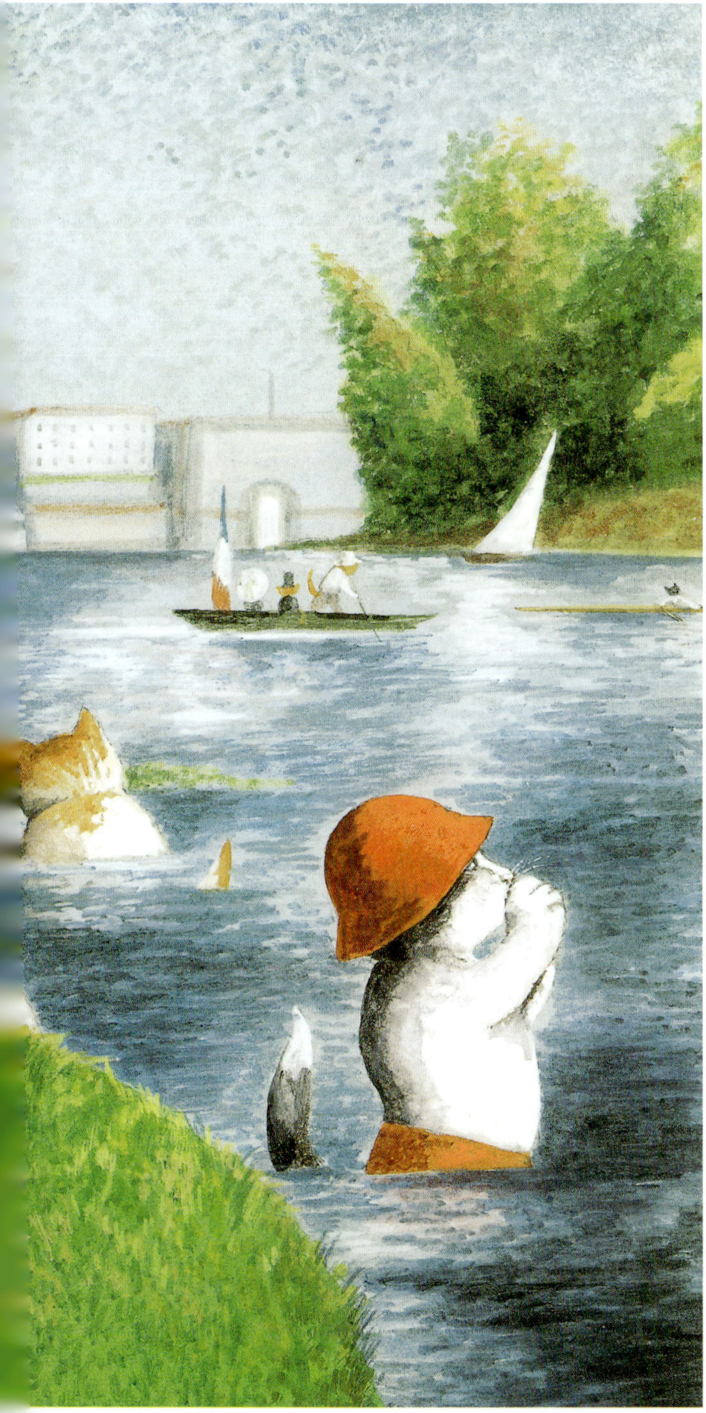

GEORGES SEURAT

Bathers at Asnières (1884)

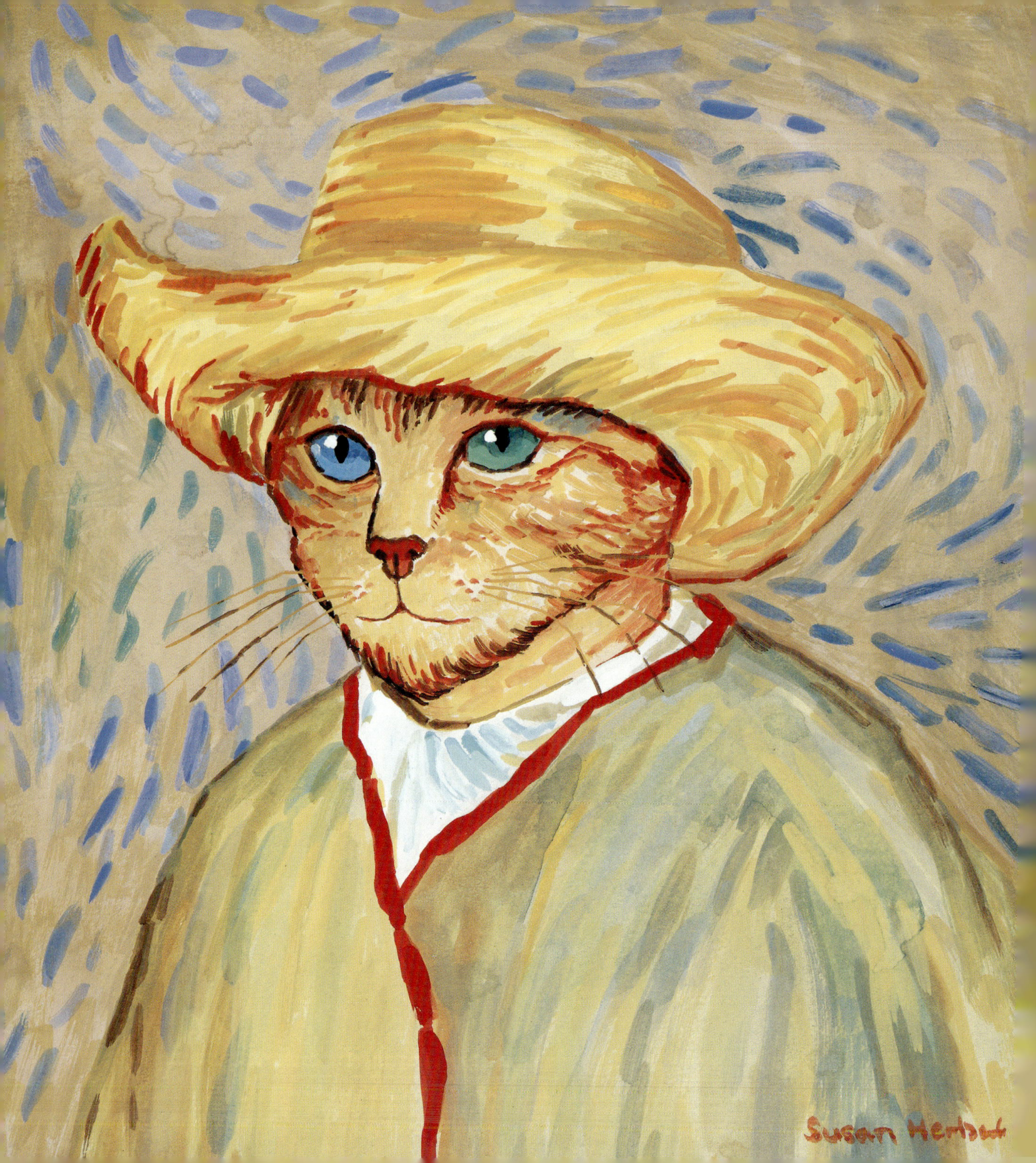
Susan Herbert

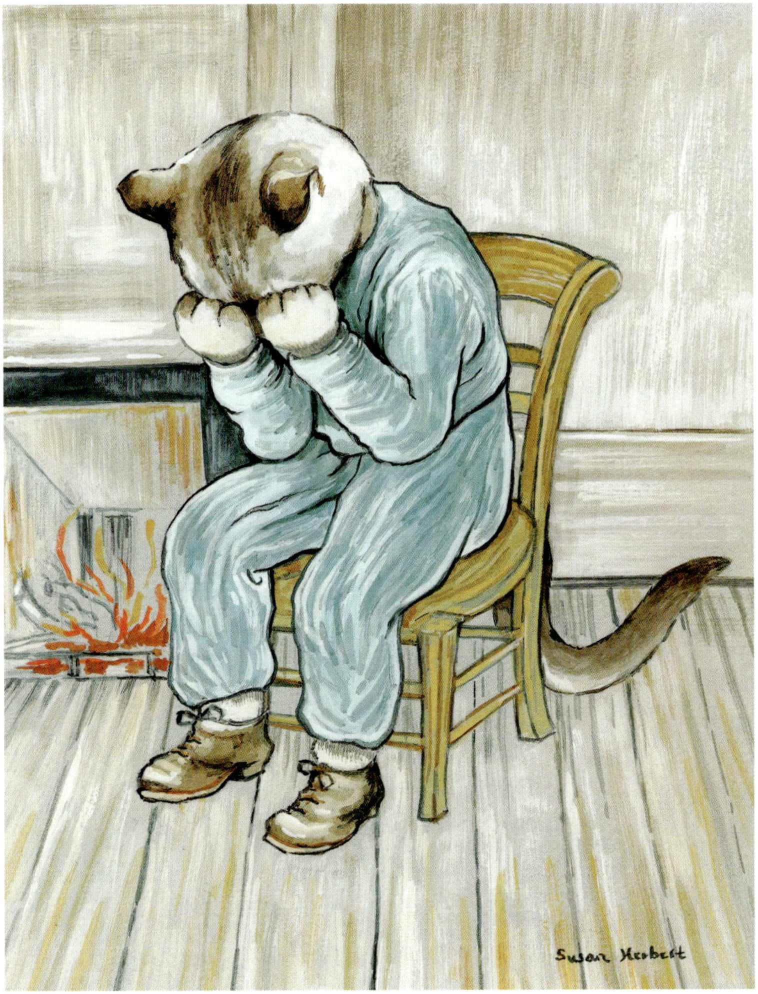

Above VINCENT VAN GOGH, *Sorrowing Old Man ('At Eternity's Gate')* (1890)
Opposite VINCENT VAN GOGH, *Self-Portrait* (1887)

VINCENT VAN GOGH

Self-Portrait with Bandaged Ear and Pipe (1889)

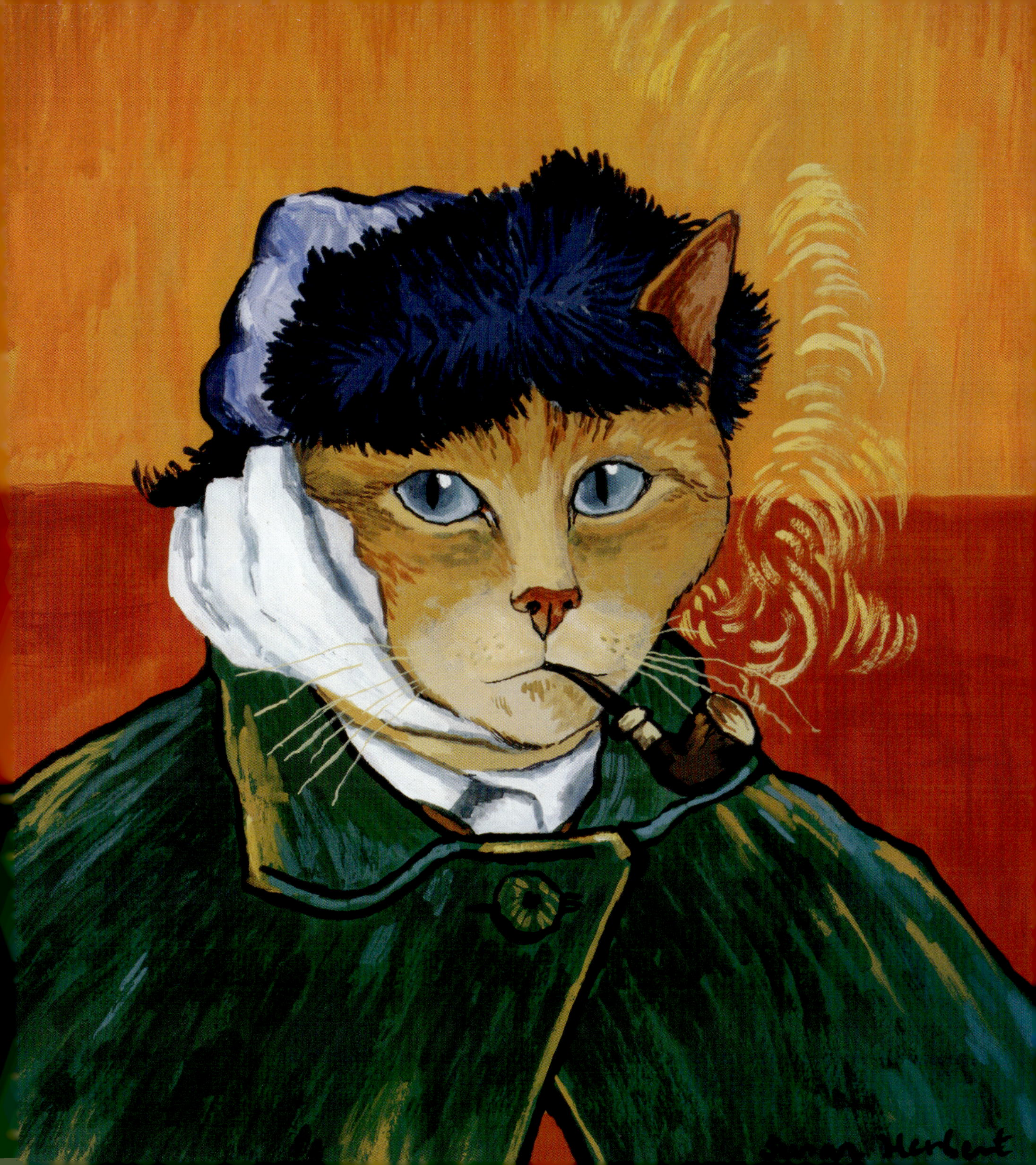

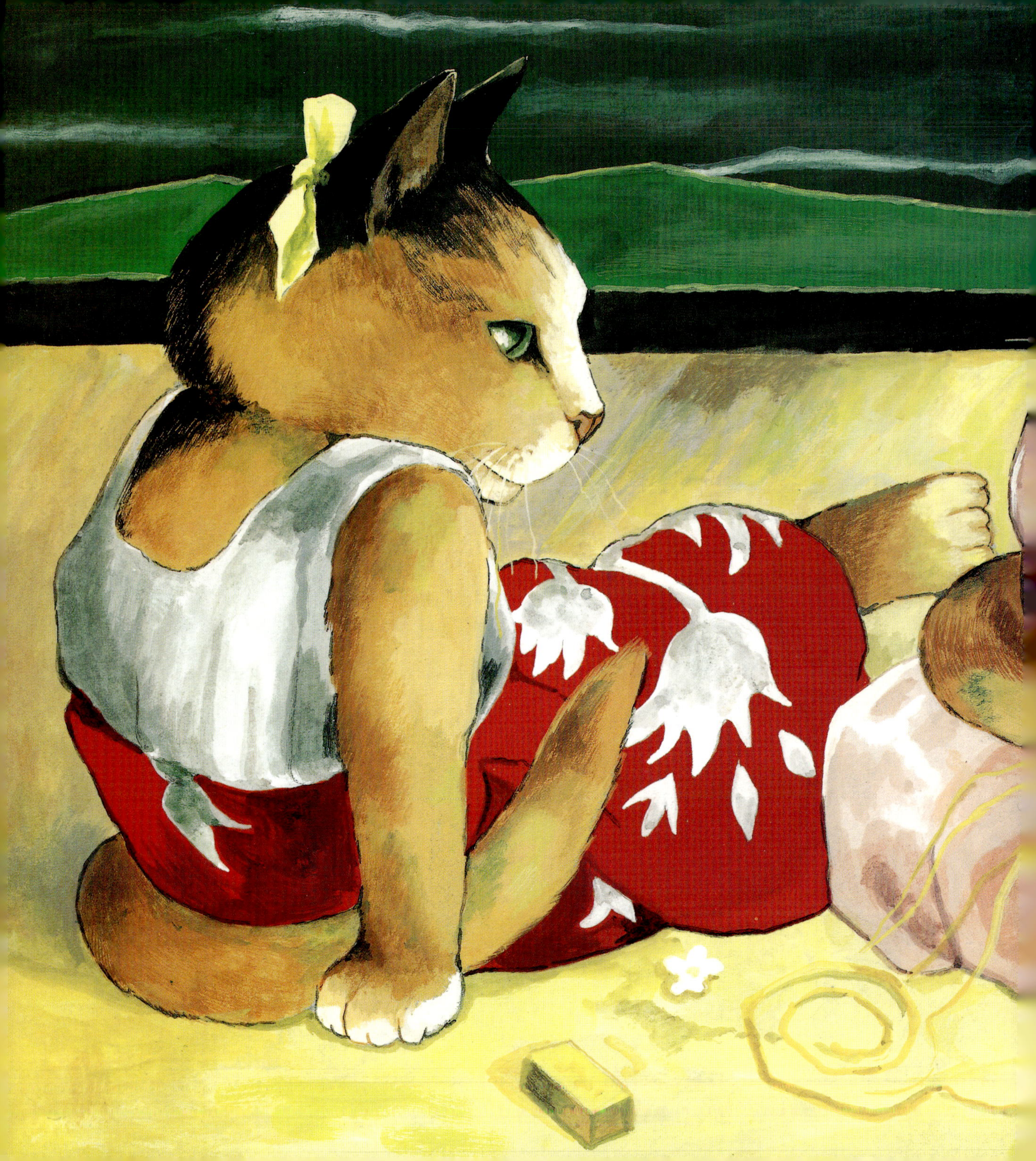

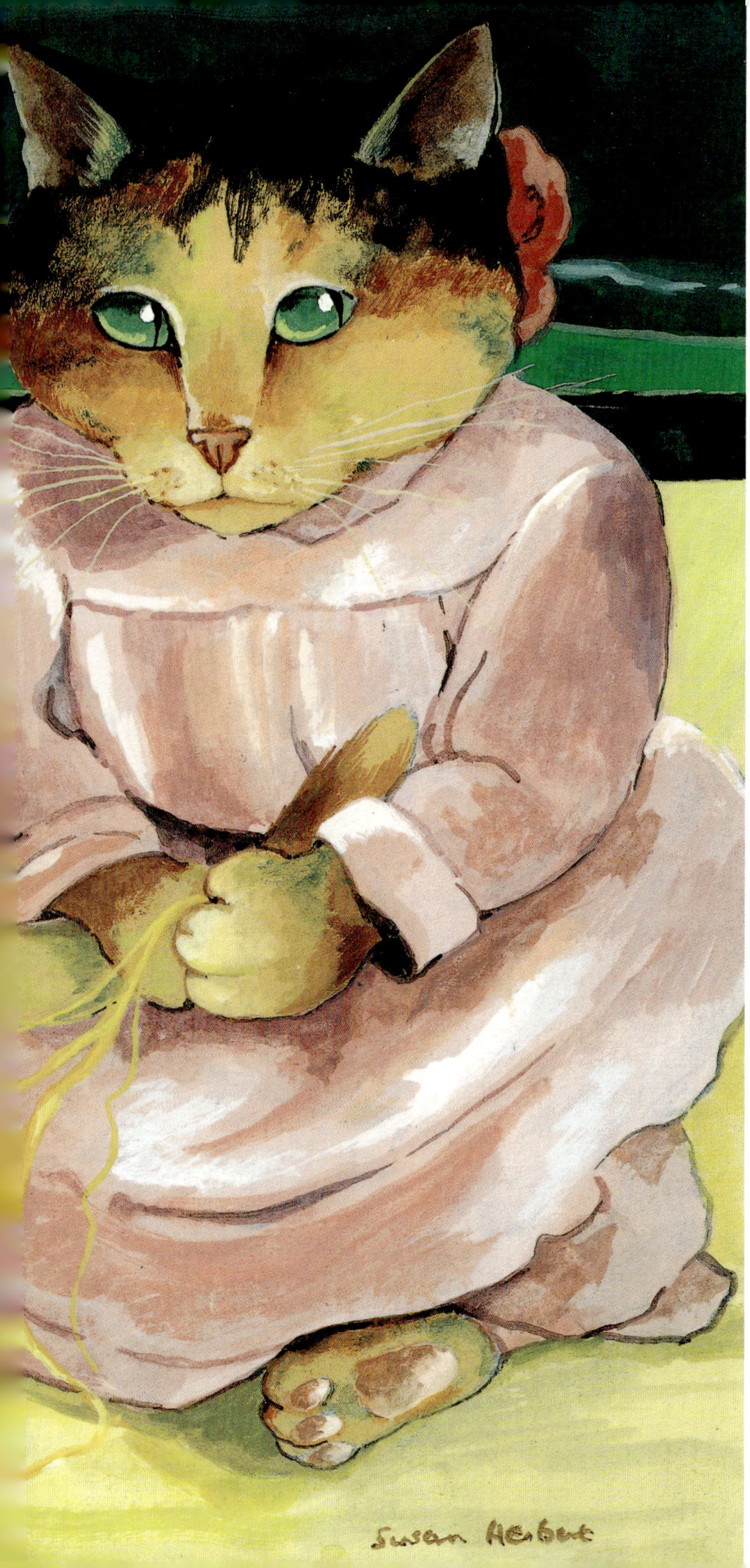

PAUL GAUGUIN

Tahitian Women on the Beach (1891)

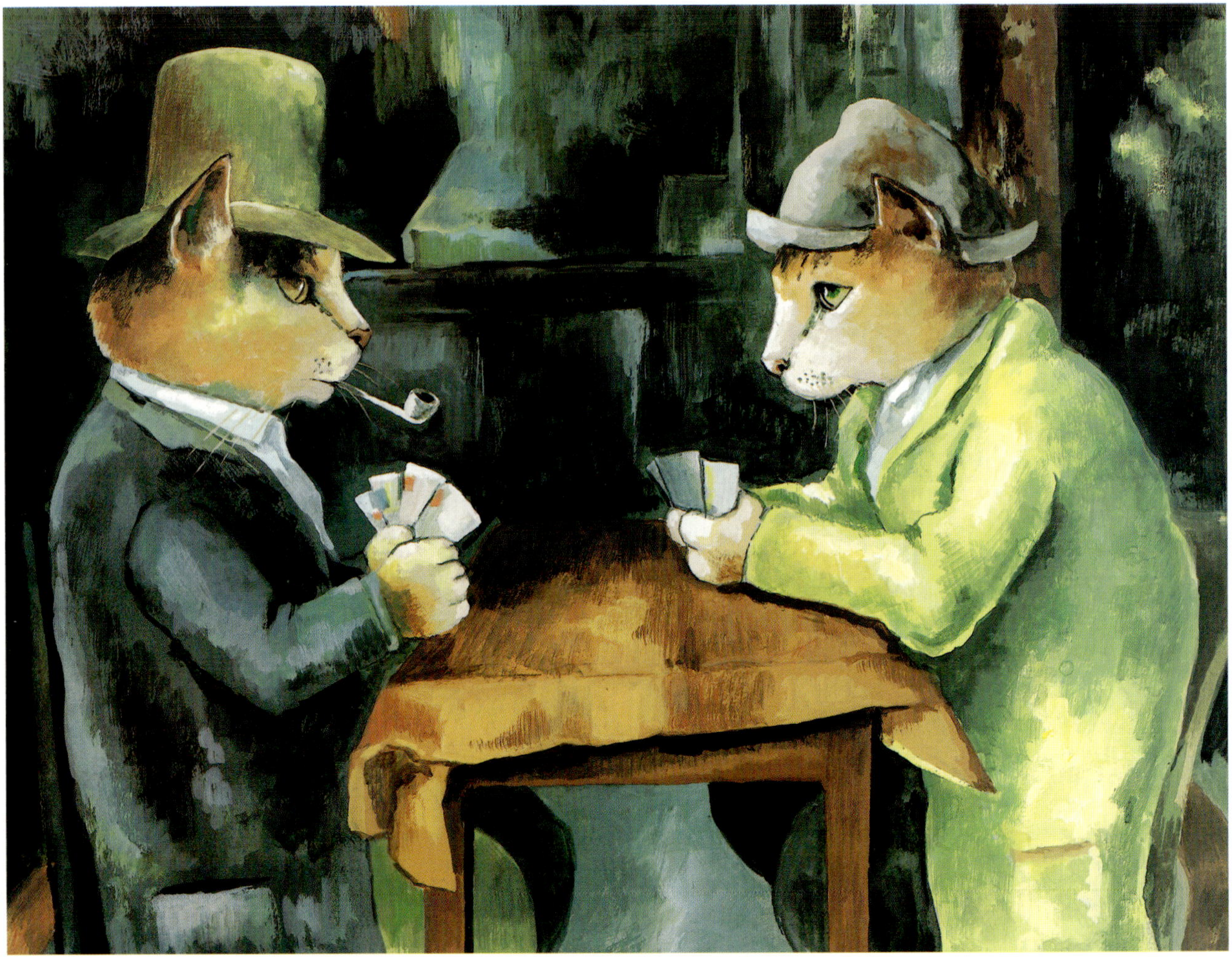

Above PAUL CÉZANNE, *The Card Players* (1890–95)

Opposite PAUL CÉZANNE, *Woman with a Coffee Pot* (1890–95)

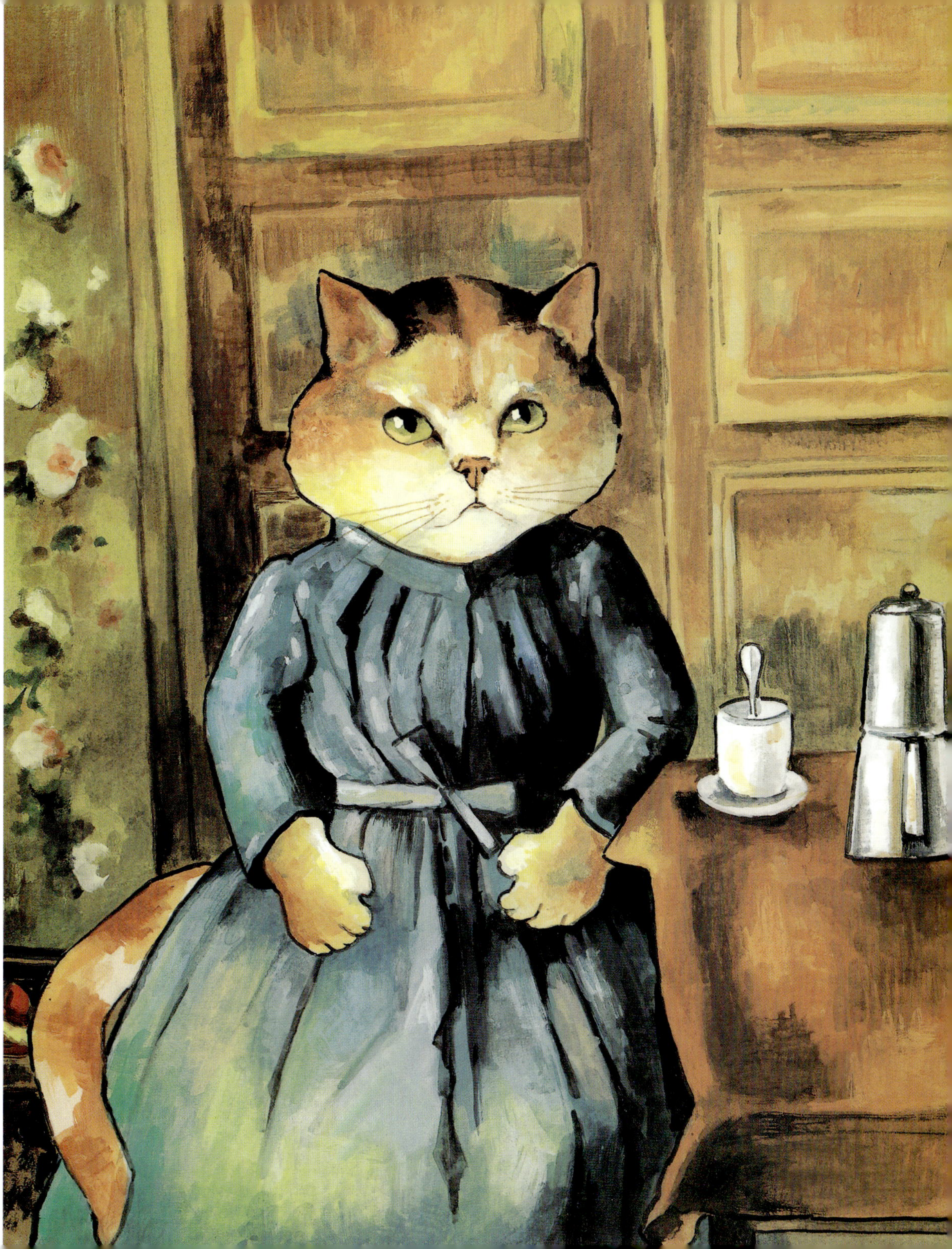

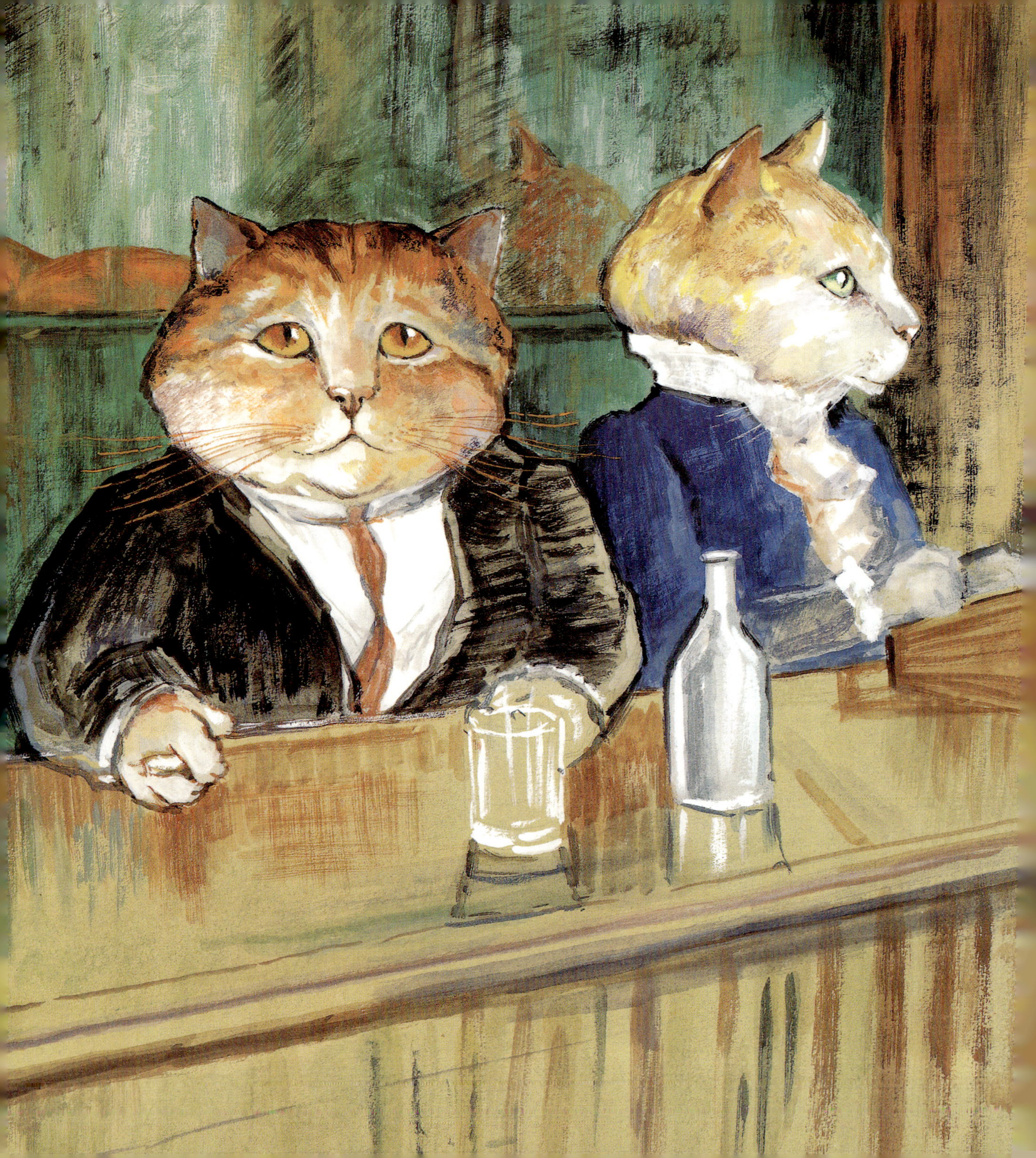

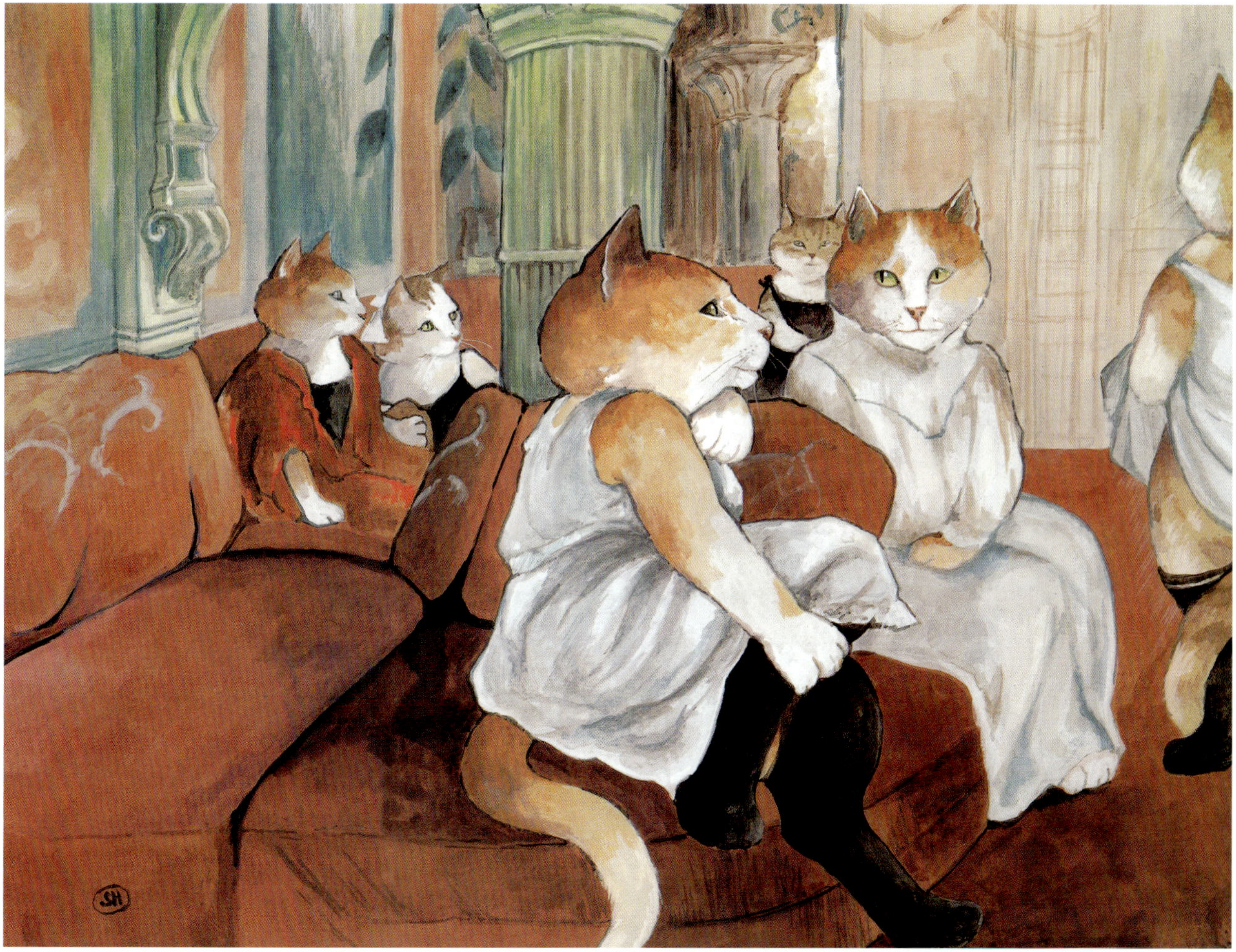

Above HENRI DE TOULOUSE-LAUTREC, *In the Salon at the Rue des Moulins* (1894)

Opposite HENRI DE TOULOUSE-LAUTREC, *At the Bar* (1898)

Overleaf JOHN BYAM LISTON SHAW, *The Blessed Damozel* (1895)

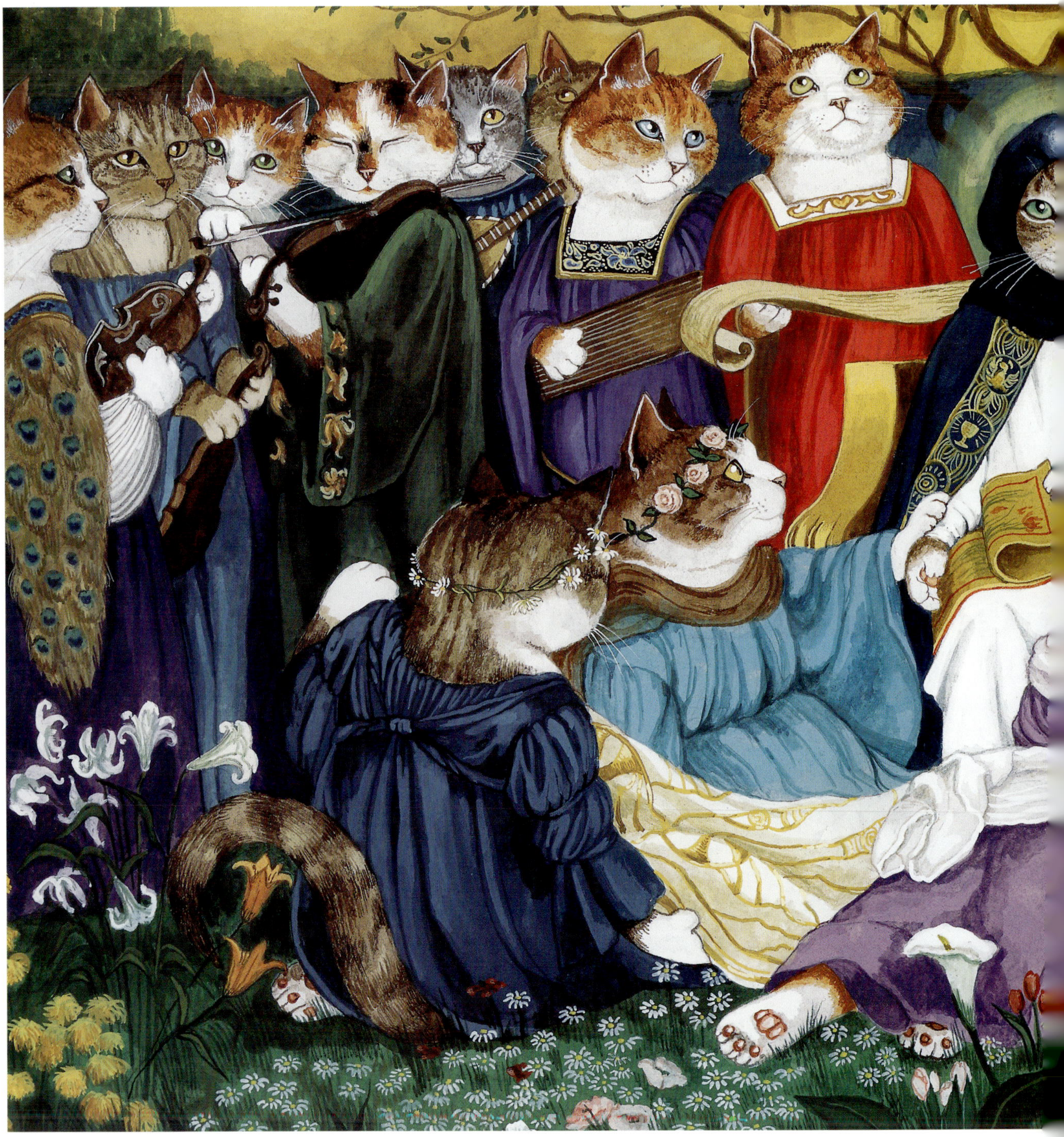

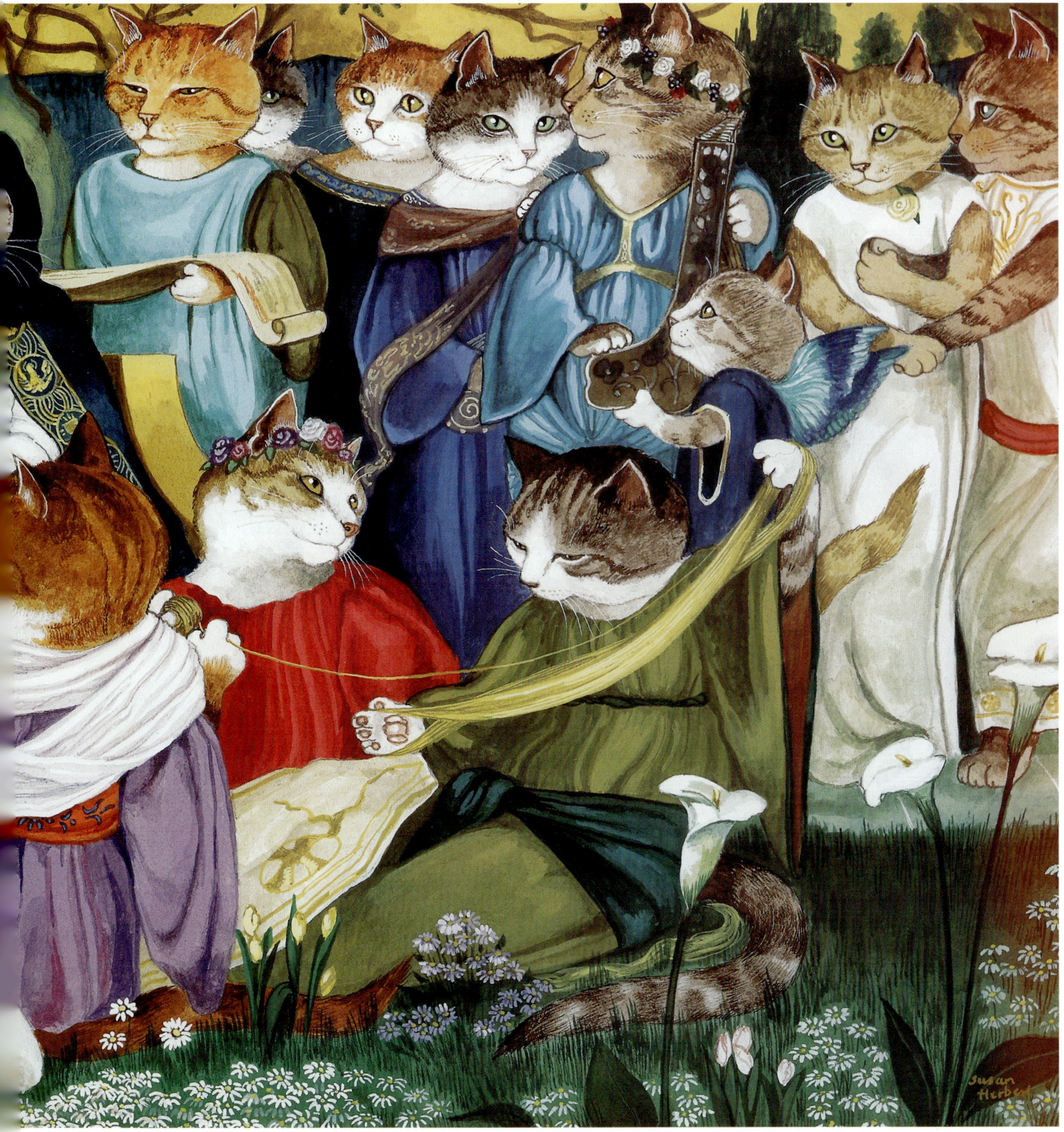

SIR EDWARD BURNE-JONES

The Mirror of Venus (1875)

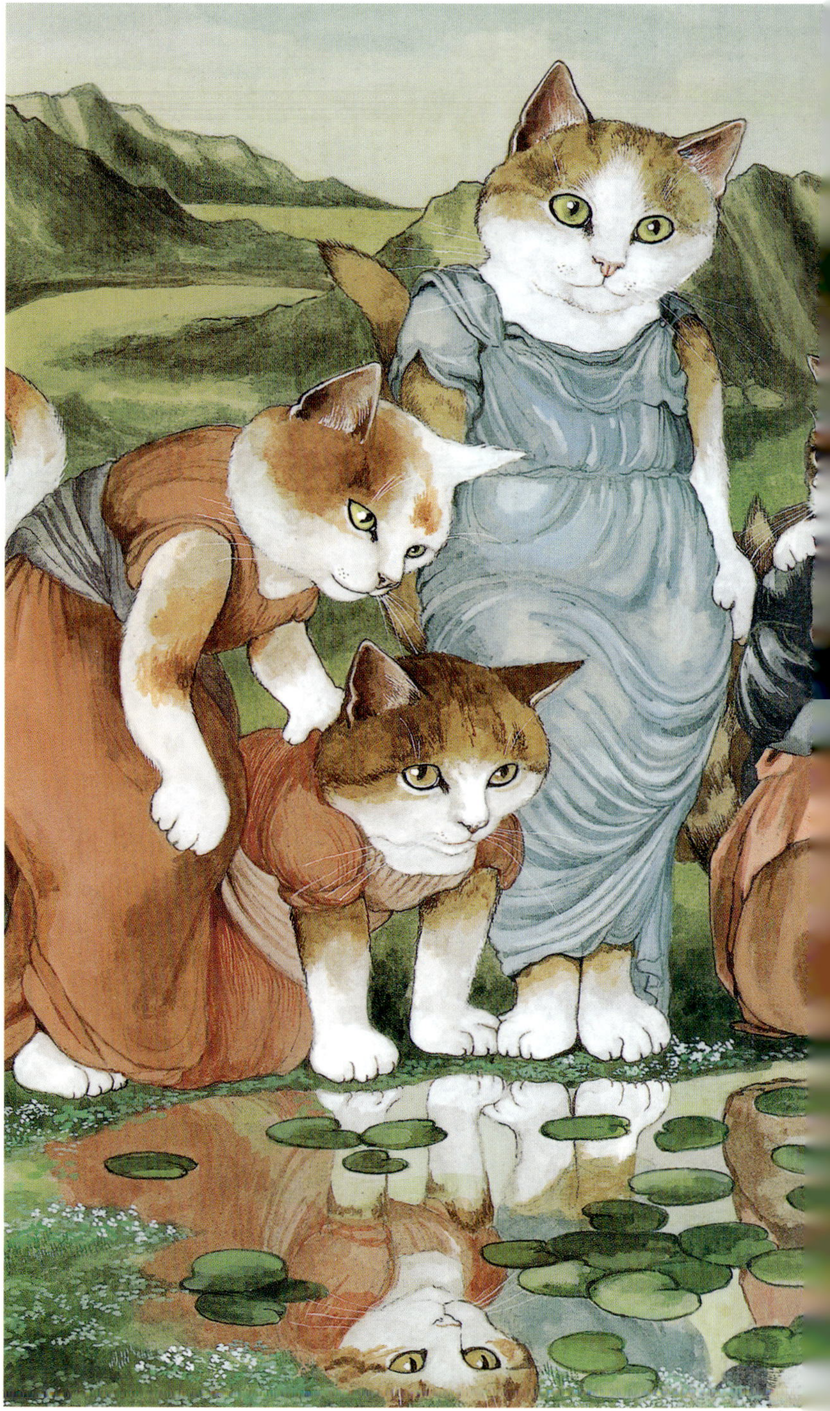

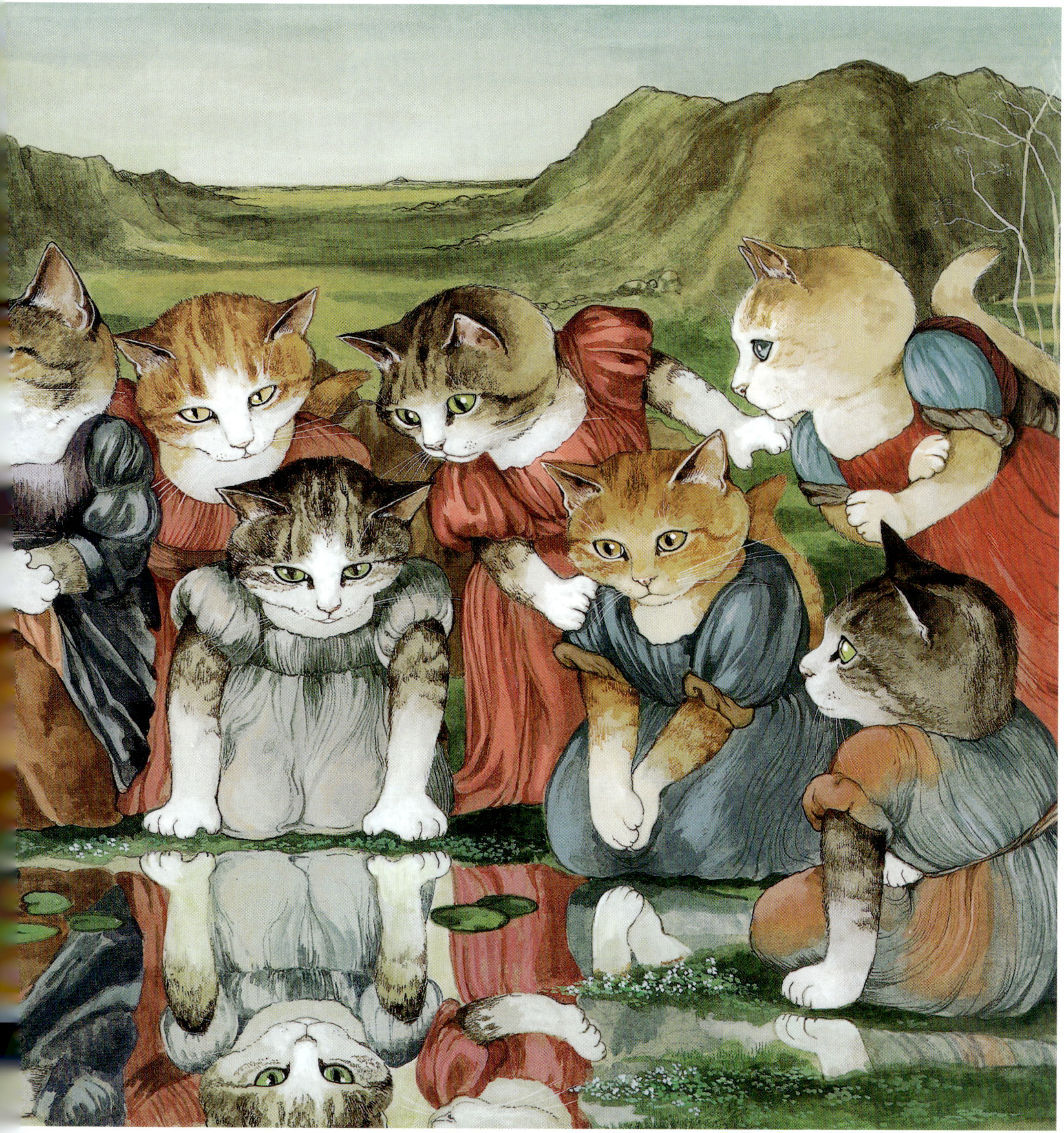

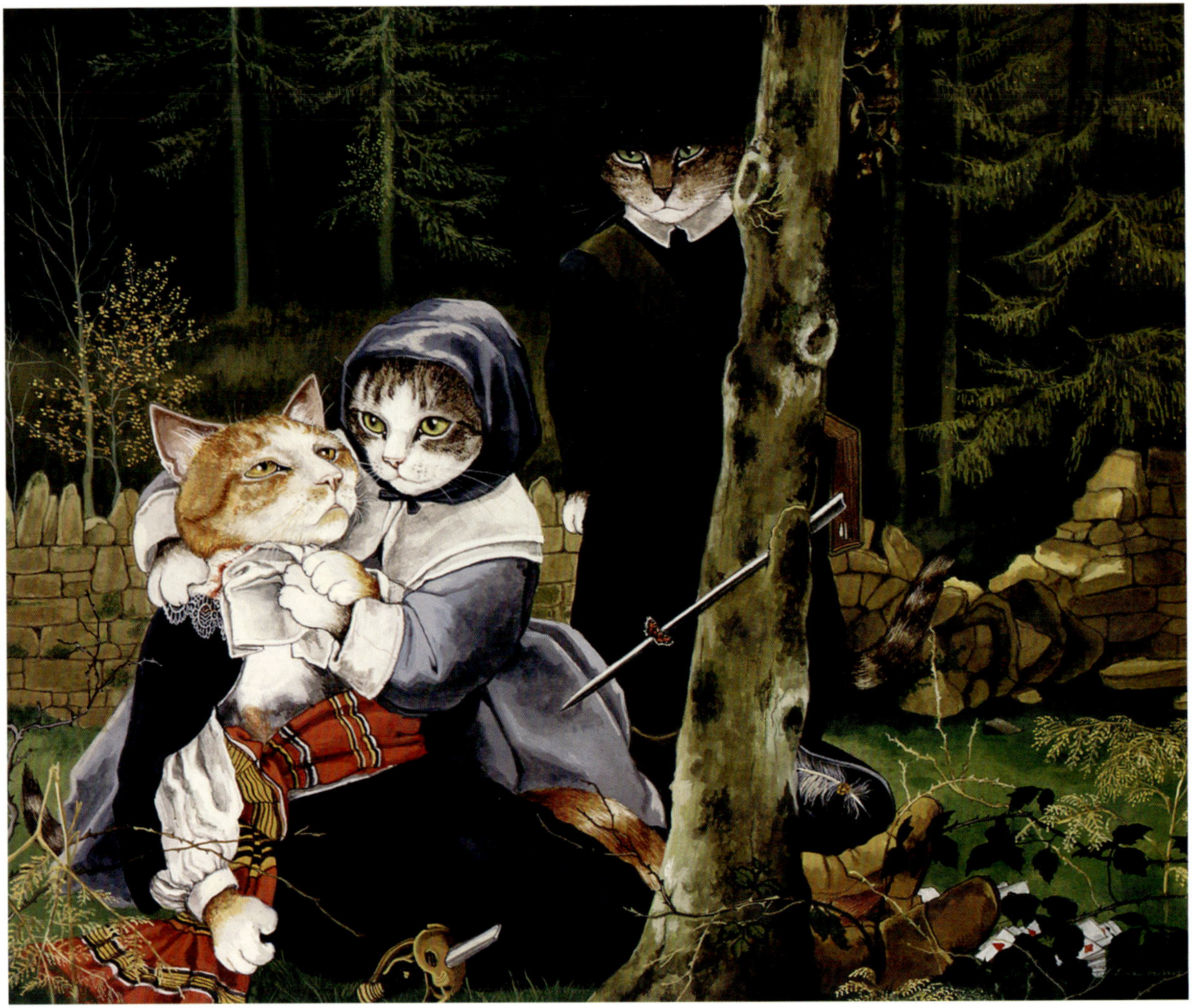

Above WILLIAM SHAKESPEARE BURTON, *The Wounded Cavalier* (1855)

Opposite KATE ELIZABETH BUNCE, *Melody (Musica)* (c. 1895–97)

Overleaf JOHN WILLIAM WATERHOUSE, *Hylas and the Nymphs* (1896)

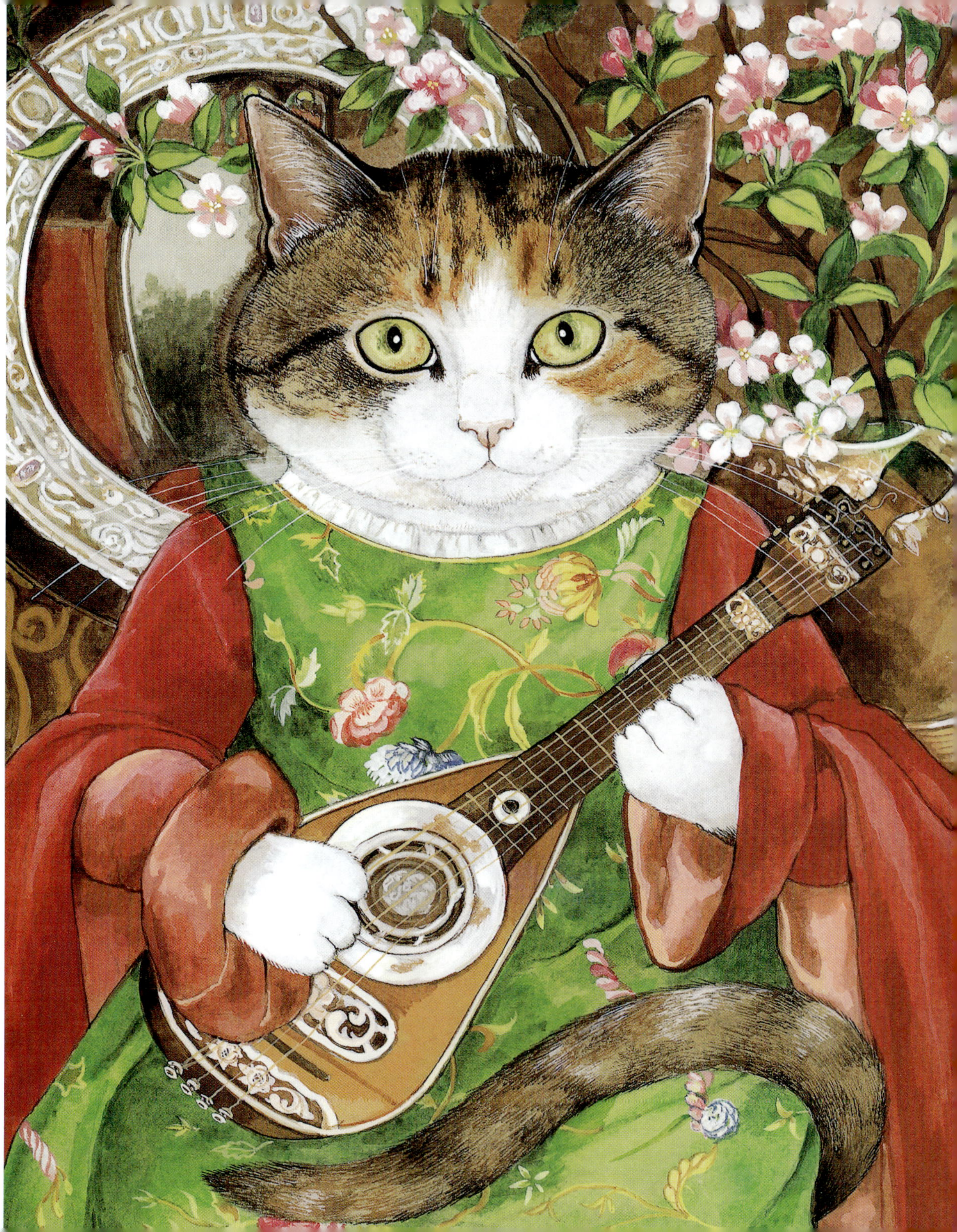

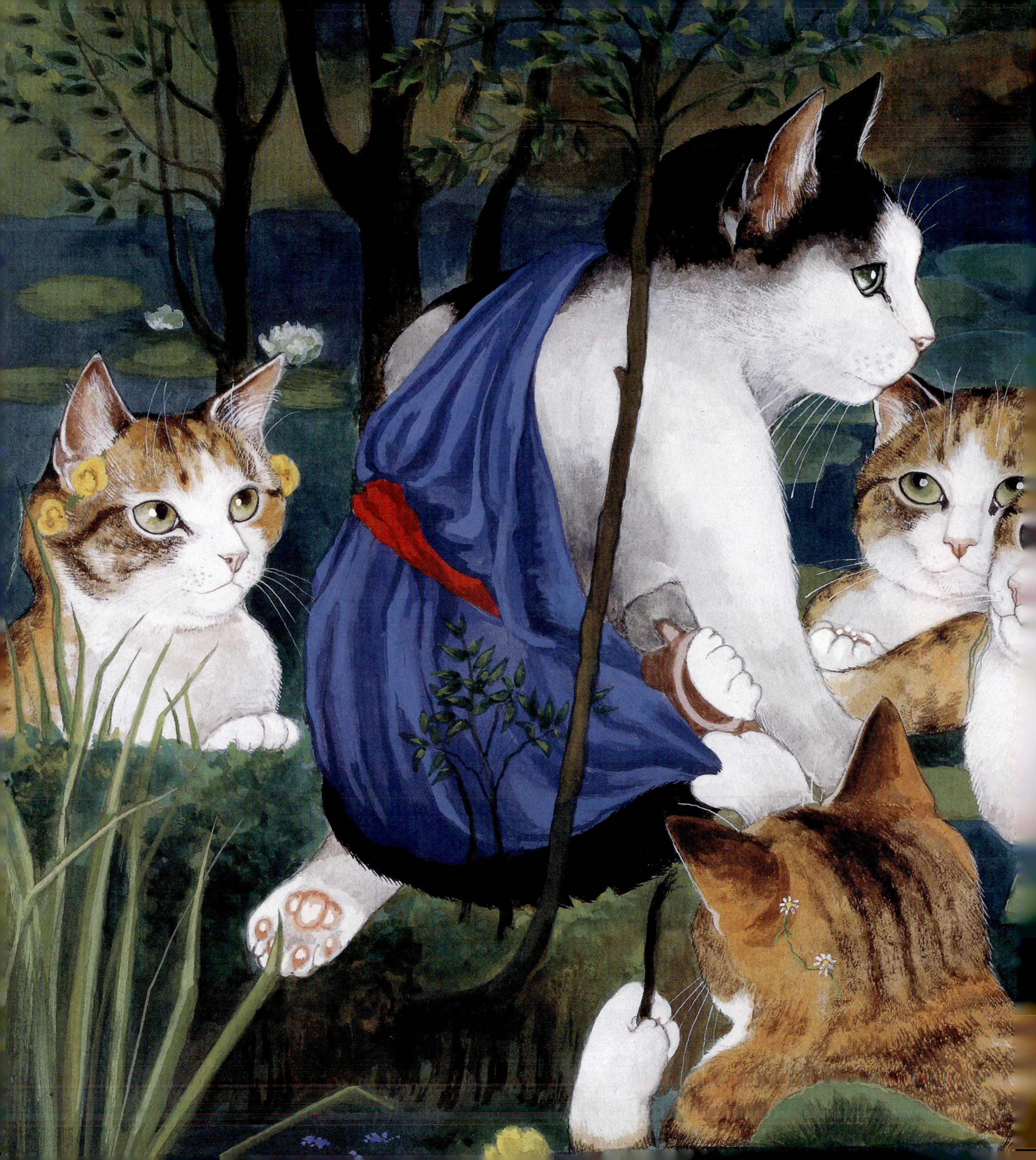

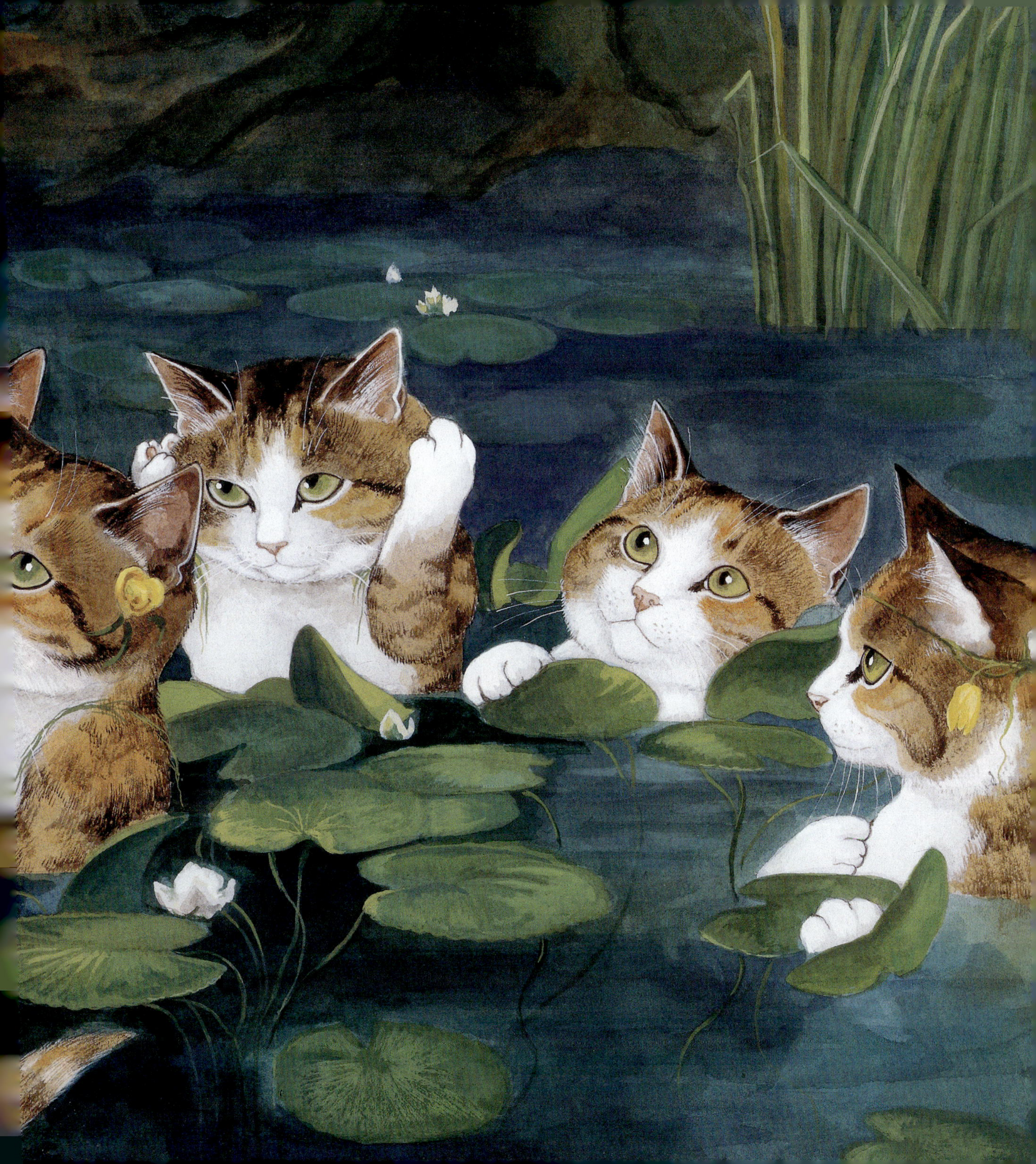

CATS ON STAGE

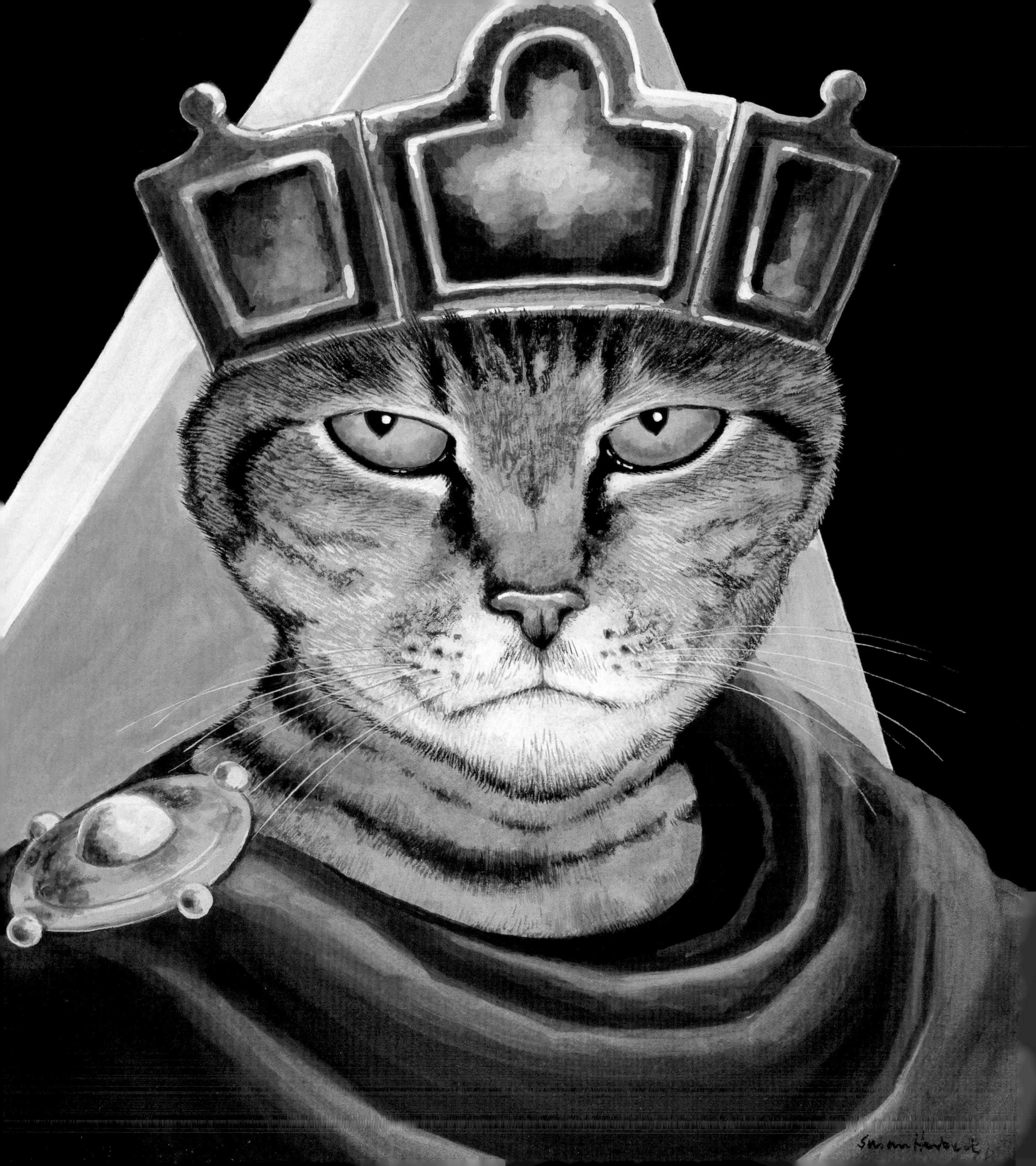

MACBETH

Act I, Scene IV

Stars, hide your fires!
Let not light see my black and deep desires.

MACBETH

Act I, Scene III

All hail Macbeth, that shalt be king hereafter!

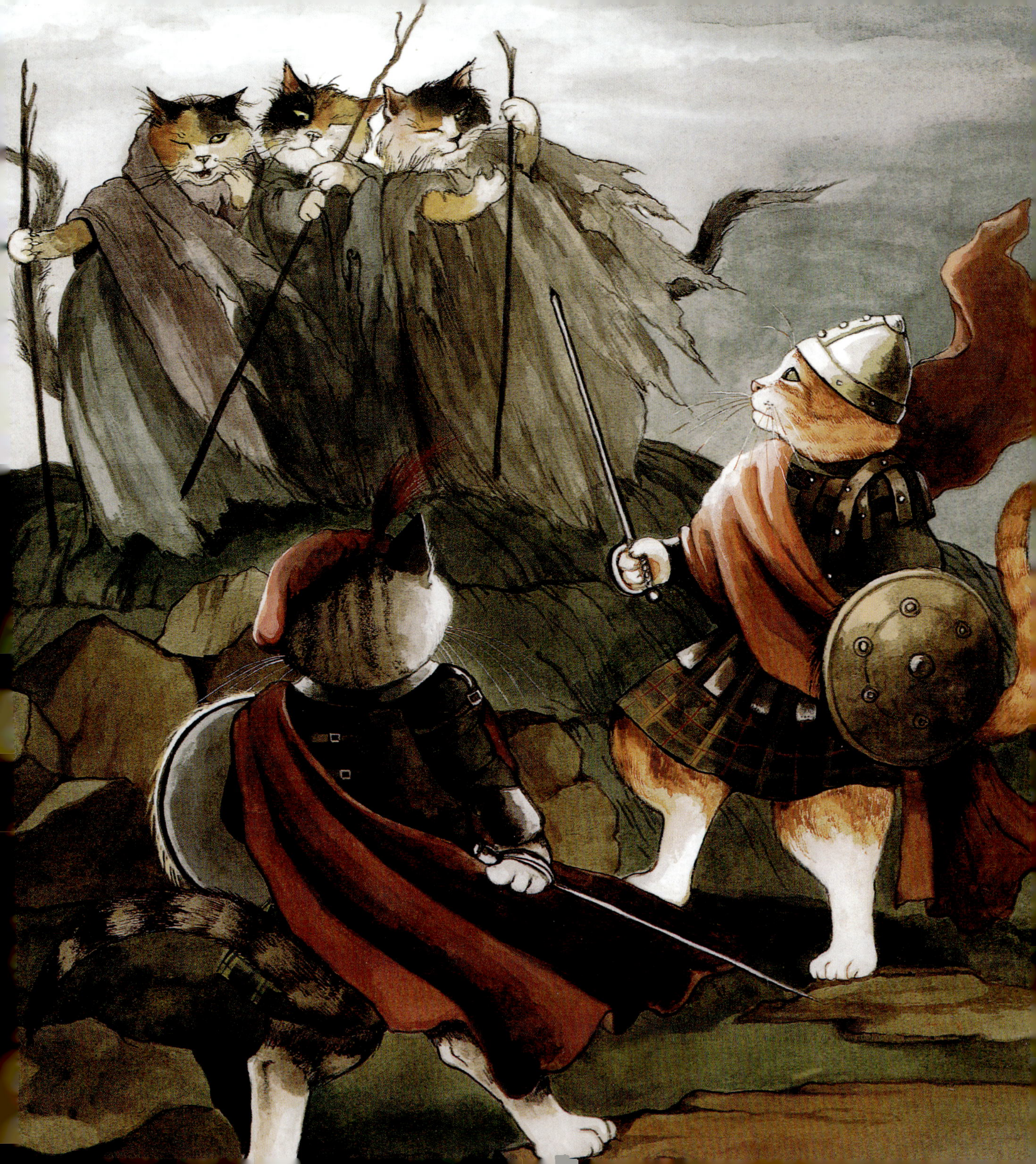

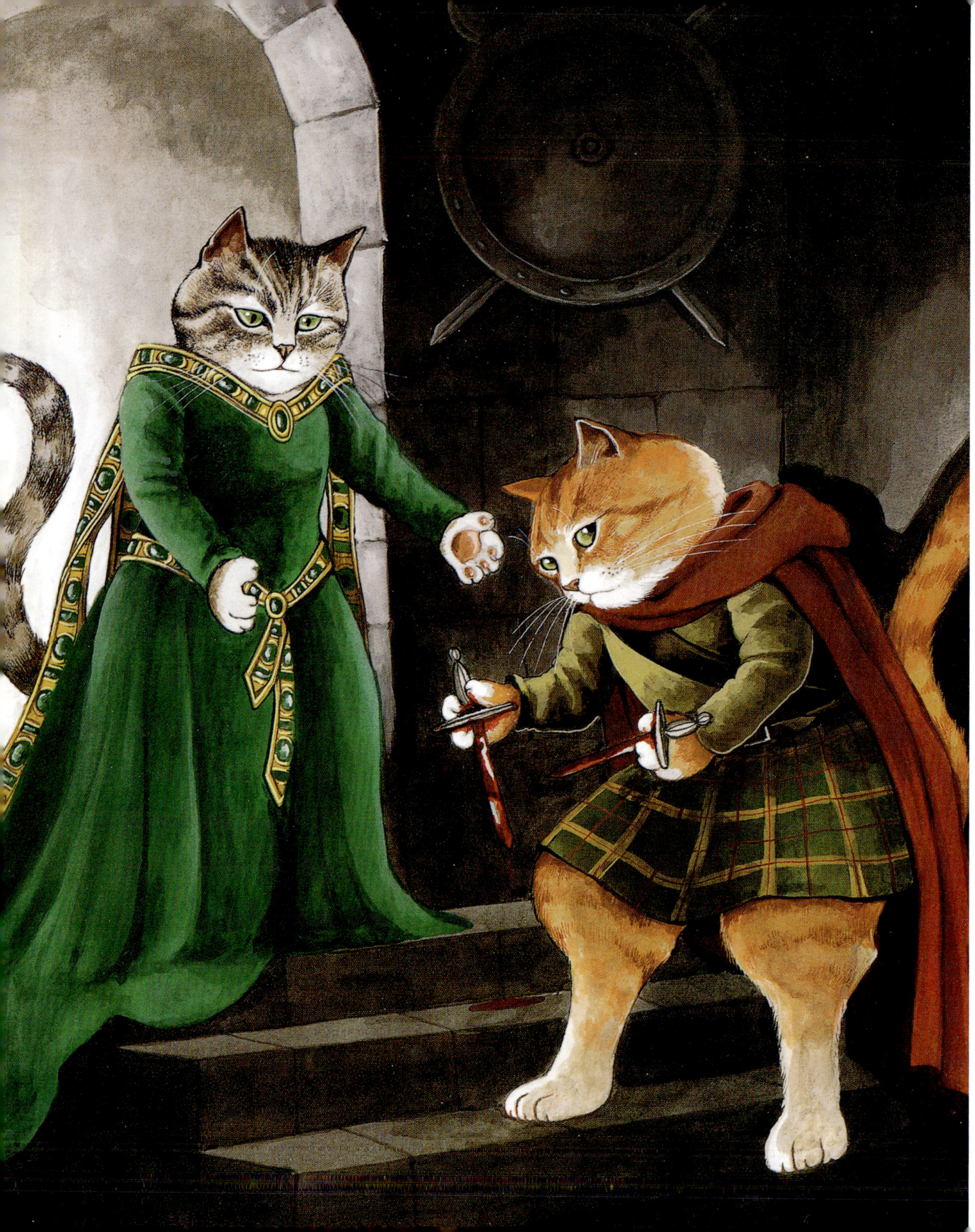

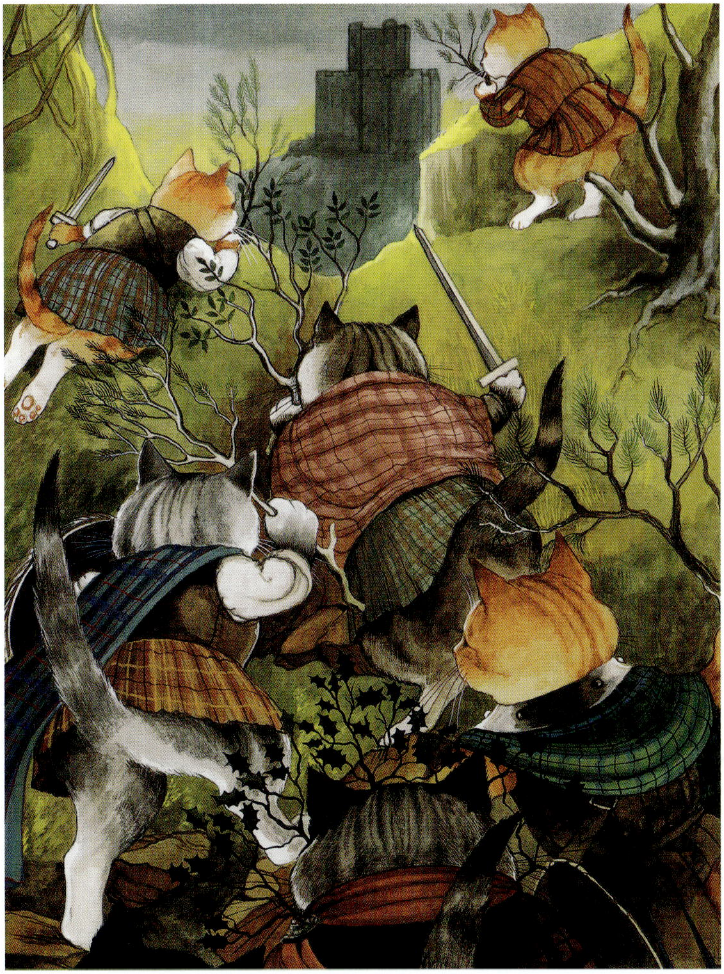

Opposite MACBETH, Act II, Scene II

Above MACBETH, Act V, Scene V

MUCH ADO ABOUT NOTHING

Act II, Scene I

I will in the interim undertake one of Hercules' labours, which is, to bring Signior Benedick and the Lady Beatrice into a mountain of affection th' one with th' other.

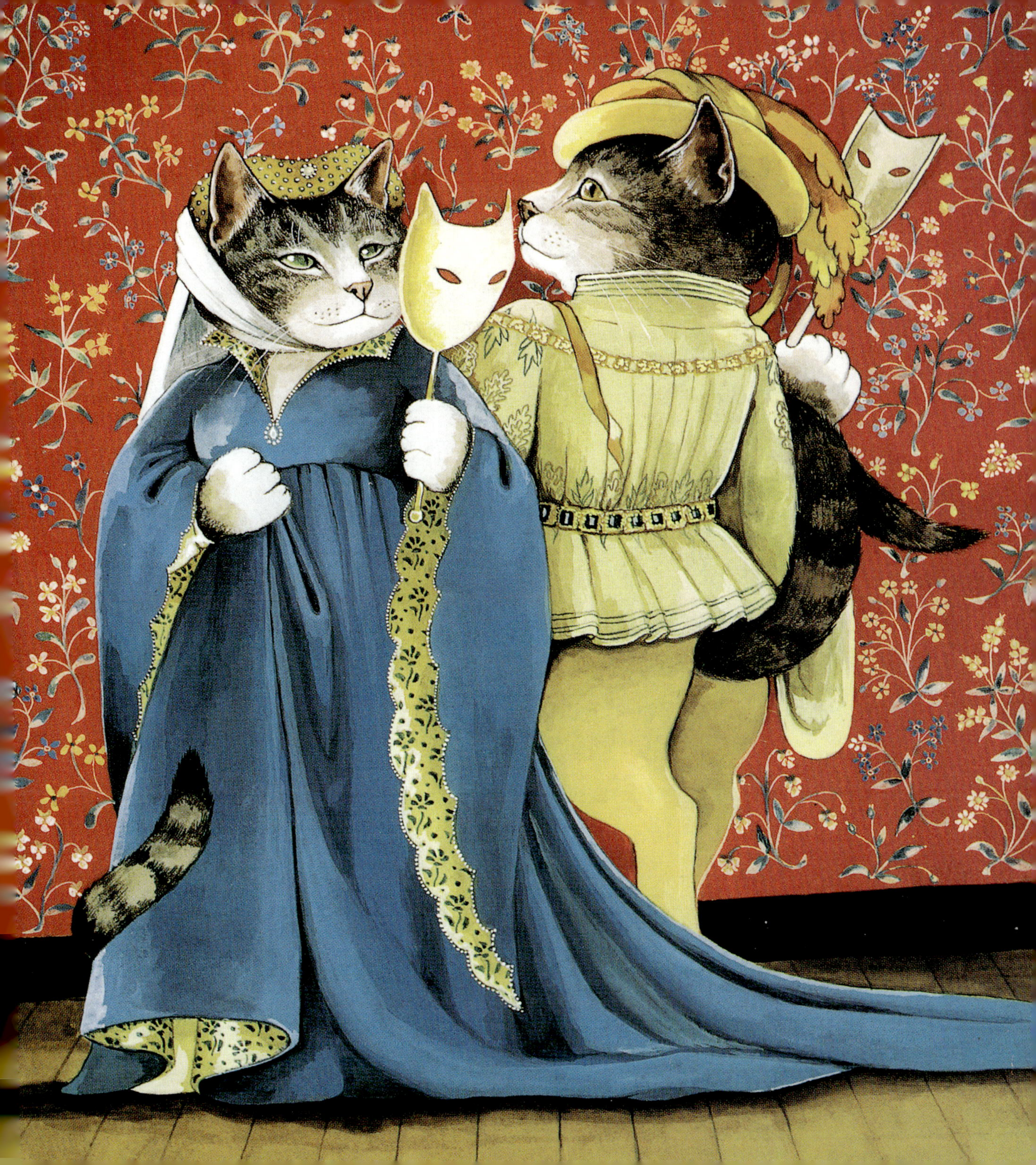

A MIDSUMMER NIGHT'S DREAM

Act II, Scene I

Ill met by moonlight, proud Titania.

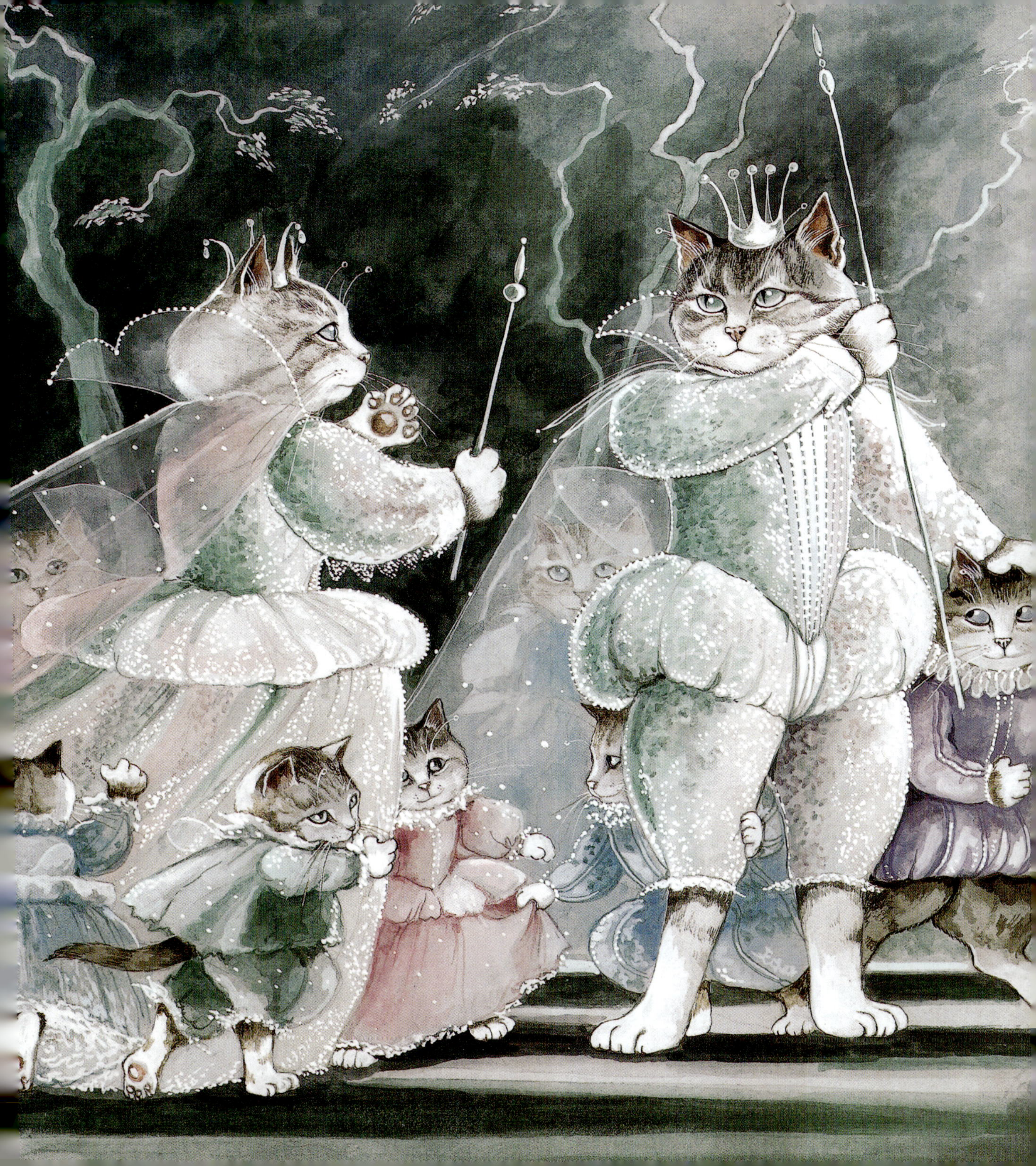

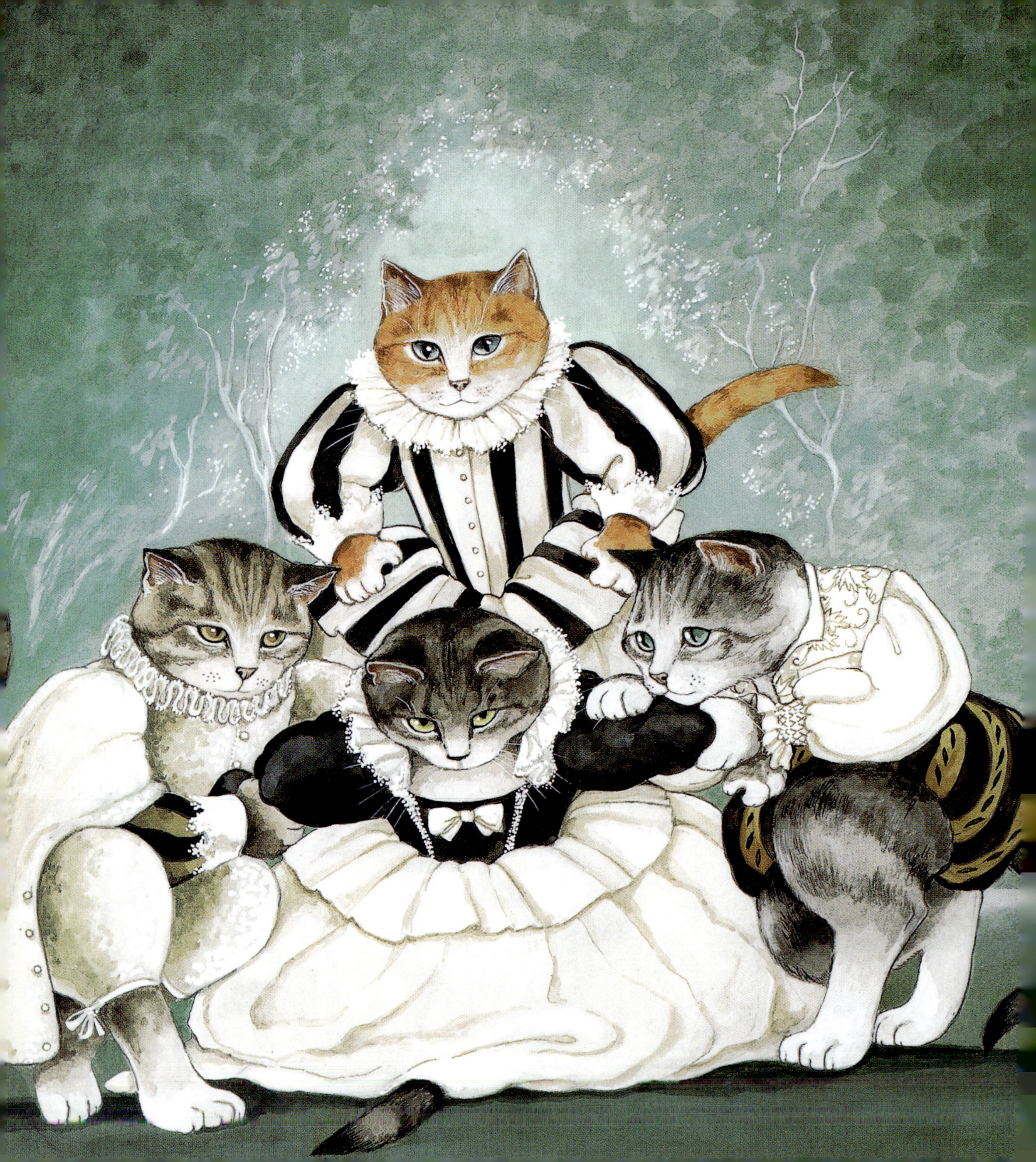

A MIDSUMMER NIGHT'S DREAM

Act III, Scene II

O me! you juggler! you cankerblossom!
You thief of love! What! Have you come by night,
And stol'n my love's heart from him?

A MIDSUMMER NIGHT'S DREAM

Act IV, Scene I

Come, sit thee down upon this flow'ry bed,
While I thy amiable cheeks do coy,
And stick musk-roses in thy sleek smooth head,
And kiss thy fair large ears, my gentle joy.

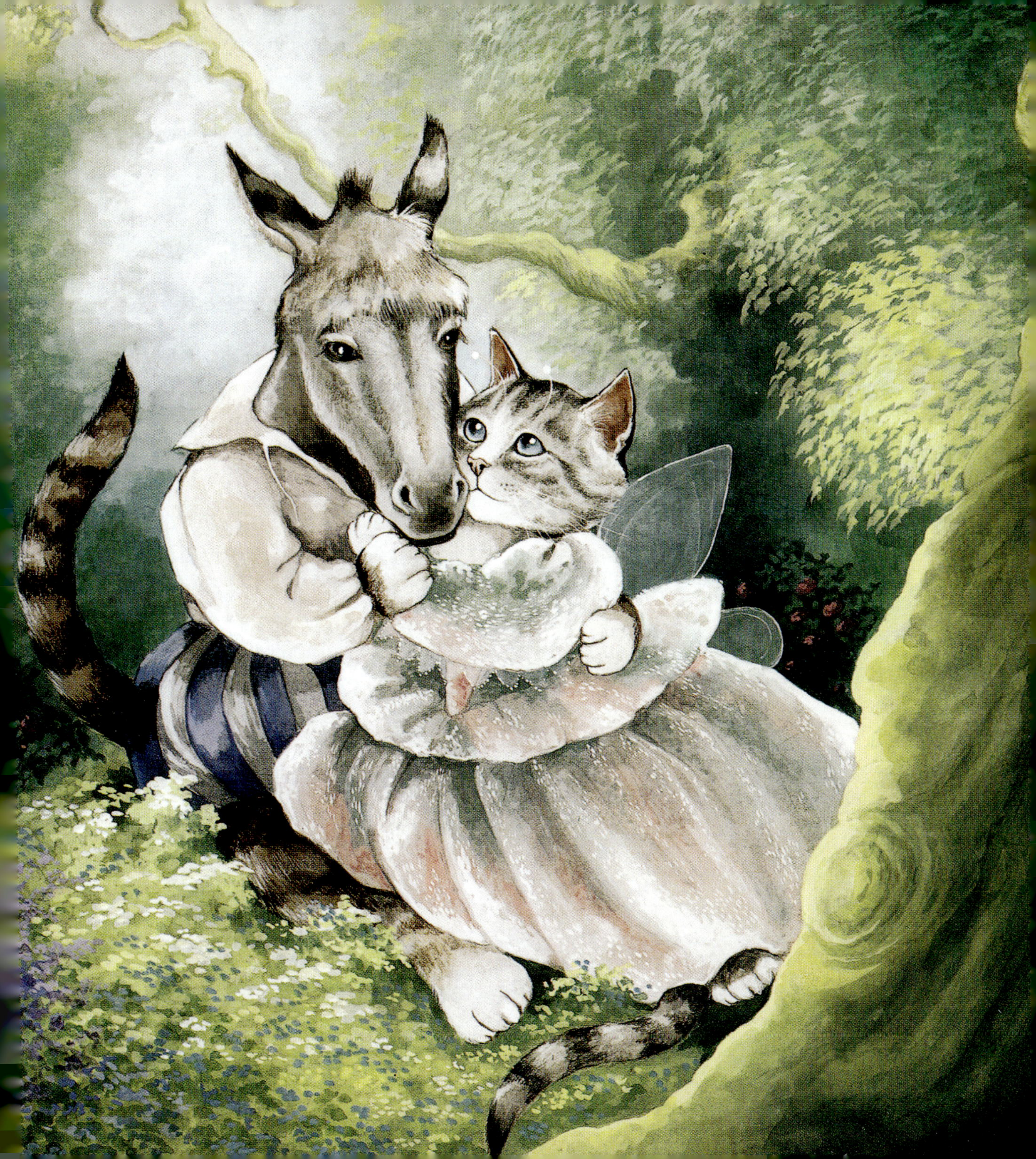

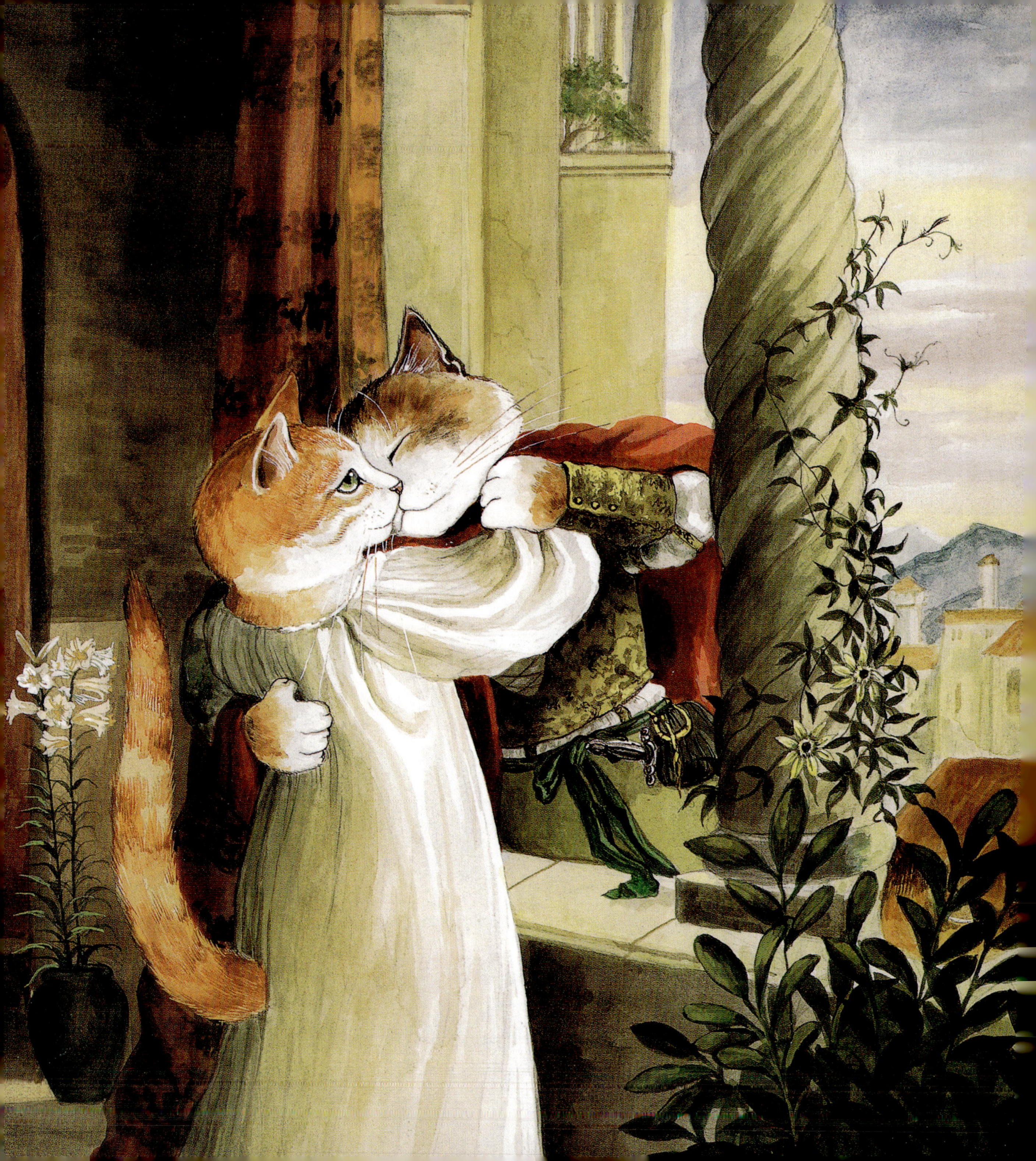

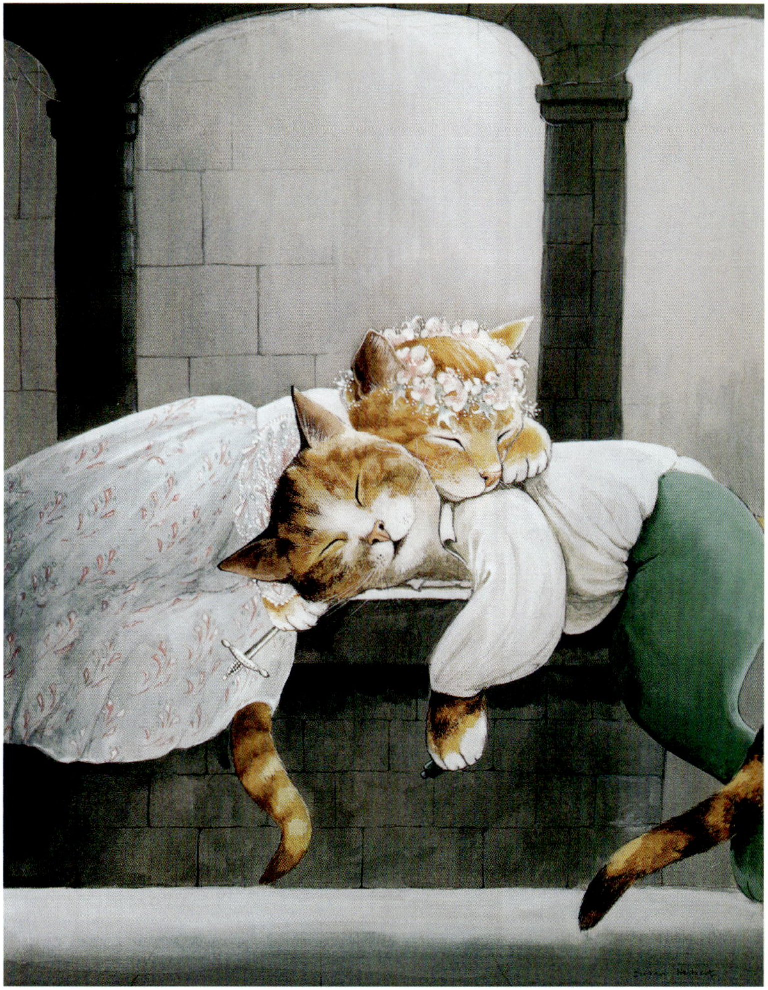

Opposite ROMEO AND JULIET, Act II, Scene II
Above ROMEO AND JULIET, Act V, Scene III

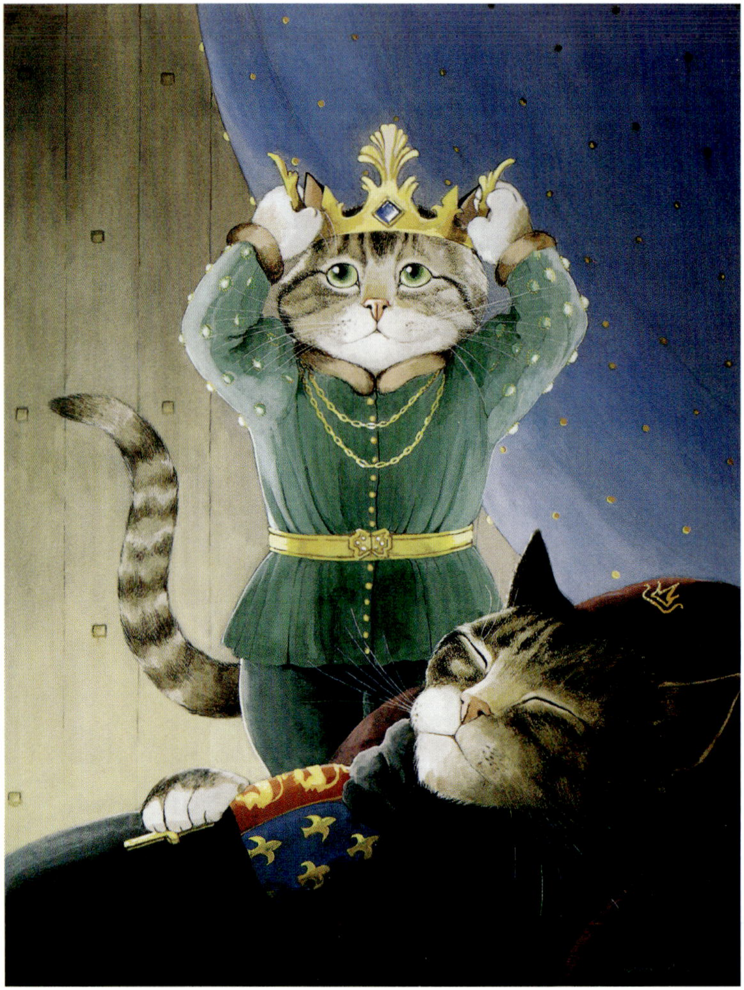

Above HENRY IV, PART II, Act IV, Scene V

Opposite HENRY V, Act III, Scene I

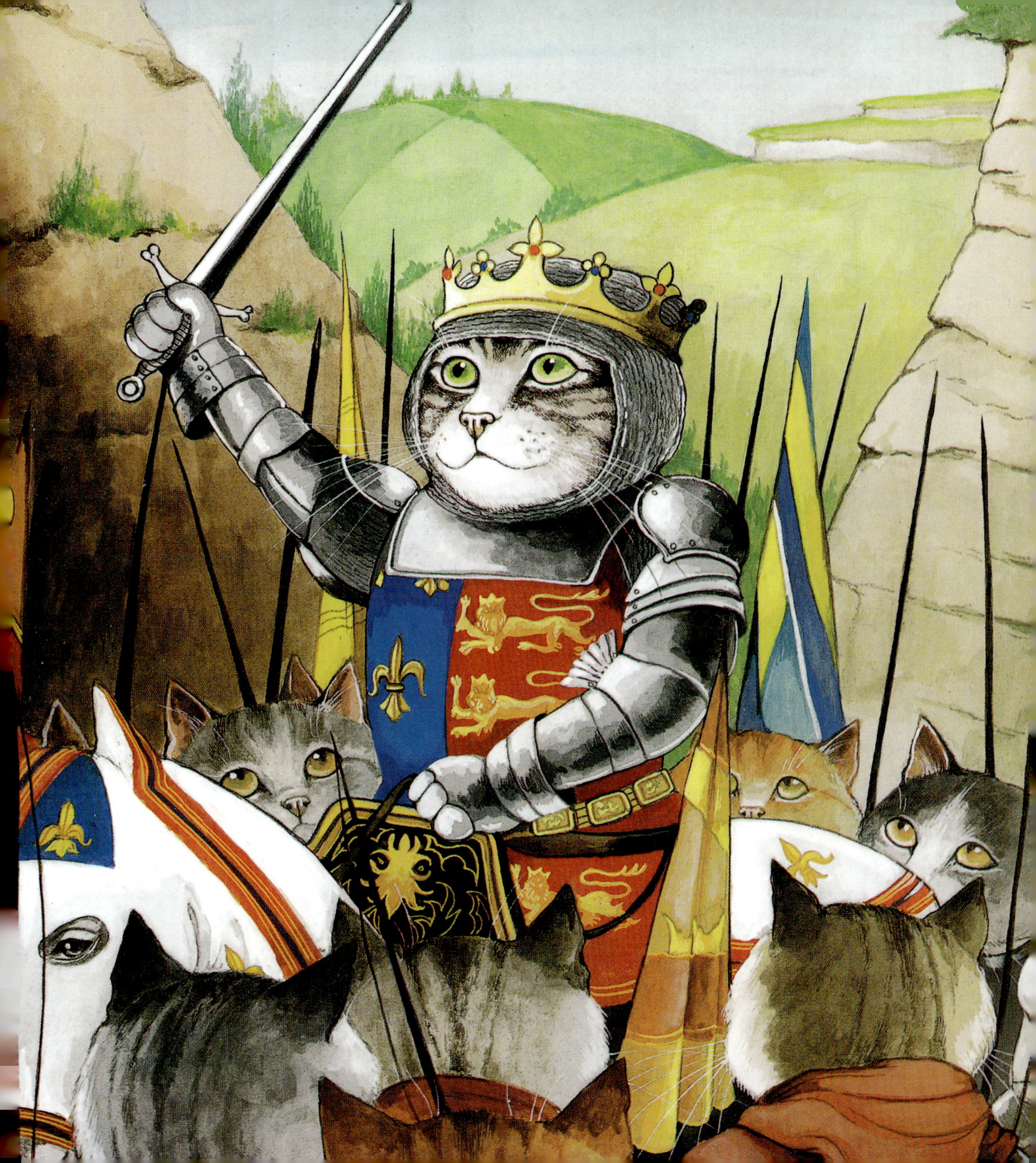

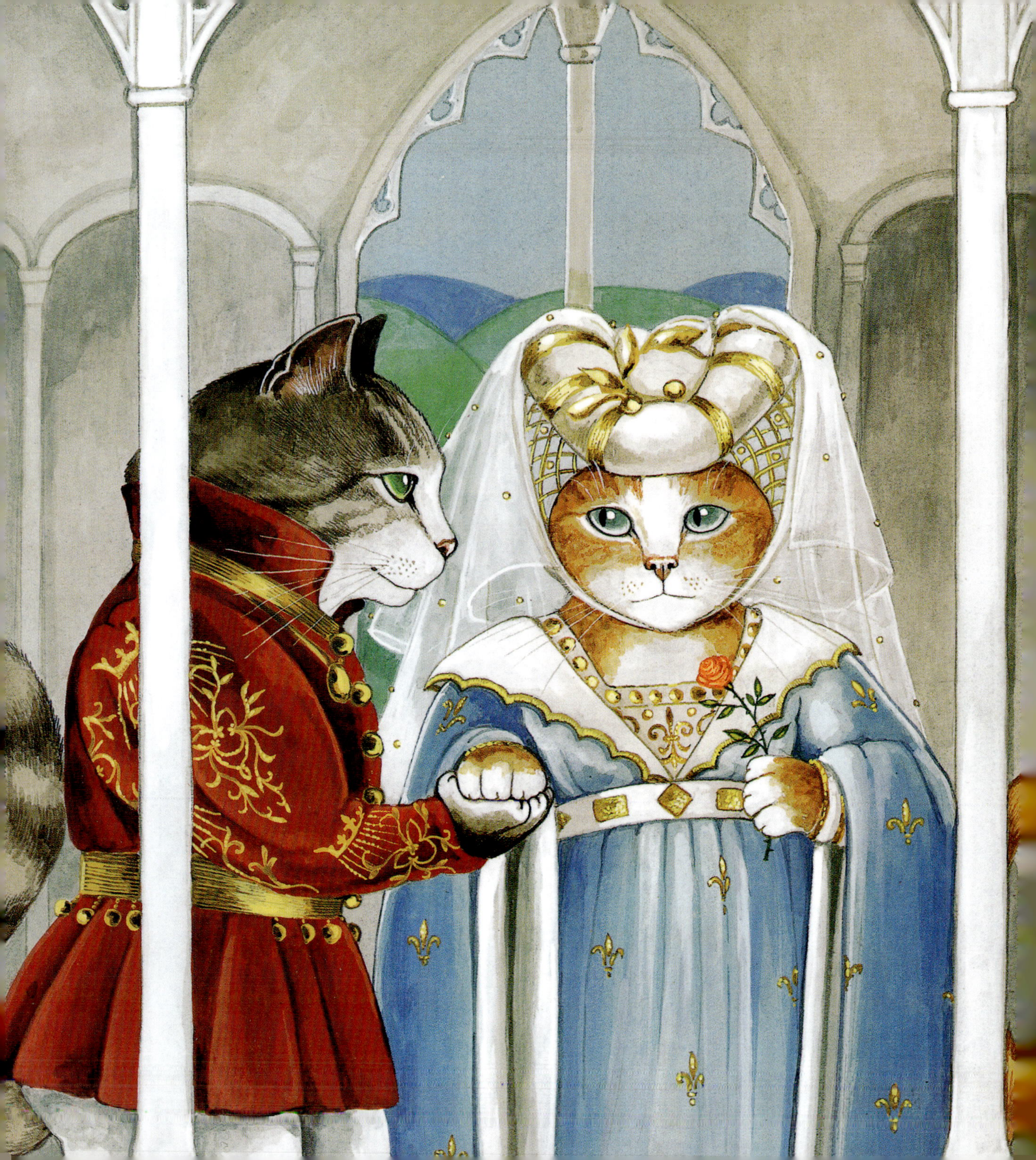

HENRY V

Act V, Scene II

And therefore tell me, most fair Katherine, will you have me? Put off your maiden blushes; avouch the thoughts of your heart with the looks of an empress; take me by the hand and say 'Harry of England, I am thine.'

THE TAMING OF THE SHREW

Act III, Scene II

I will be master of what is mine own –
She is my goods, my chattels, she is my house,
My household stuff, my field, my barn,
My horse, my ox, my ass, my any thing,

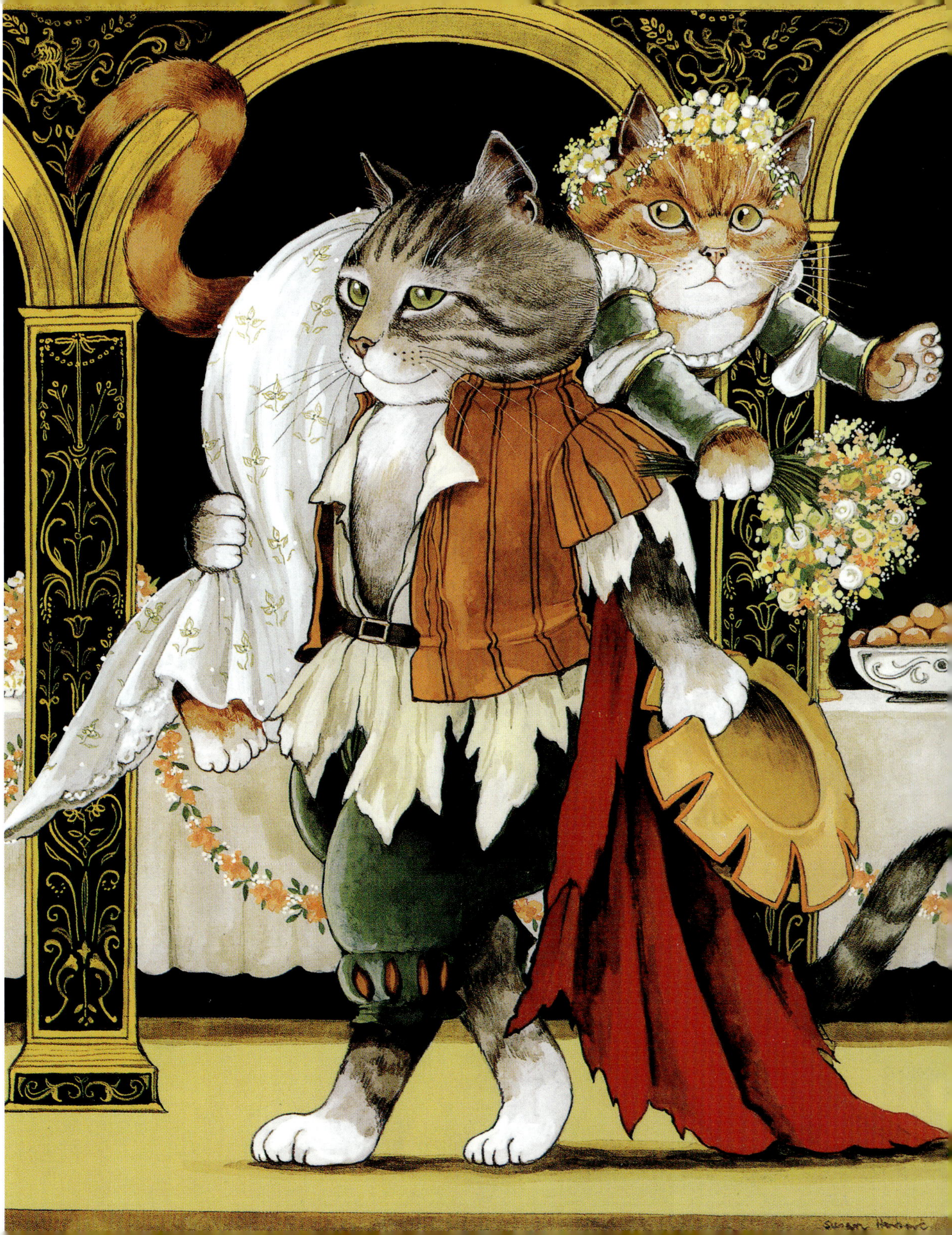

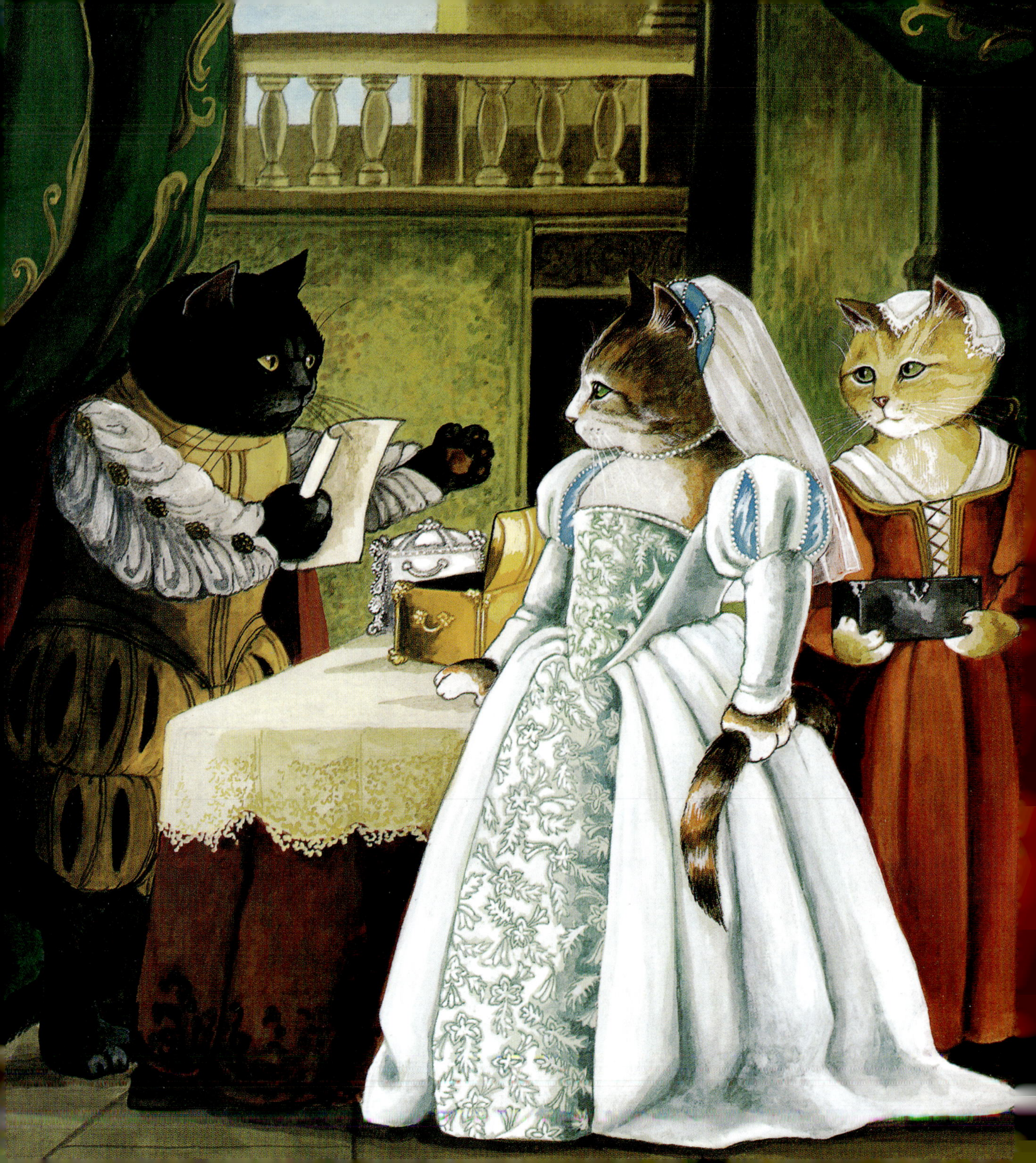

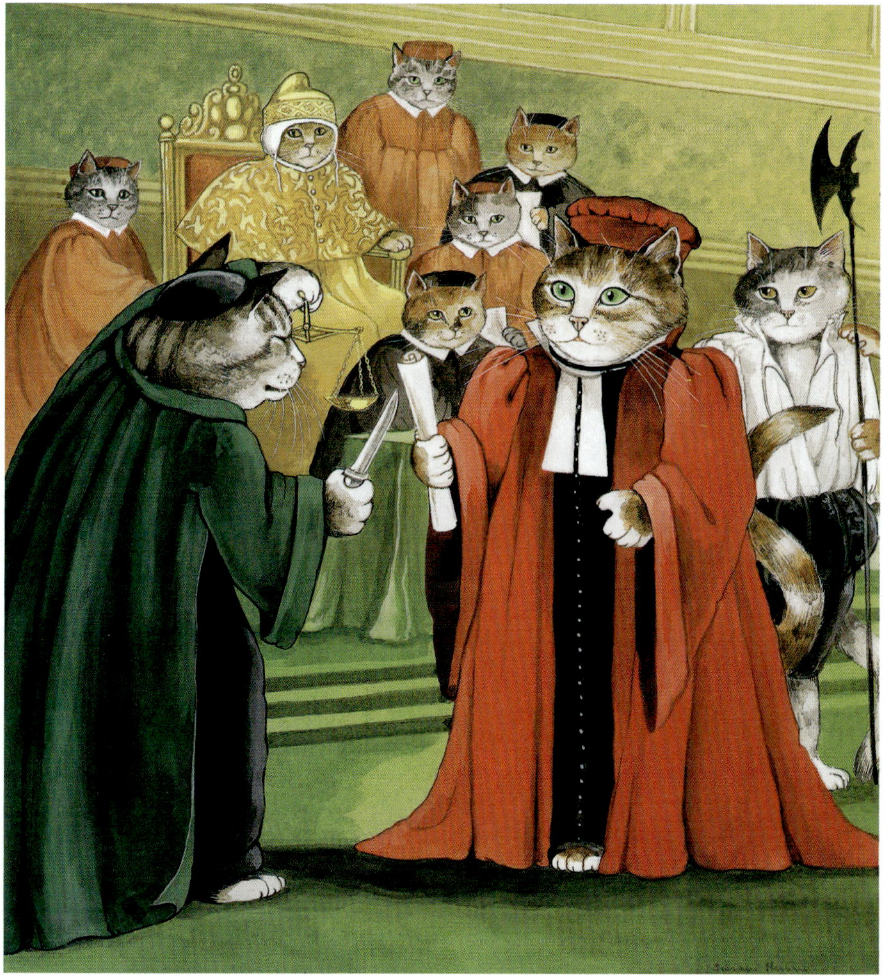

Opposite THE MERCHANT OF VENICE, Act II, Scene VII

Above THE MERCHANT OF VENICE, Act IV, Scene I

RICHARD II

Act I, Scene I

Wrath-kindled gentlemen, be rul'd by me;
Let's purge this choler without letting blood –
This we prescribe, though no physician;
Deep malice makes too deep incision.
Forget, forgive; conclude and be agreed:
Our doctors say this is no month to bleed.

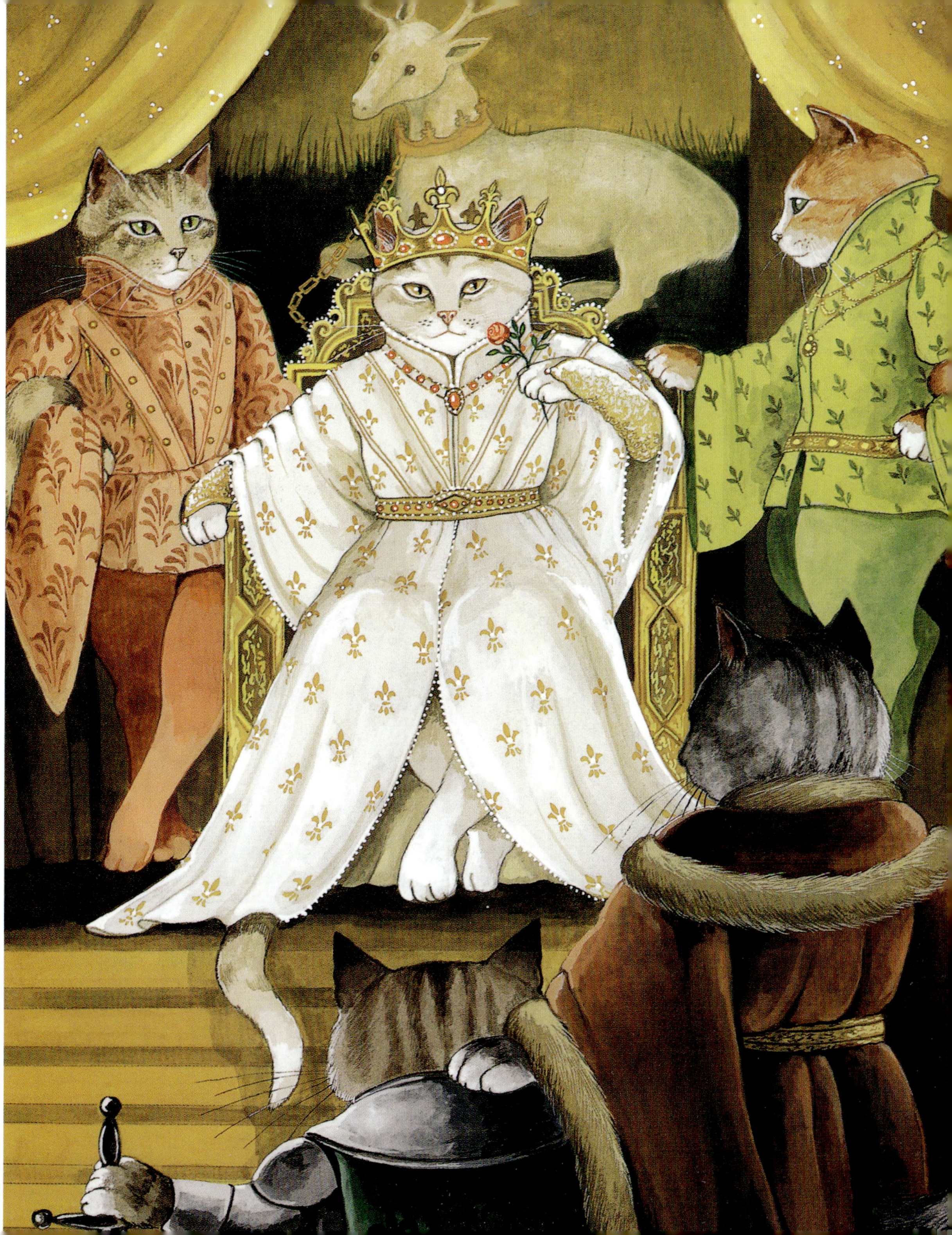

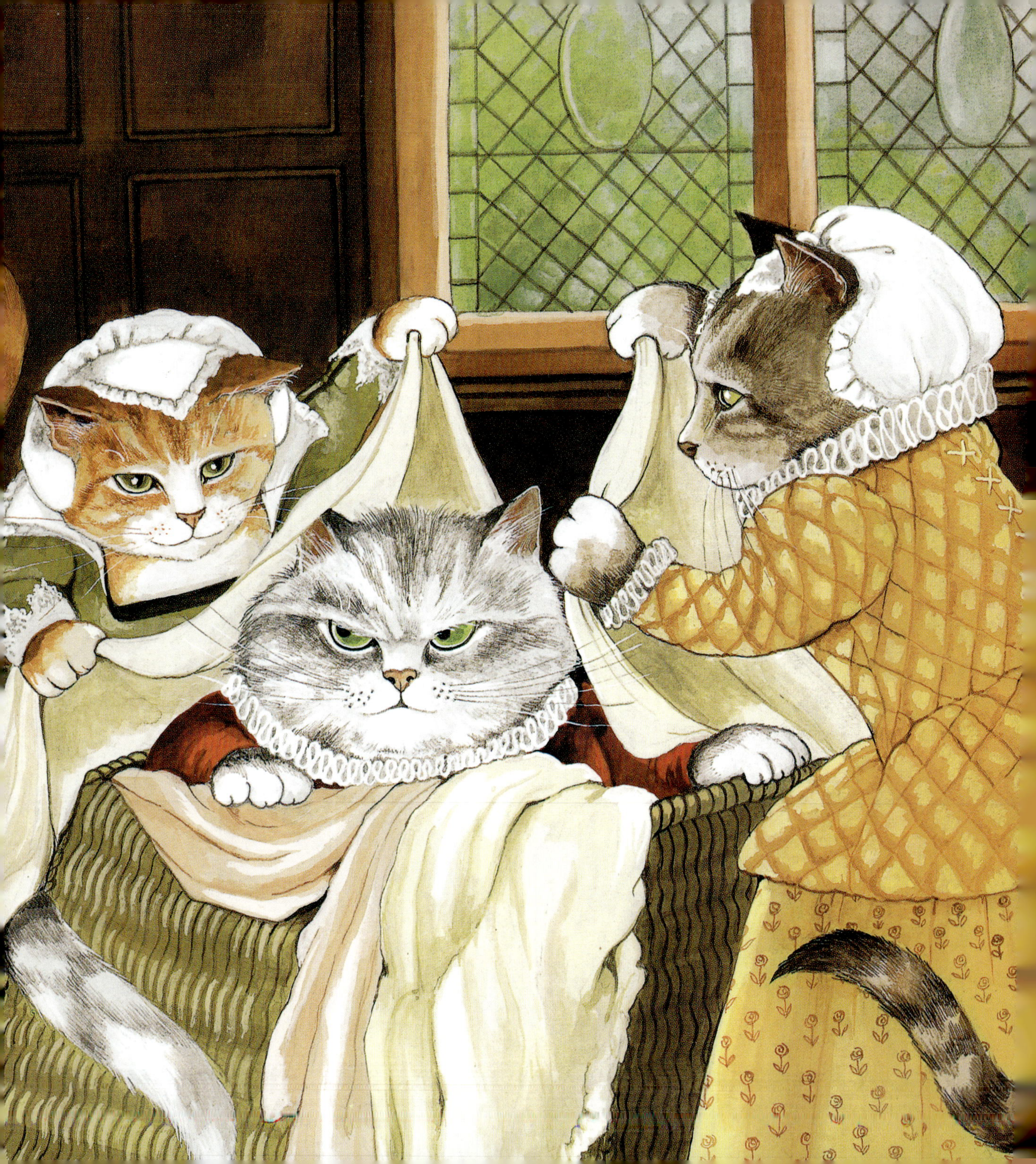

THE MERRY WIVES OF WINDSOR

Act III, Scene V

By the Lord, a buck-basket! Ramm'd me in with foul shirts and smocks, socks, foul stockings, greasy napkins, that, Master Brook, there was the rankest compound of villainous smell that ever offended nostril.

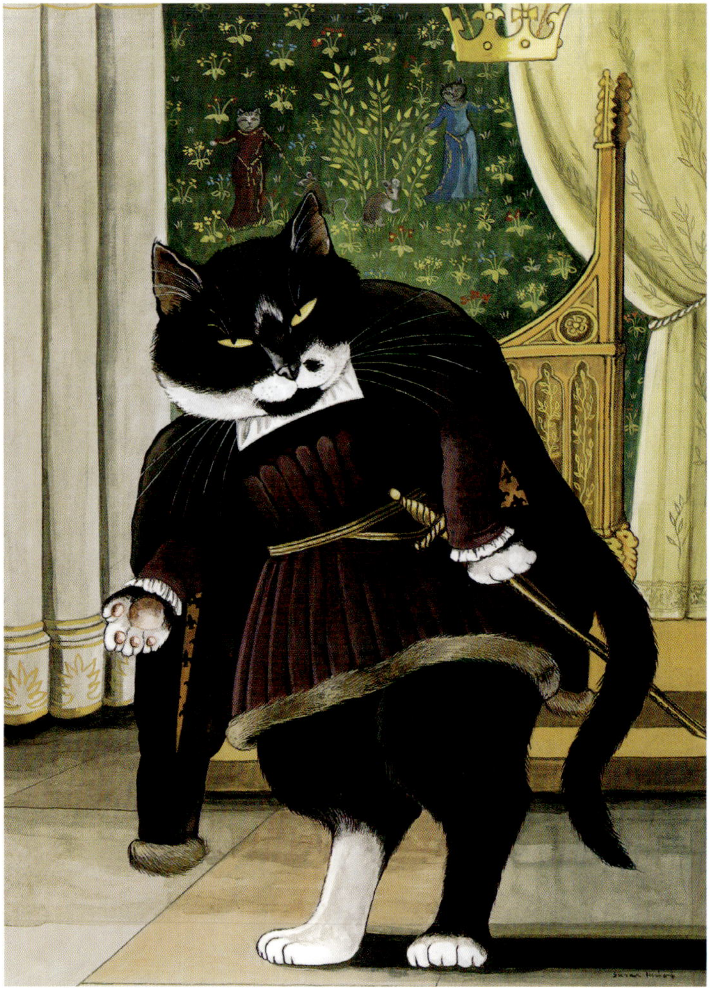

Above RICHARD III, Act I, Scene I

Opposite RICHARD III, Act IV, Scene III

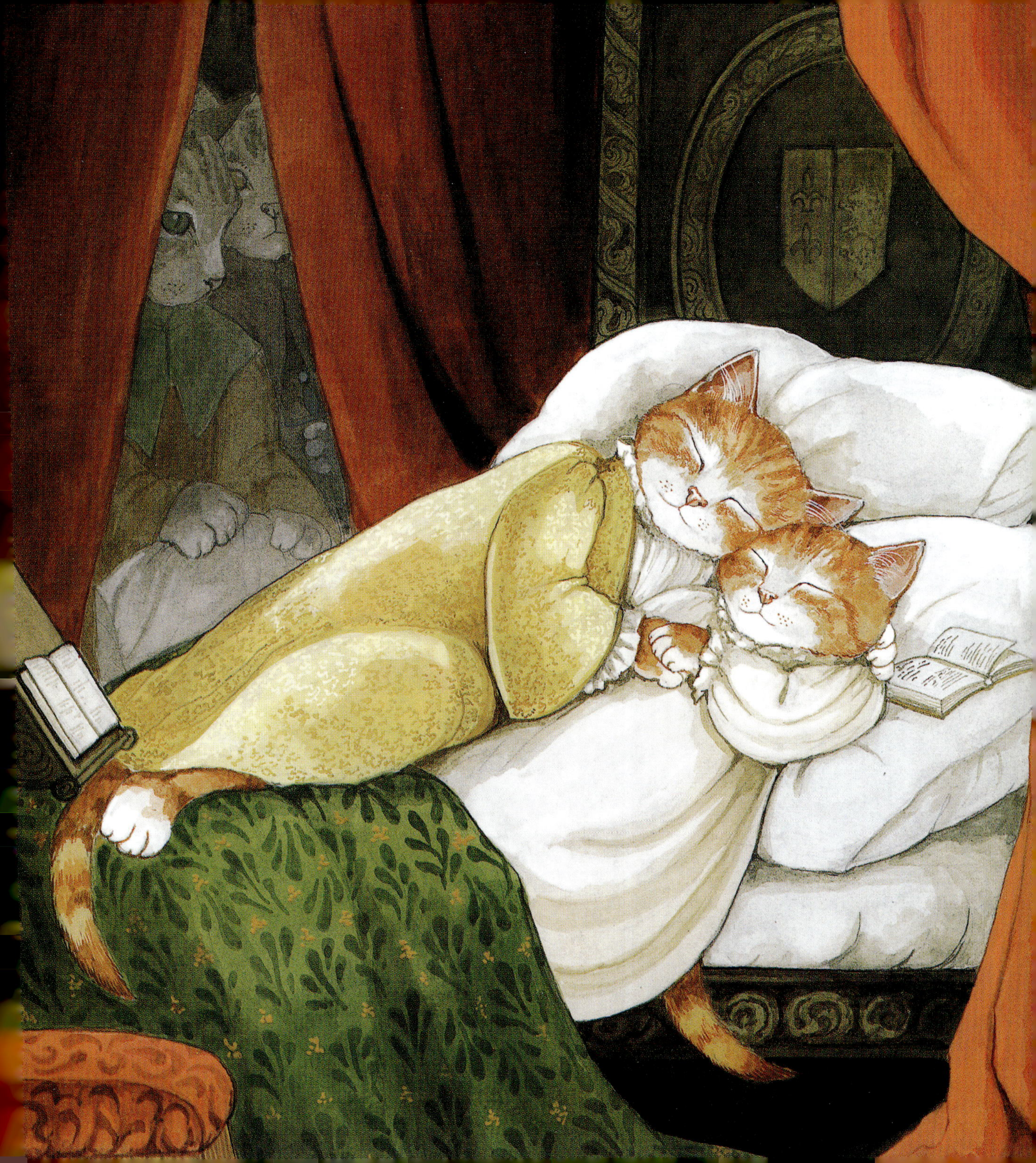

AS YOU LIKE IT

Act II, Scene VII

All the world's a stage,
And all the men and women merely players;
They have their exits and their entrances;
And one man in his time plays many parts,
His acts being seven ages.

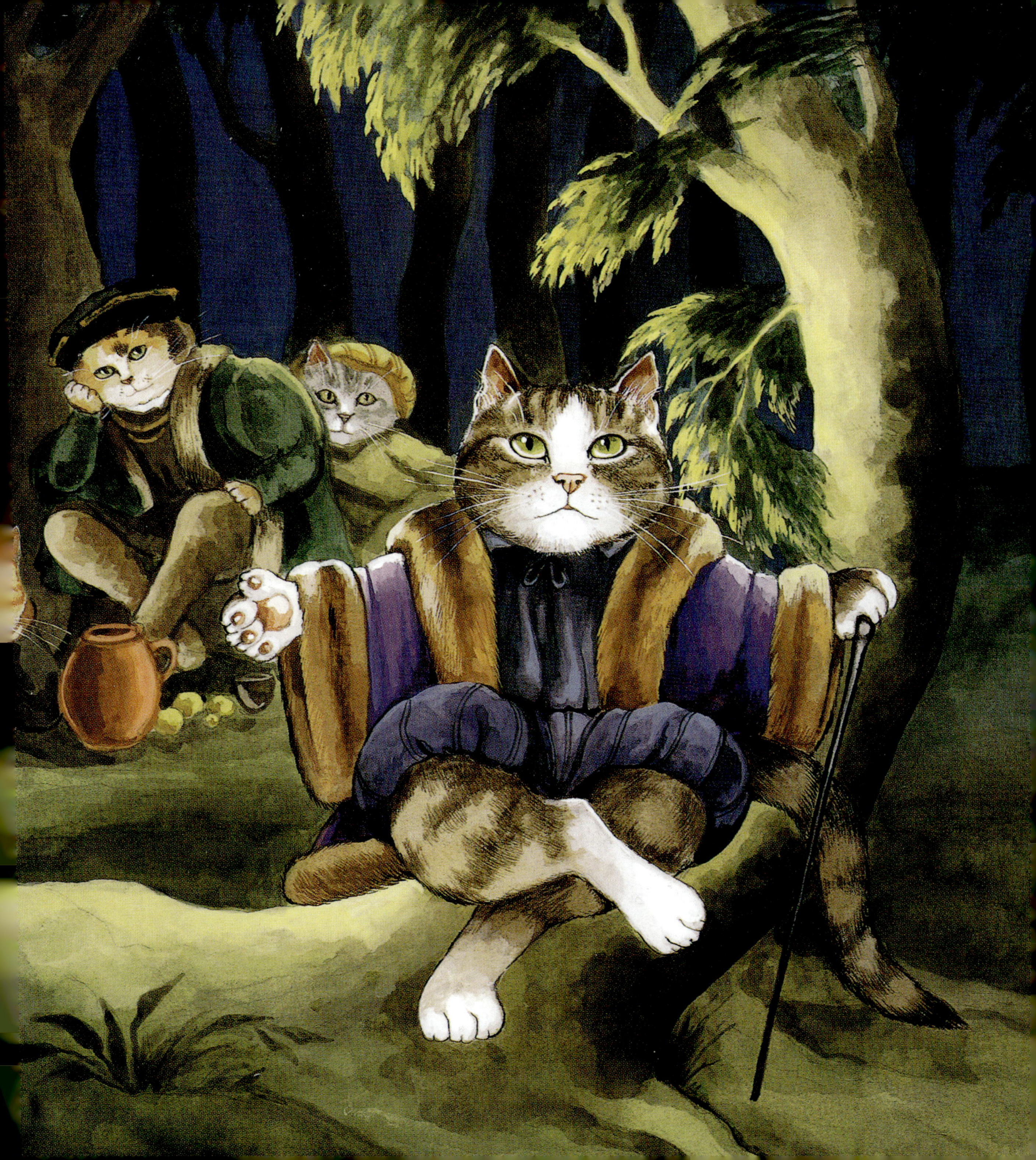

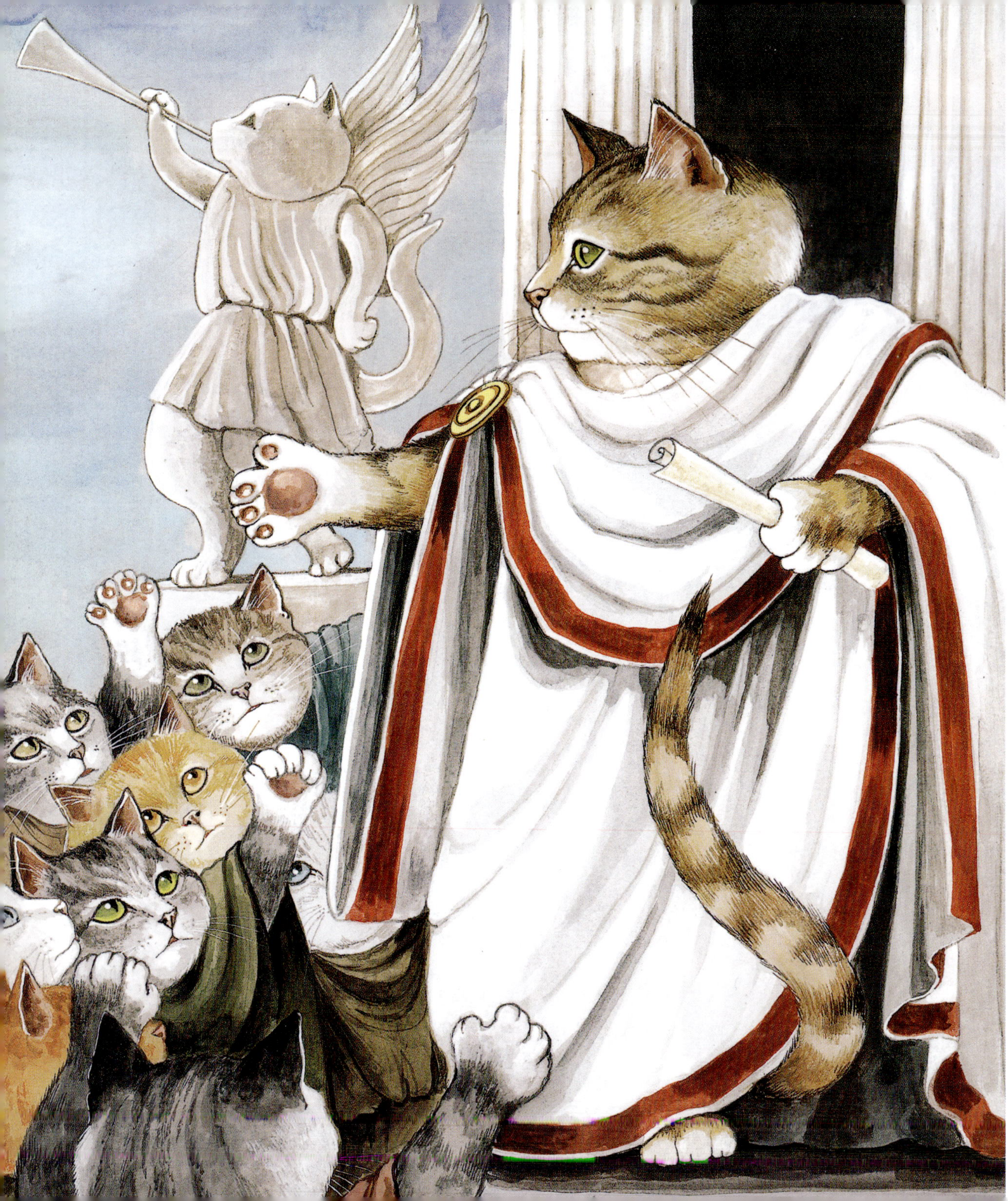

JULIUS CAESAR

Act III, Scene II

Friends, Romans, countrymen, lend me your ears;
I come to bury Caesar, not to praise him.
The evil that men do lives after them;
The good is oft interred with their bones;
So let it be with Caesar.

TWELFTH NIGHT

Act III, Scene IV

Some are born great, some achieve greatness,
and some have greatness thrust upon 'em.

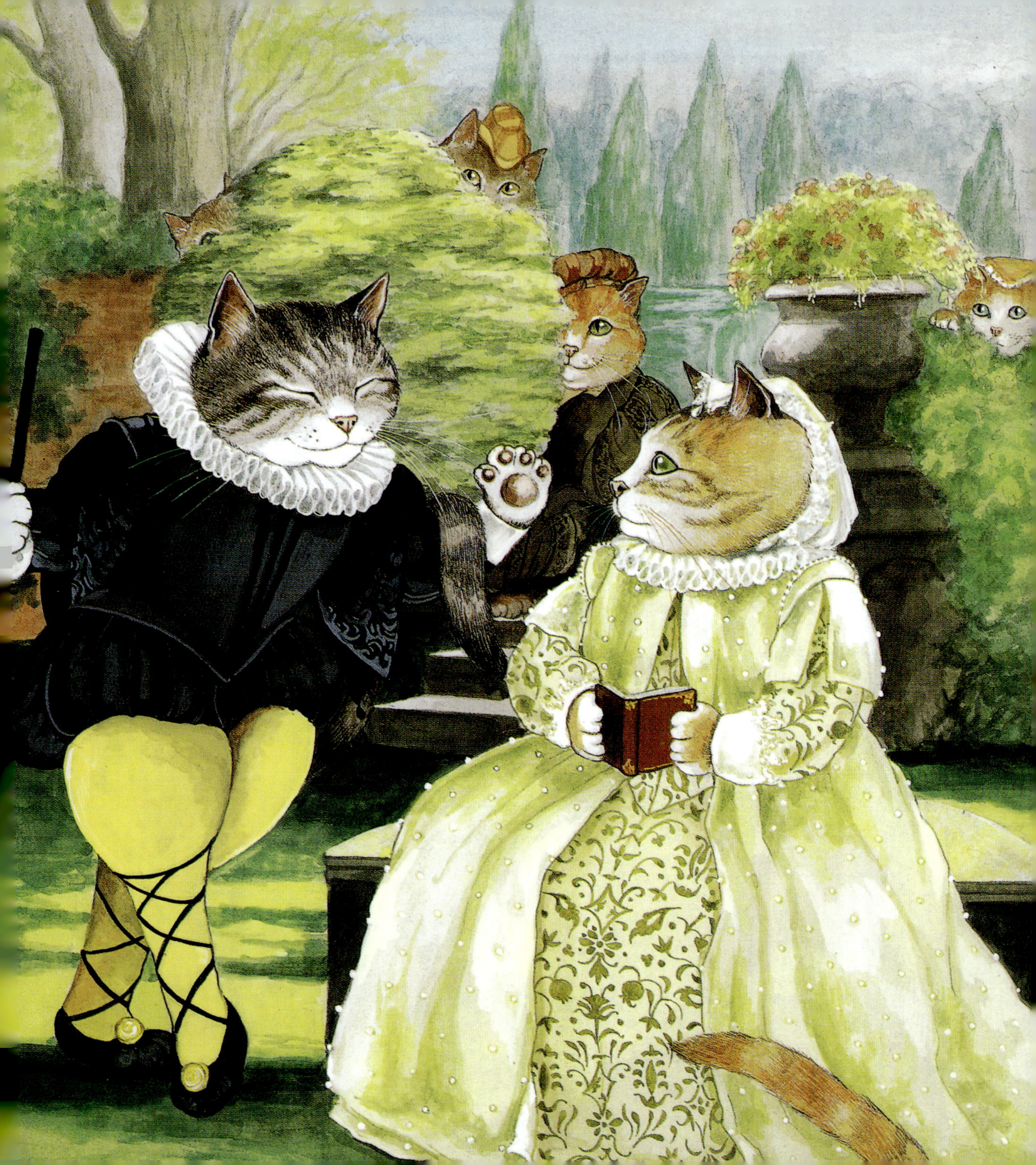

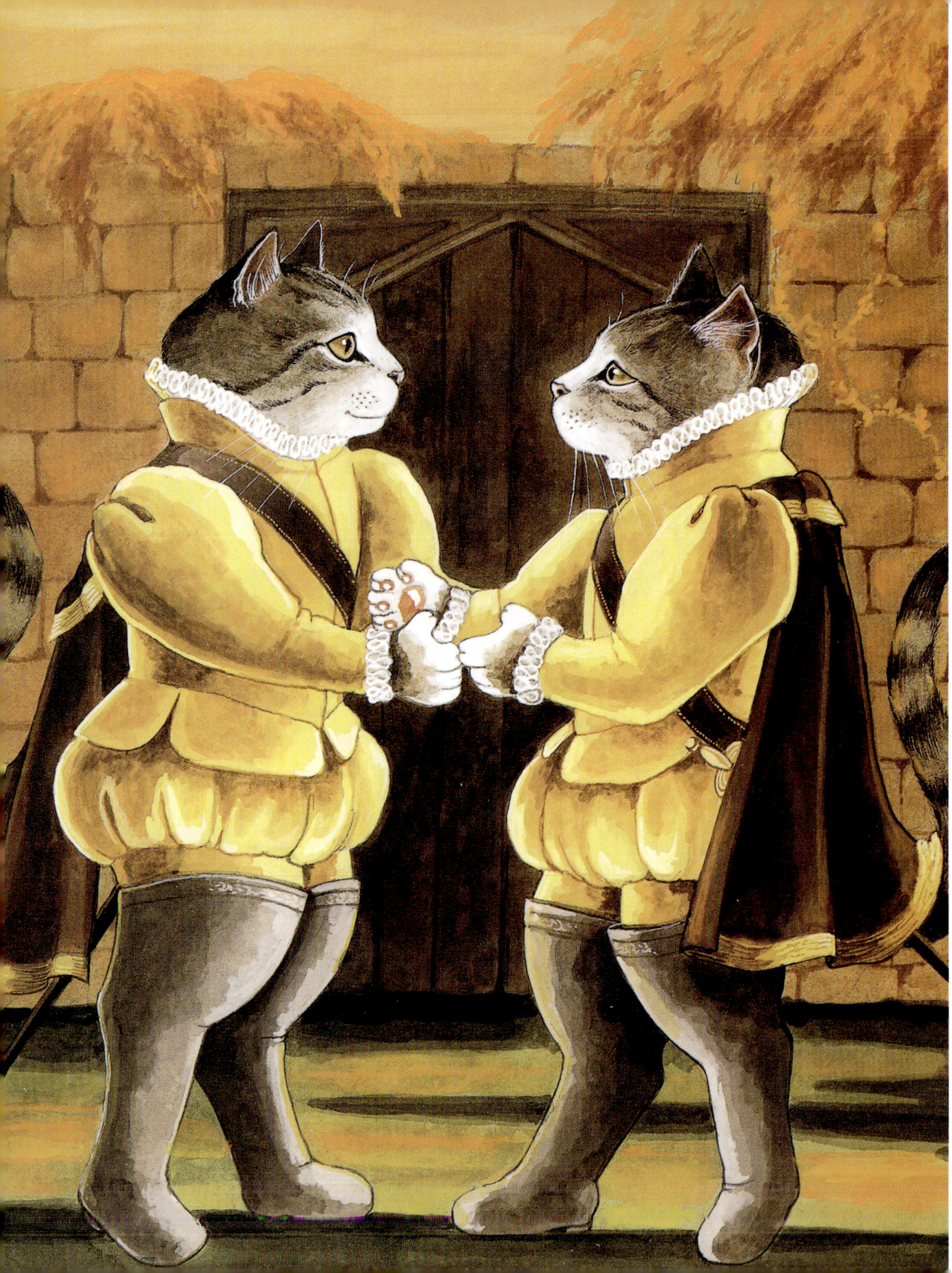

TWELFTH NIGHT

Act V, Scene I

Were you a woman, as the rest goes even,
I should my tears let fall upon your cheek,
And say 'Thrice welcome, drowned Viola!'

HAMLET

Act IV, Scene VII

There is a willow grows aslant a brook,
That shows his hoar leaves in the glassy stream;
There with fantastic garlands did she come
Of crowflowers, nettles, daisies, and long purples,
That liberal shepherds give a grosser name,
But our cold maids do dead men's fingers call them.

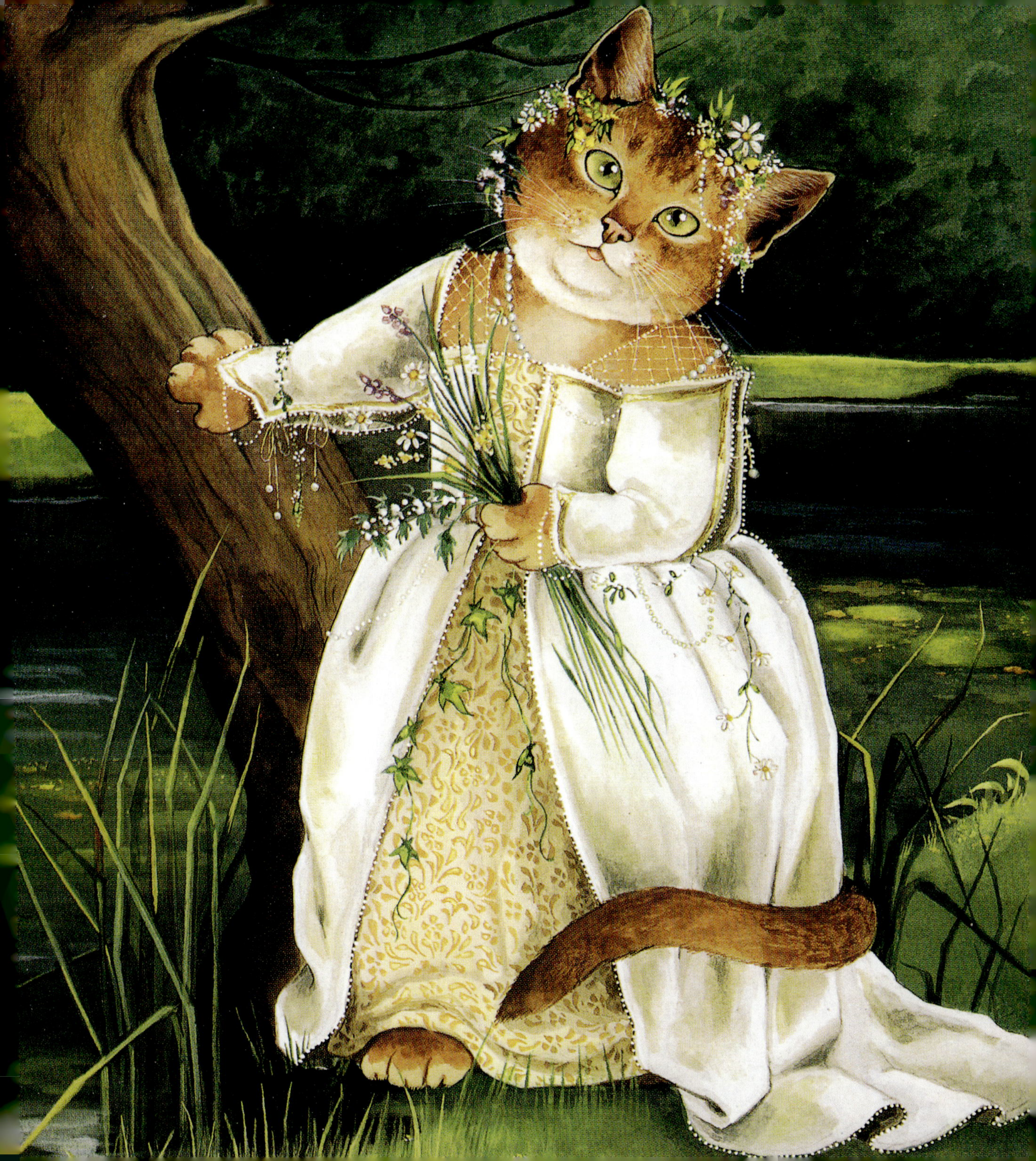

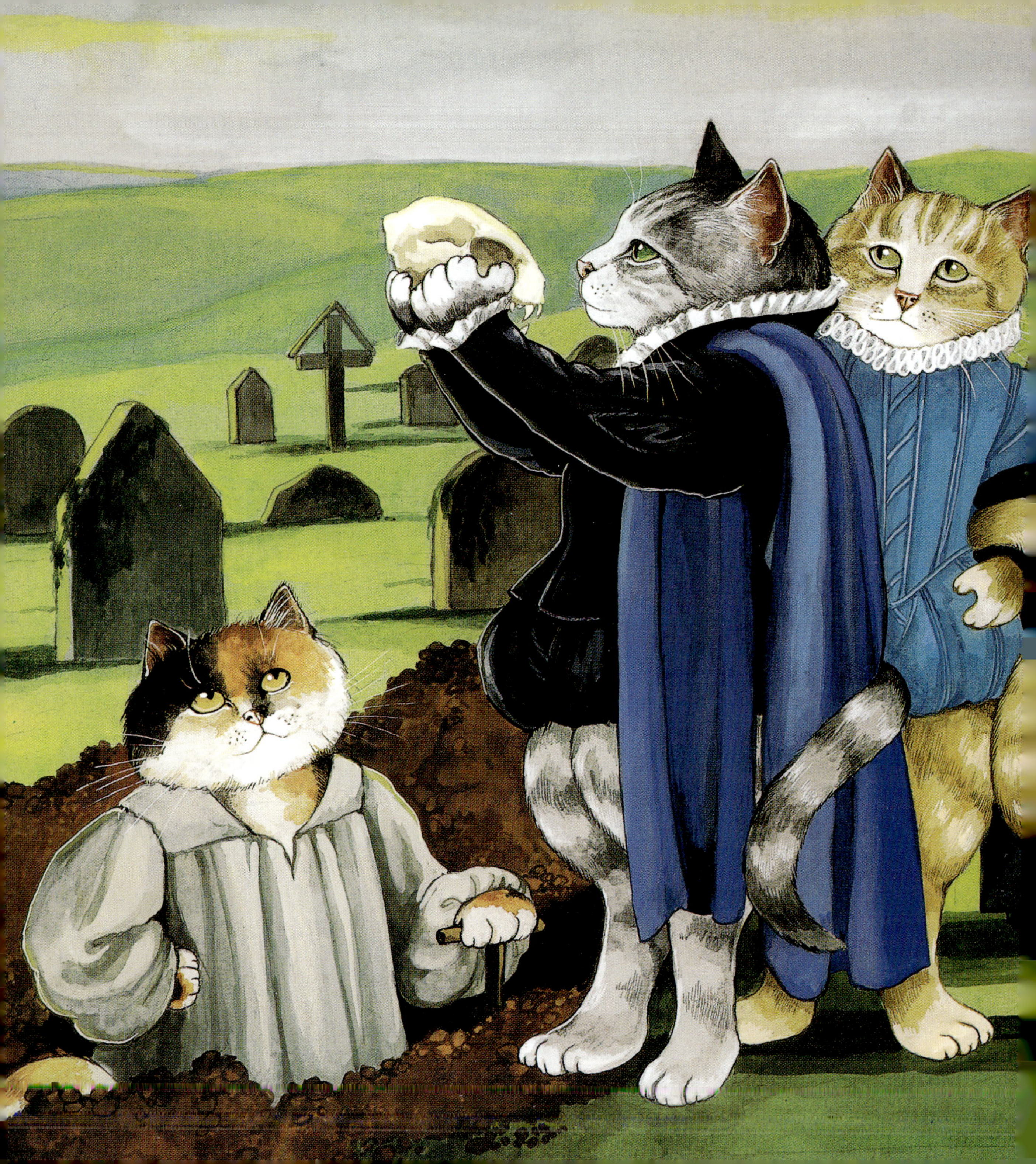

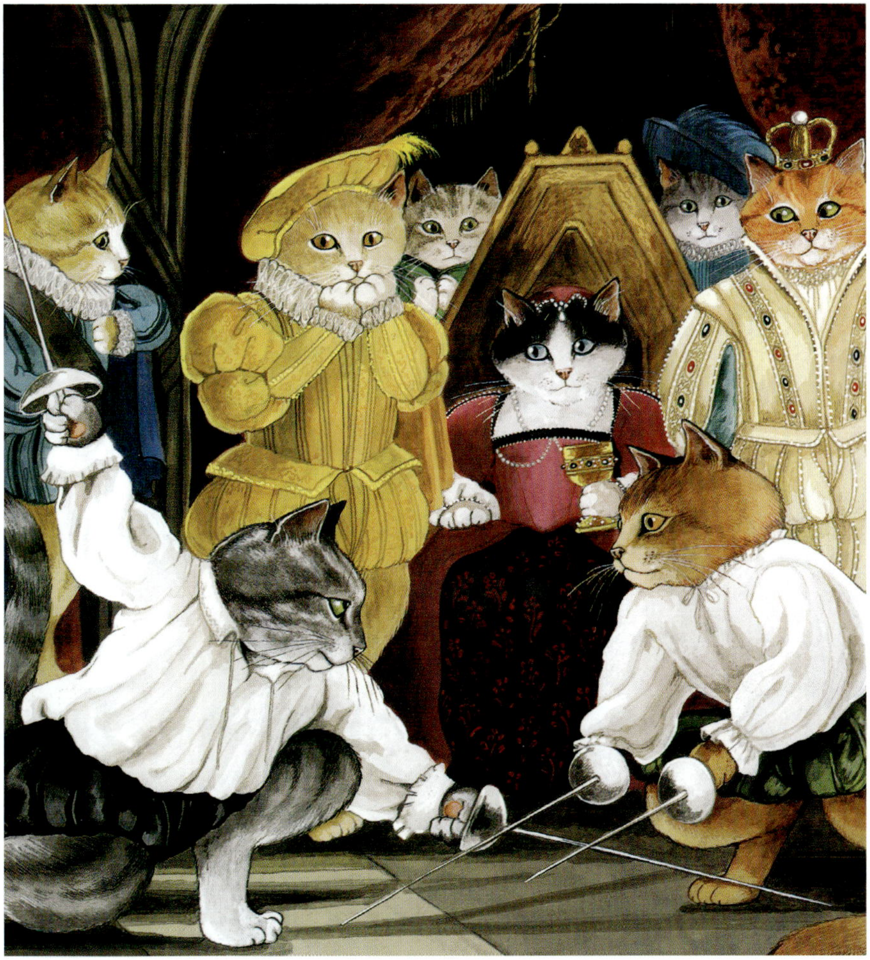

Opposite HAMLET, Act V, Scene I

Above HAMLET, Act V, Scene II

OTHELLO

Act III, Scene III

O, beware, my lord, of jealousy;
It is the green-ey'd monster which doth mock
The meat it feeds on.

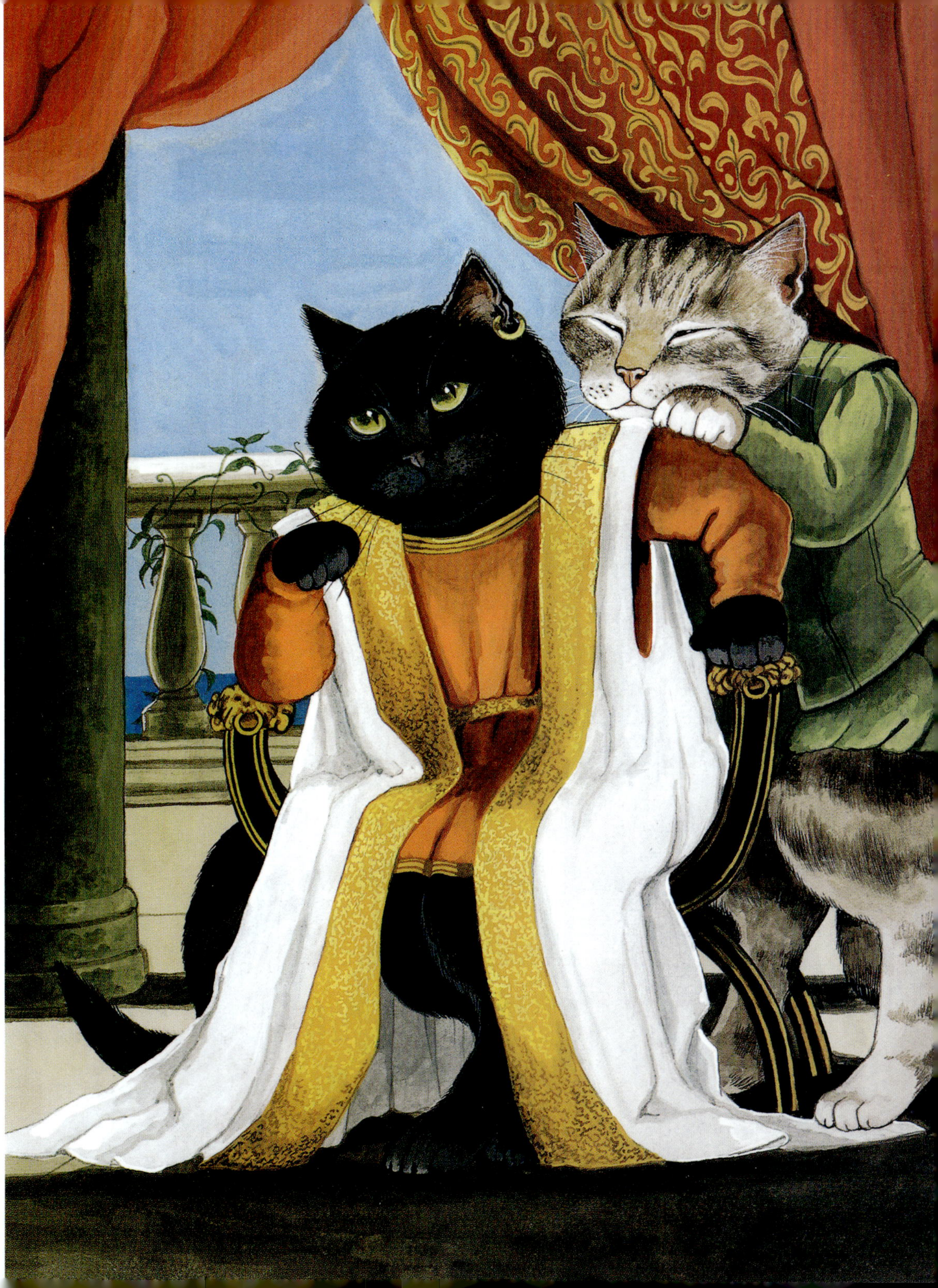

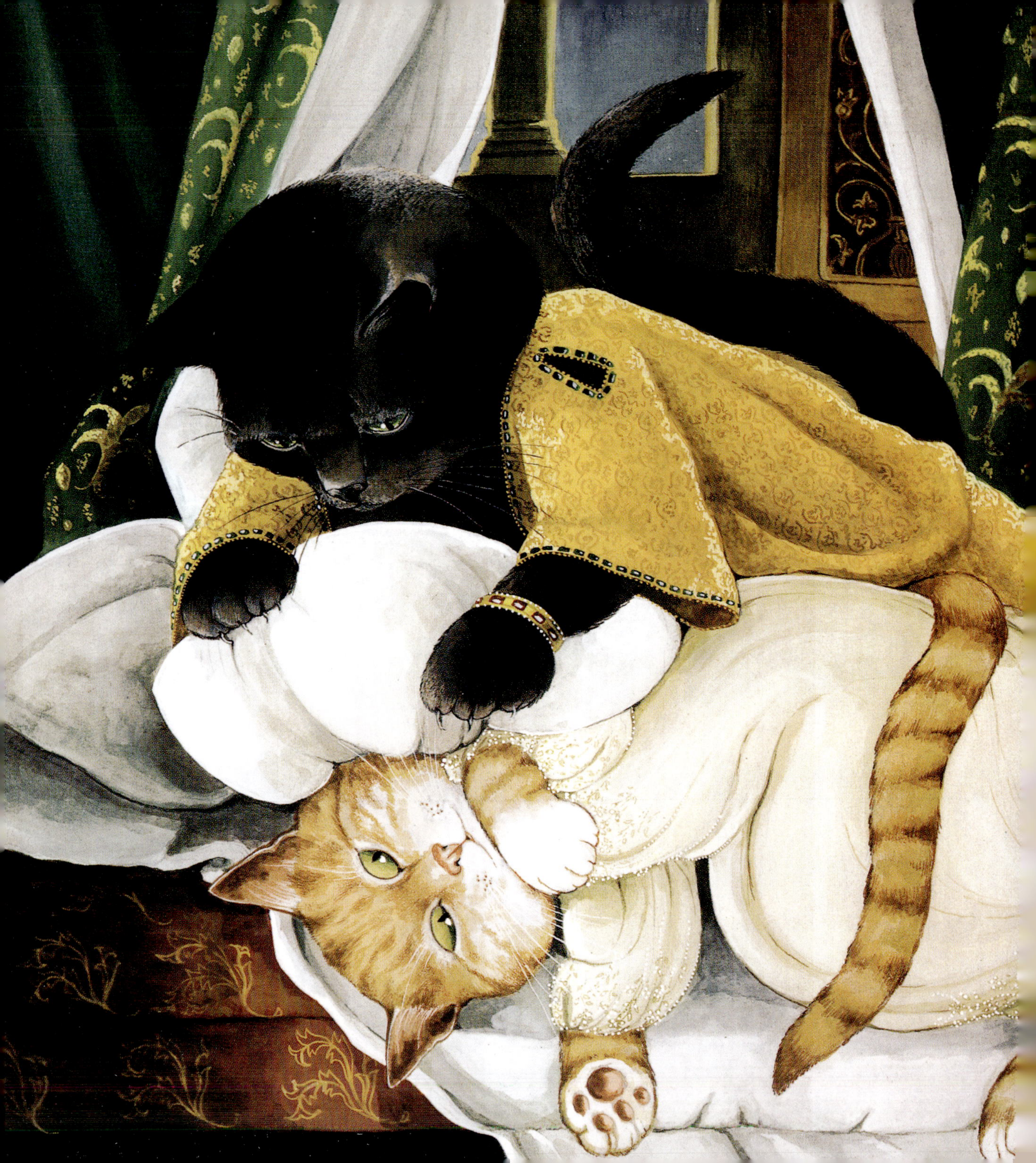

OTHELLO

Act V, Scene II

Kill me tomorrow; let me live tonight.

ANTONY AND CLEOPATRA

Act II, Scene II

Age cannot wither her, nor custom stale
Her infinite variety.

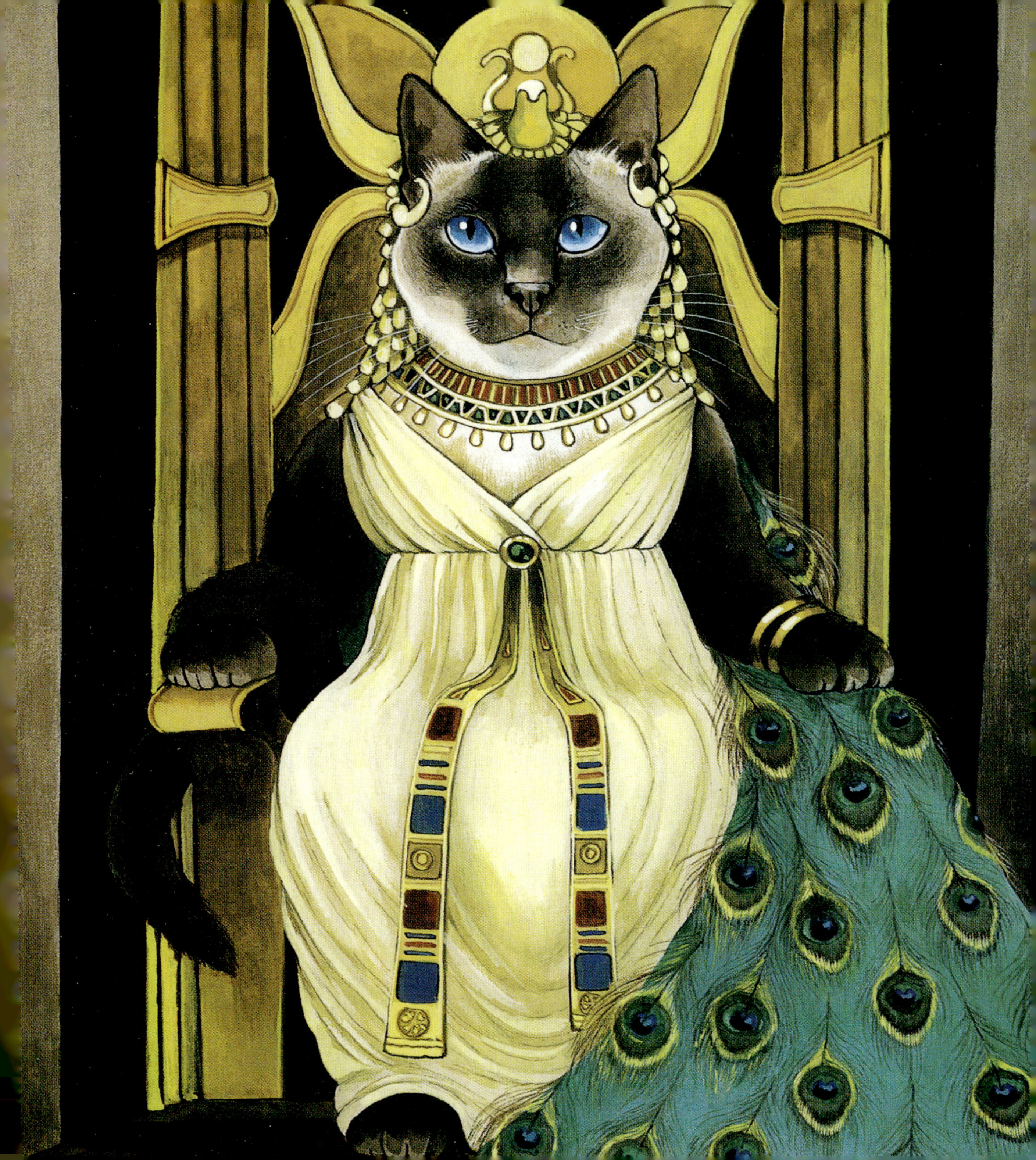

KING LEAR

Act I, Scene I

Unhappy that I am, I cannot heave
My heart into my mouth. I love your Majesty
According to my bond; nor more nor less.

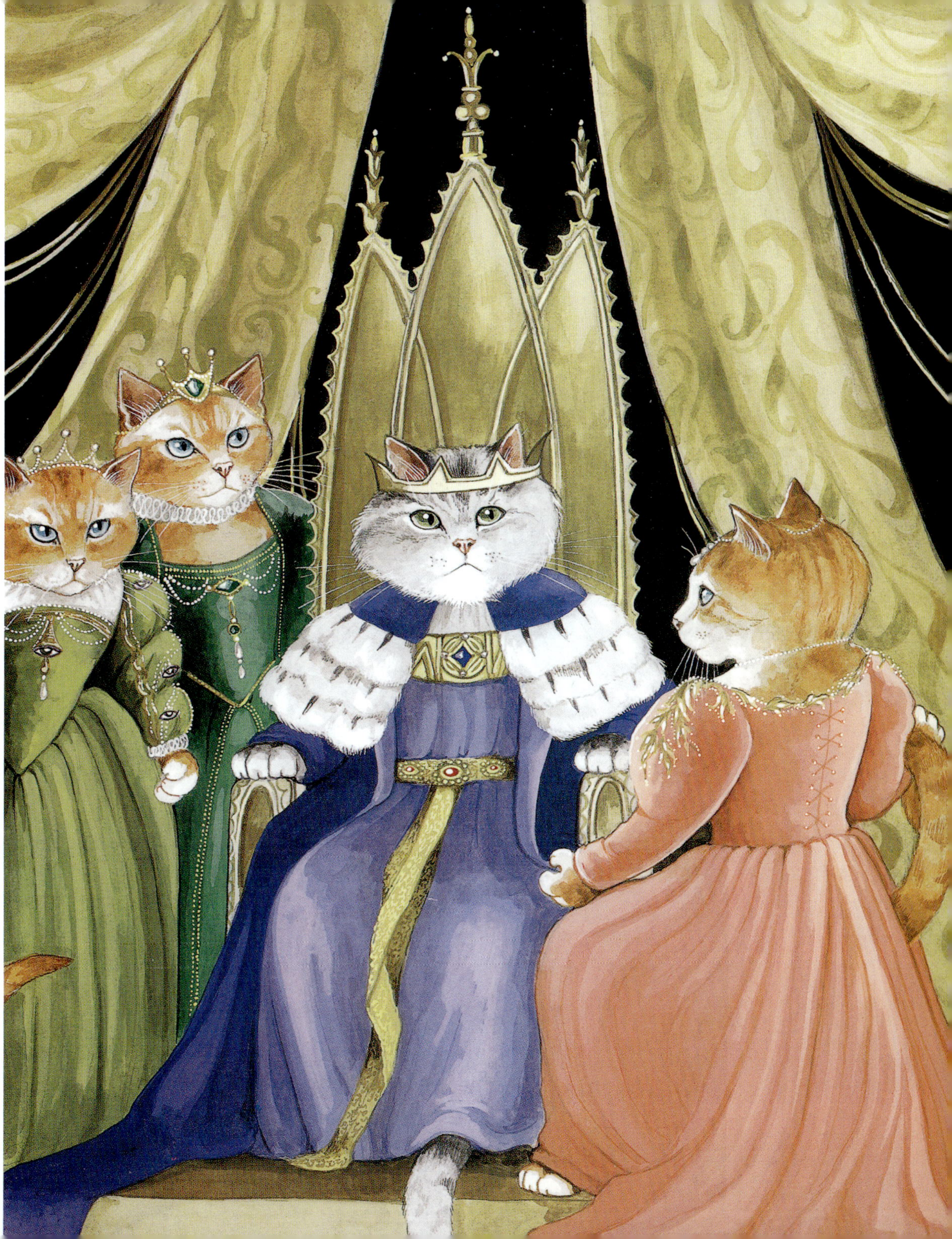

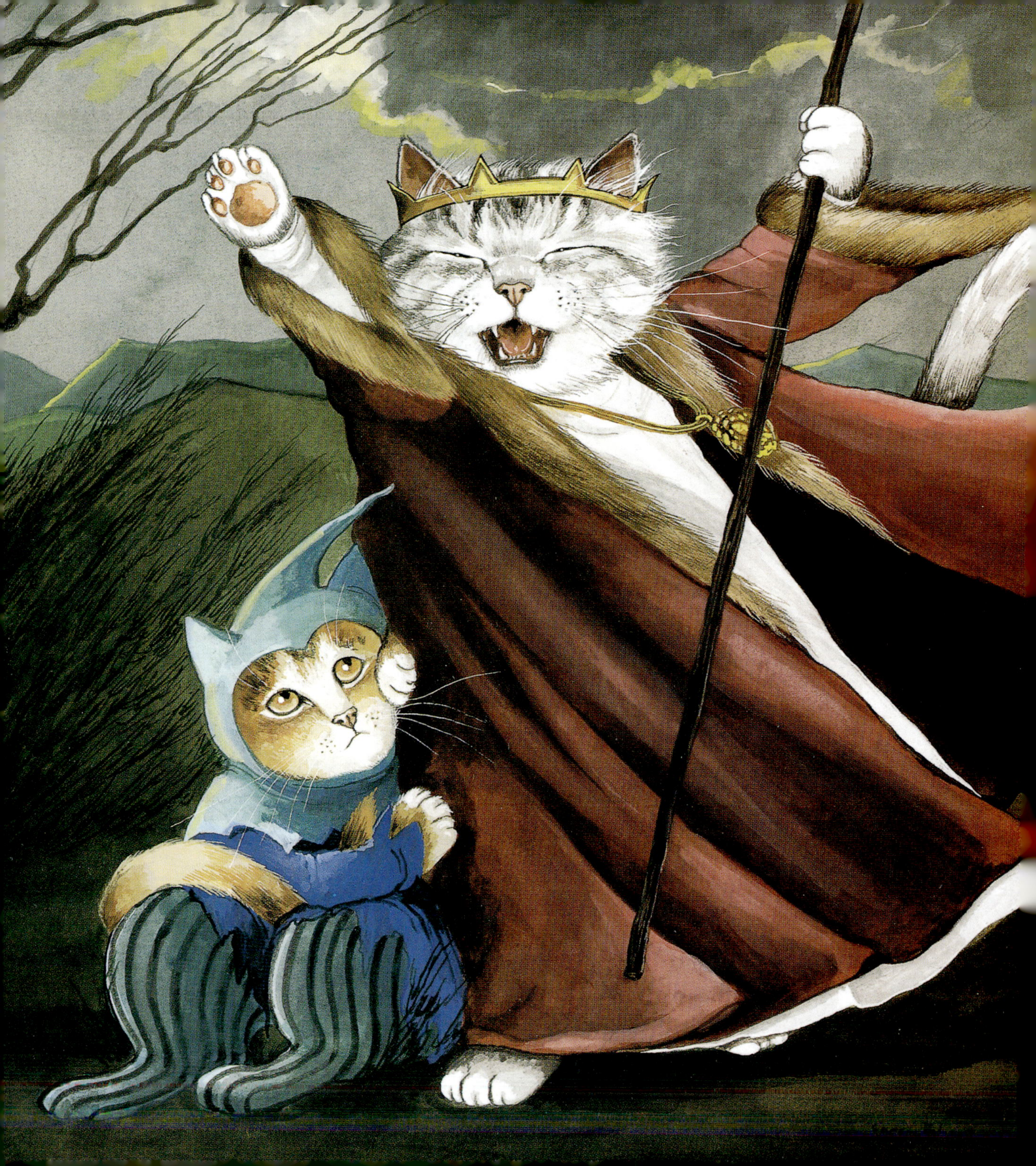

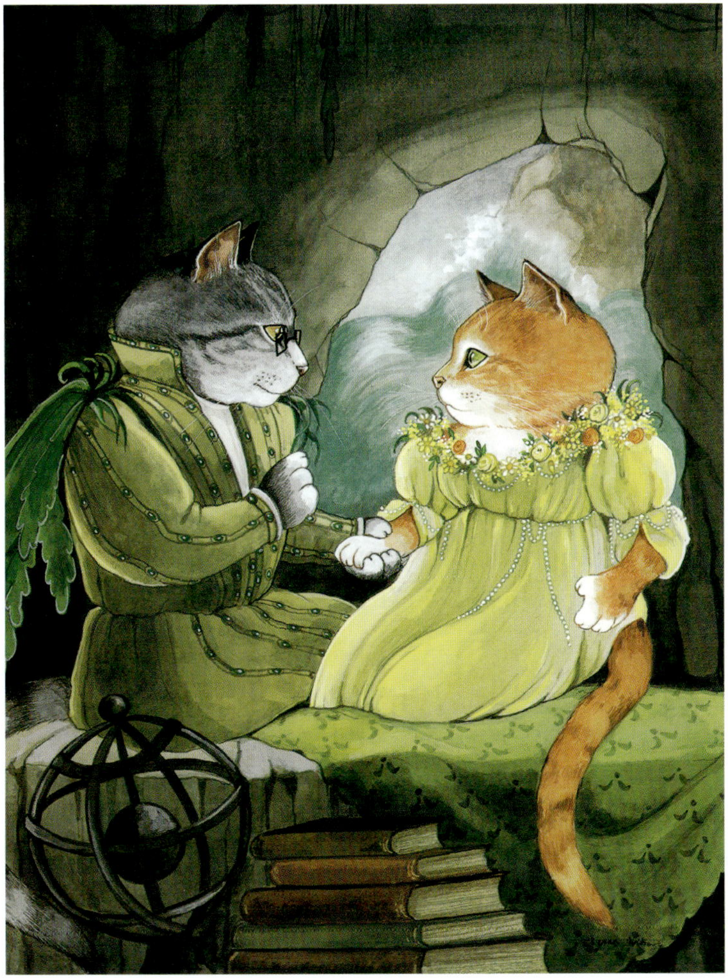

Opposite KING LEAR, Act III, Scene II

Above THE TEMPEST, Act I, Scene II

DER ROSENKAVALIER

by Richard Strauss

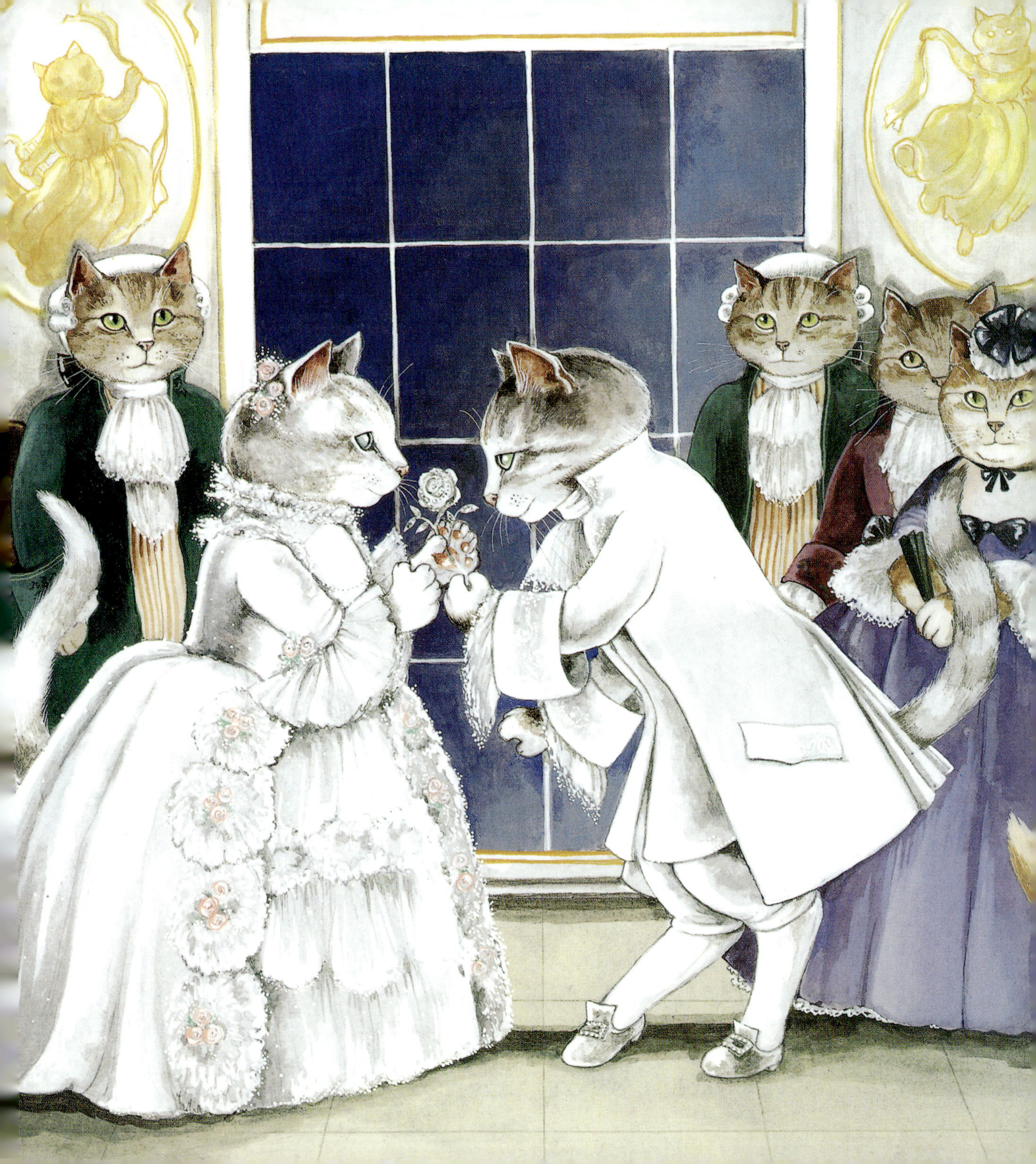

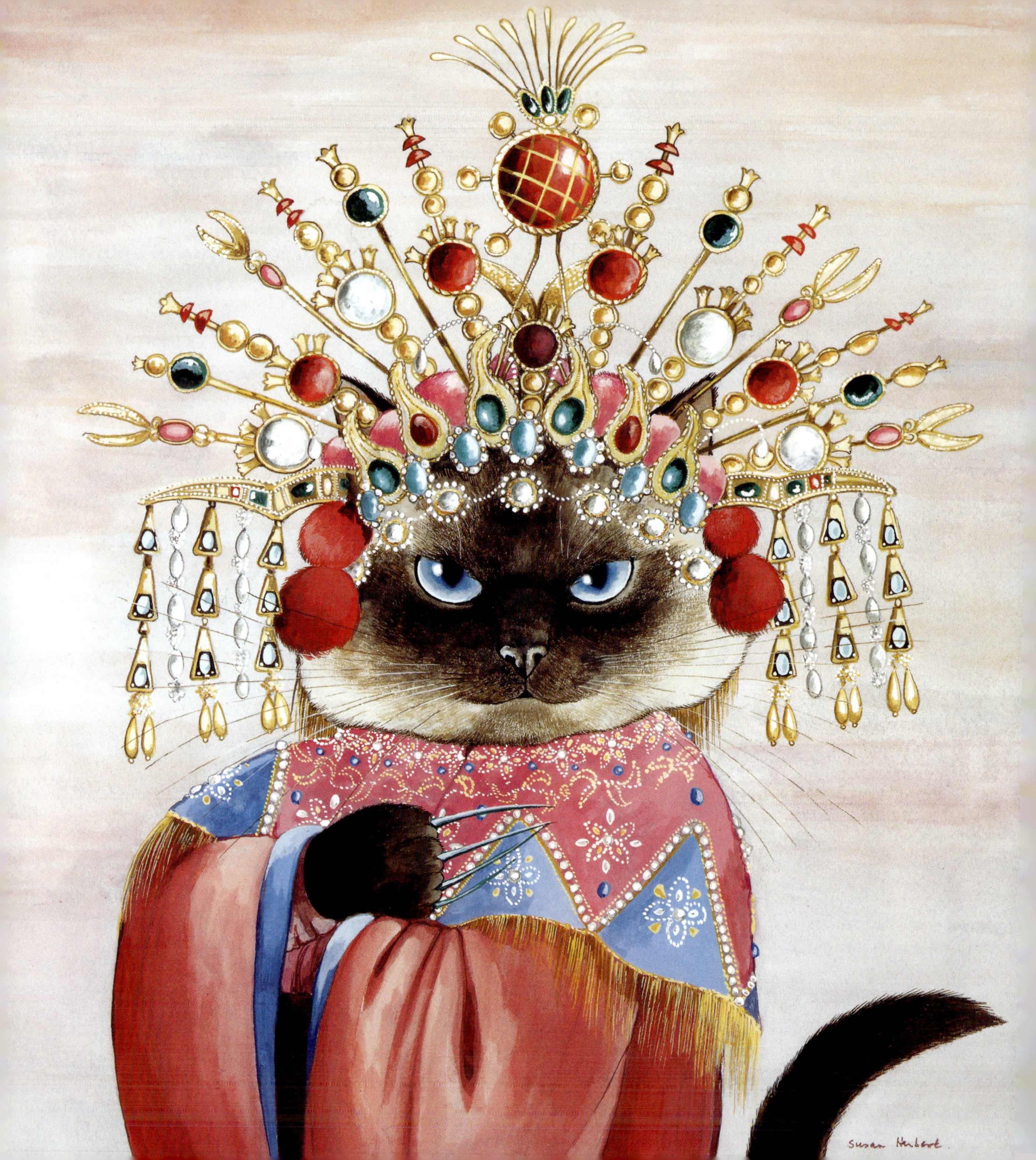
Susan Herbert

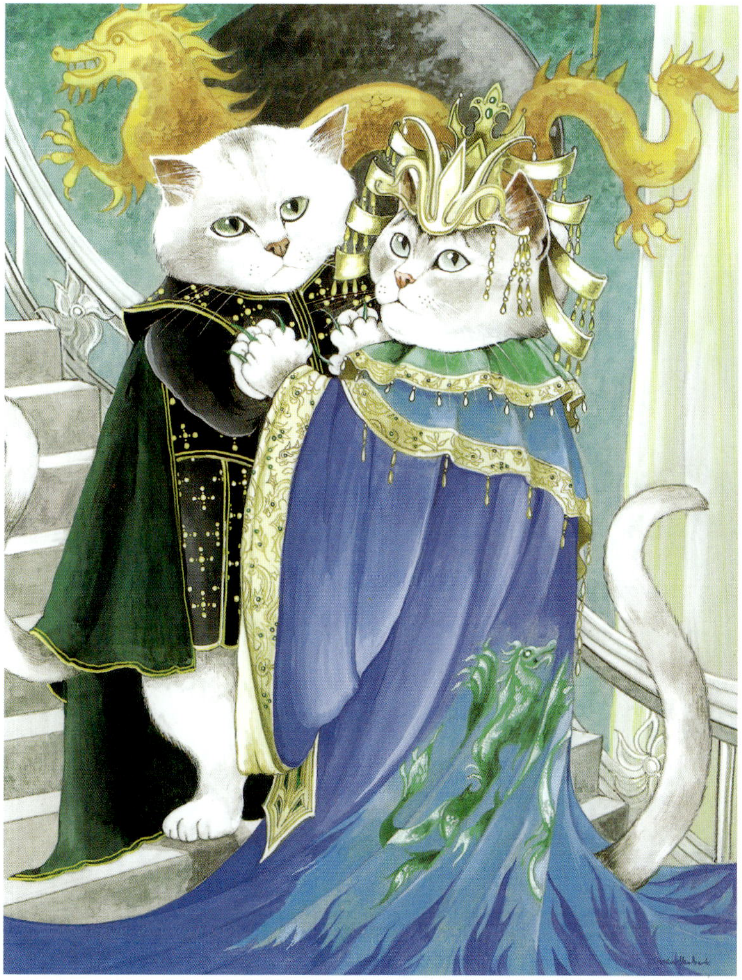

Above and opposite

TURANDOT *by Giacomo Puccini*

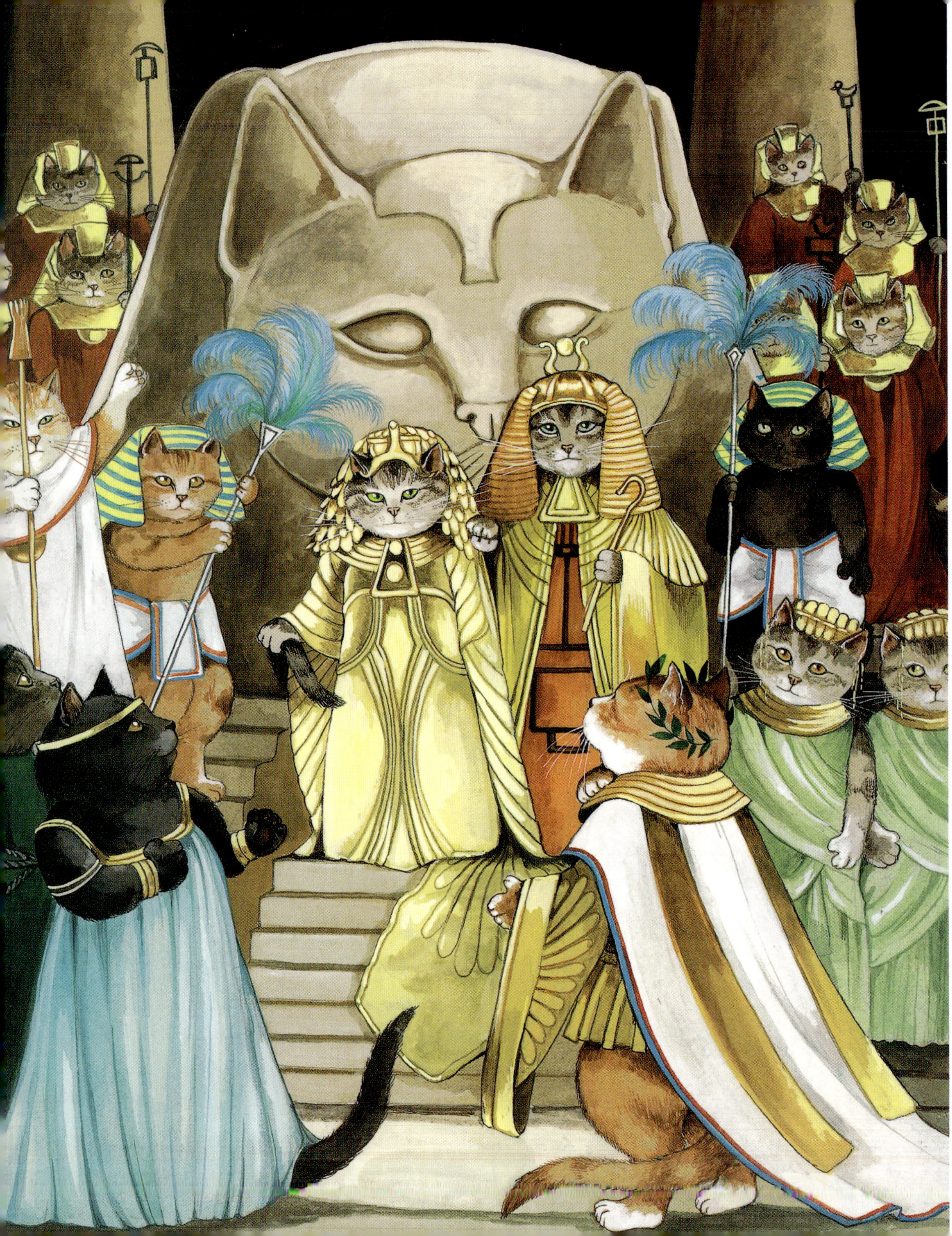

AIDA

by Giuseppe Verdi

THE MAGIC FLUTE

by Wolfgang Amadeus Mozart

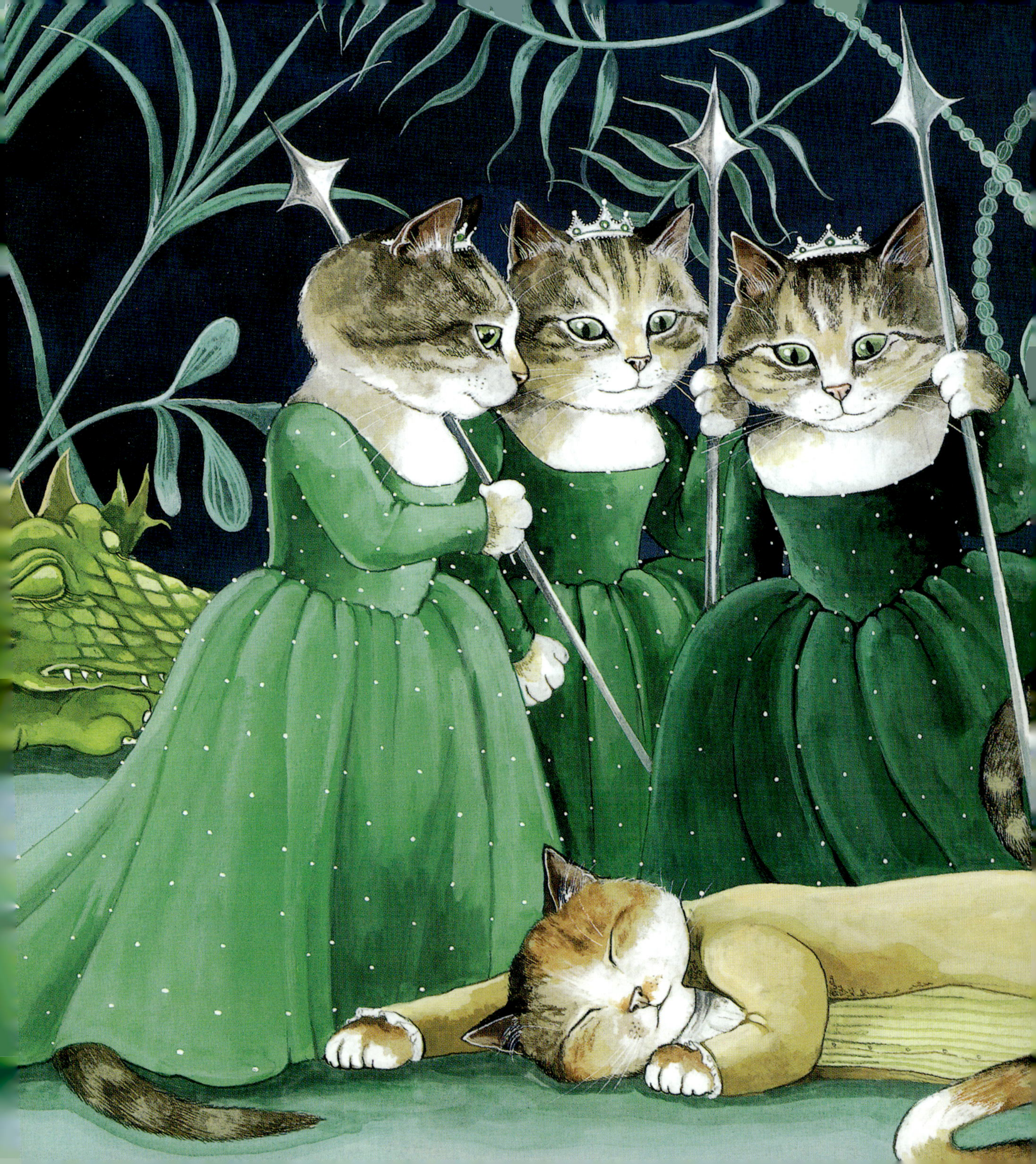

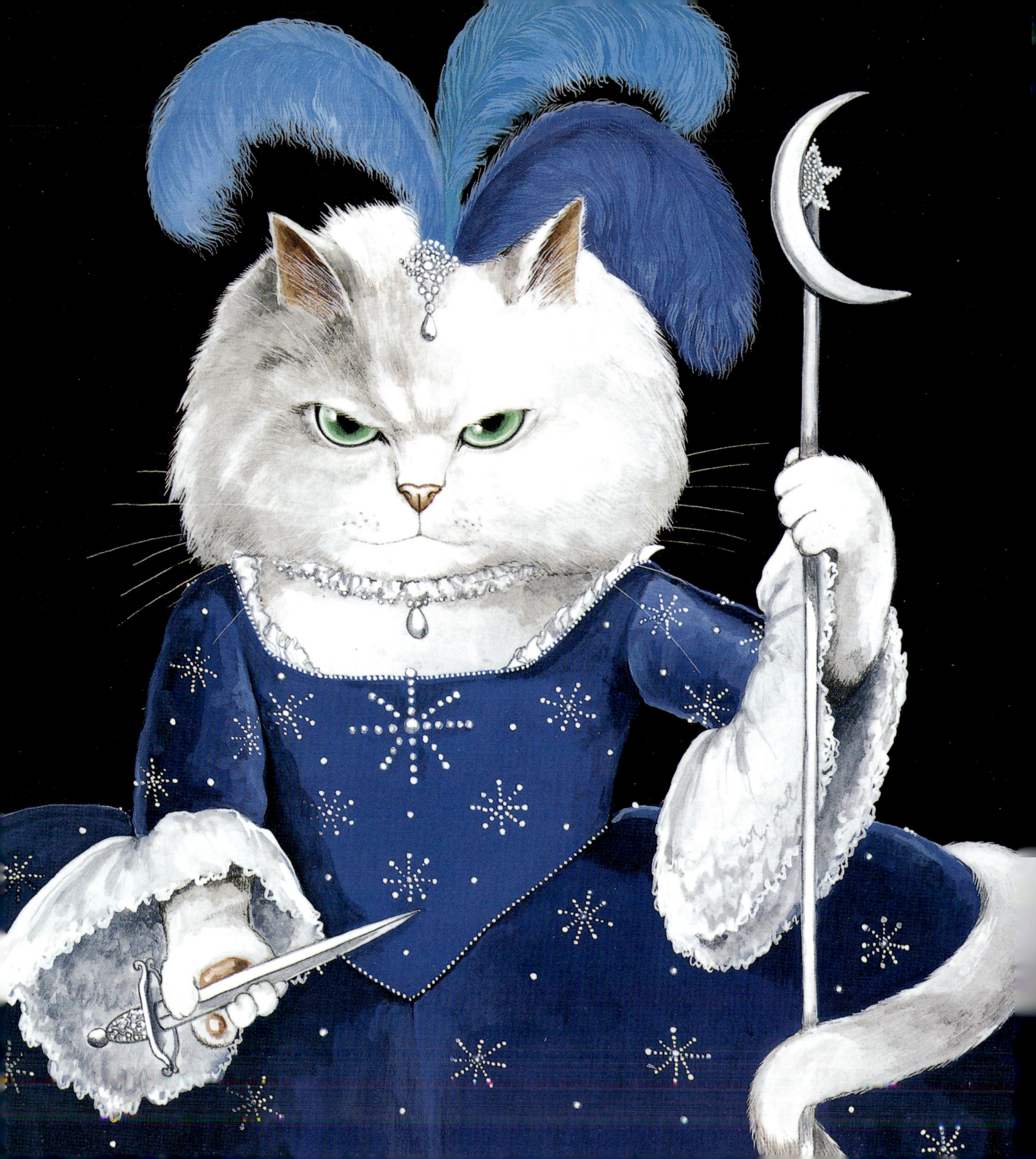

THE MAGIC FLUTE

by Wolfgang Amadeus Mozart

DIE FLEDERMAUS

by Johann Strauss the Younger

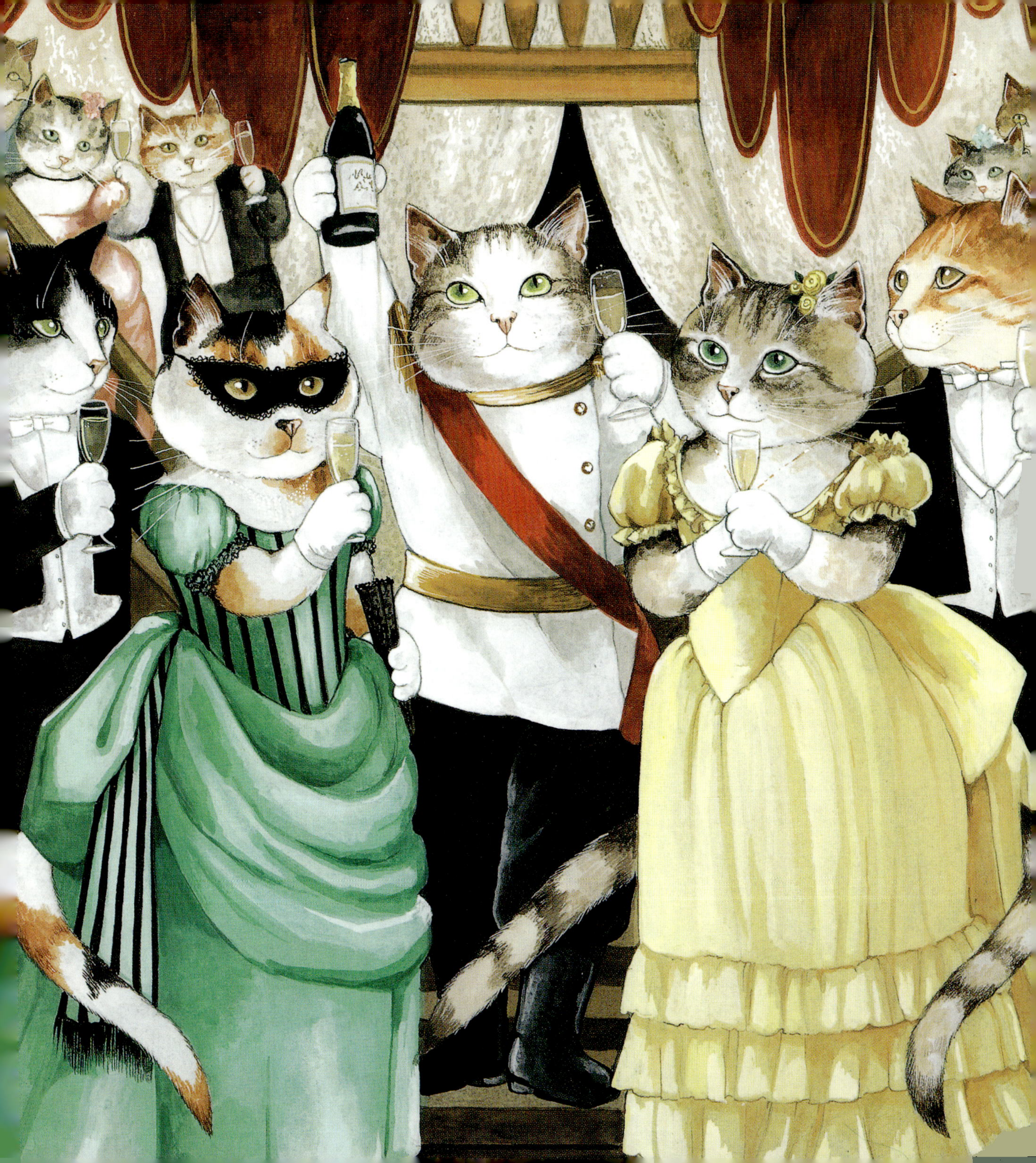

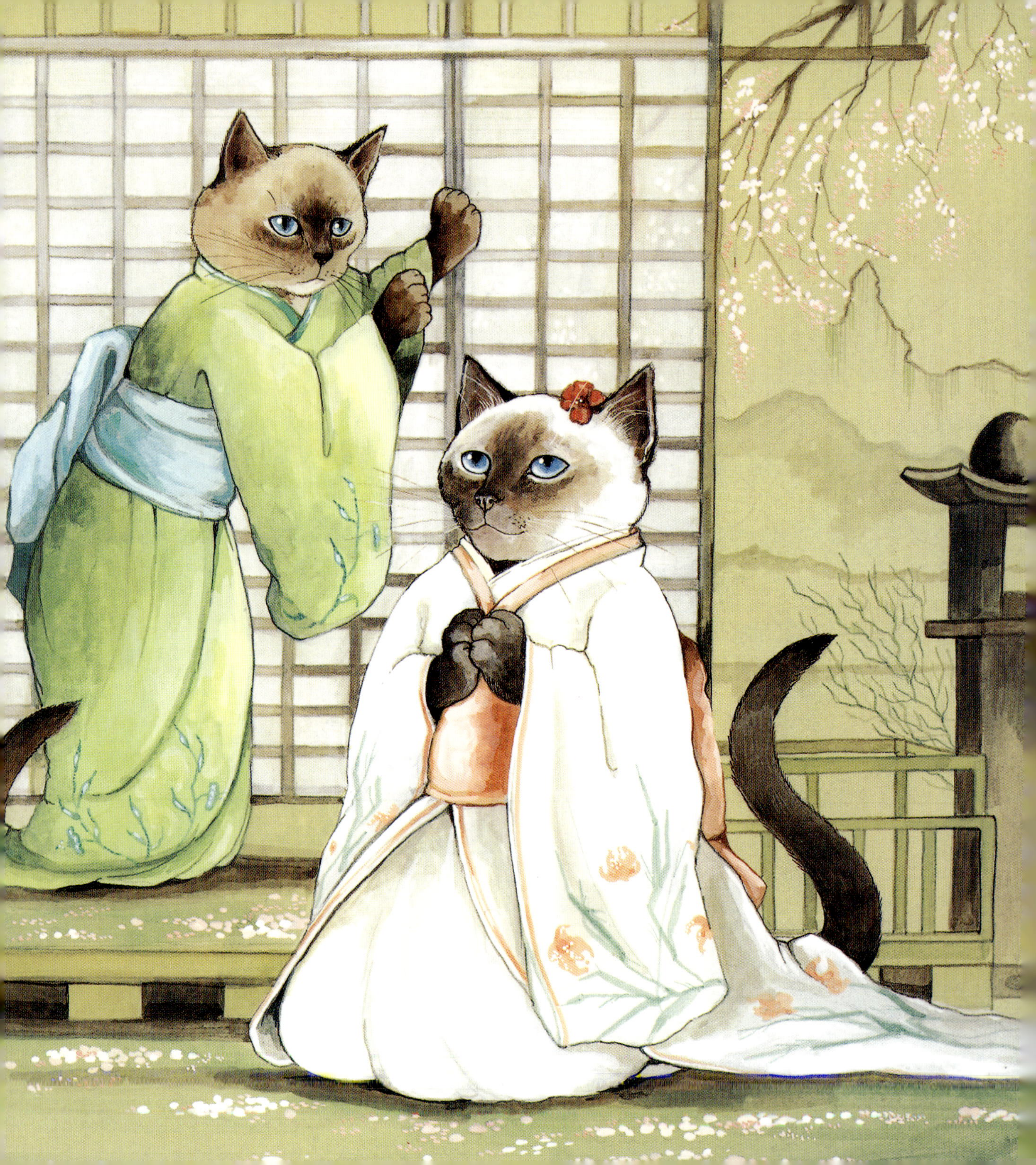

MADAME BUTTERFLY

by Giacomo Puccini

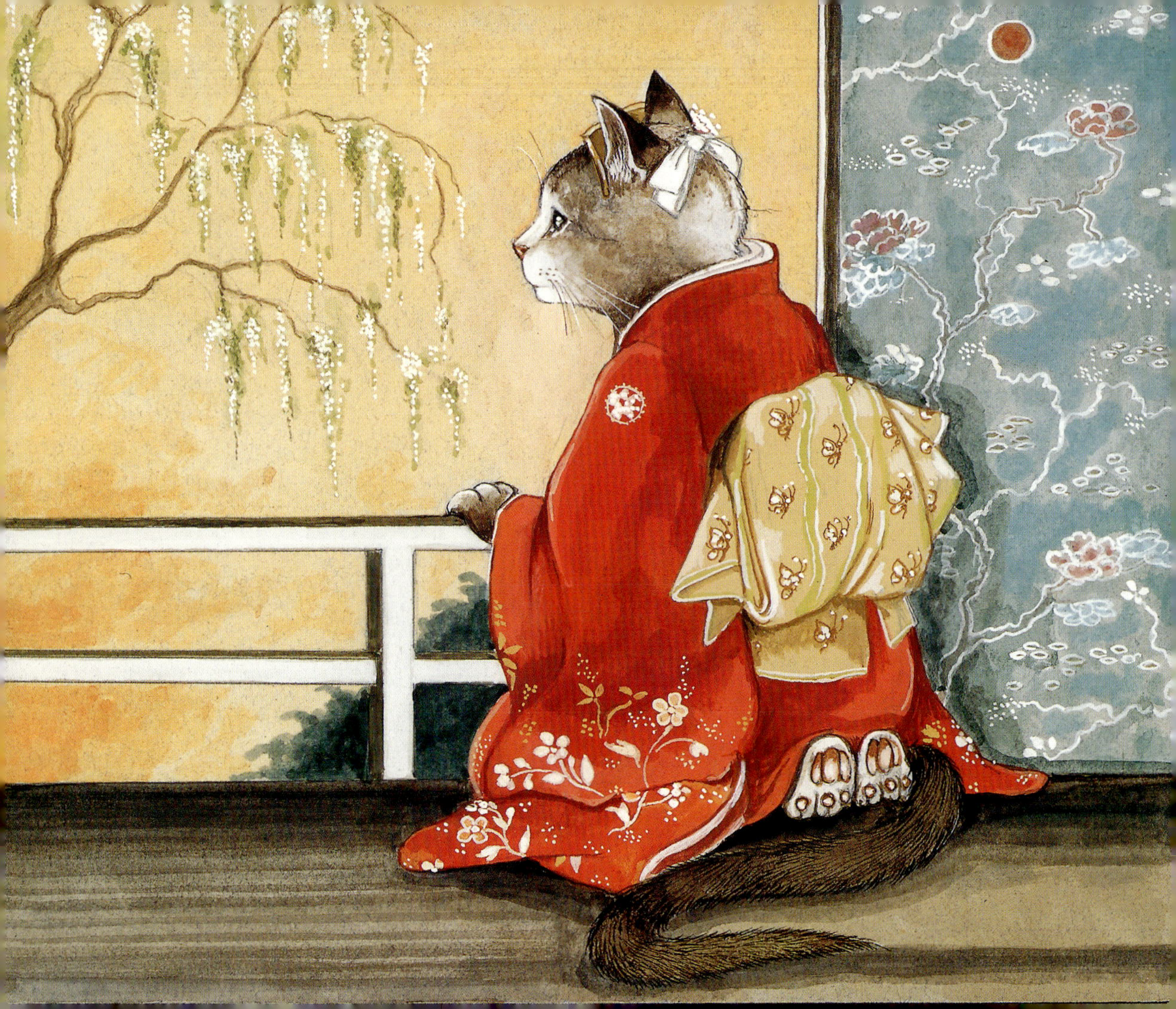

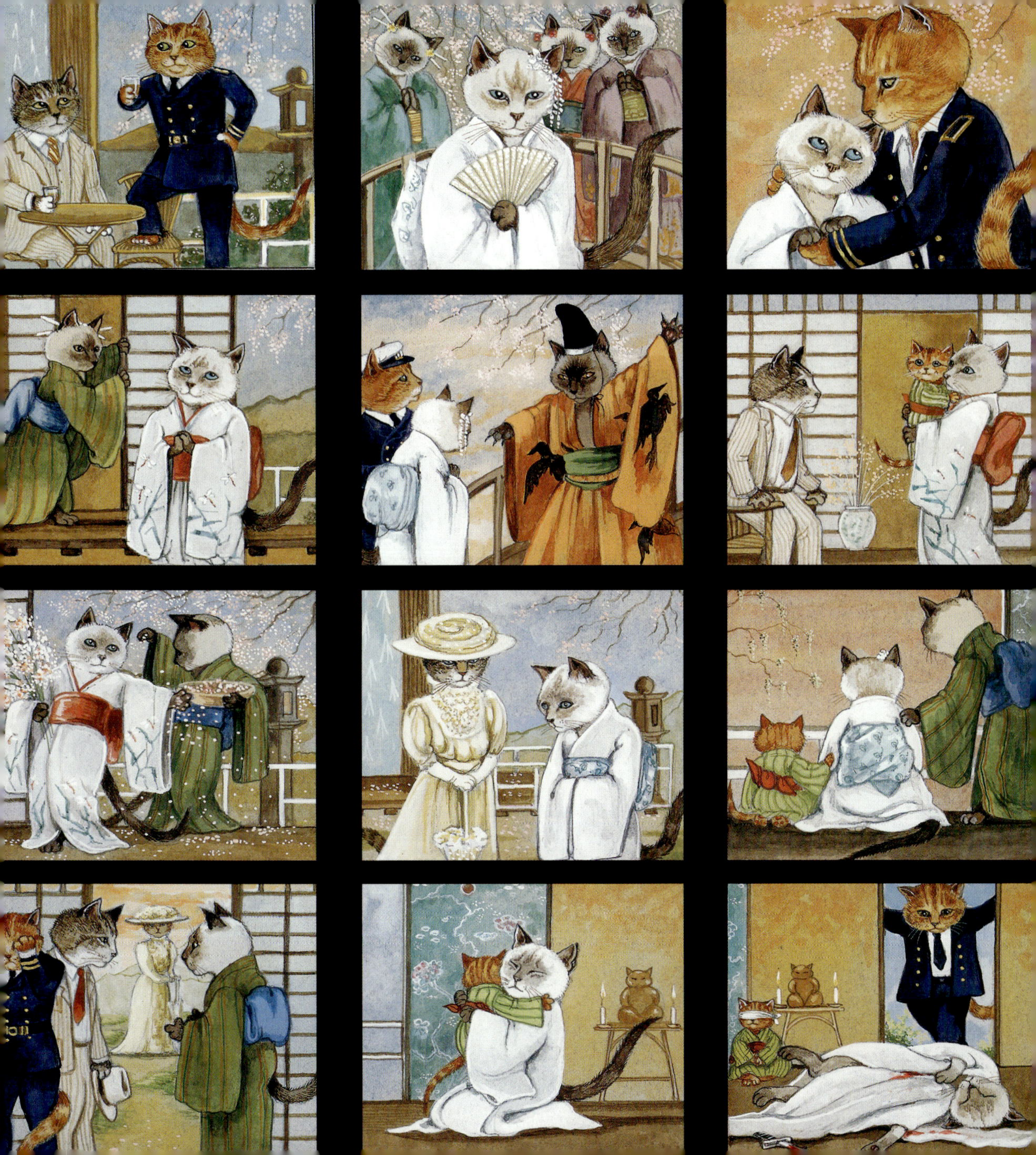

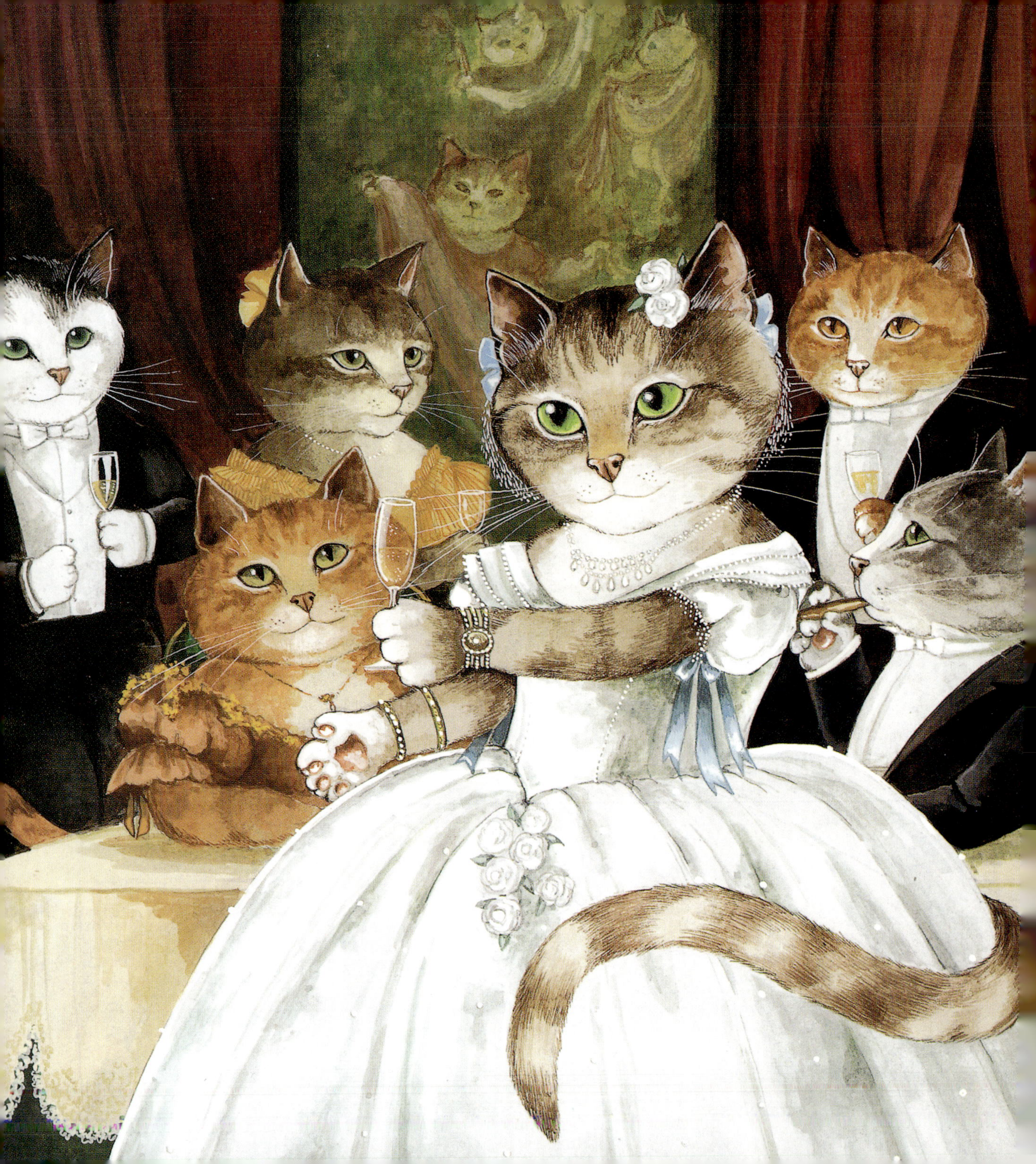

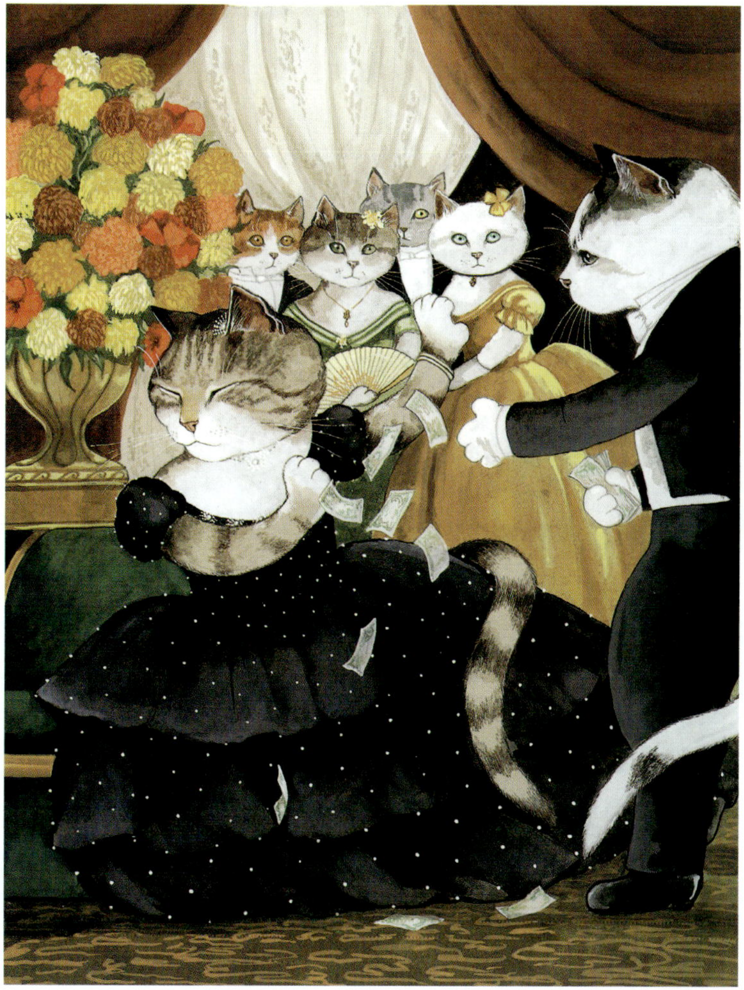

Above and opposite

LA TRAVIATA *by Giuseppe Verdi*

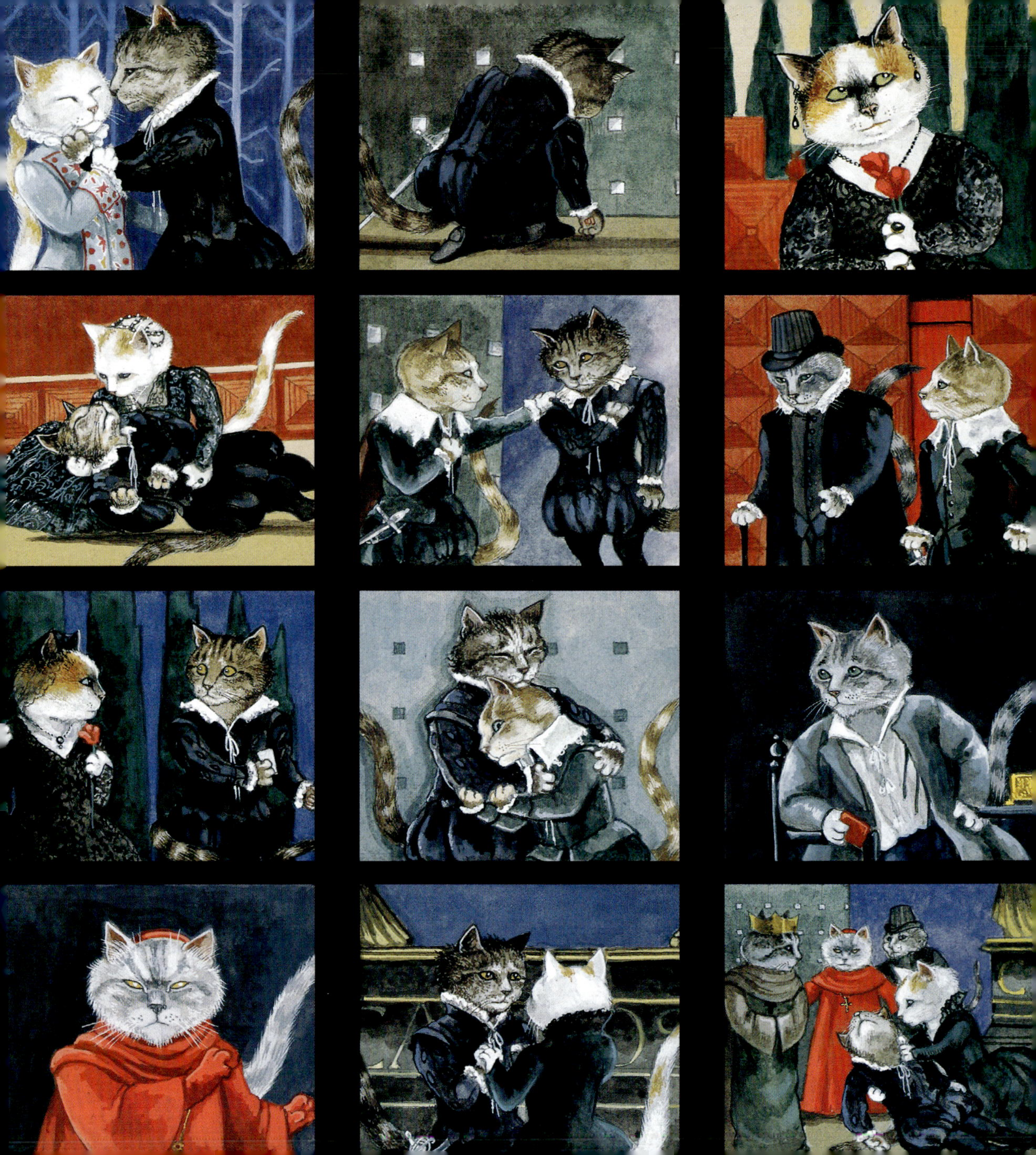

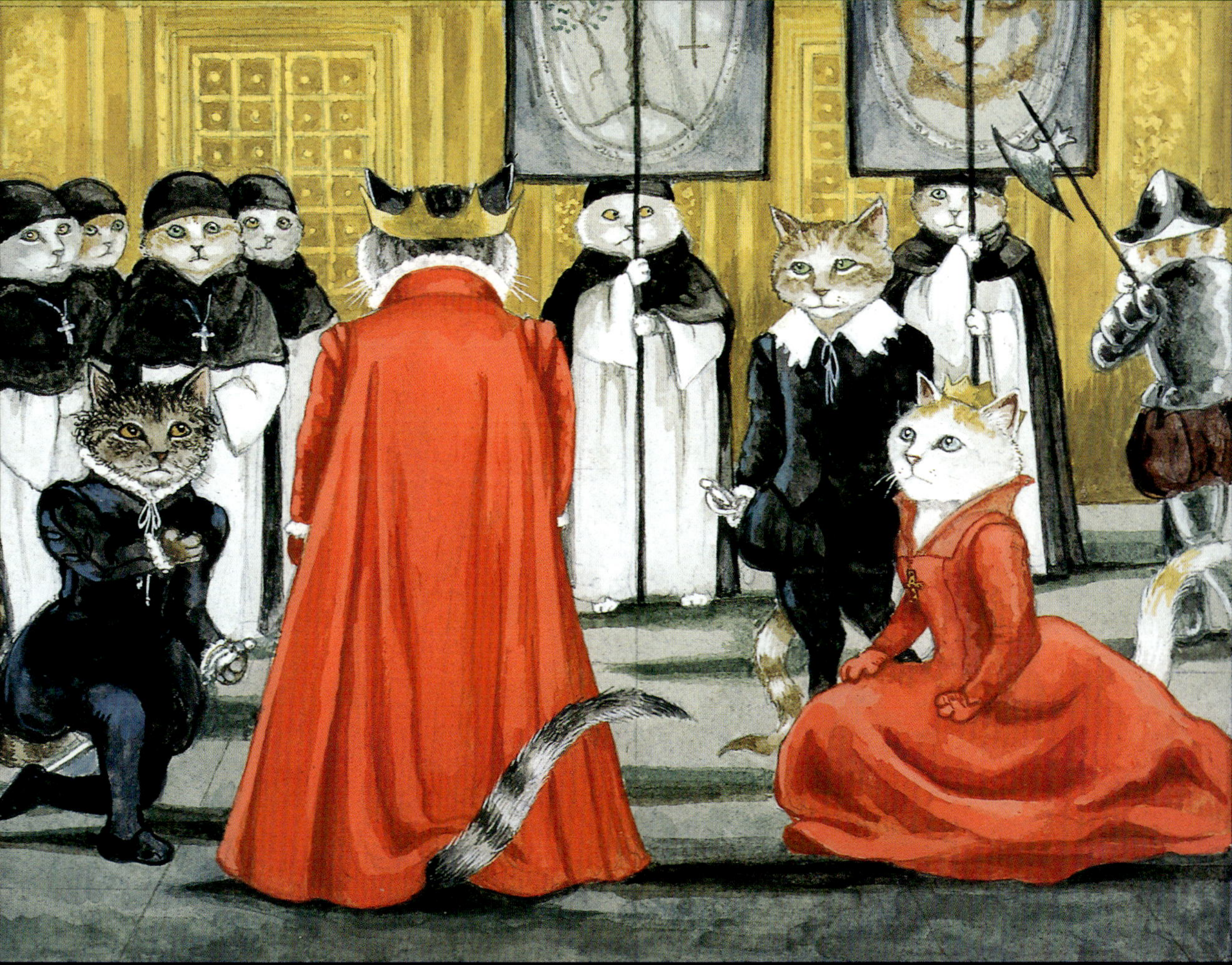

DON CARLOS *by Giuseppe Verdi*

COSÌ FAN TUTTE

by Wolfgang Amadeus Mozart

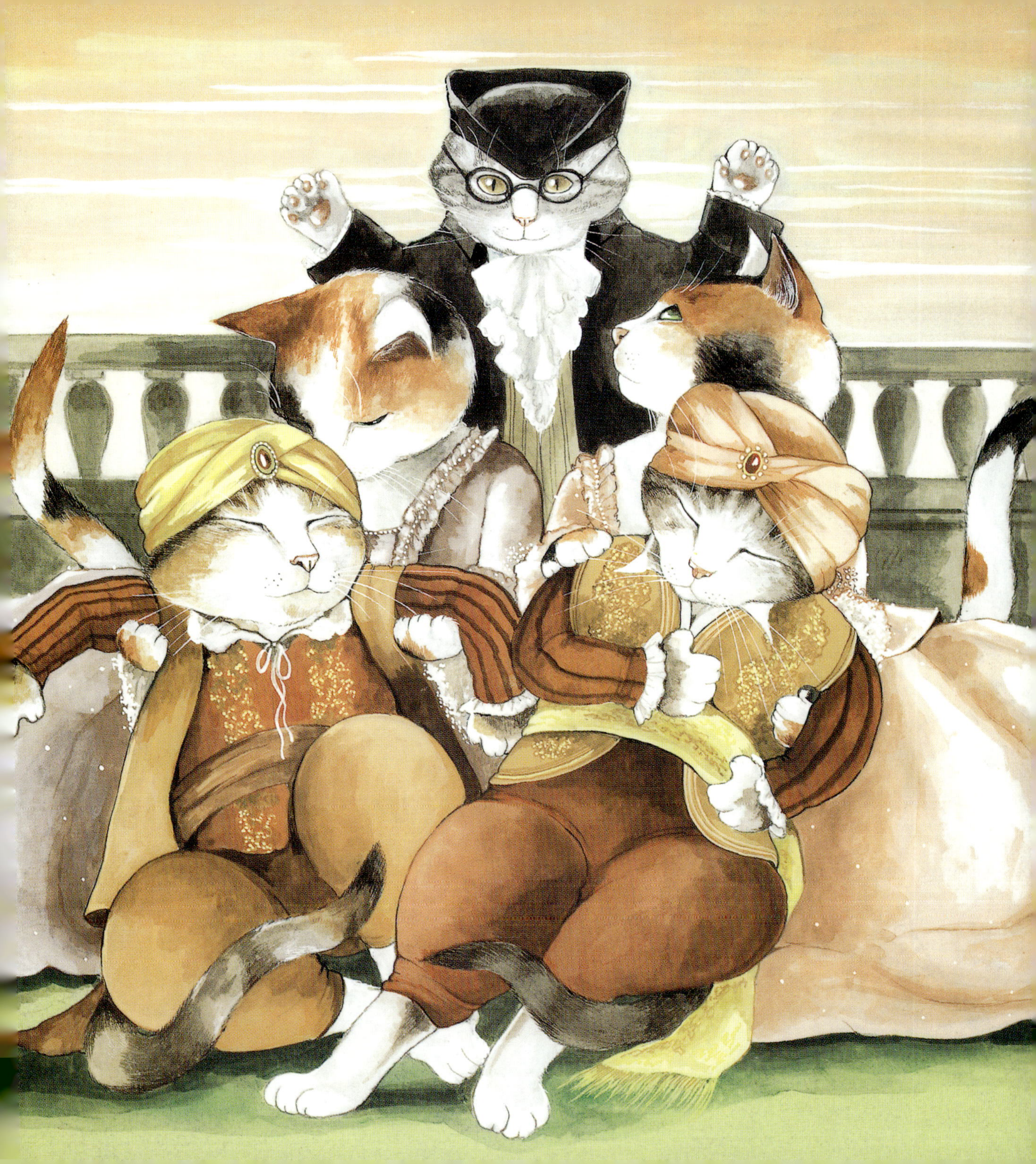

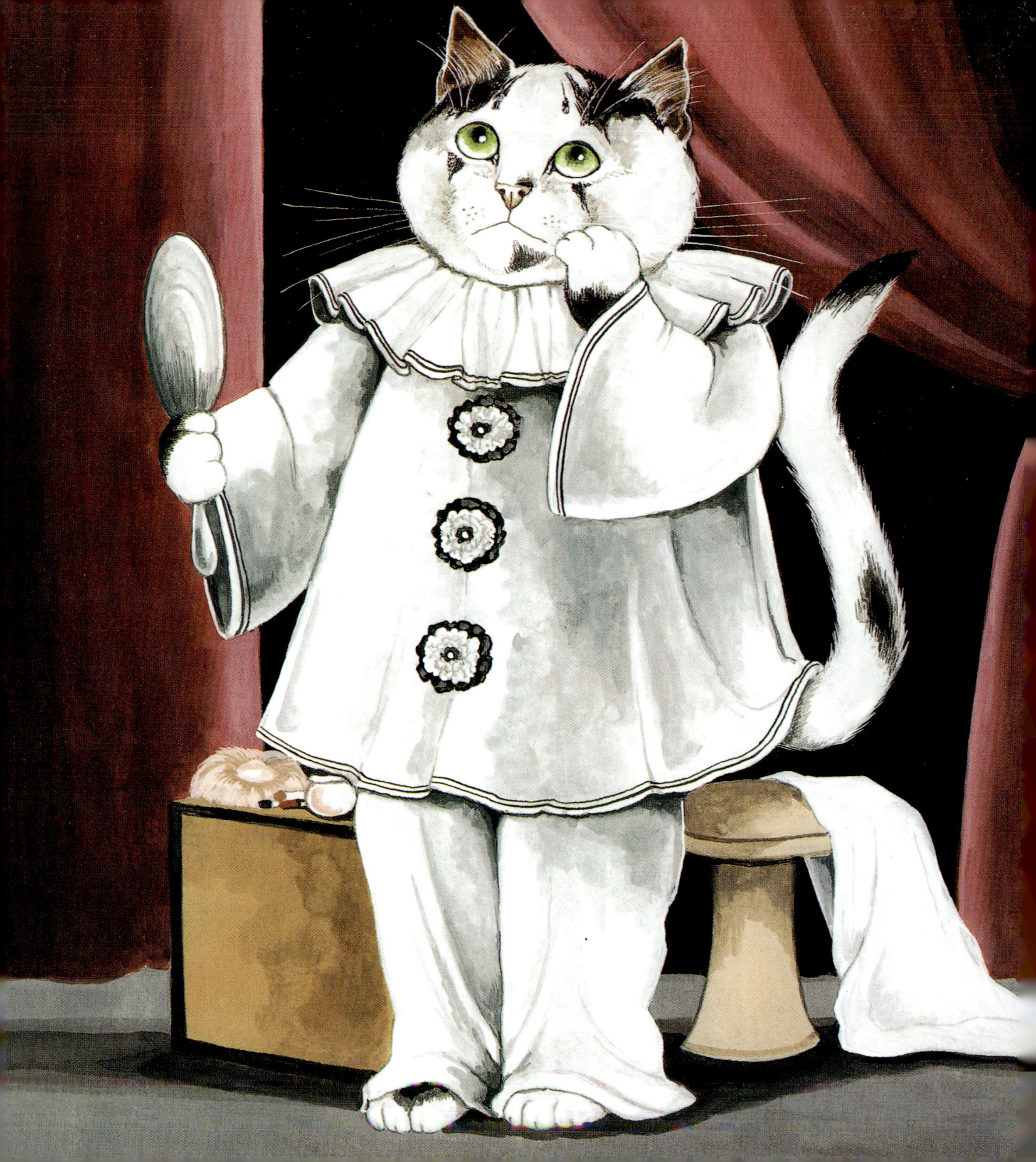

PAGLIACCI

by Ruggiero Leoncavallo

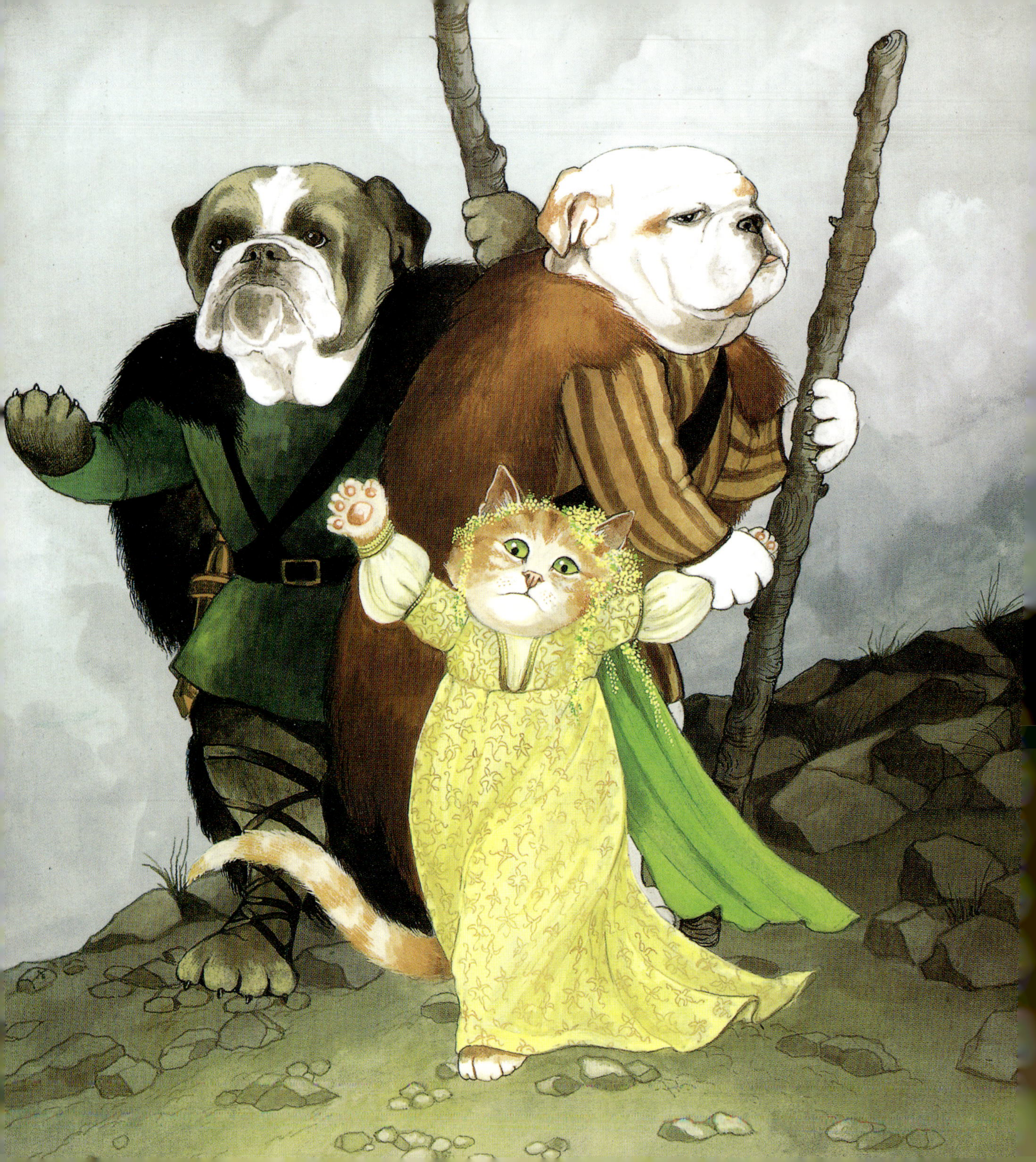

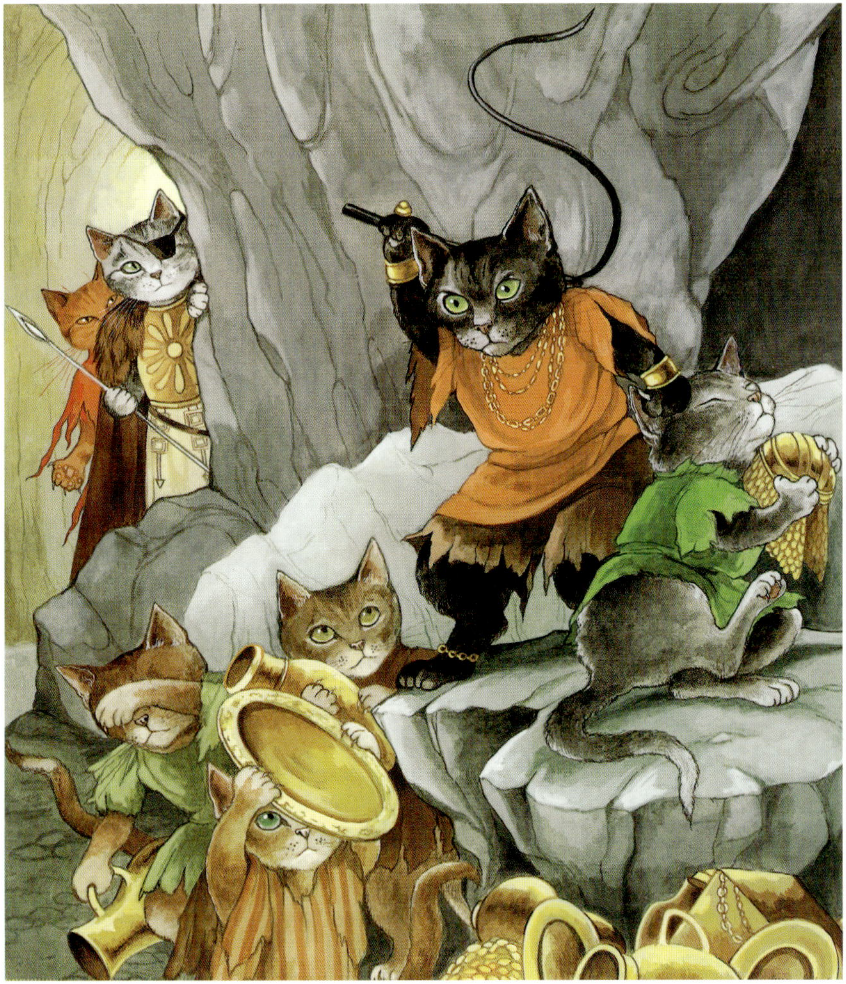

Above and opposite

DAS RHEINGOLD *by Richard Wagner*

BORIS GODUNOV

by Modest Mussorgsky

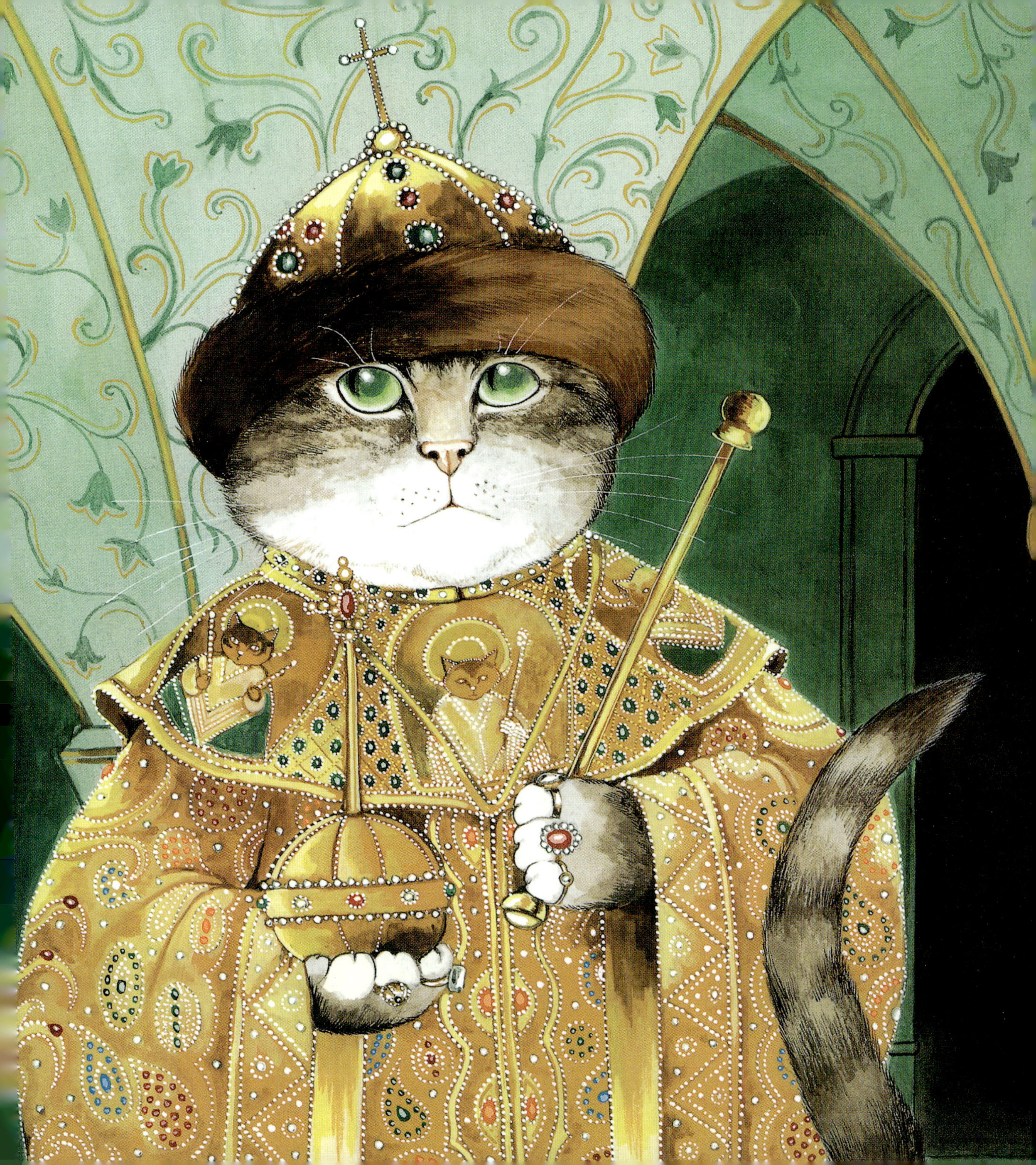

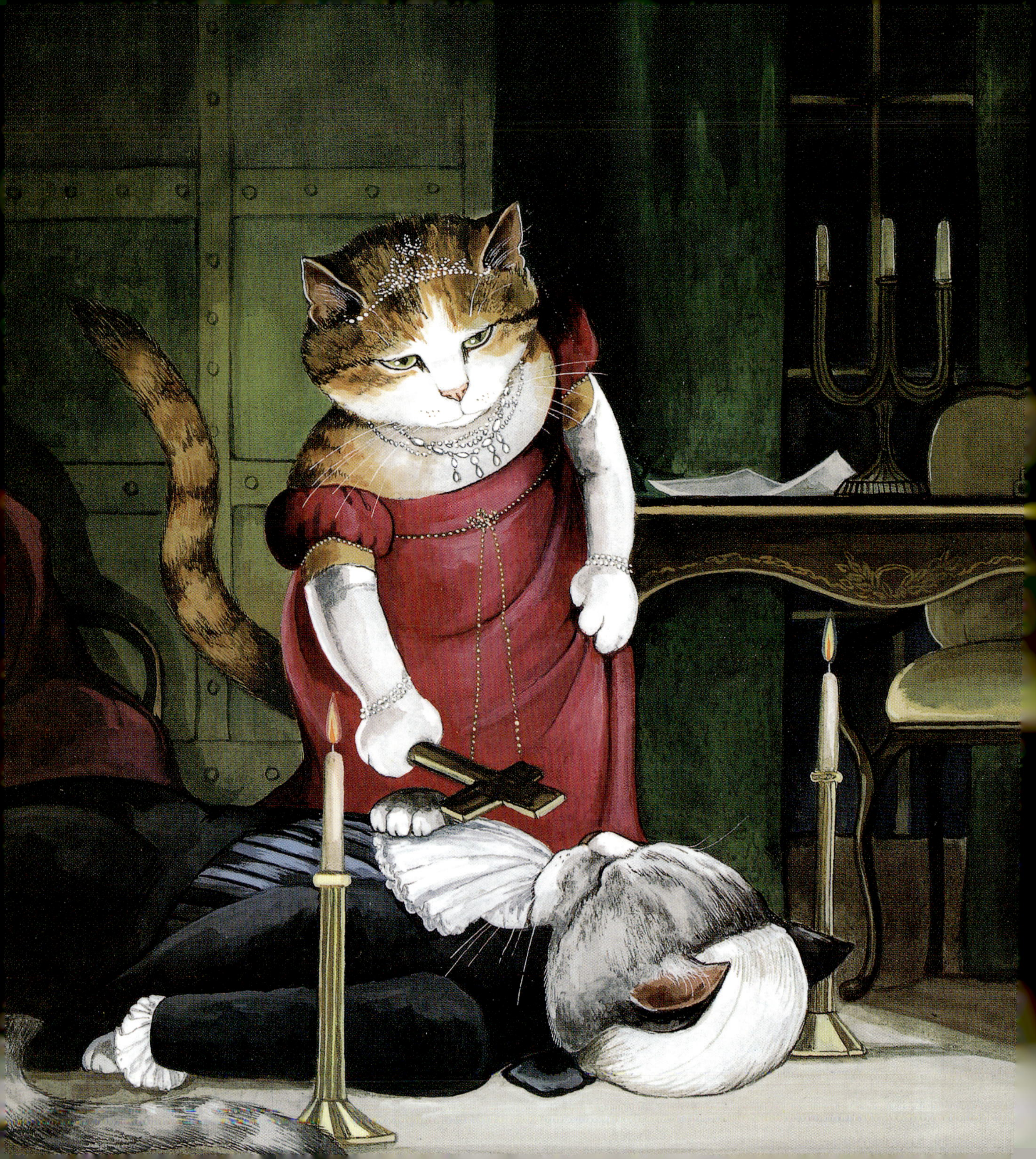

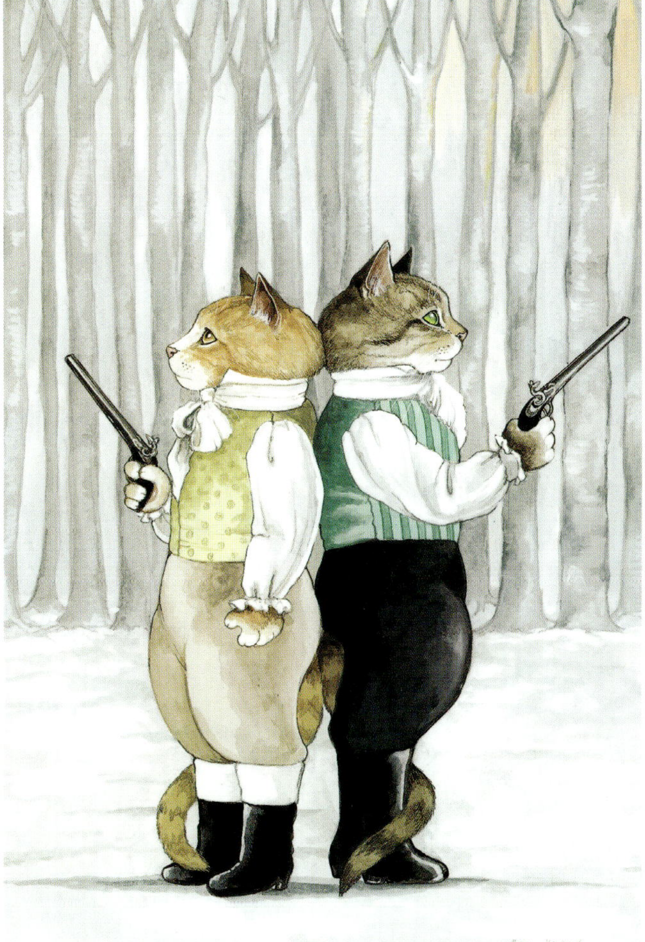

Above EUGENE ONEGIN *by Pyotr Ilyich Tchaikovsky*

Opposite TOSCA *by Giacomo Puccini*

DIE WALKÜRE

by Richard Wagner

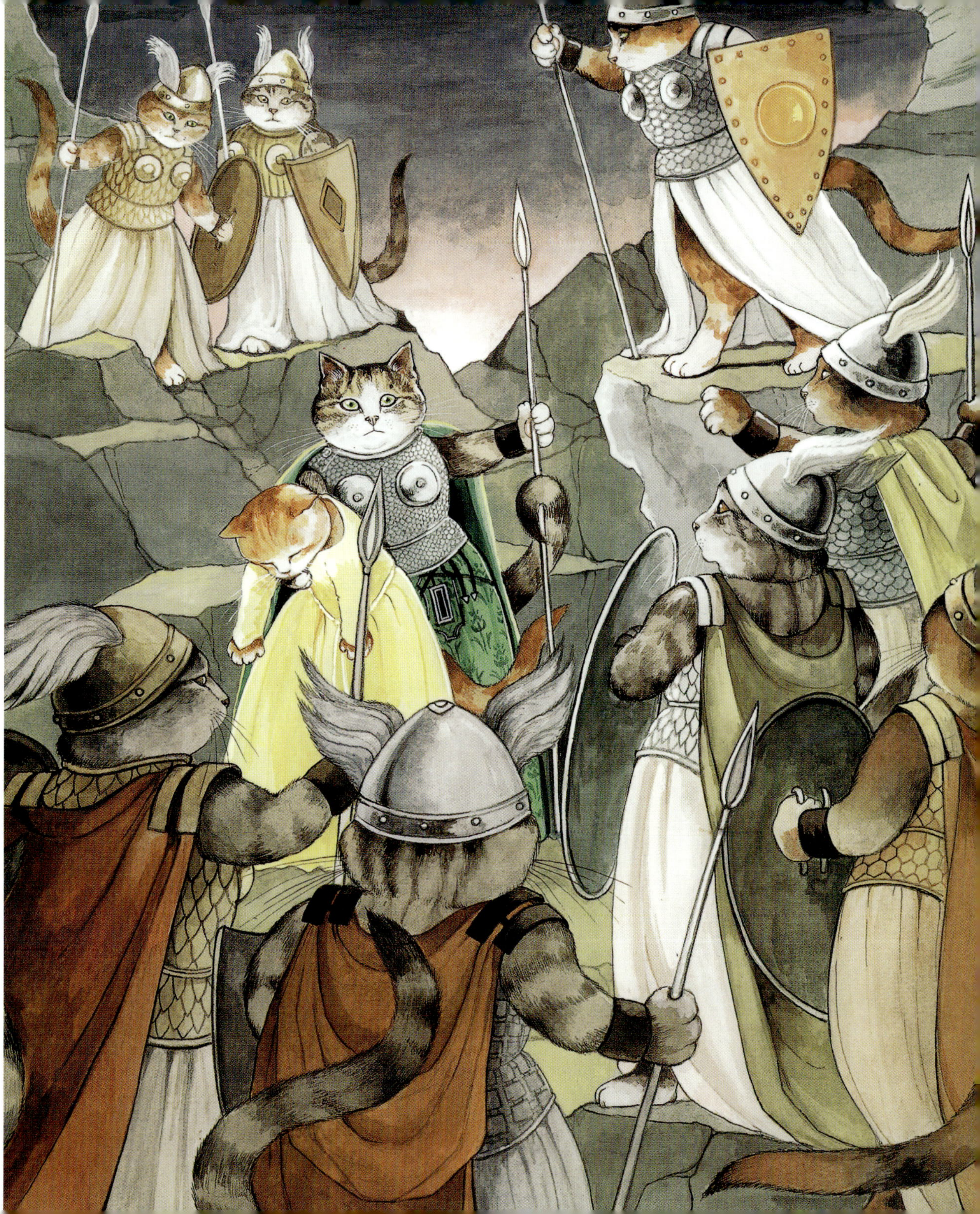

THE MASTERSINGERS OF NUREMBERG

by Richard Wagner

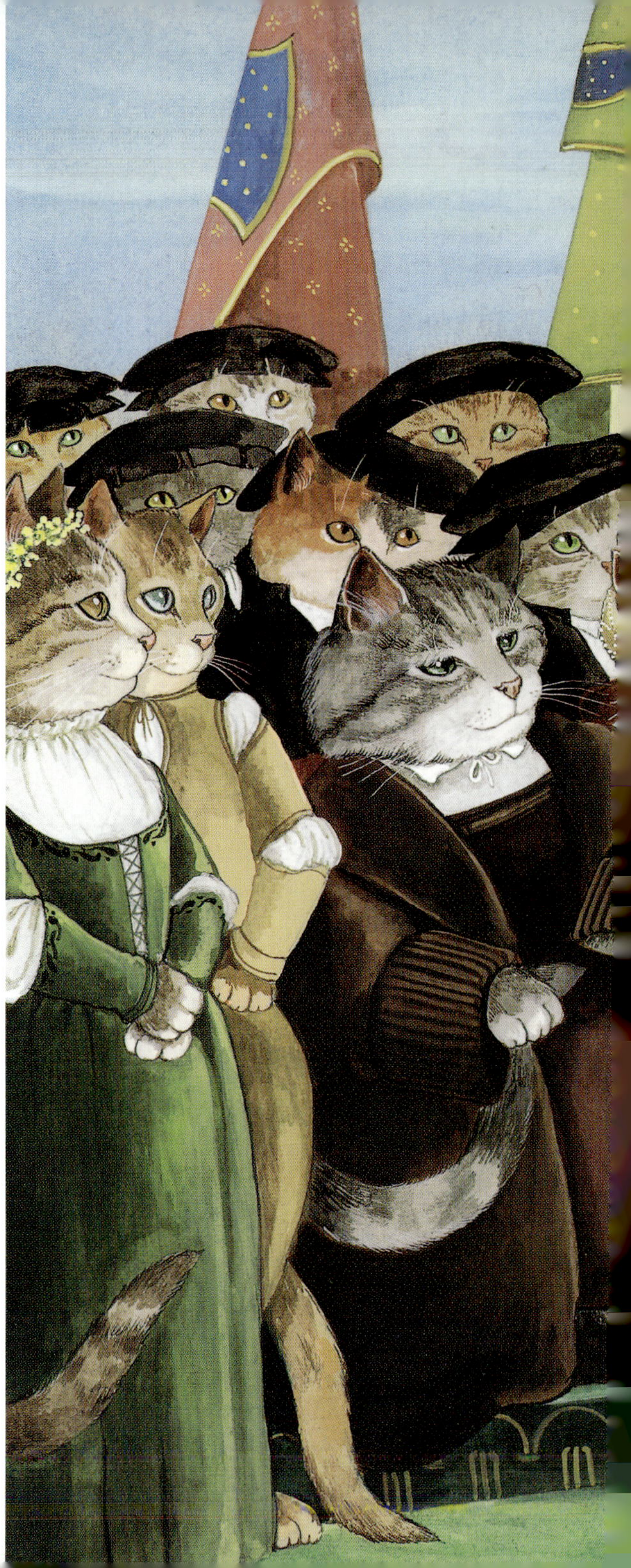

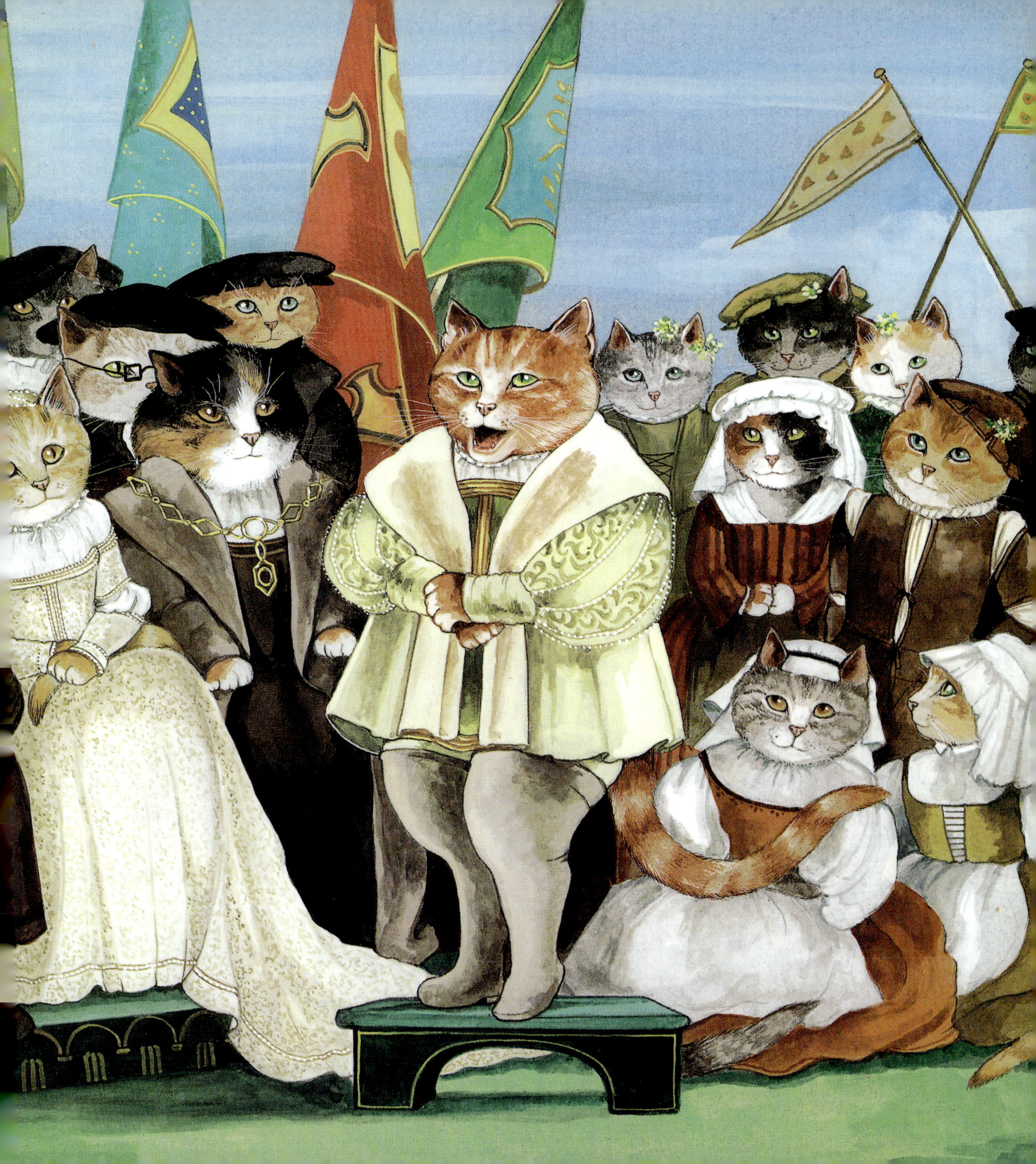

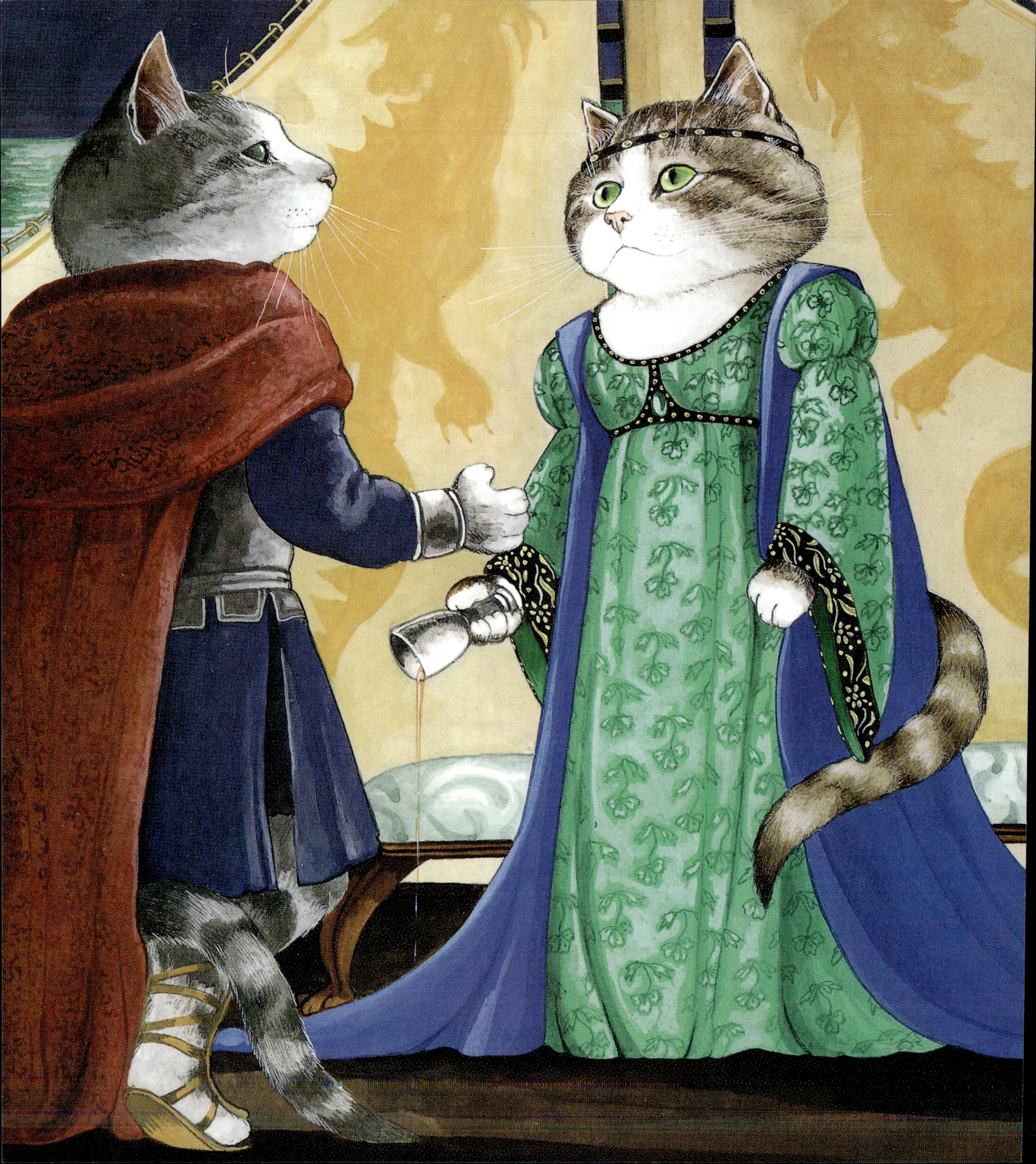

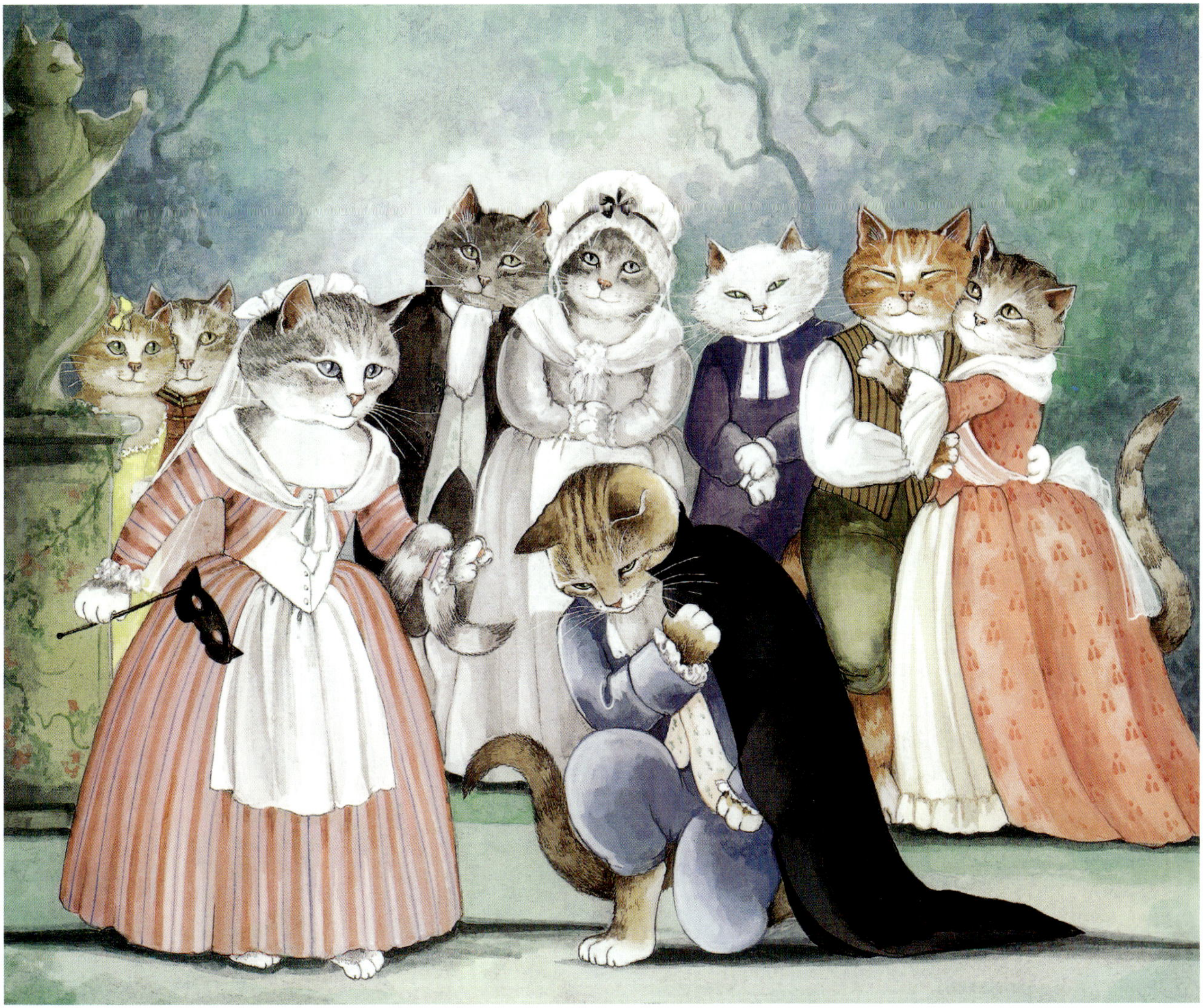

Above THE MARRIAGE OF FIGARO *by Wolfgang Amadeus Mozart*

Opposite TRISTAN UND ISOLDE *by Richard Wagner*

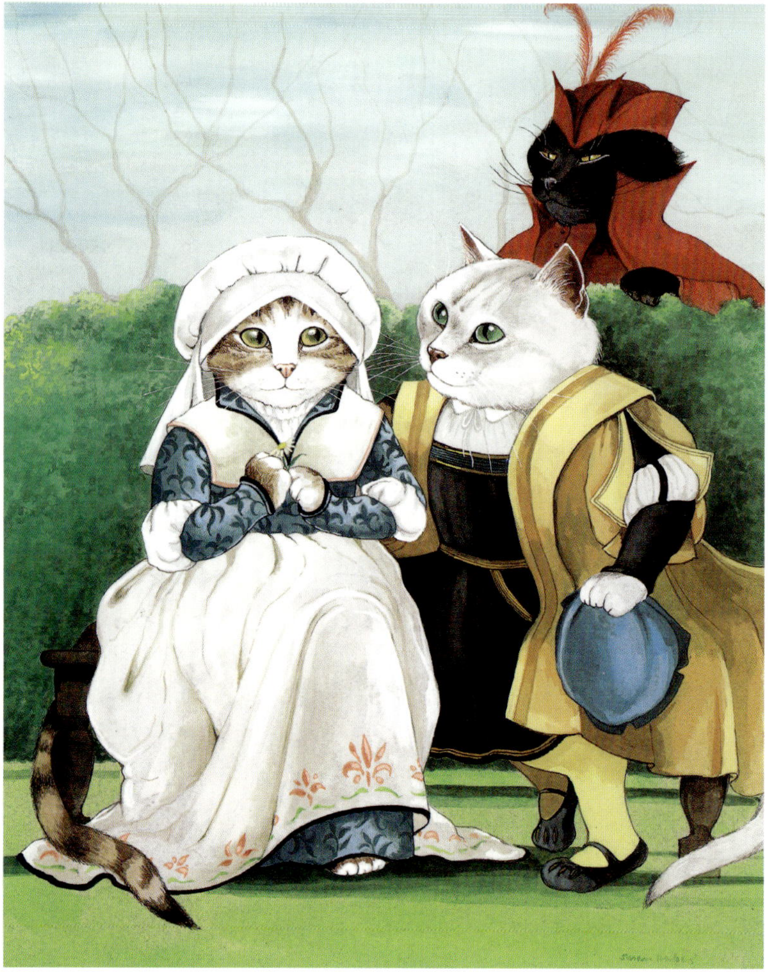

Above FAUST *by Charles Gounod*

Opposite RIGOLETTO *by Giuseppe Verdi*

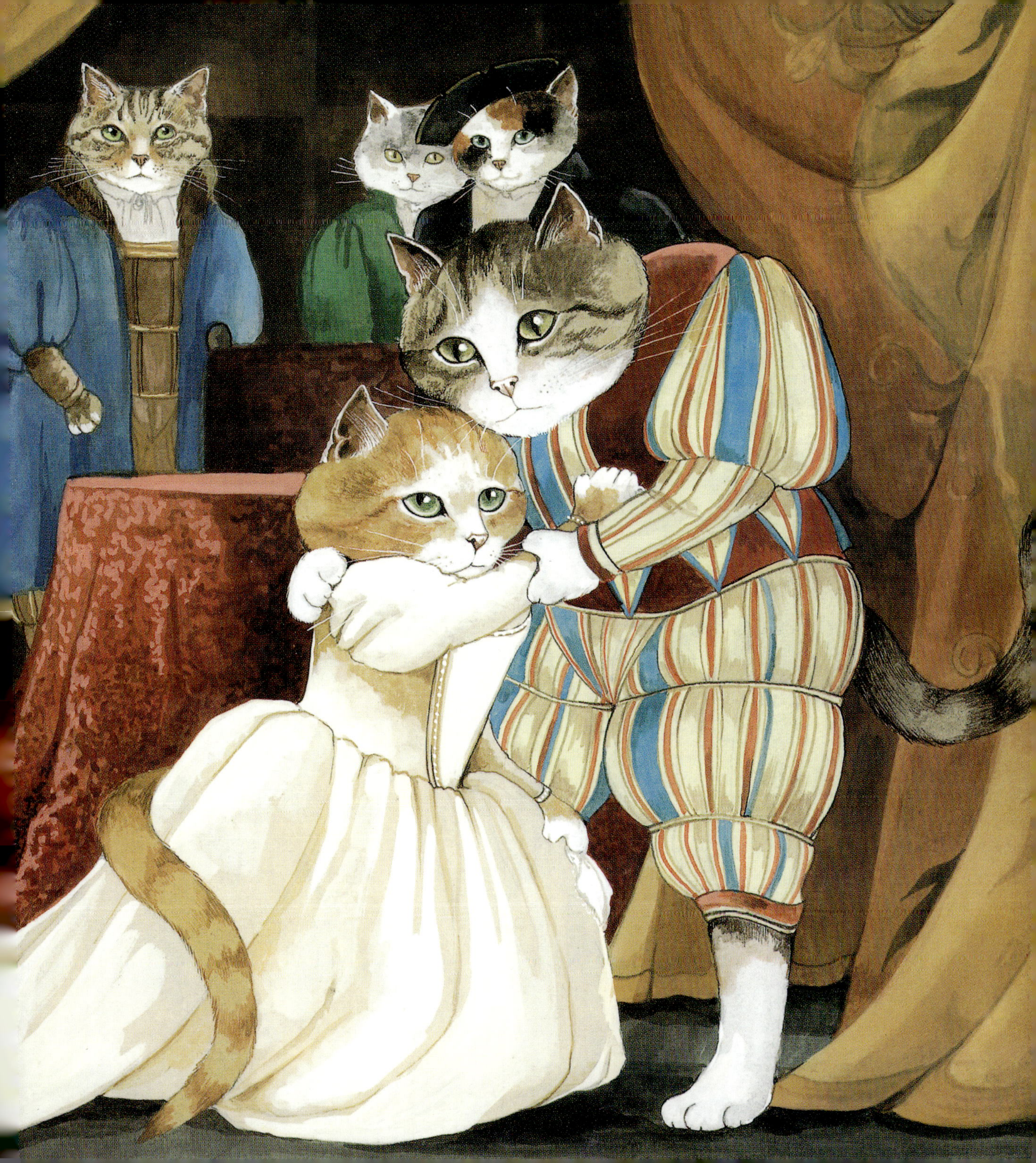

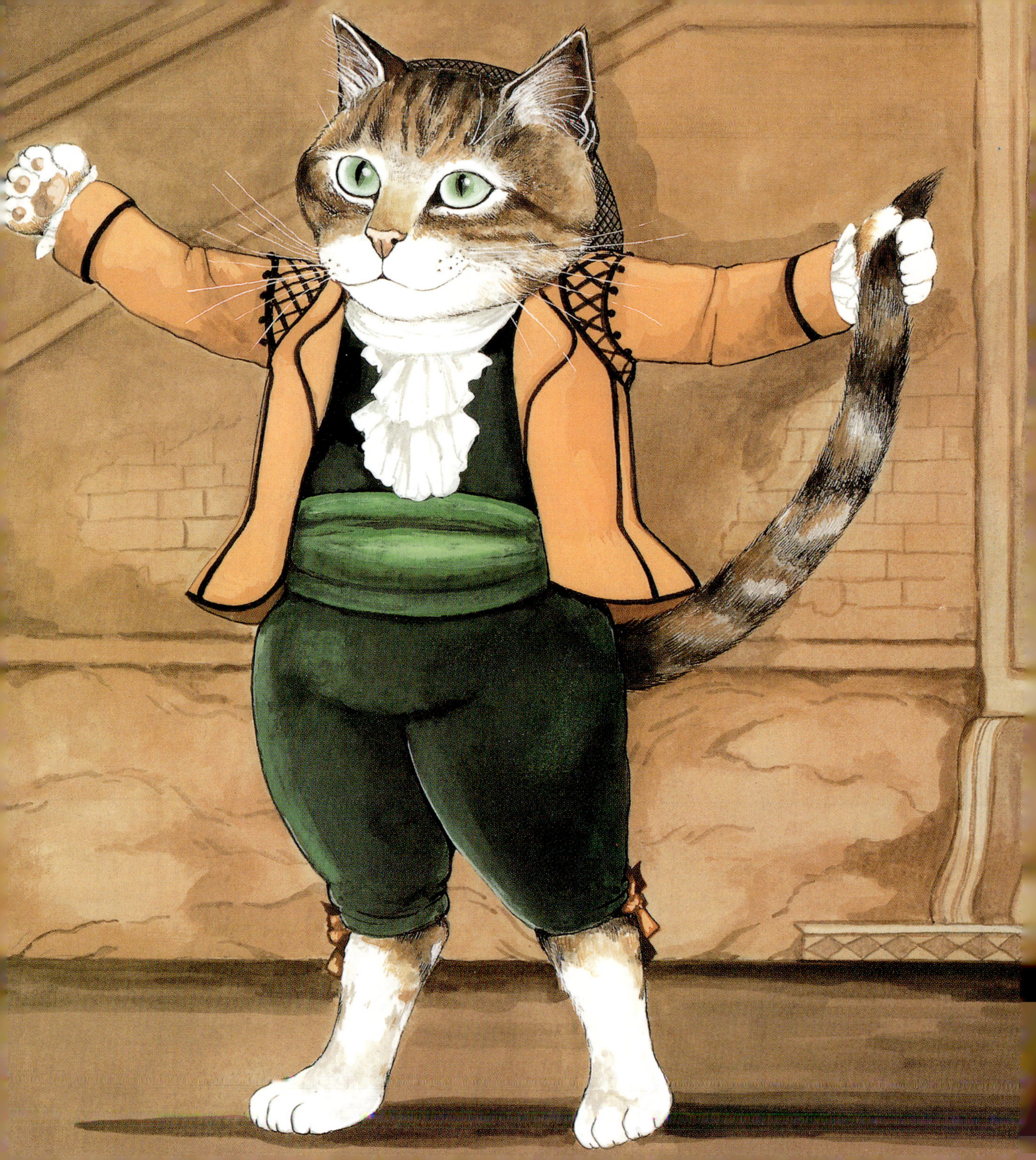

THE BARBER OF SEVILLE

by Gioachino Rossini

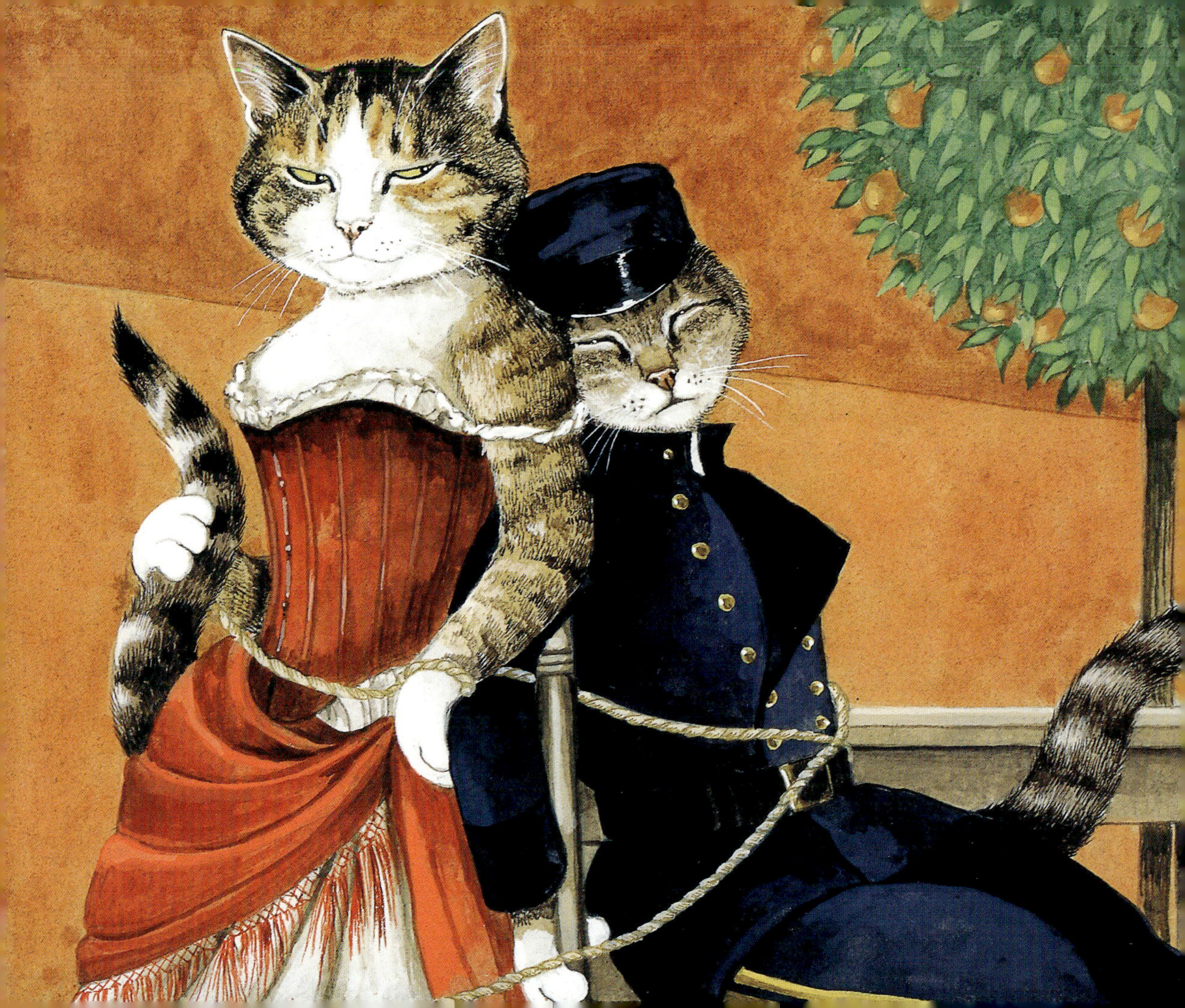

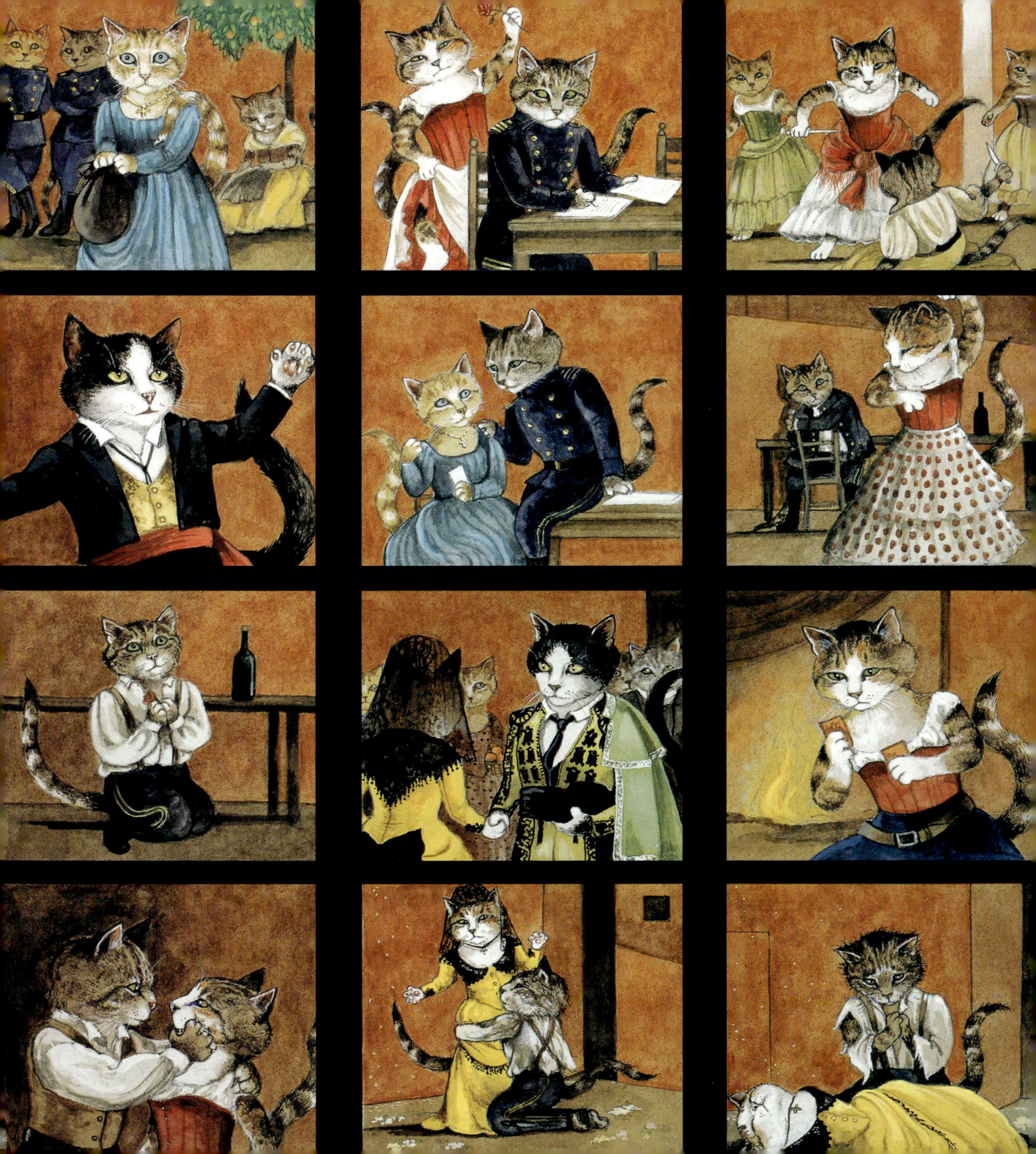

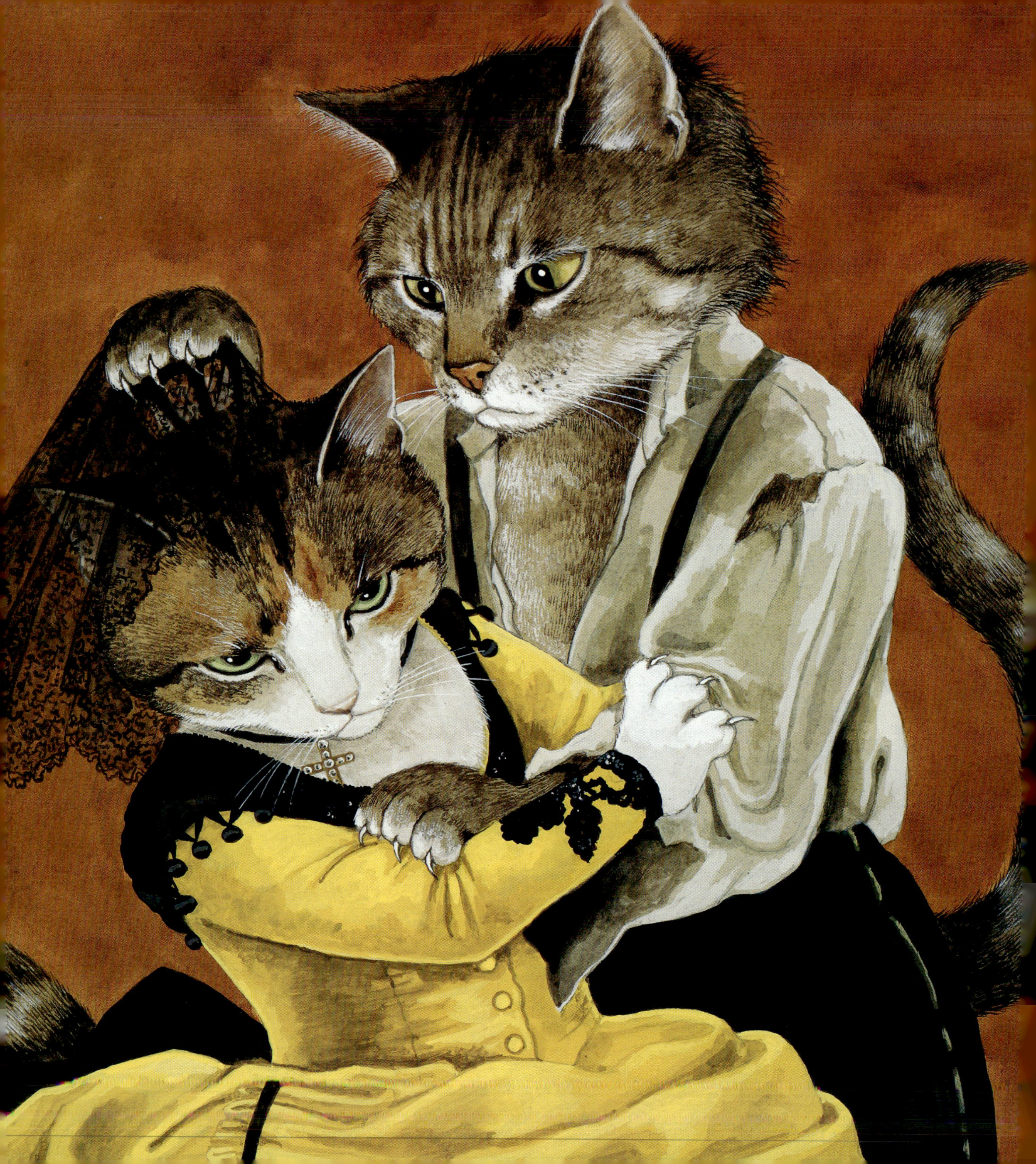

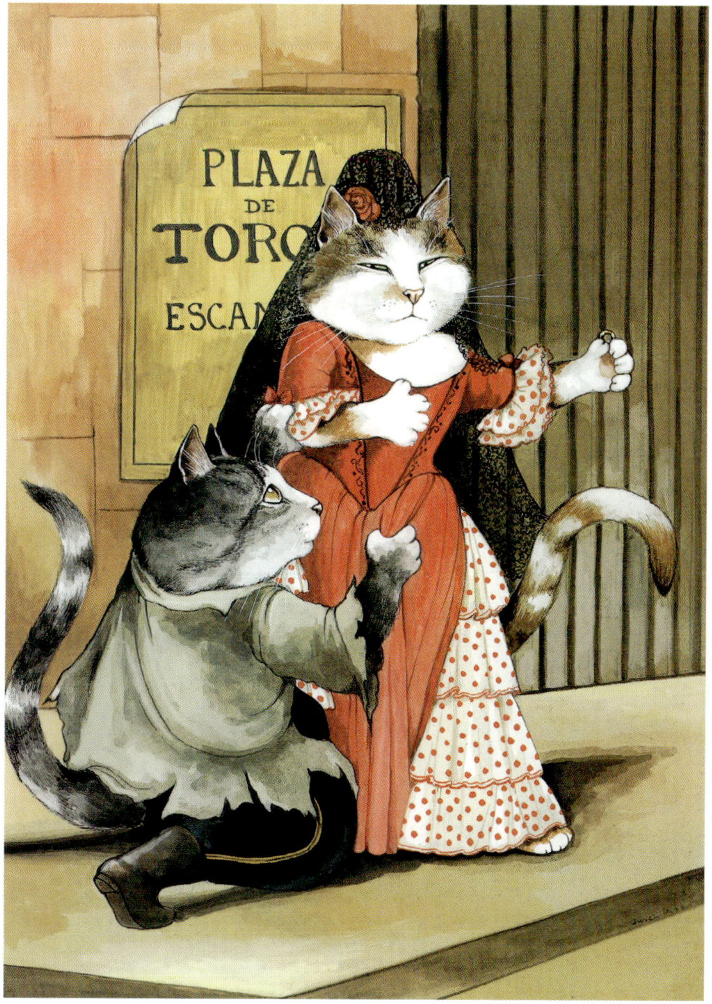

Above and opposite

CARMEN *by Georges Bizet*

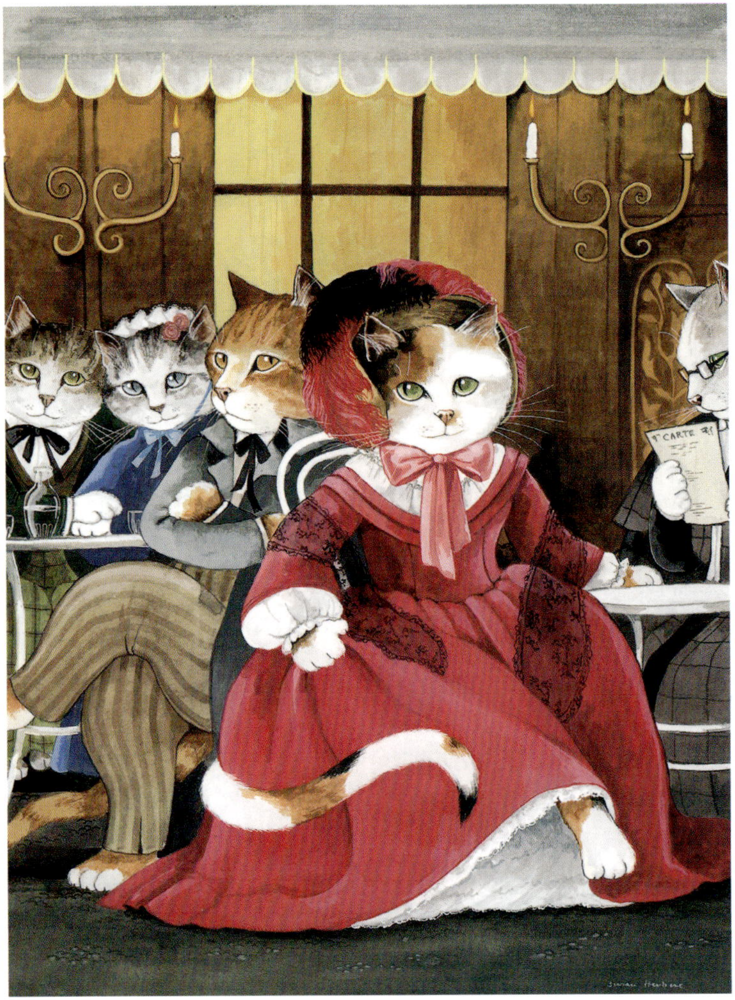

Above and opposite

LA BOHÈME *by Giacomo Puccini*

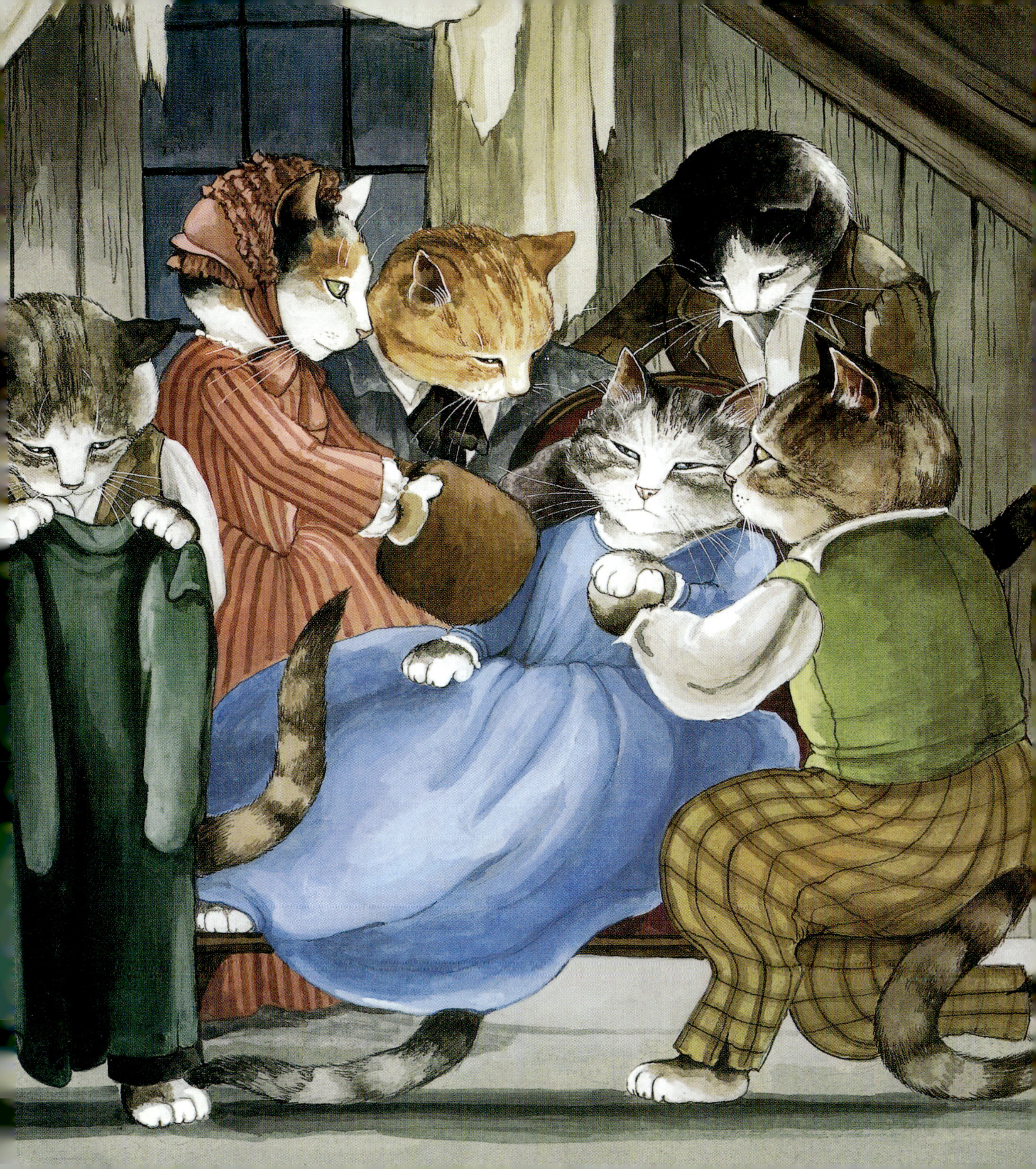

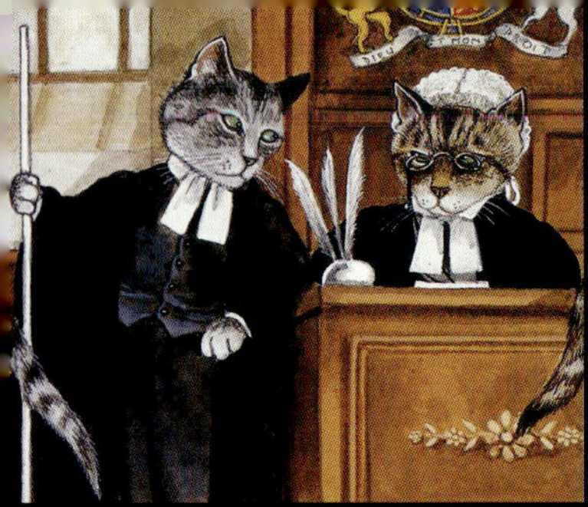
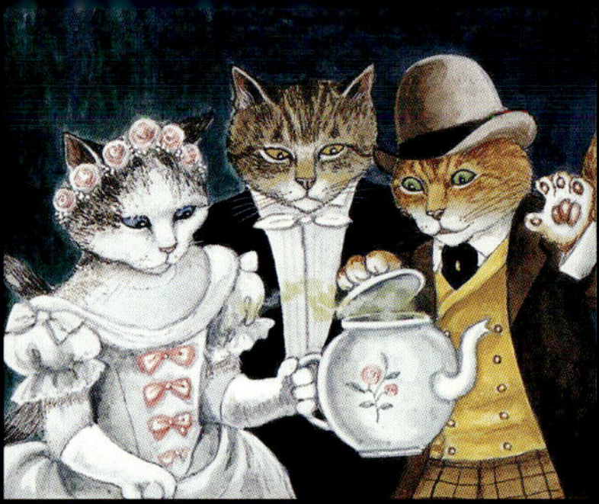
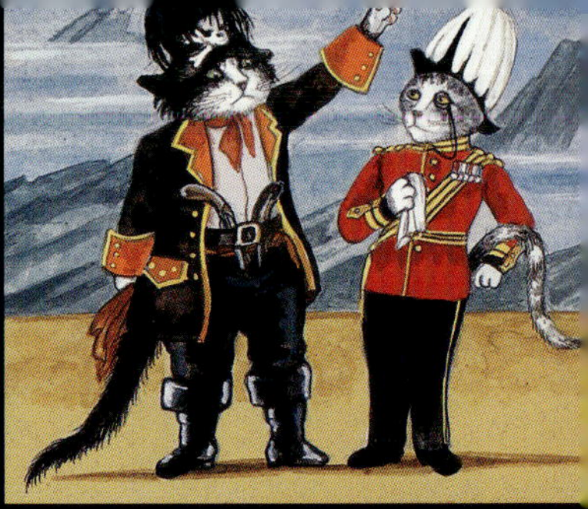
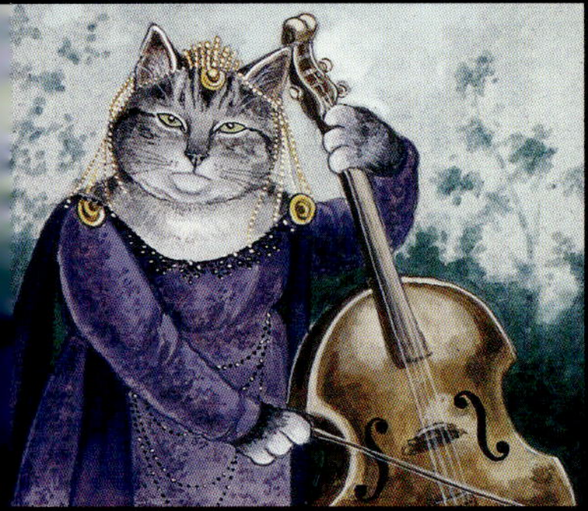
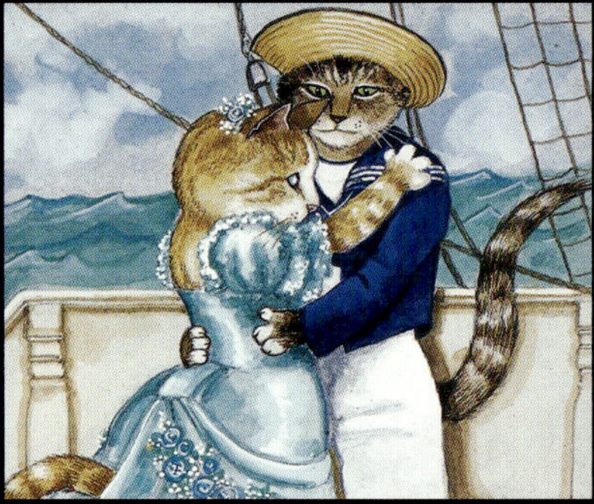
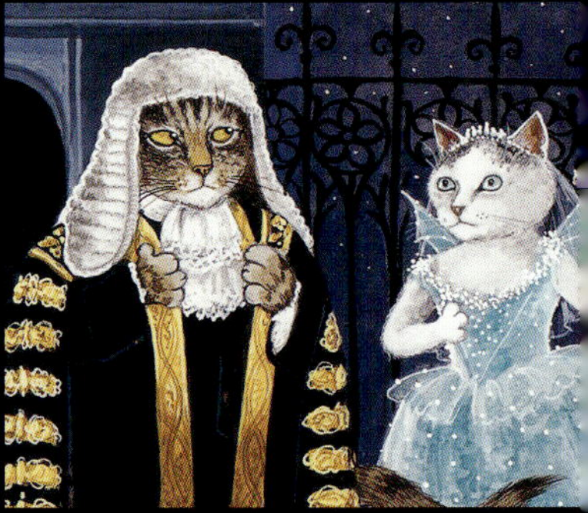
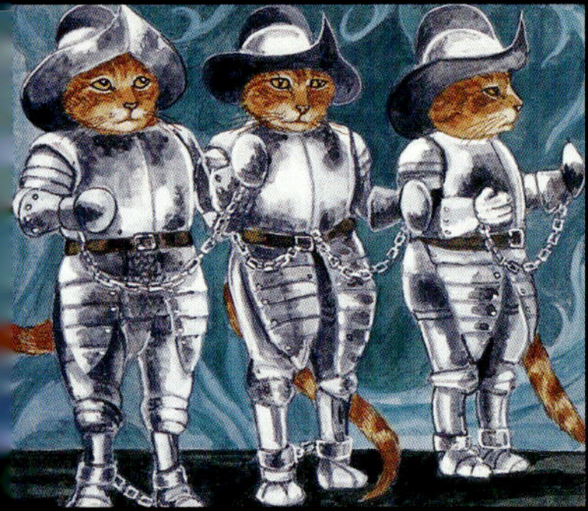
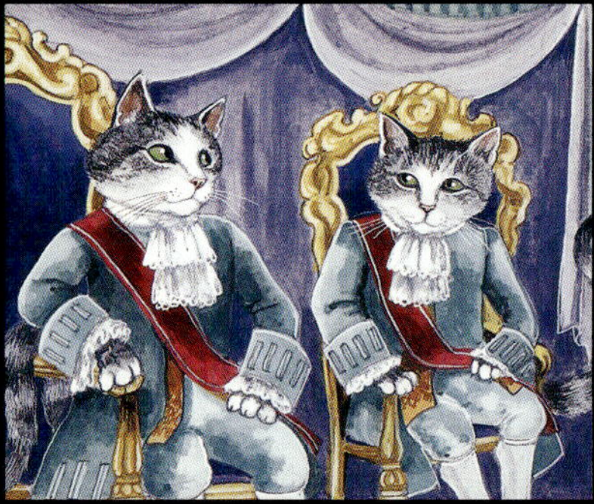
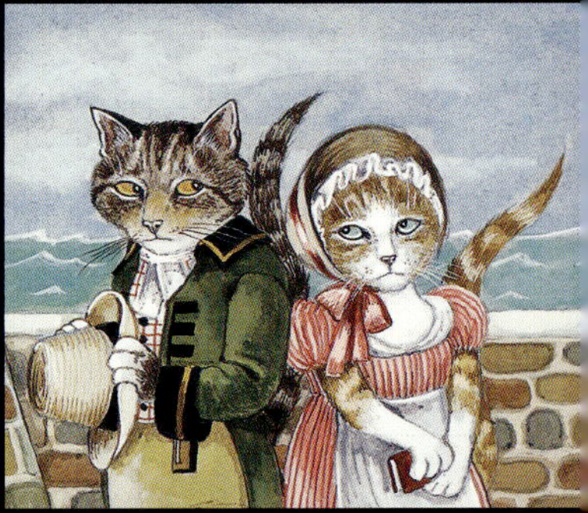
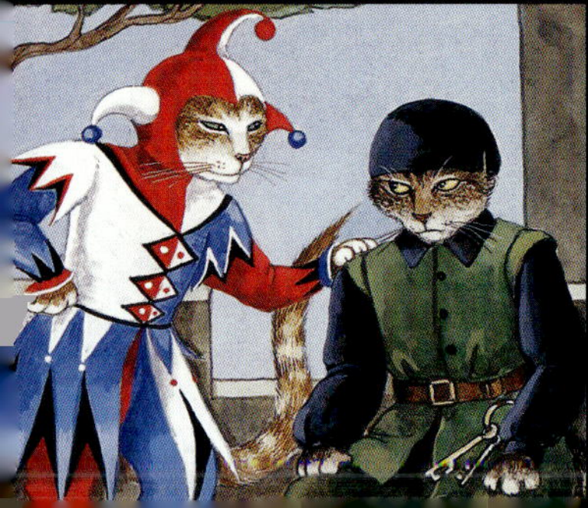
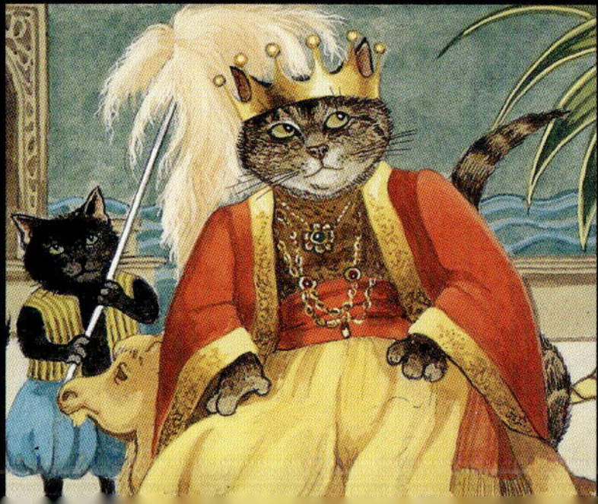
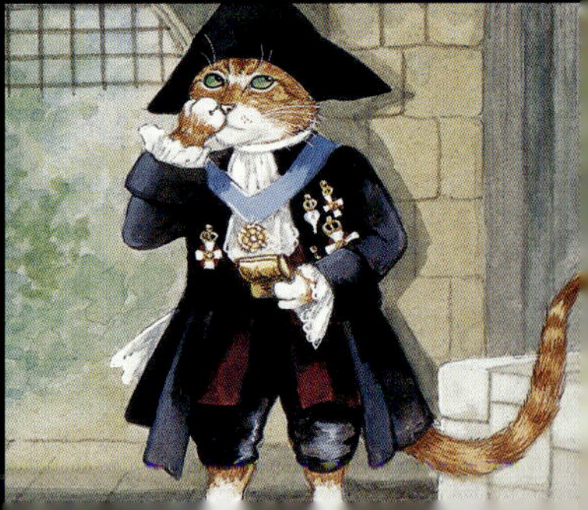

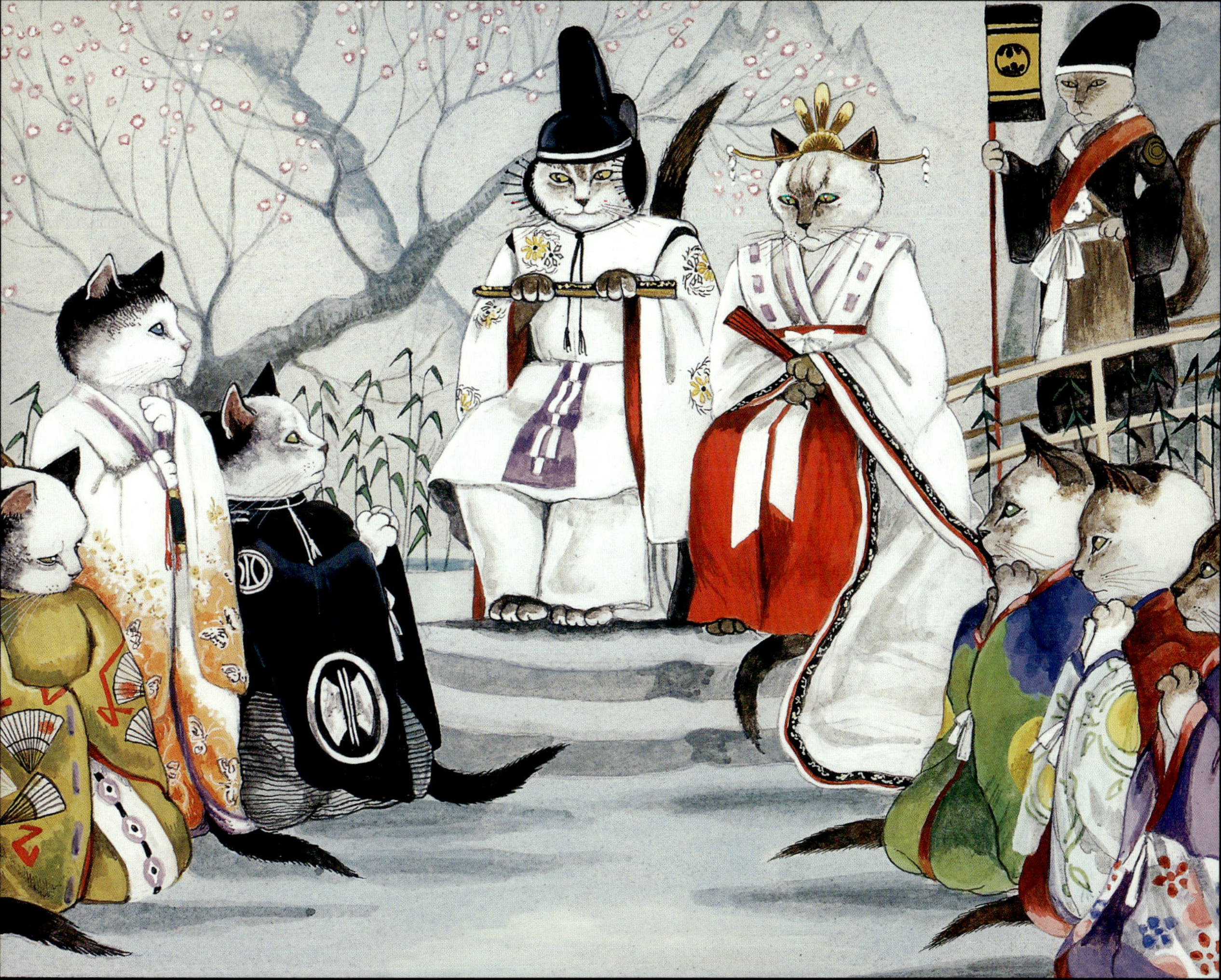

THE MIKADO (above)

and other comic operas by Gilbert and Sullivan

CATS IN THE MOVIES

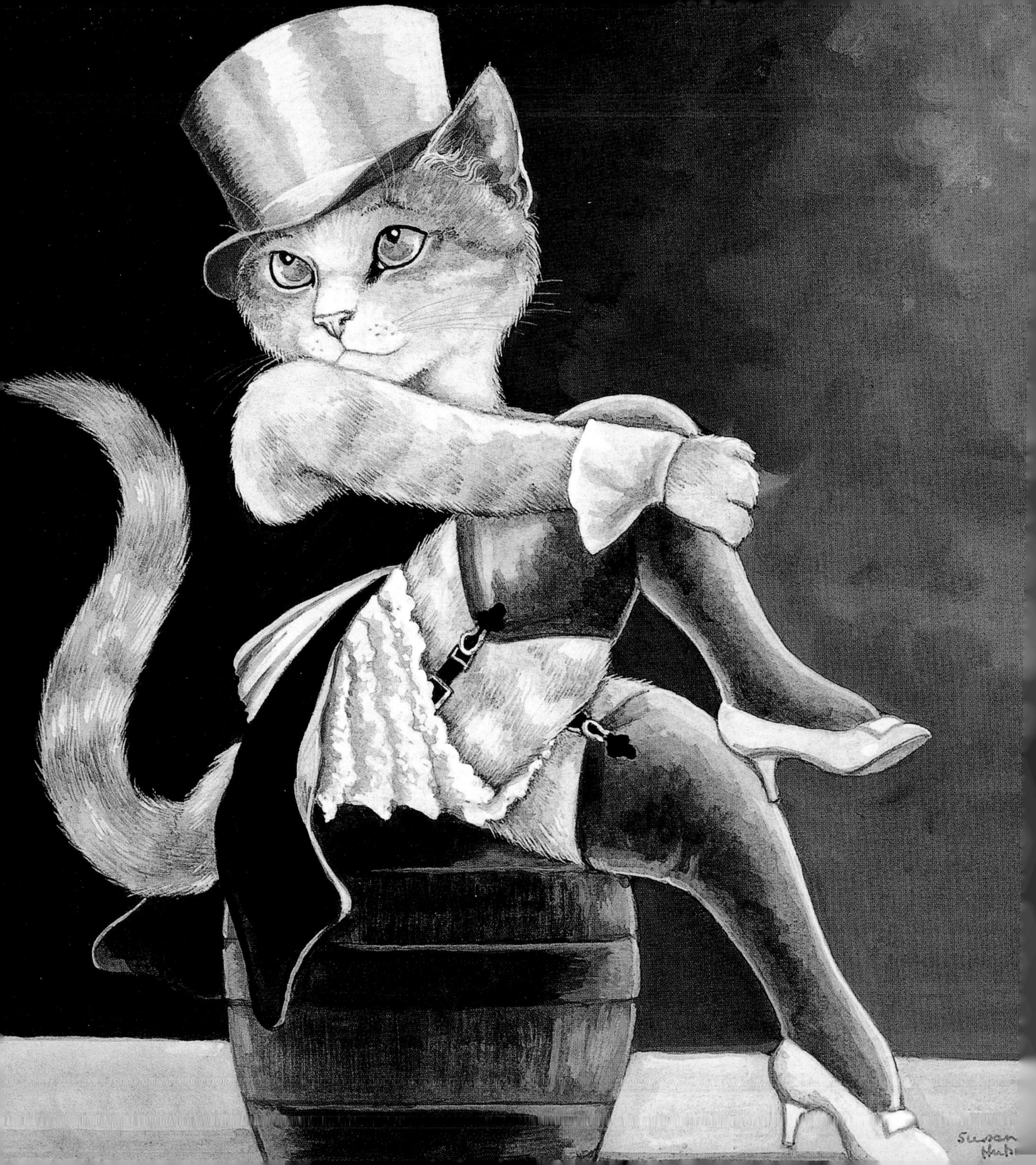

Marlene Dietrich in

THE BLUE ANGEL (1930)

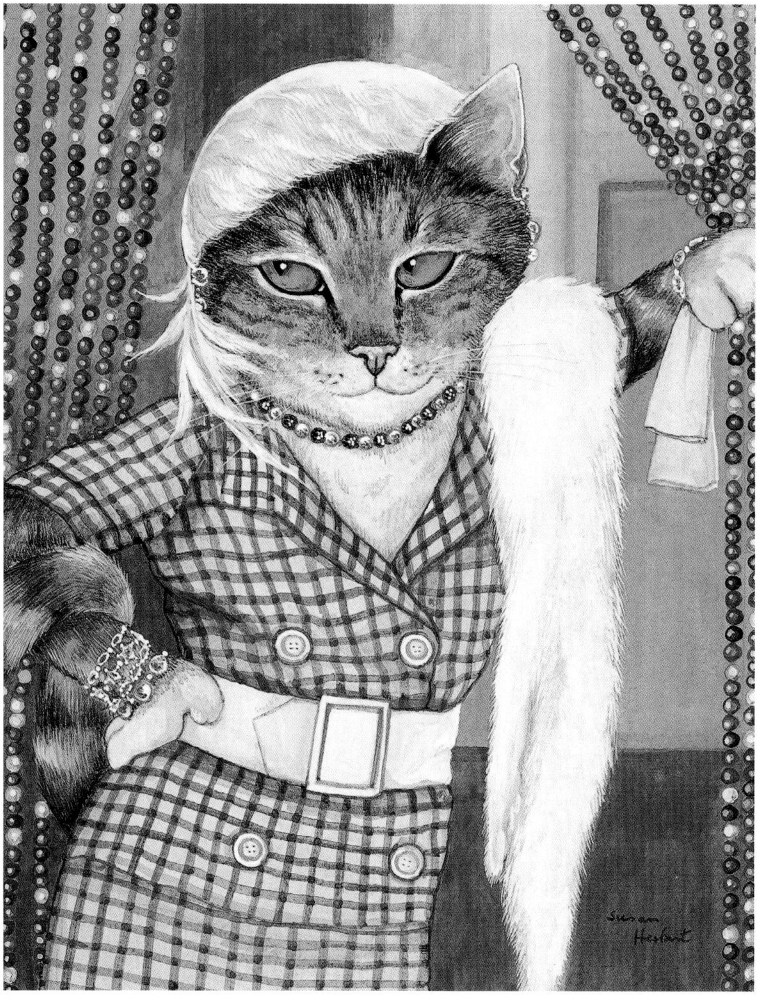

Above *Joan Crawford in* RAIN (1932)

Opposite *Mae West in* BELLE OF THE NINETIES (1934)

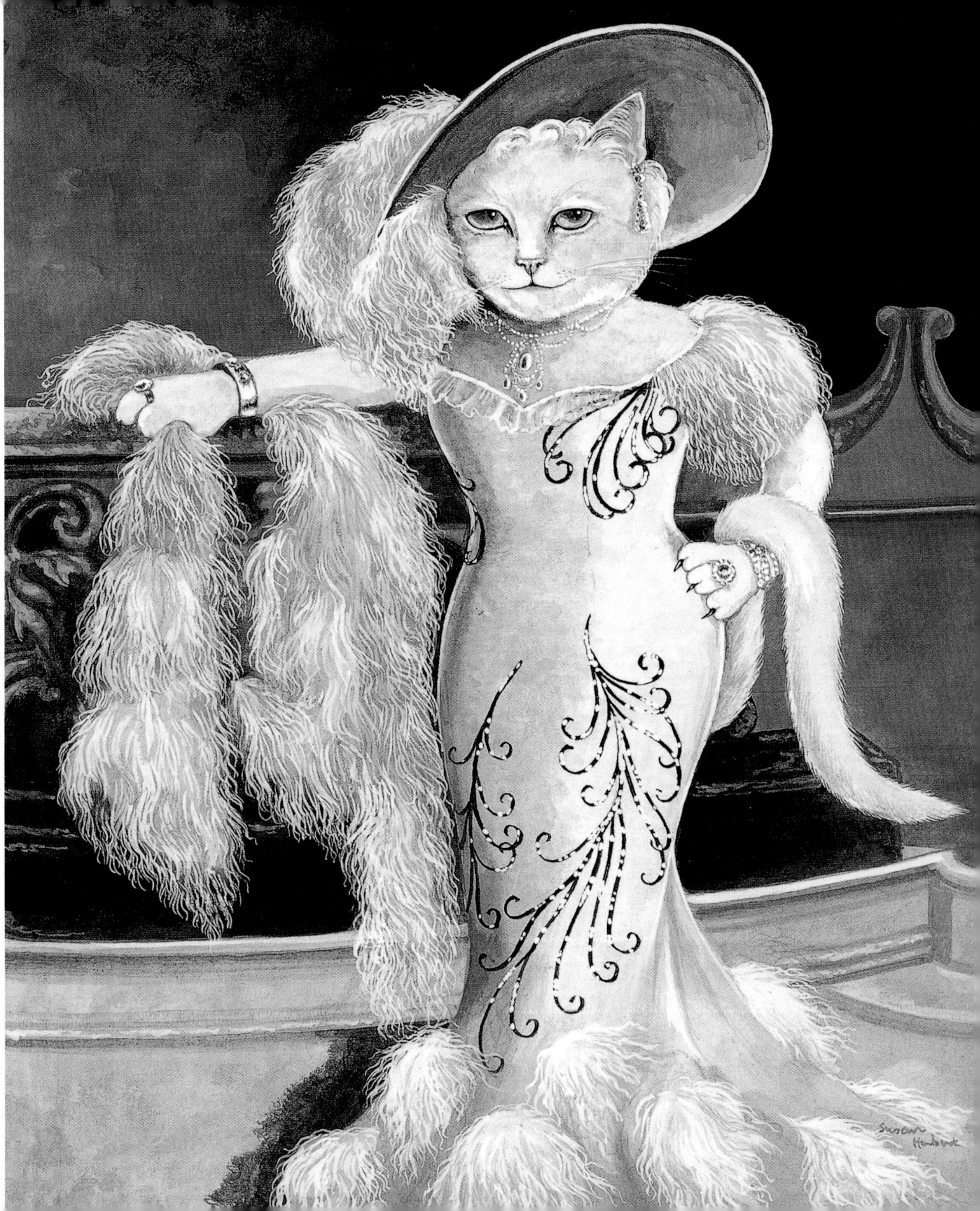
Susan Herbert

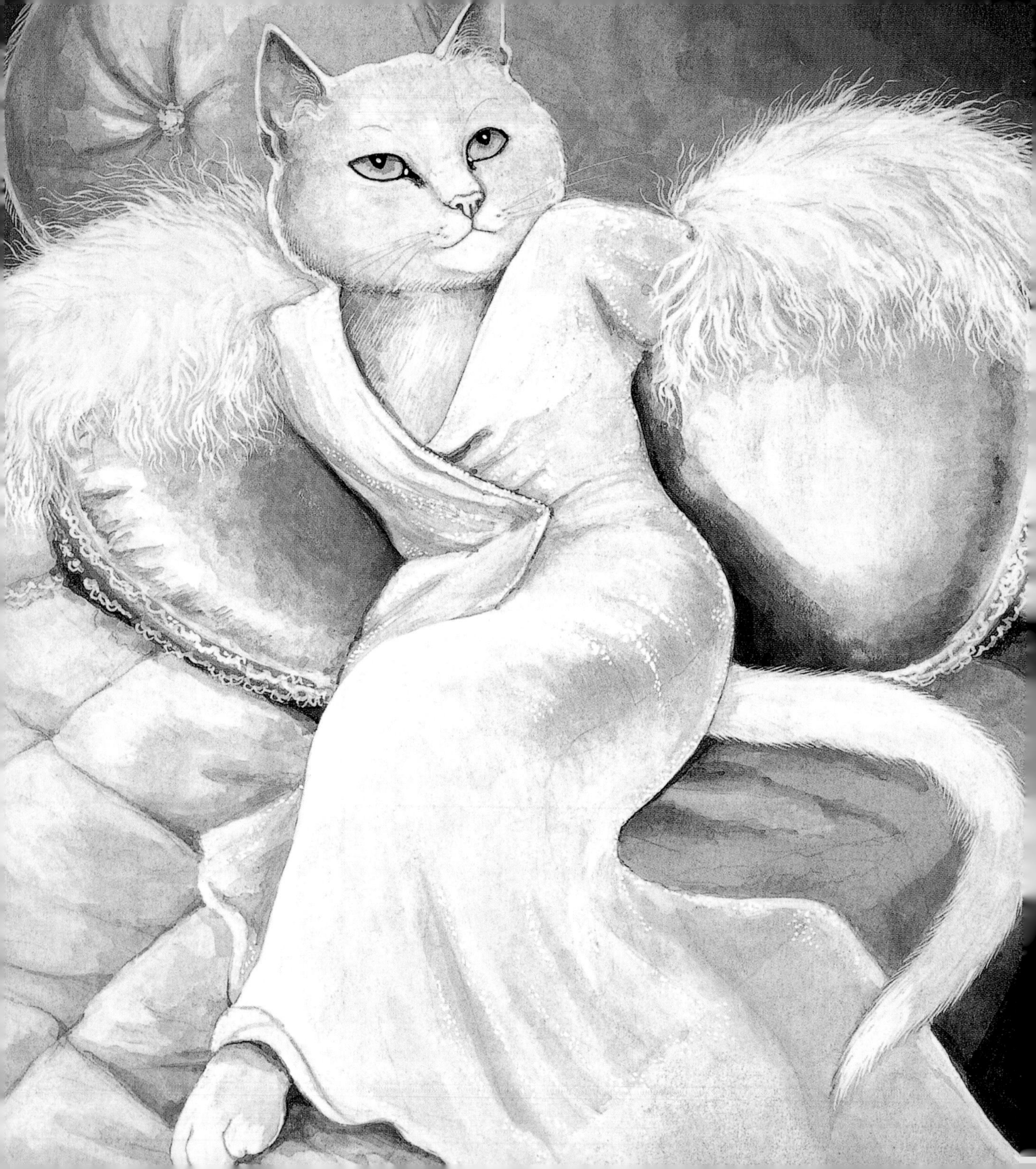

Jean Harlow in

DINNER AT EIGHT (1933)

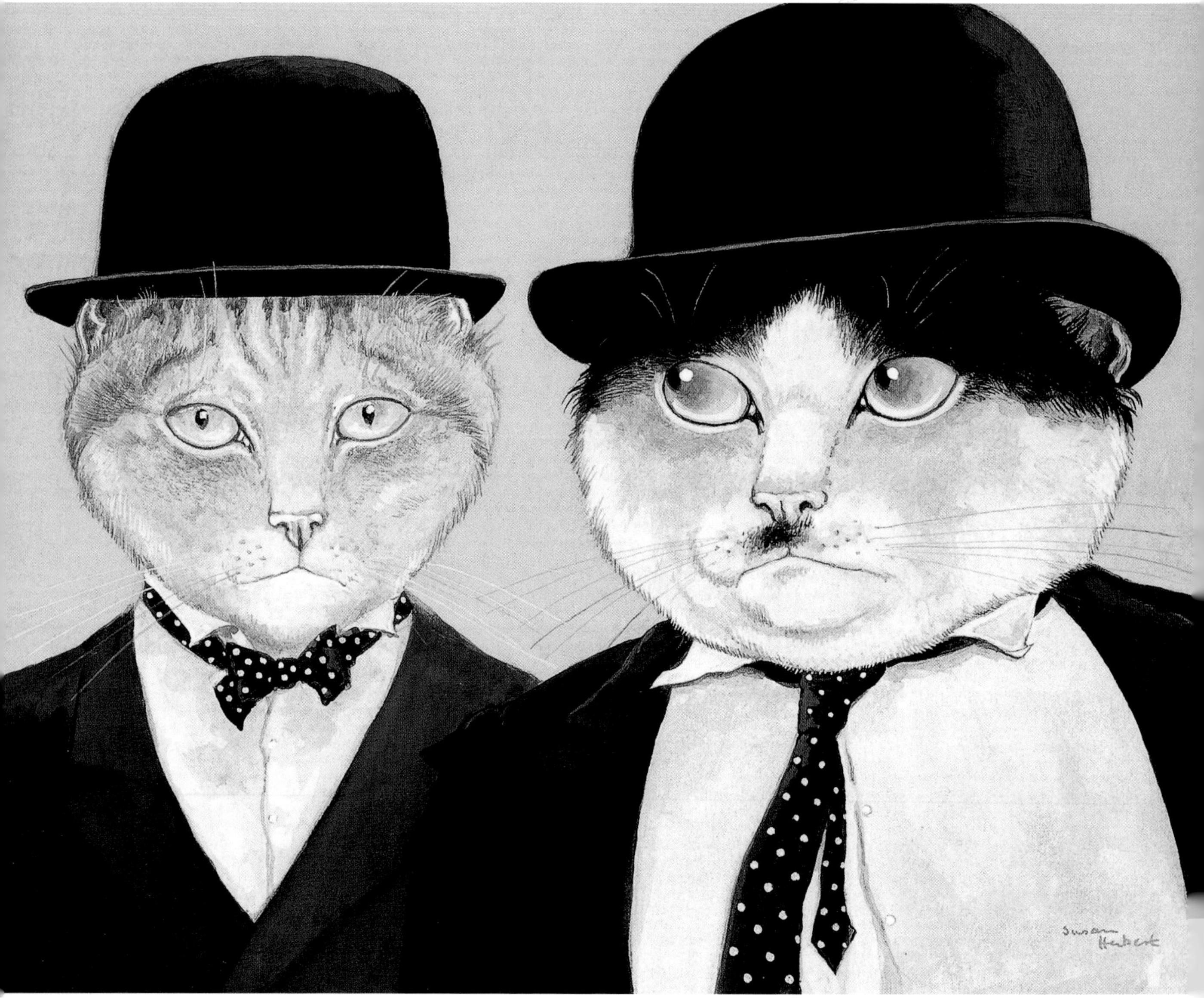

LAUREL AND HARDY

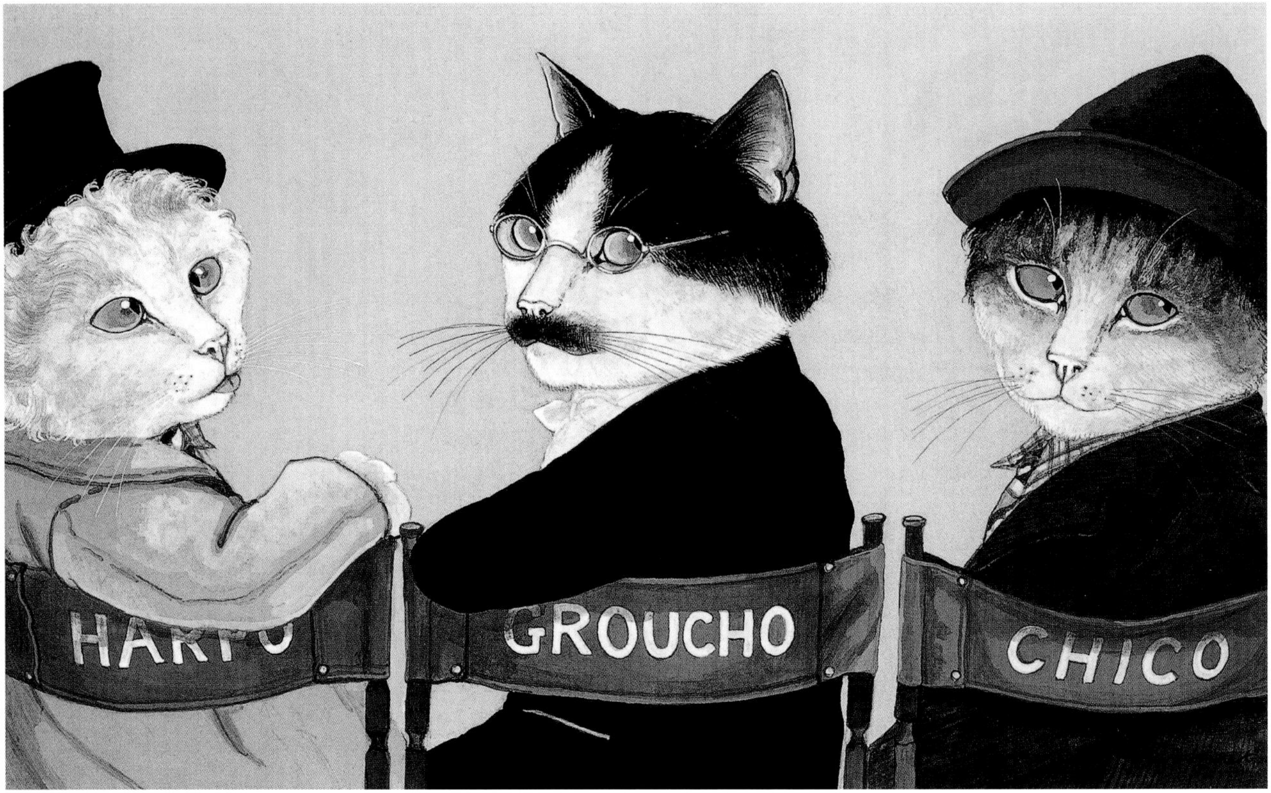

Above *The Marx Brothers in* A NIGHT AT THE OPERA (1935)

Opposite *Charlie Chaplin and Jackie Gleason in* THE KID (1921)

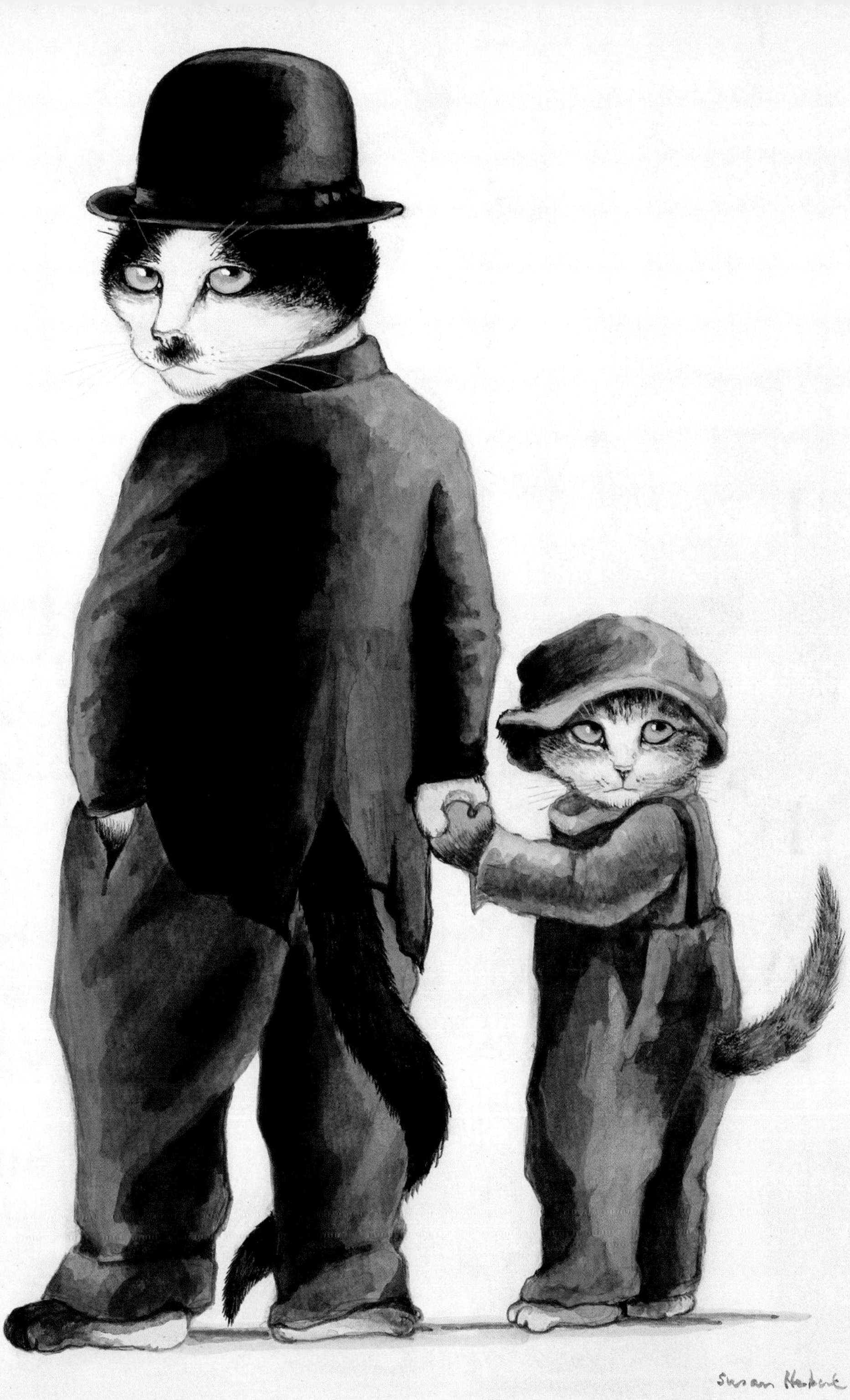

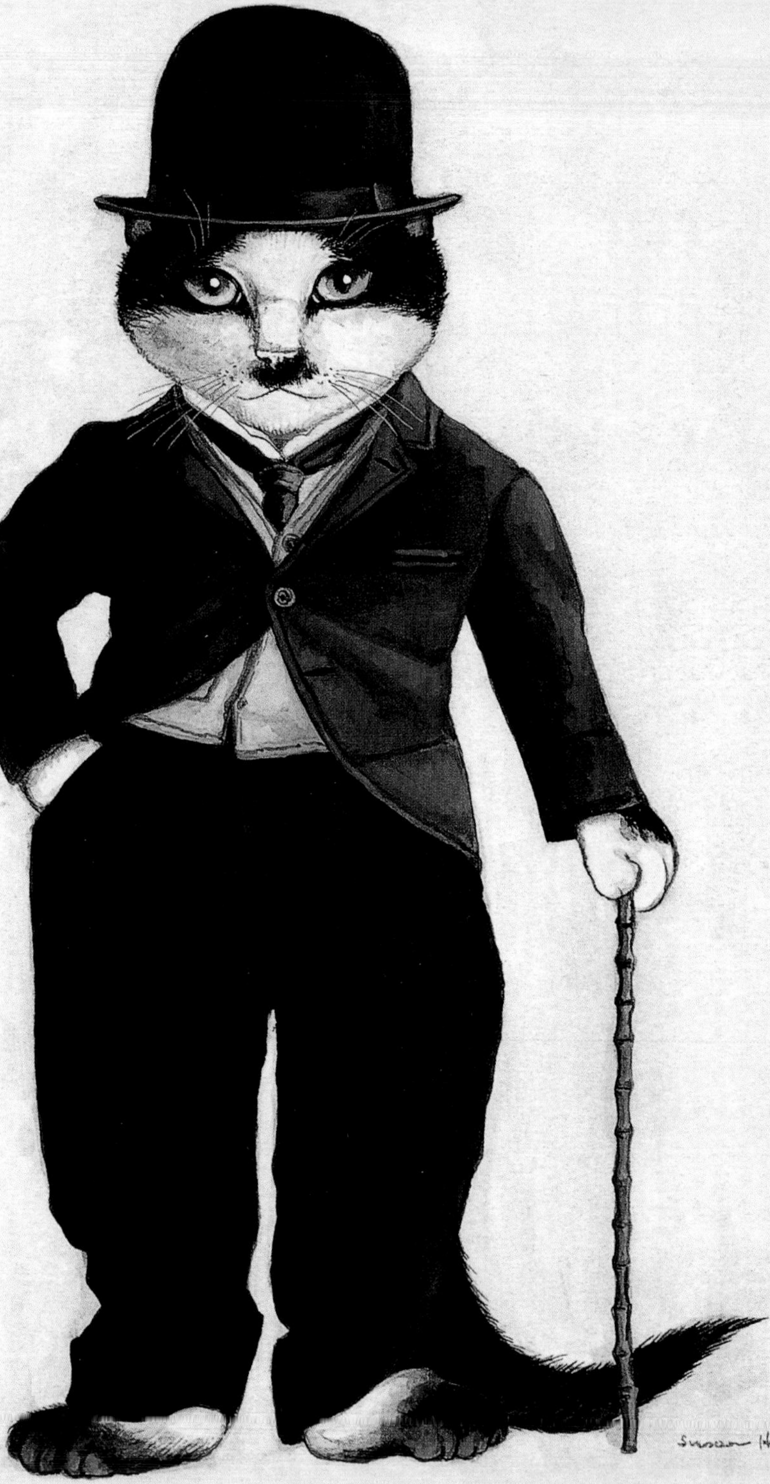
Susan Herbert

Charlie Chaplin in

THE TRAMP (1915)

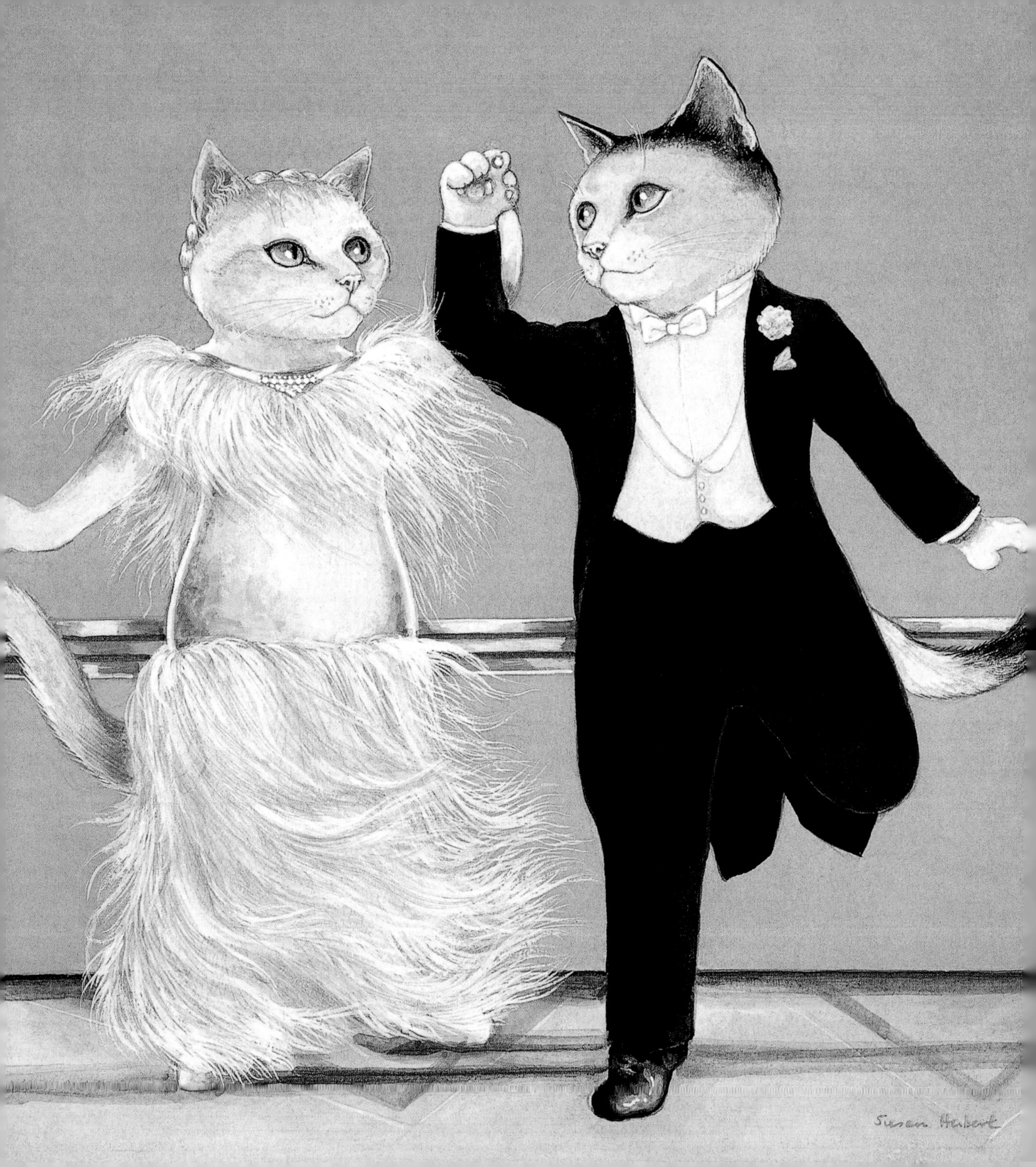
Susan Herbert

Fred Astaire and Ginger Rogers in

TOP HAT (1935)

A Busby Berkeley dance sequence from
GOLD DIGGERS OF 1935 (1935)

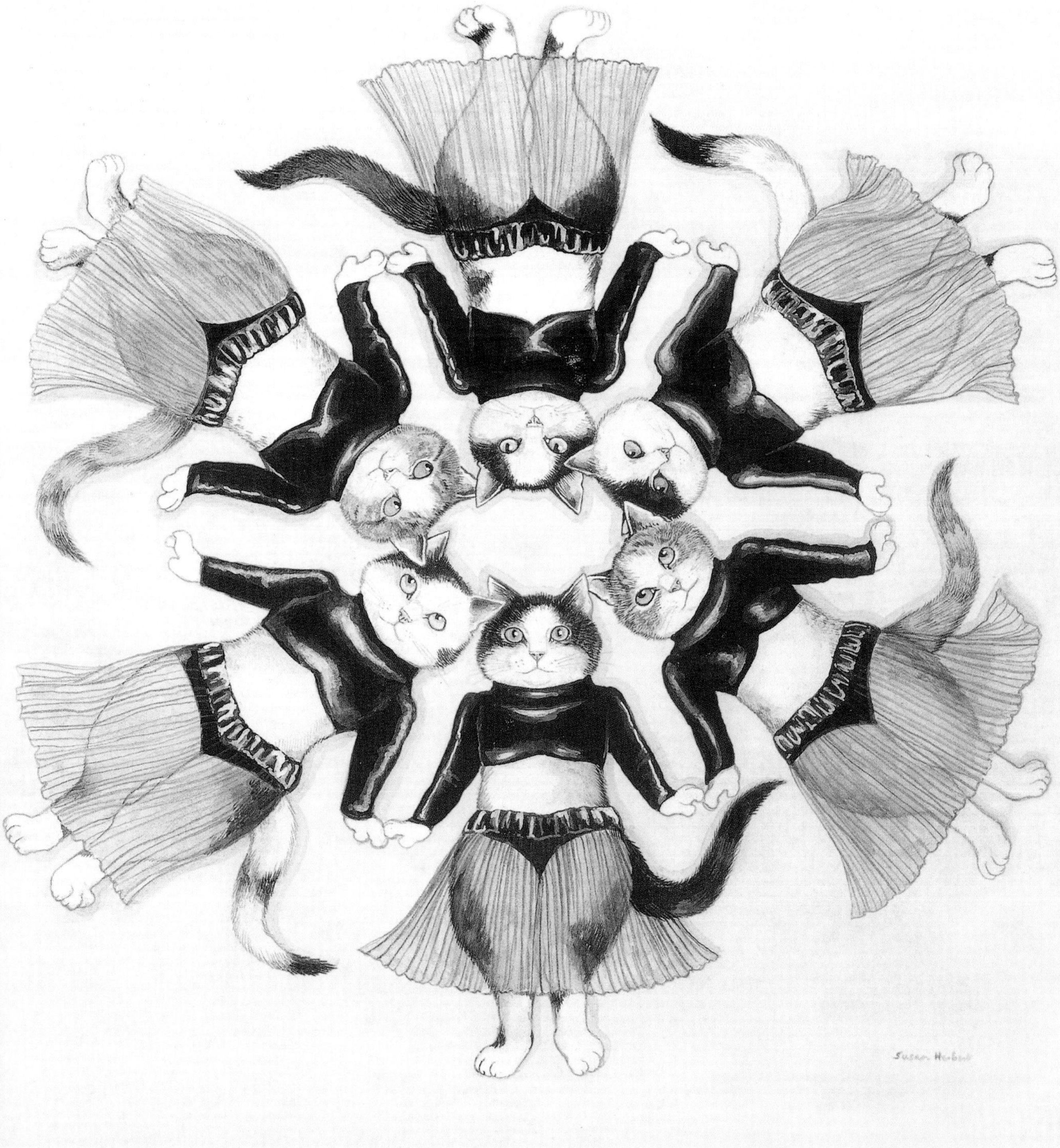
Susan Herbert

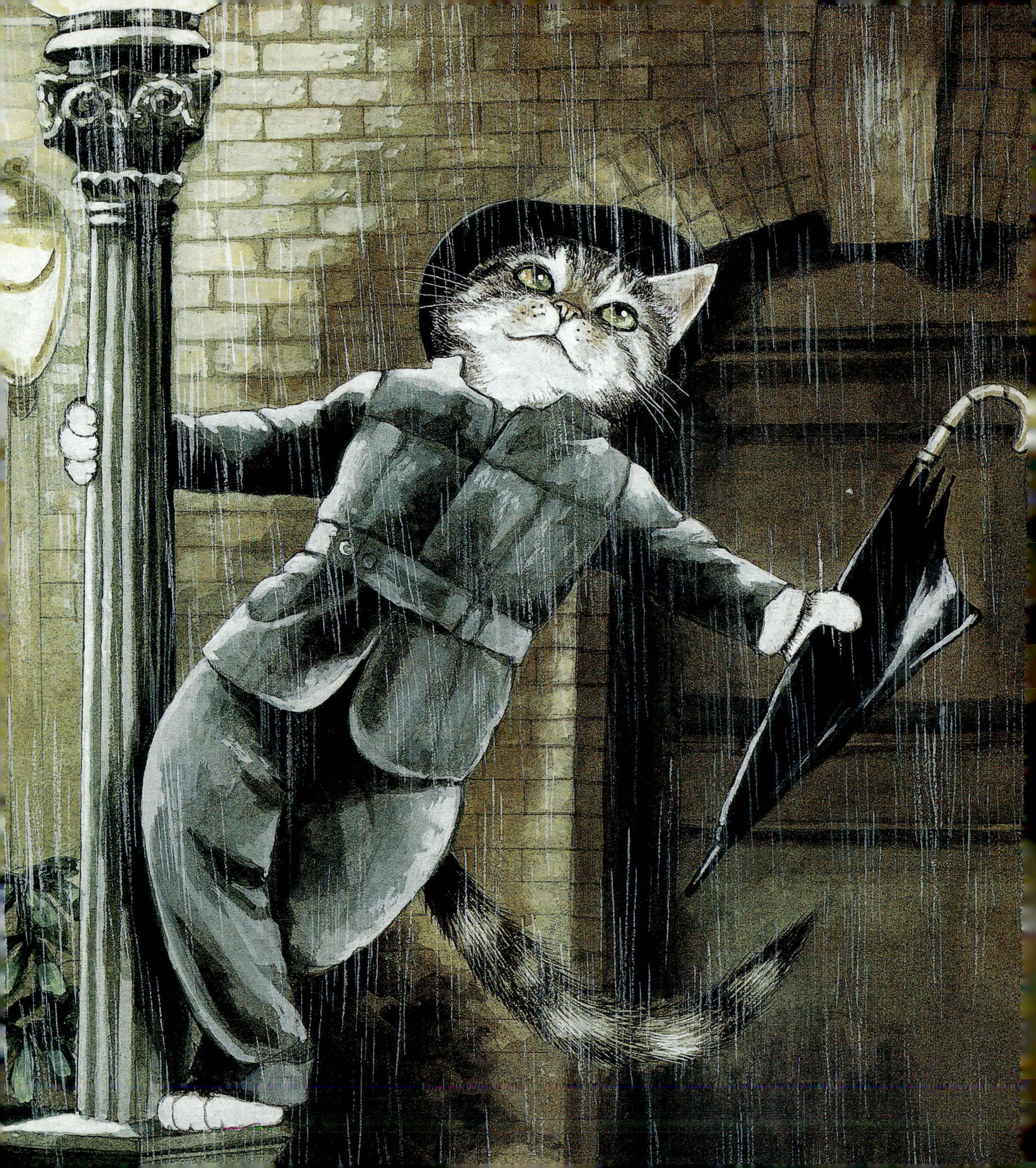

Gene Kelly in

SINGIN' IN THE RAIN (1952)

Deborah Kerr and Yul Brynner in

THE KING AND I (1956)

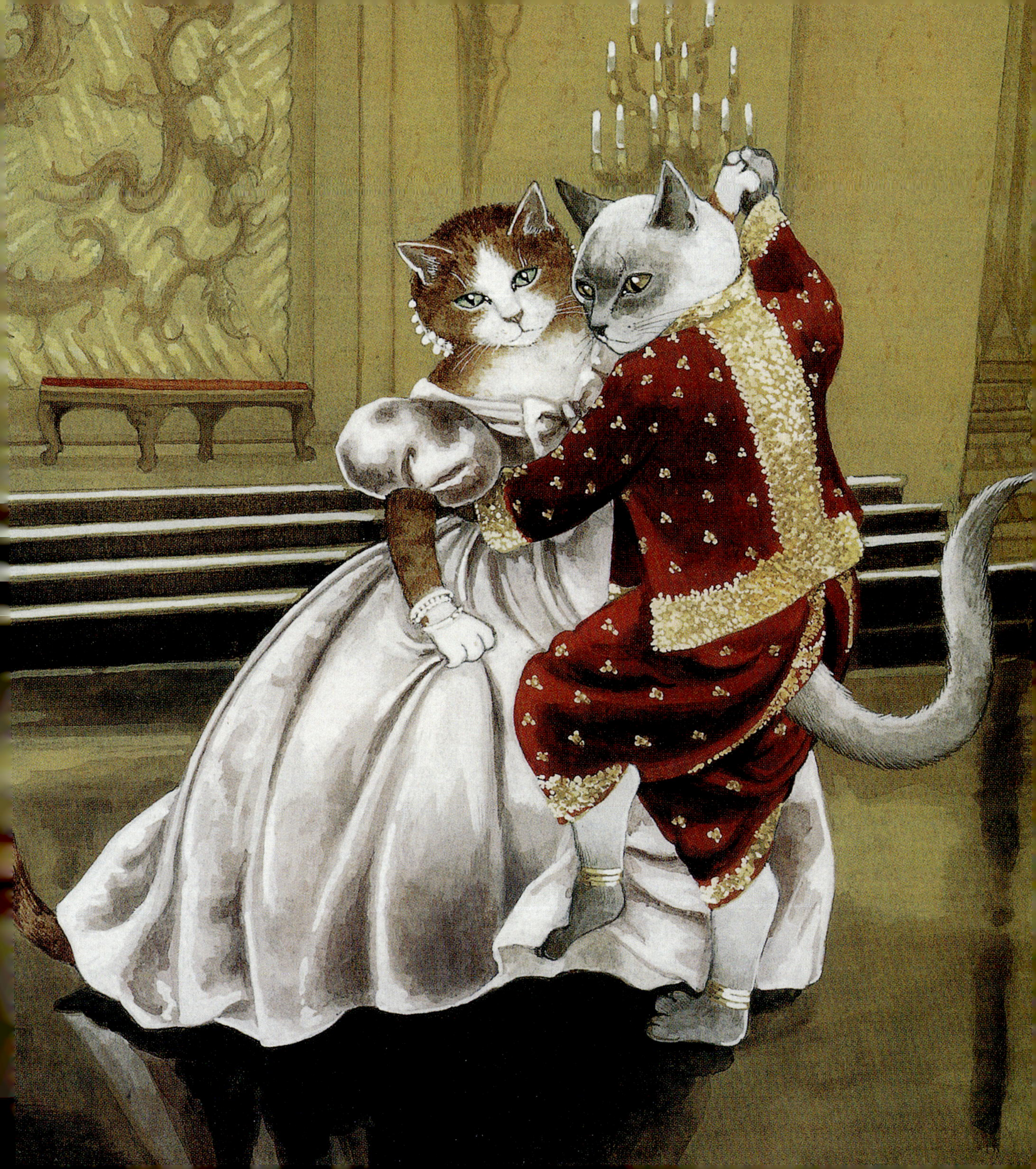

THE WIZARD OF OZ (1939)

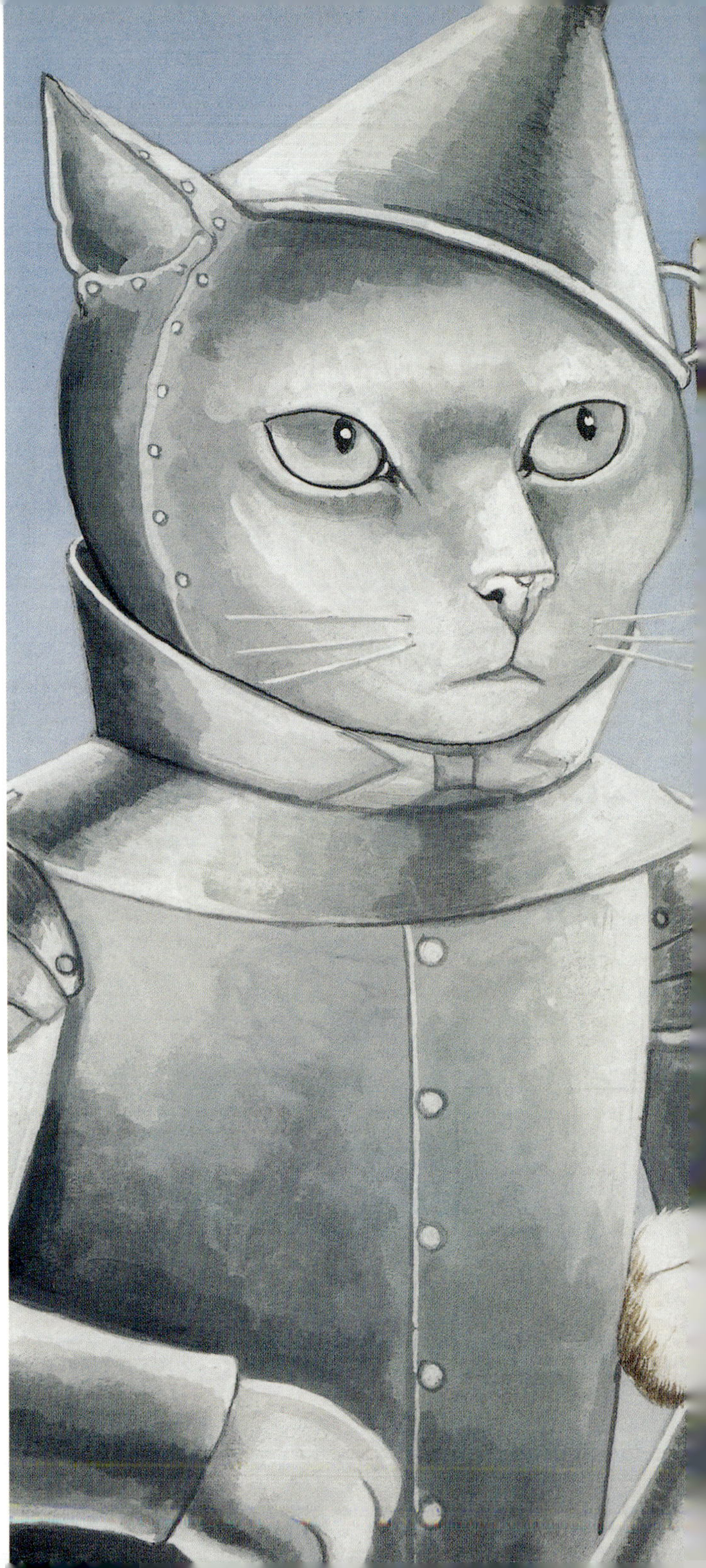

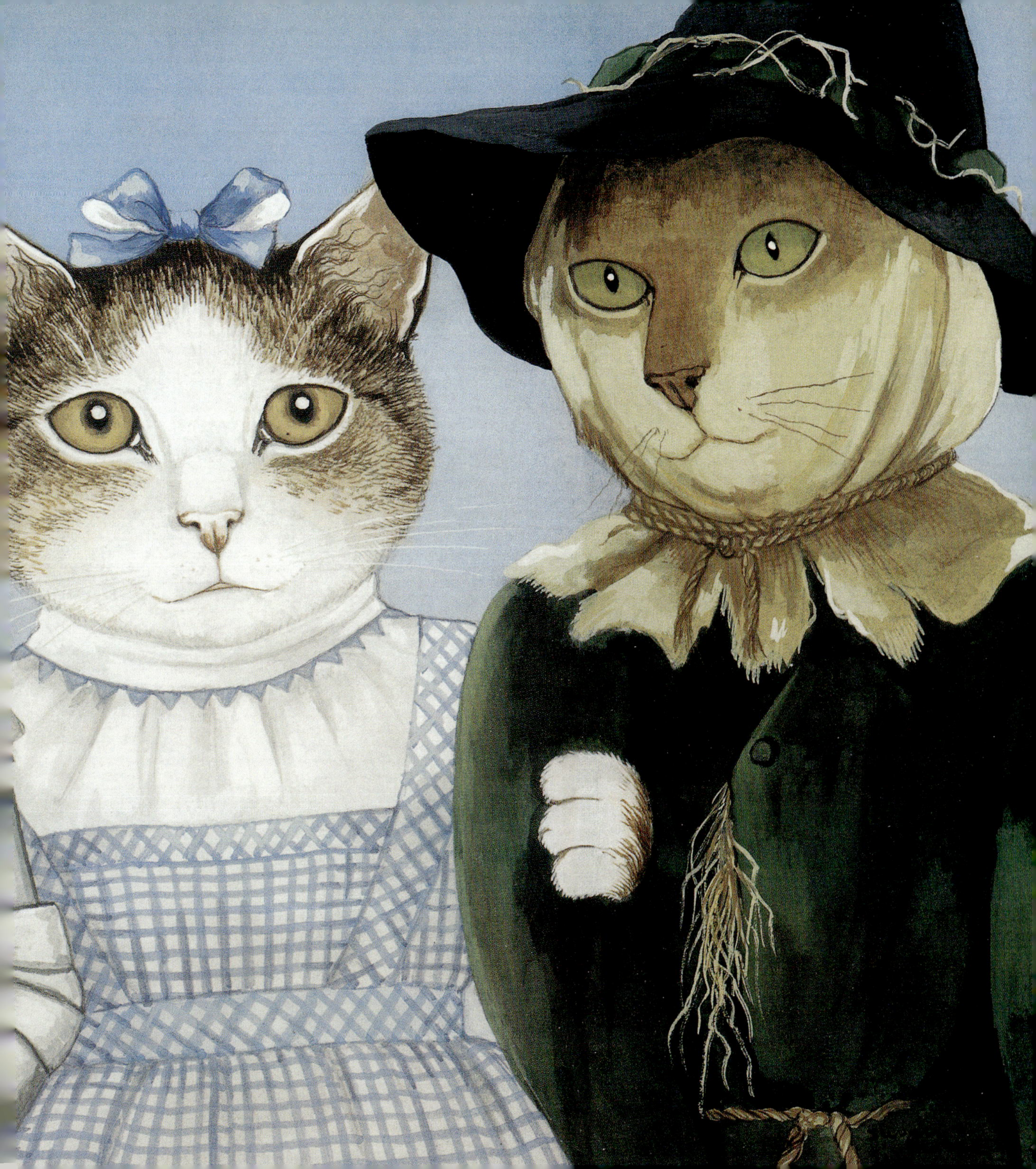

Ronald Colman in

A TALE OF TWO CITIES (1935)

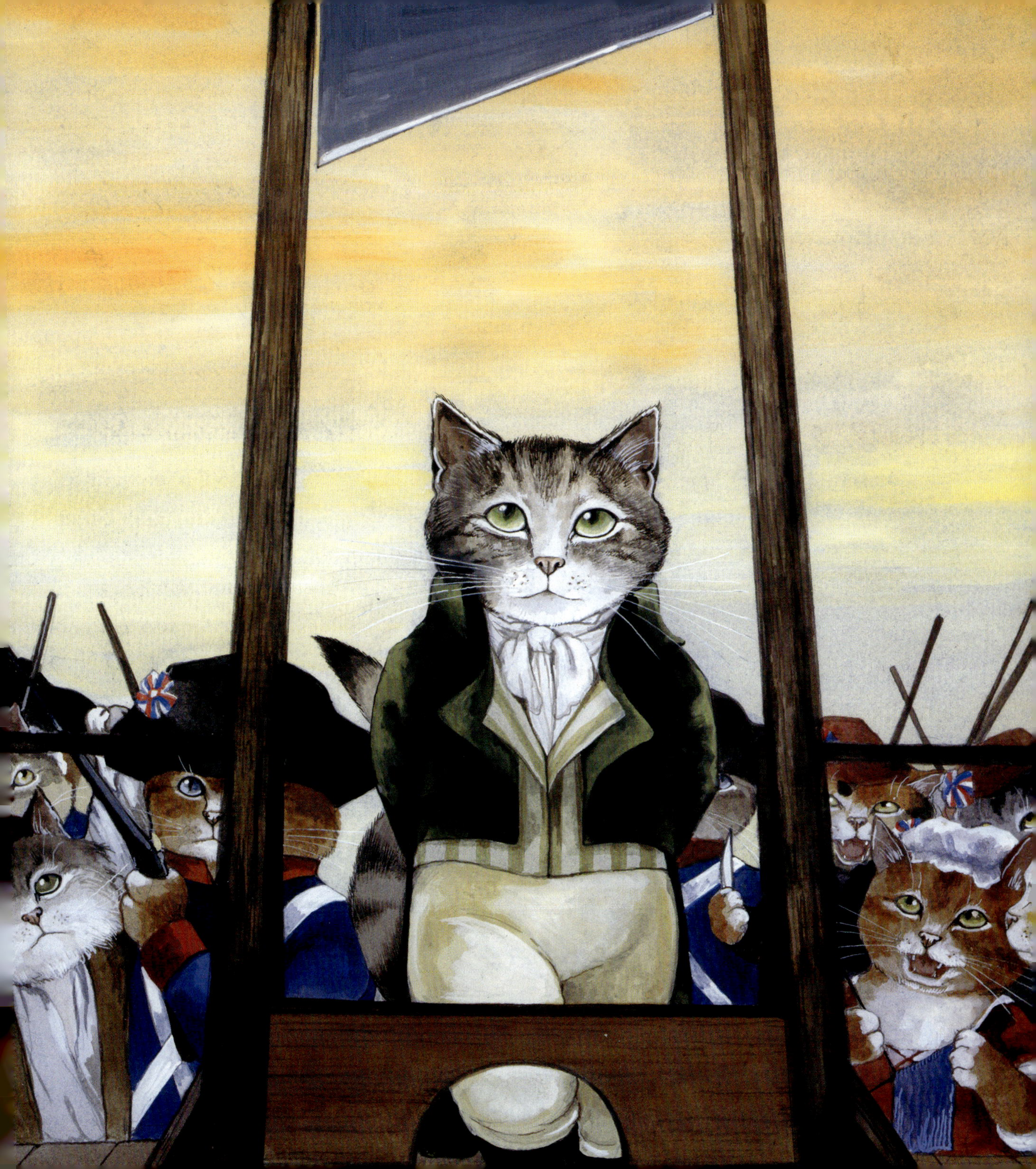

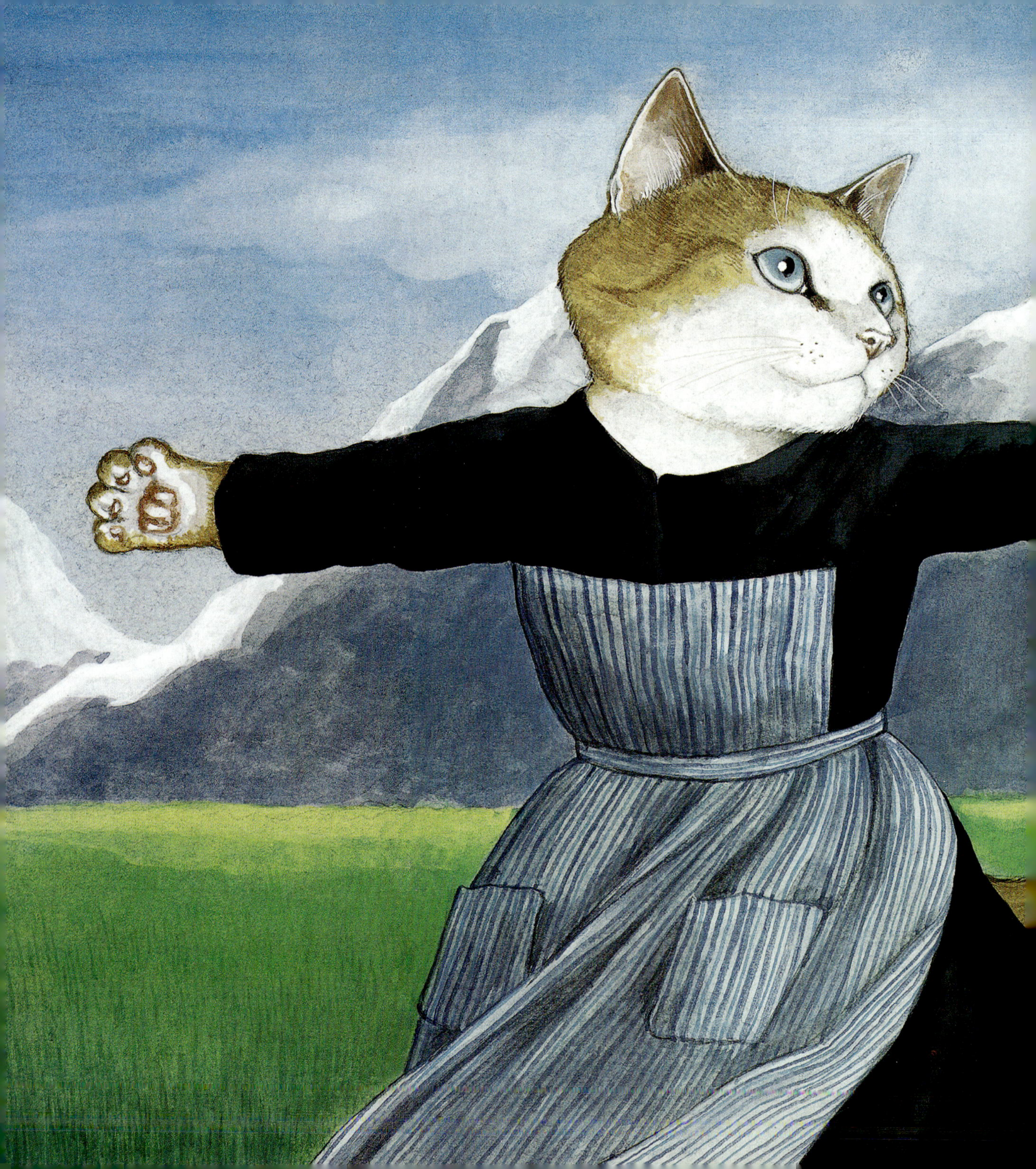

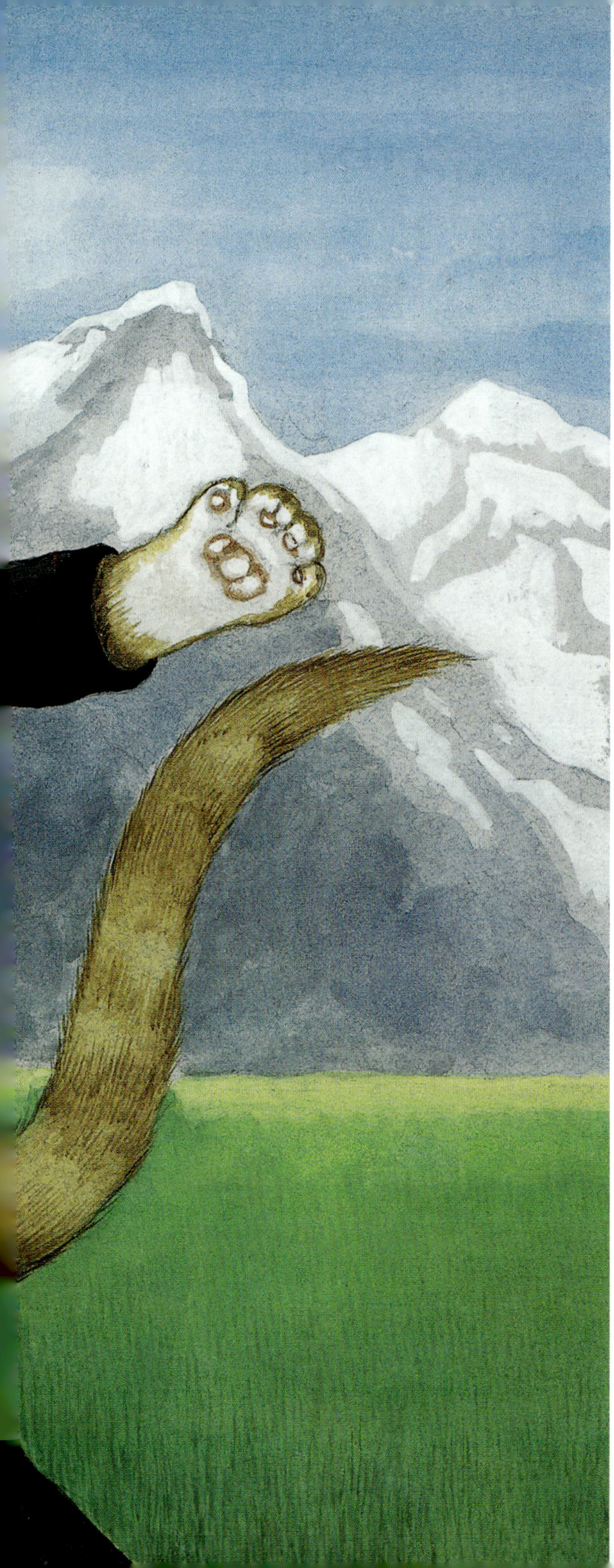

Julie Andrews in

THE SOUND OF MUSIC (1965)

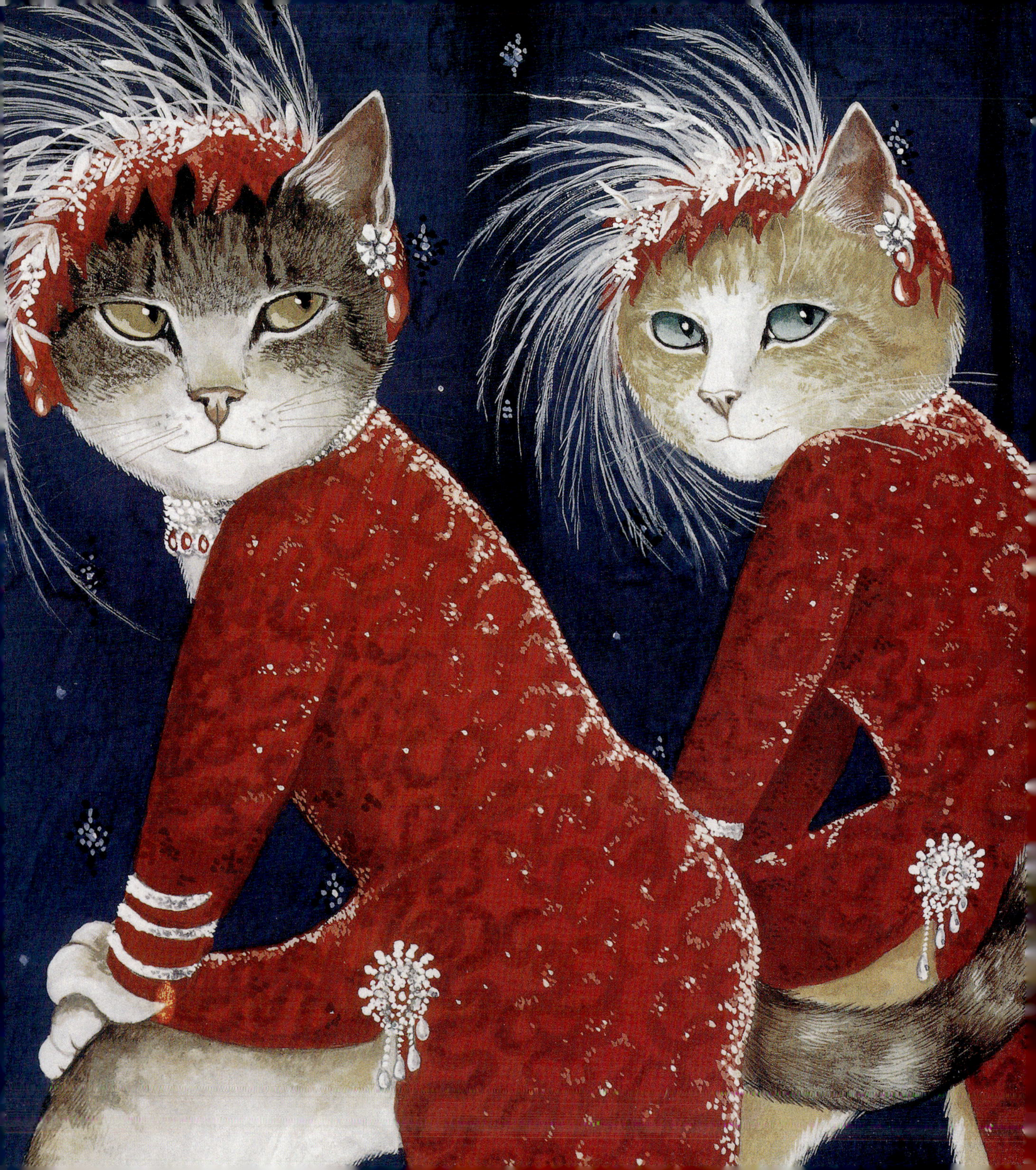

Jane Russell and Marilyn Monroe in
GENTLEMEN PREFER BLONDES (1953)

WEST SIDE STORY (1961)

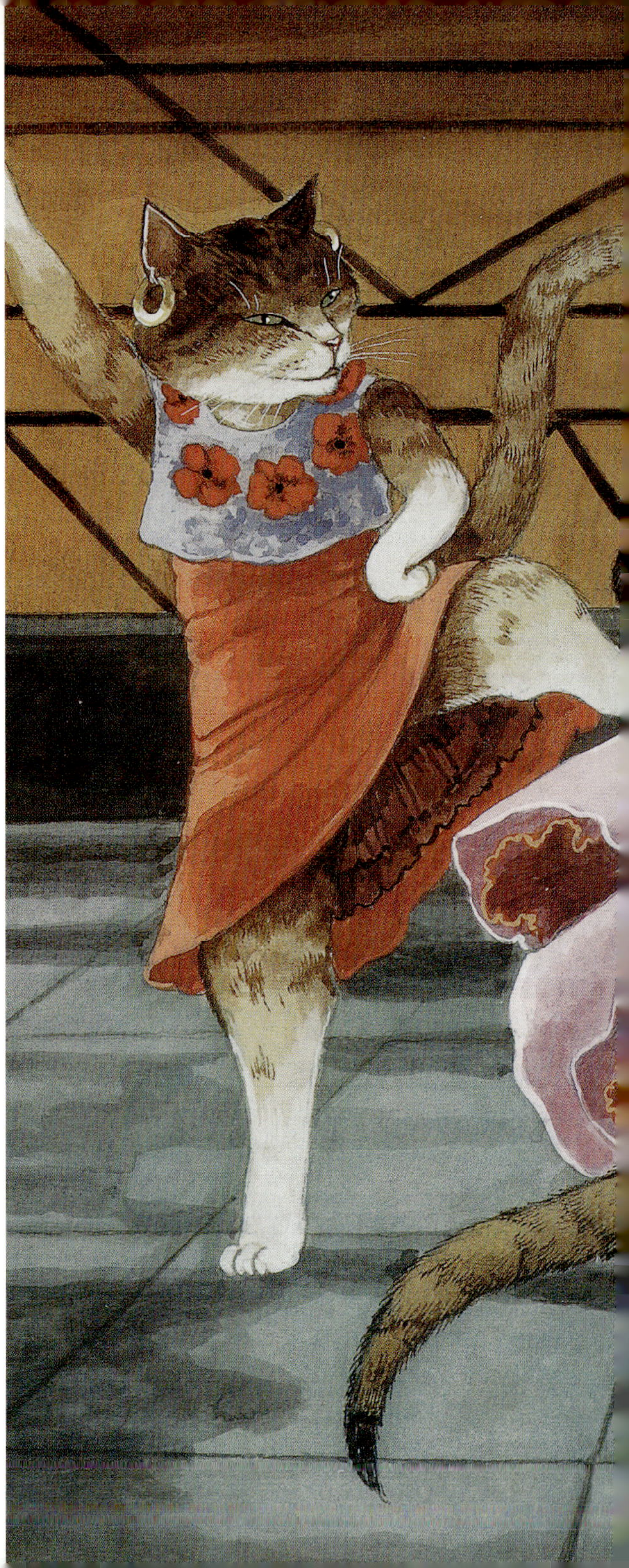

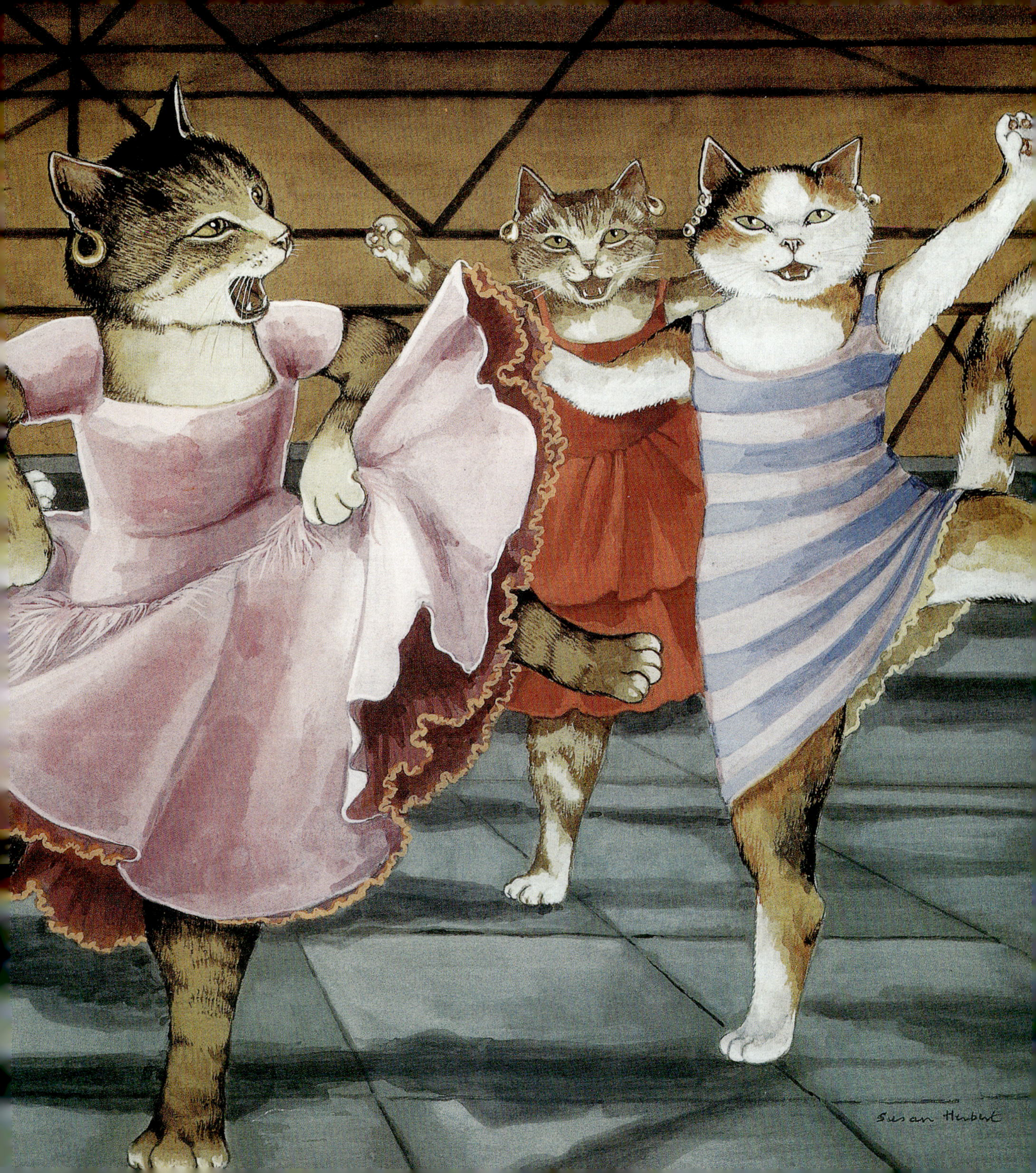
Susan Herbert

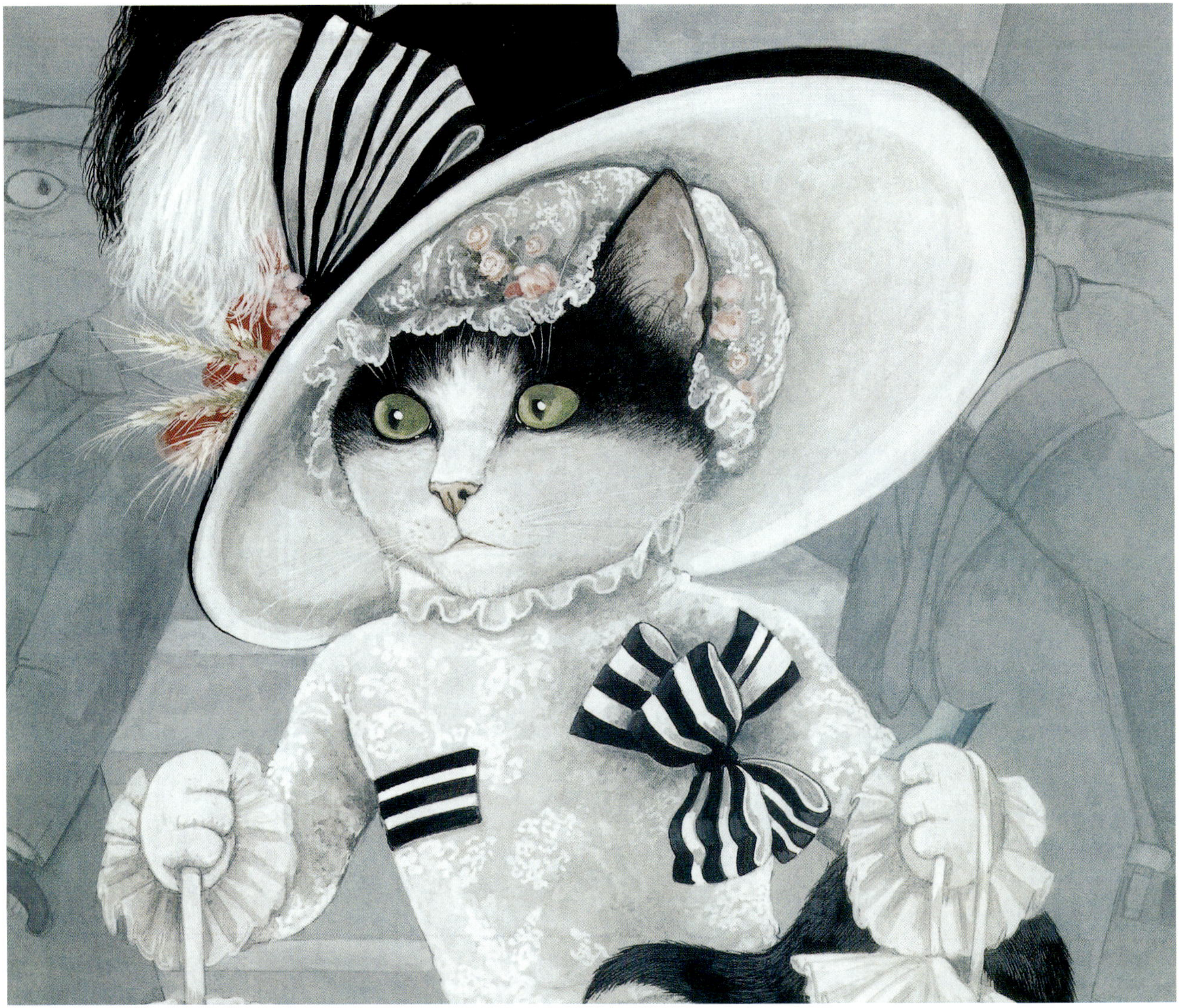

Above and opposite

Audrey Hepburn in MY FAIR LADY (1950)

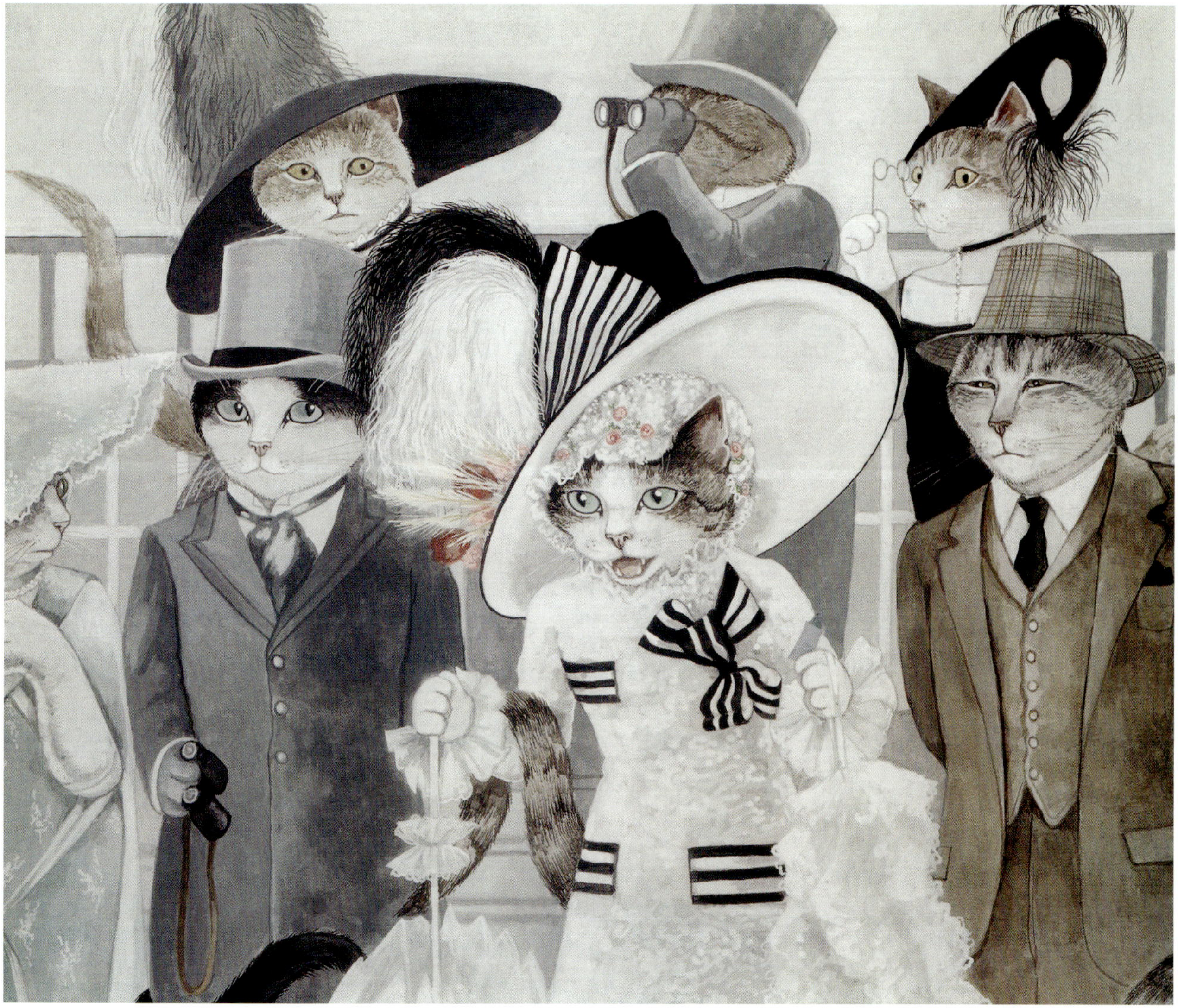

Overleaf, left *Charlton Heston in* THE TEN COMMANDMENTS (1950)

Overleaf, right *Elizabeth Taylor in* CLEOPATRA (1963)

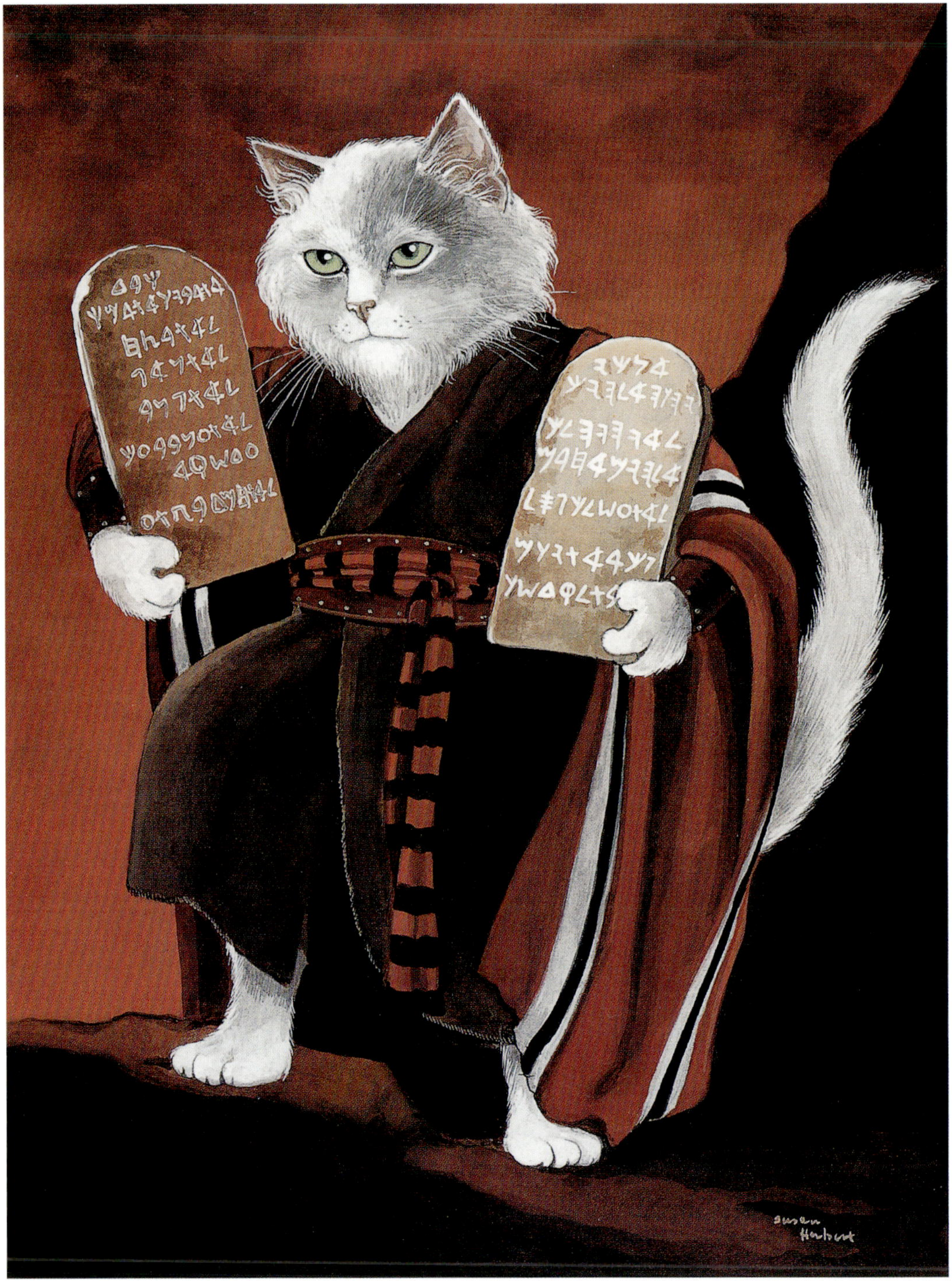
susan Herbert

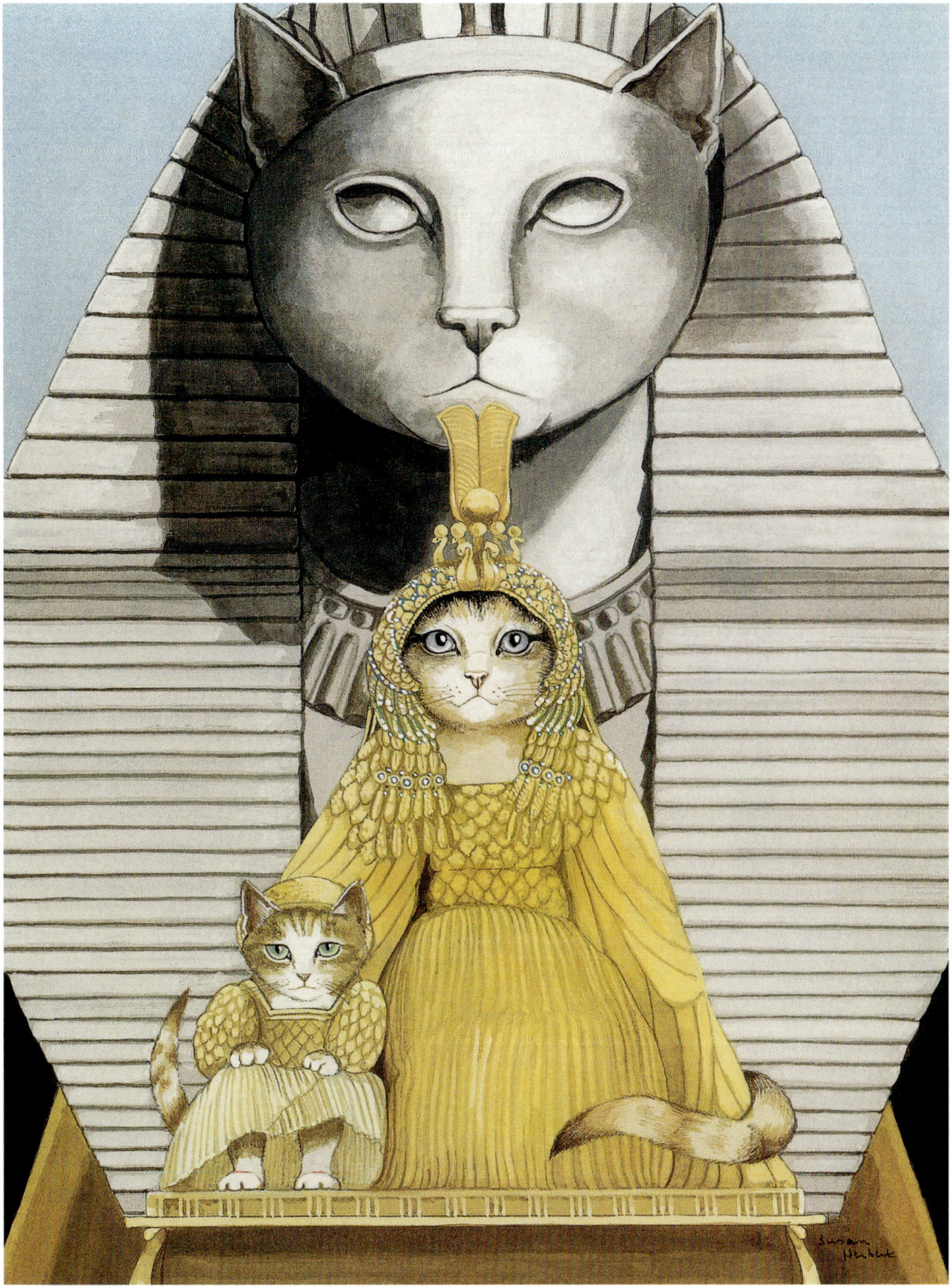

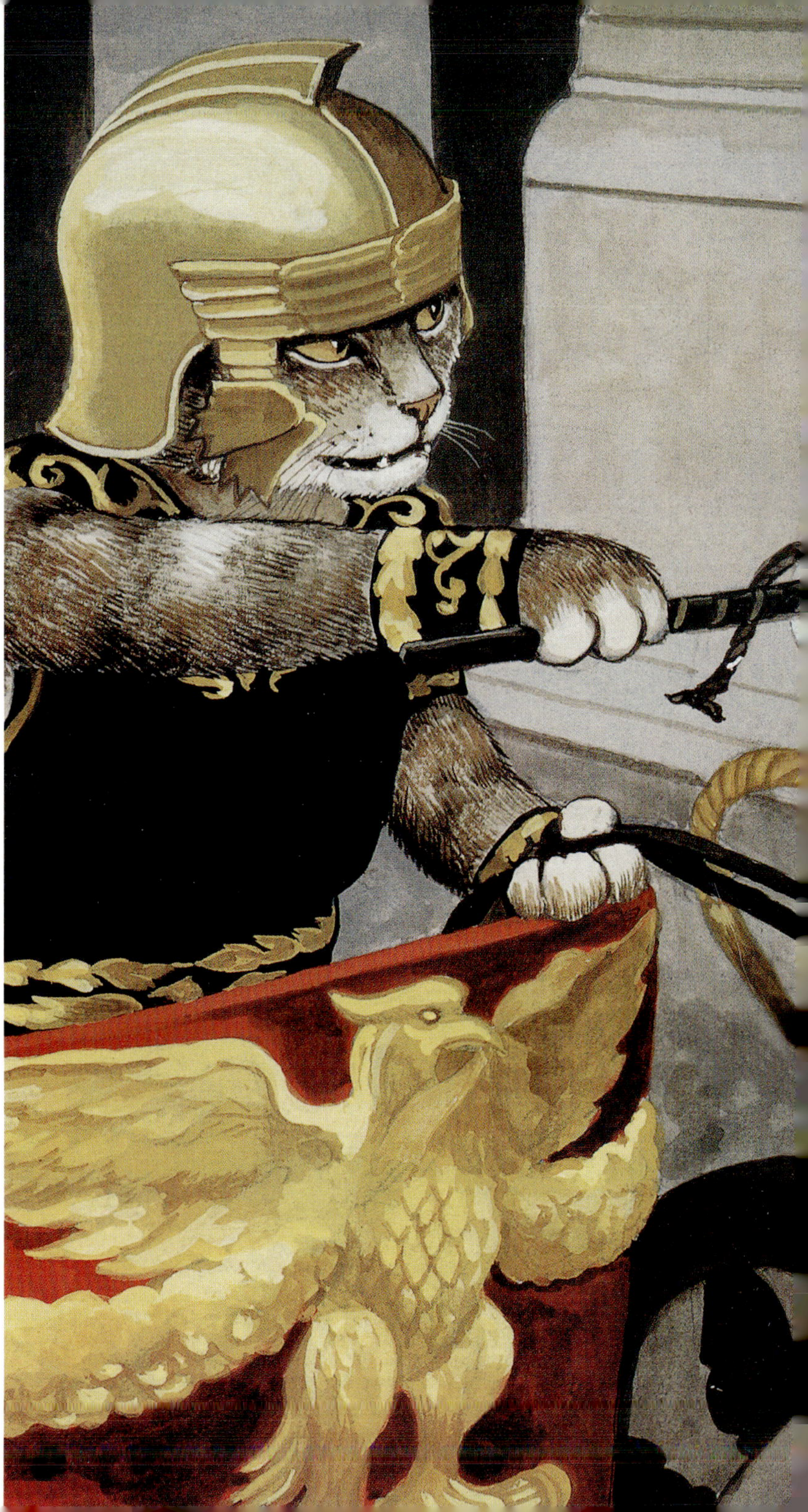

Charlton Heston
in BEN HUR (1959)

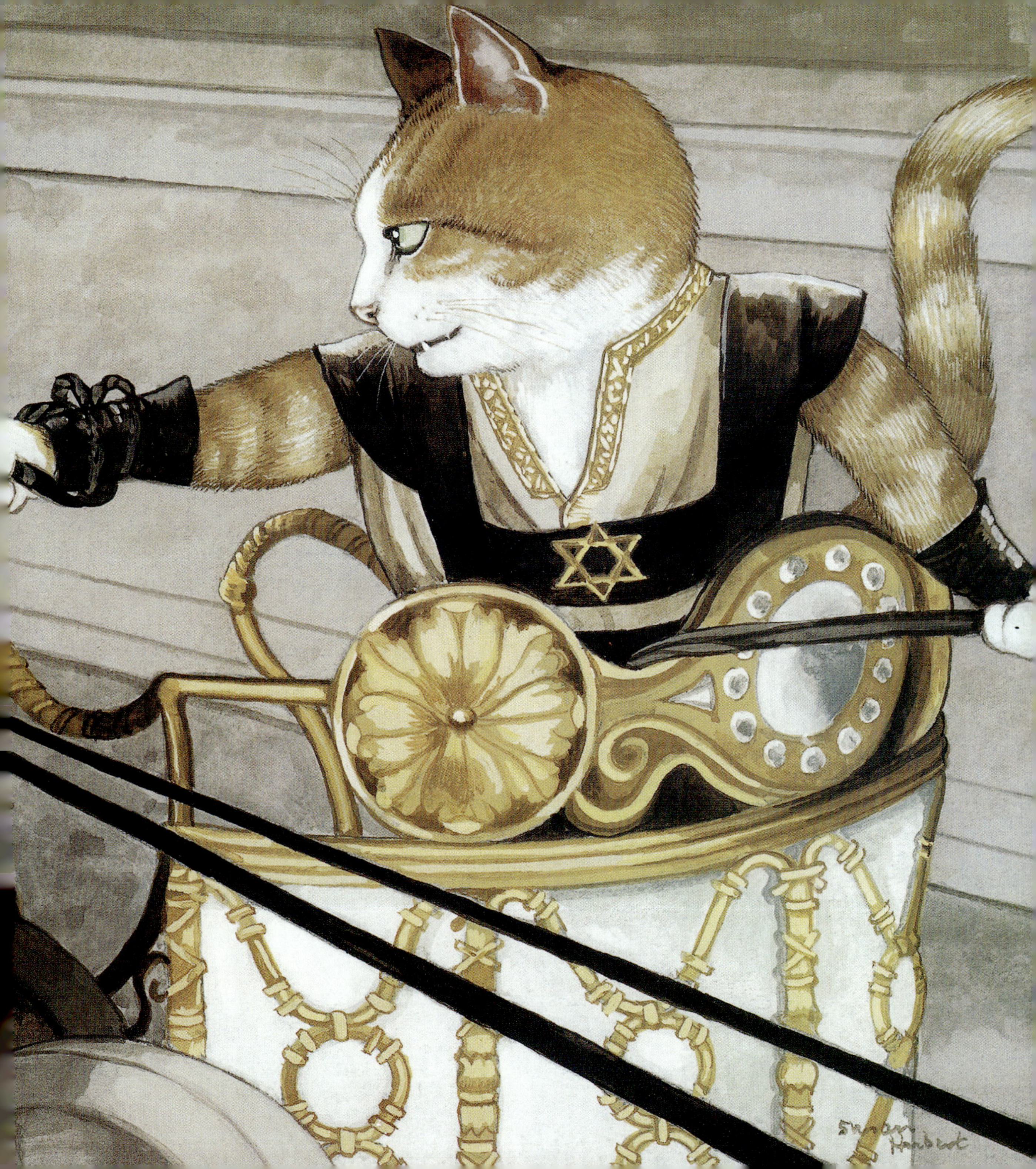

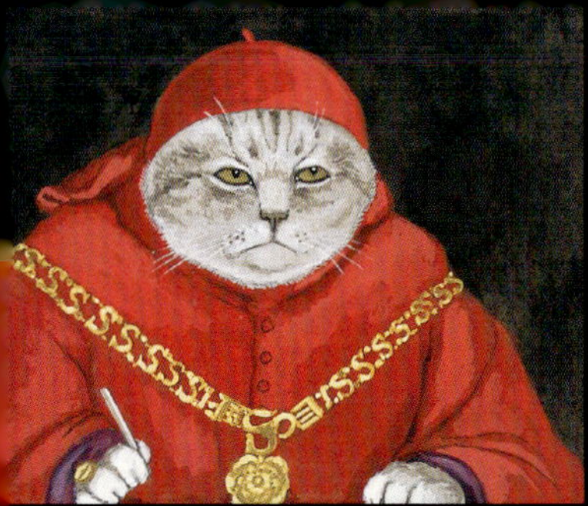
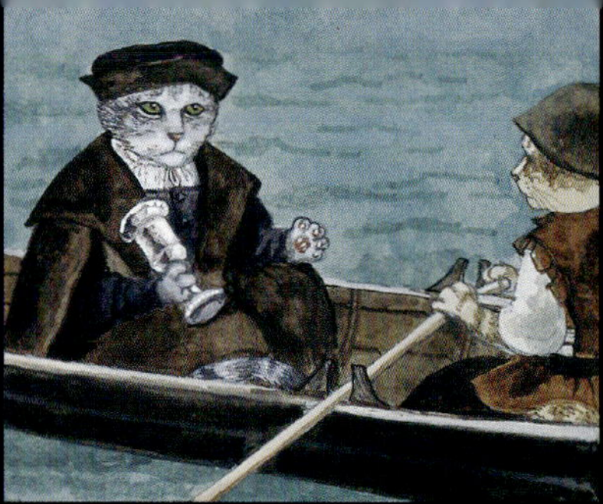
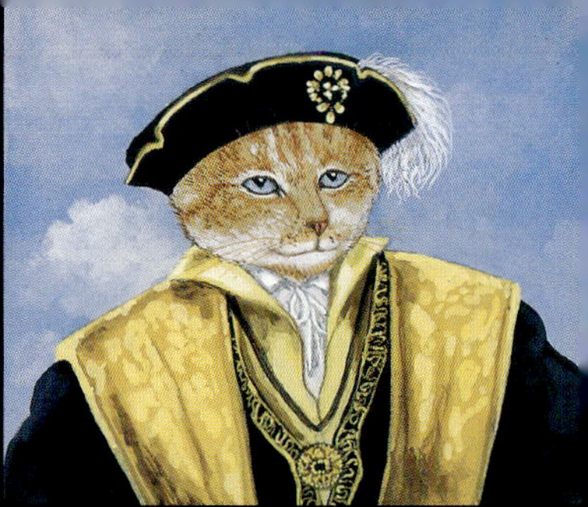
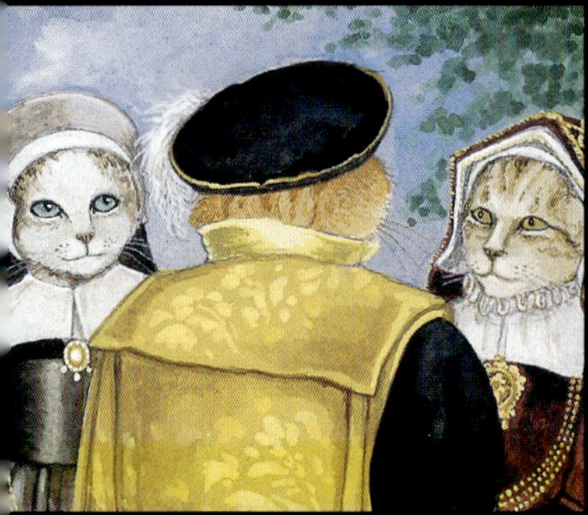
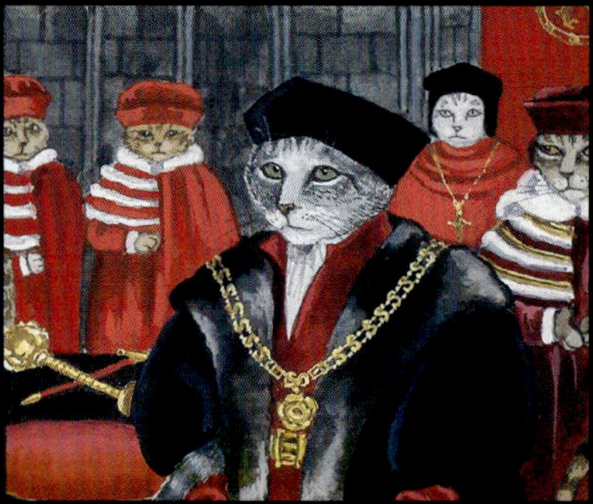
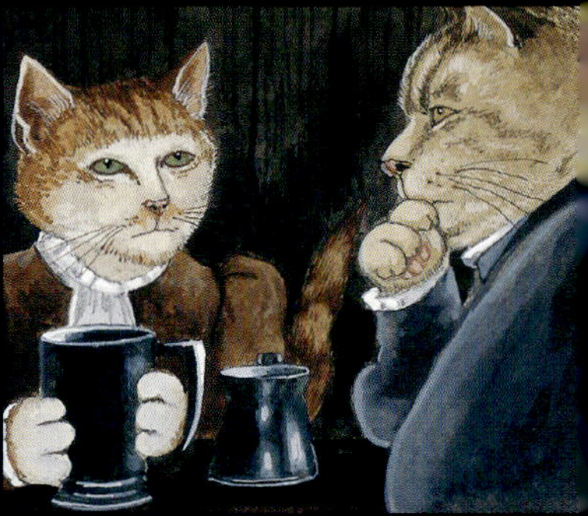
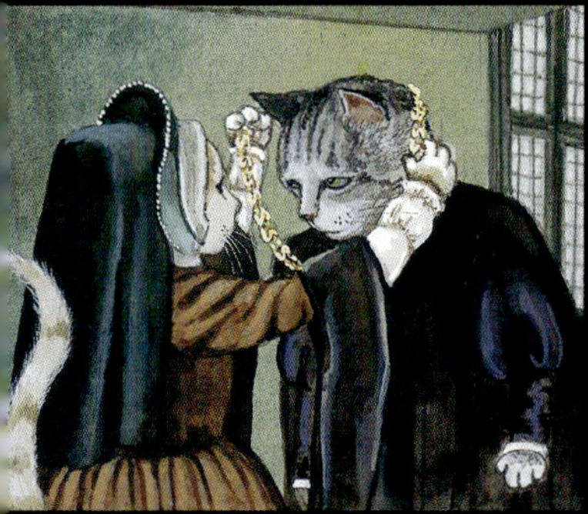
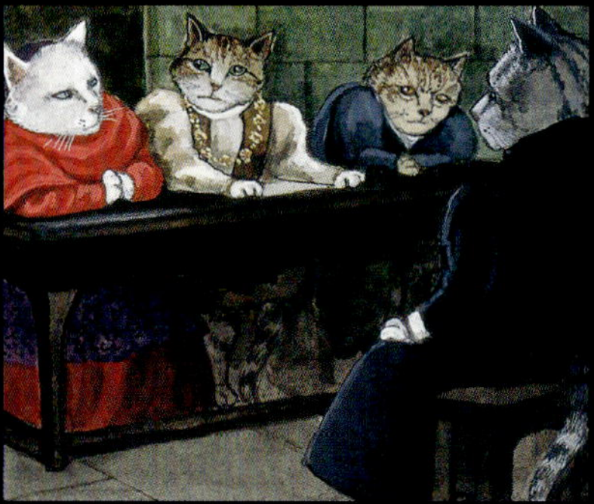
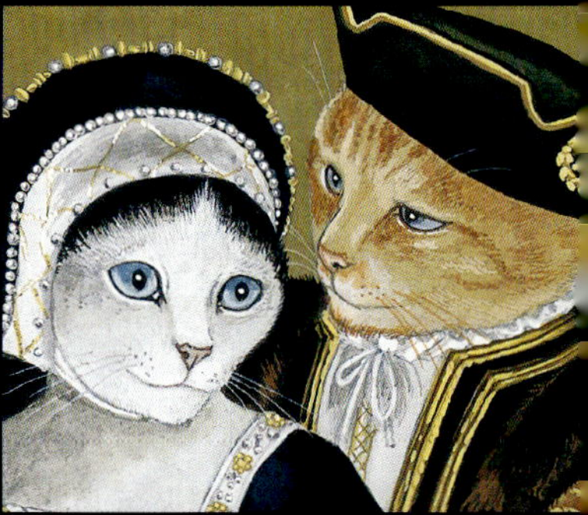
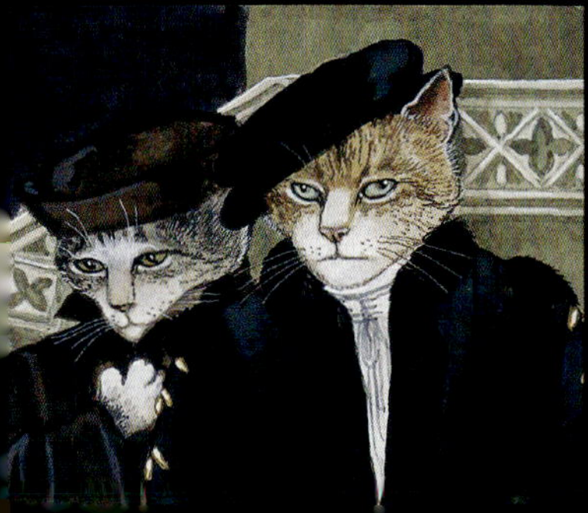
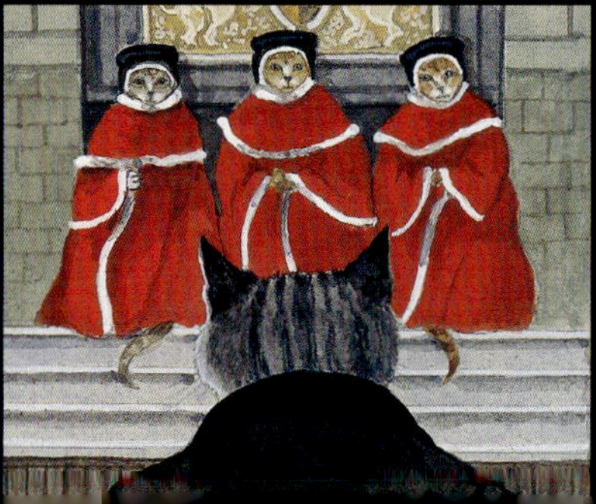
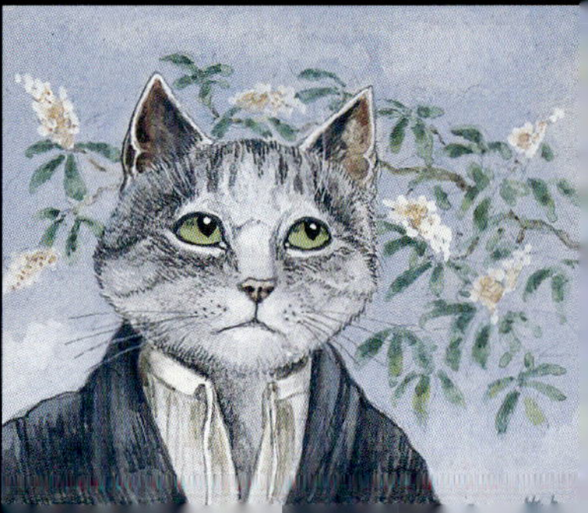

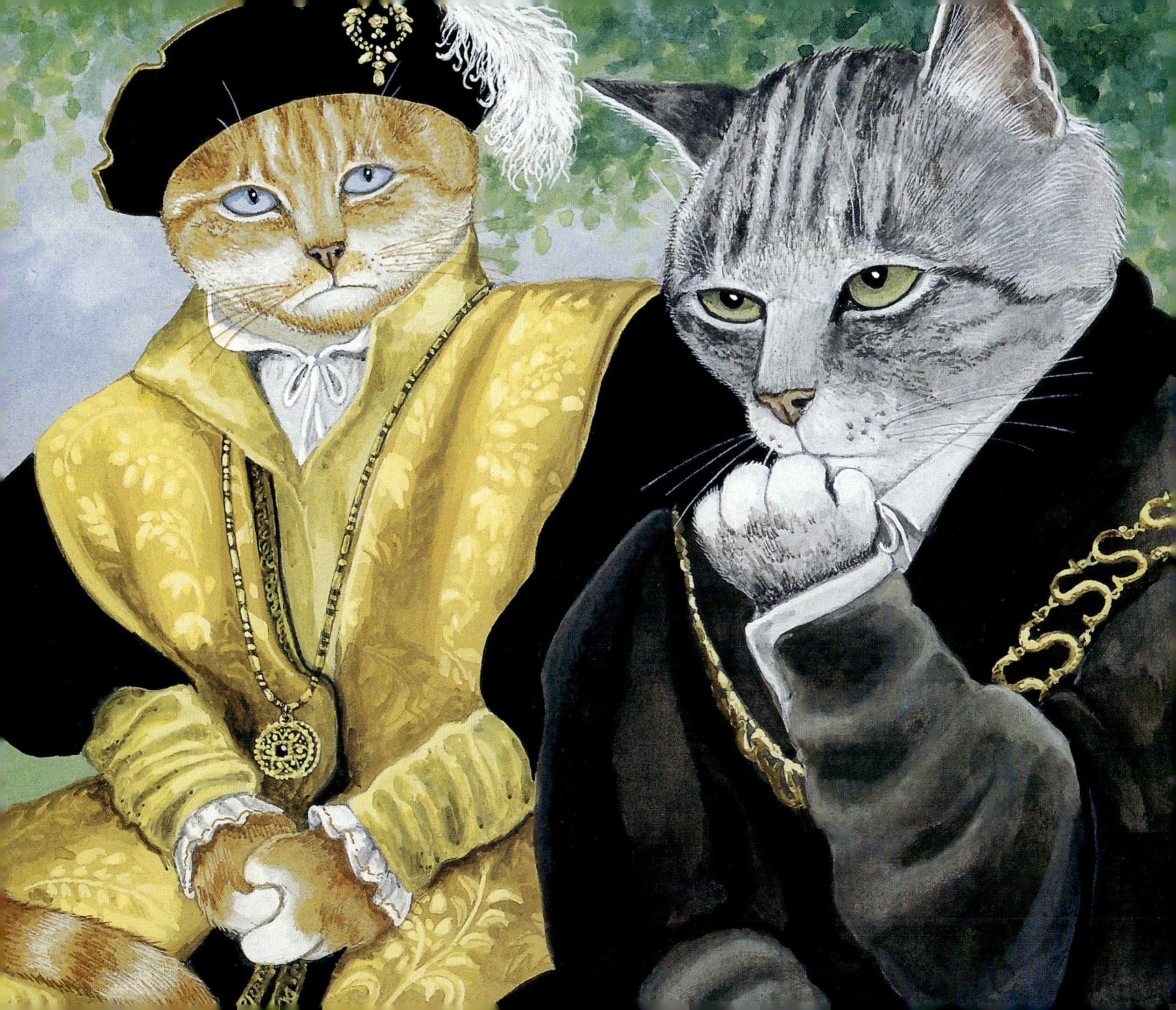

Peter O'Toole in

LAWRENCE OF ARABIA (1962)

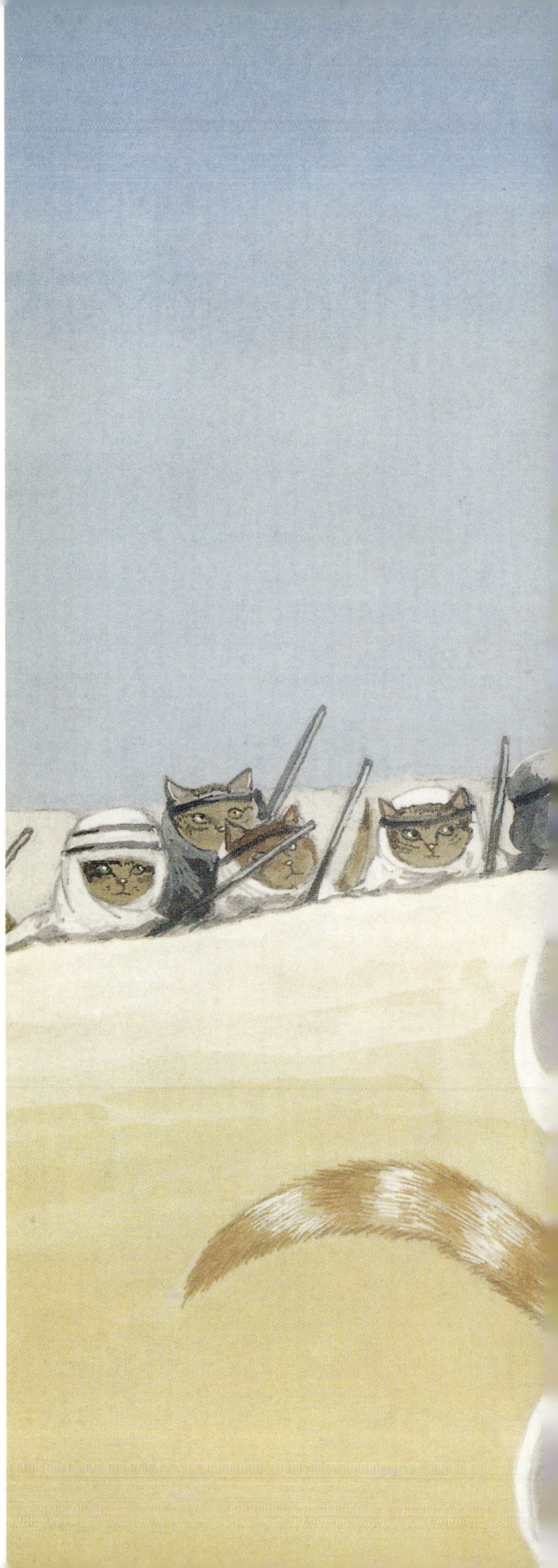

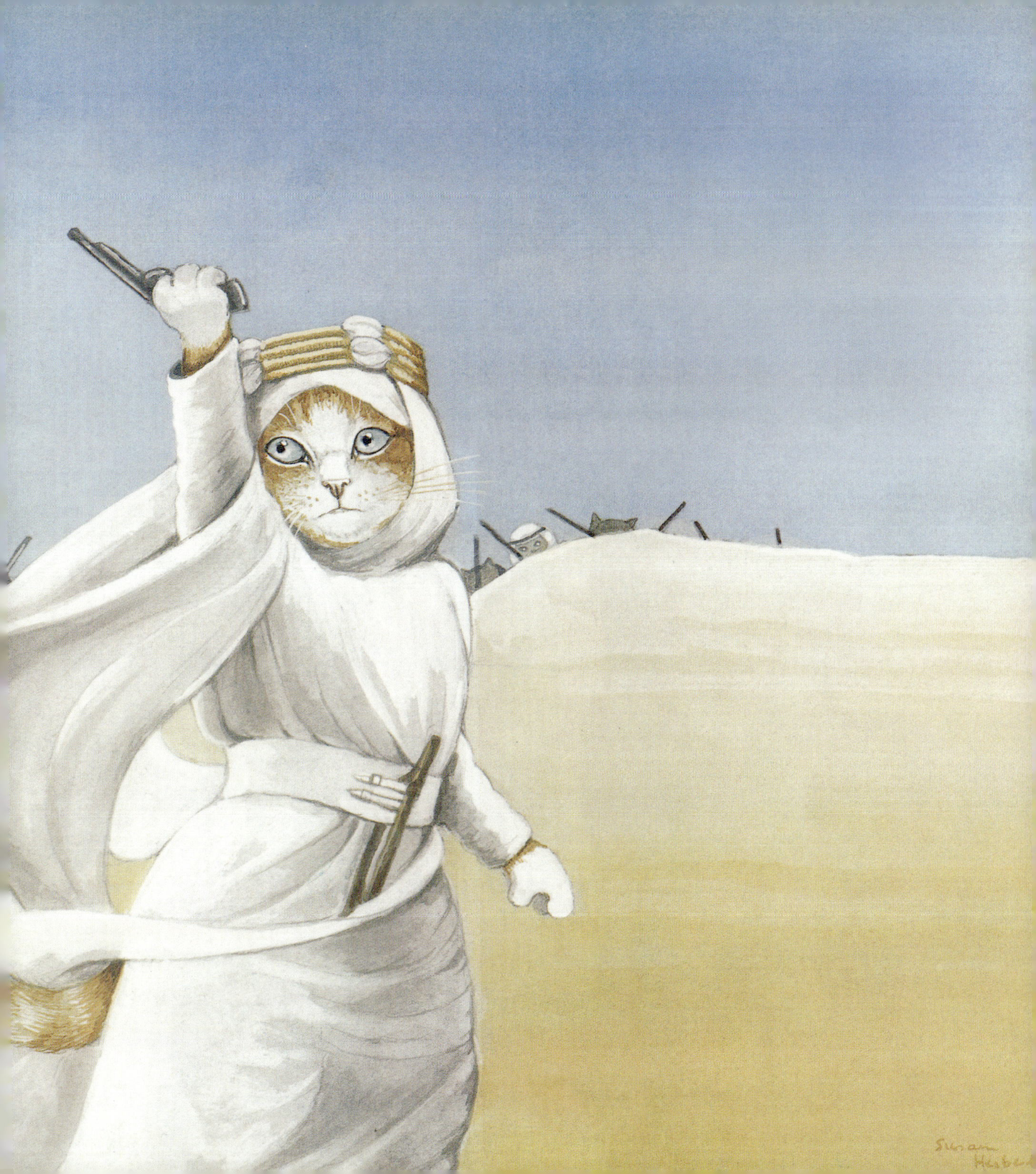

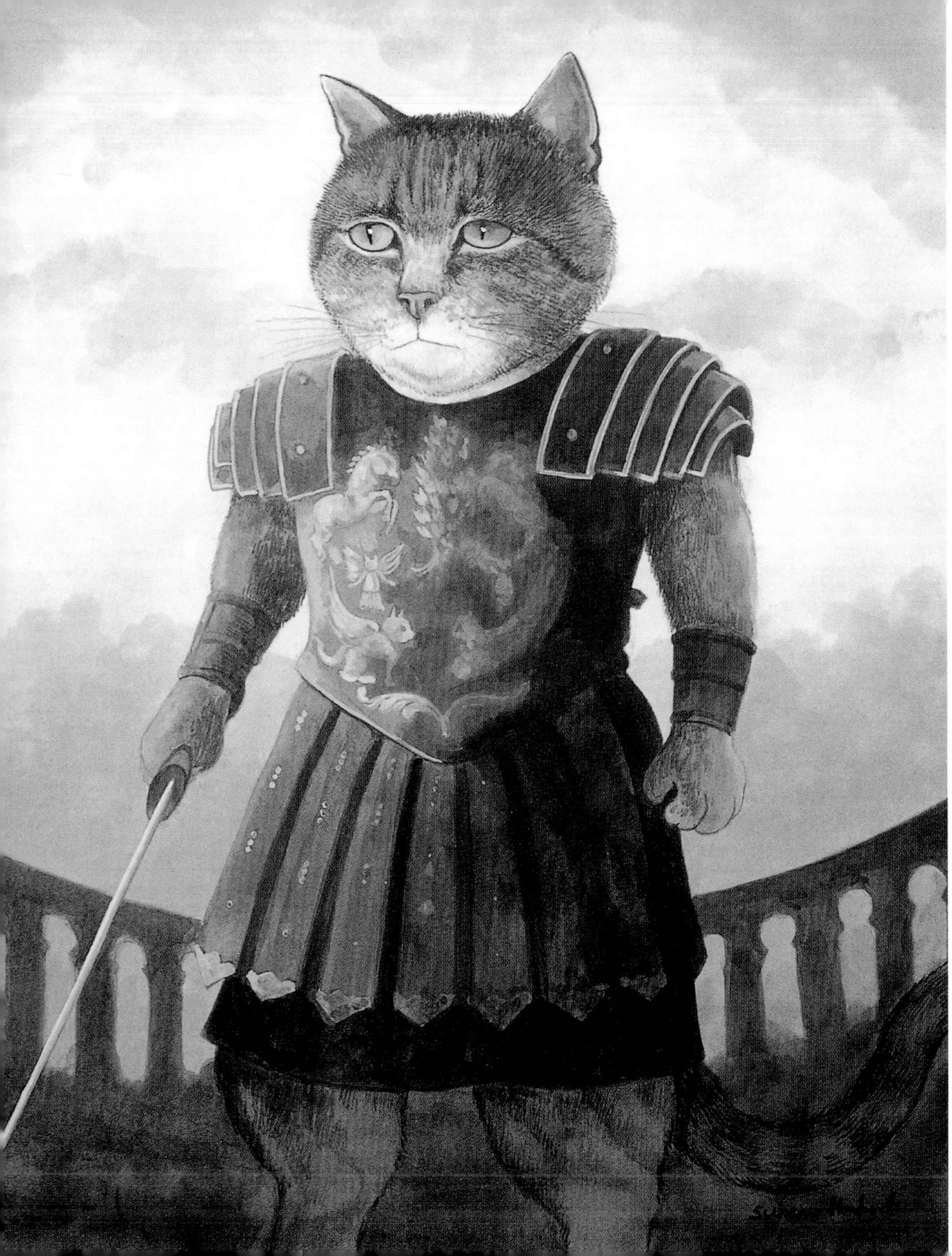

Russell Crowe in

GLADIATOR (2000)

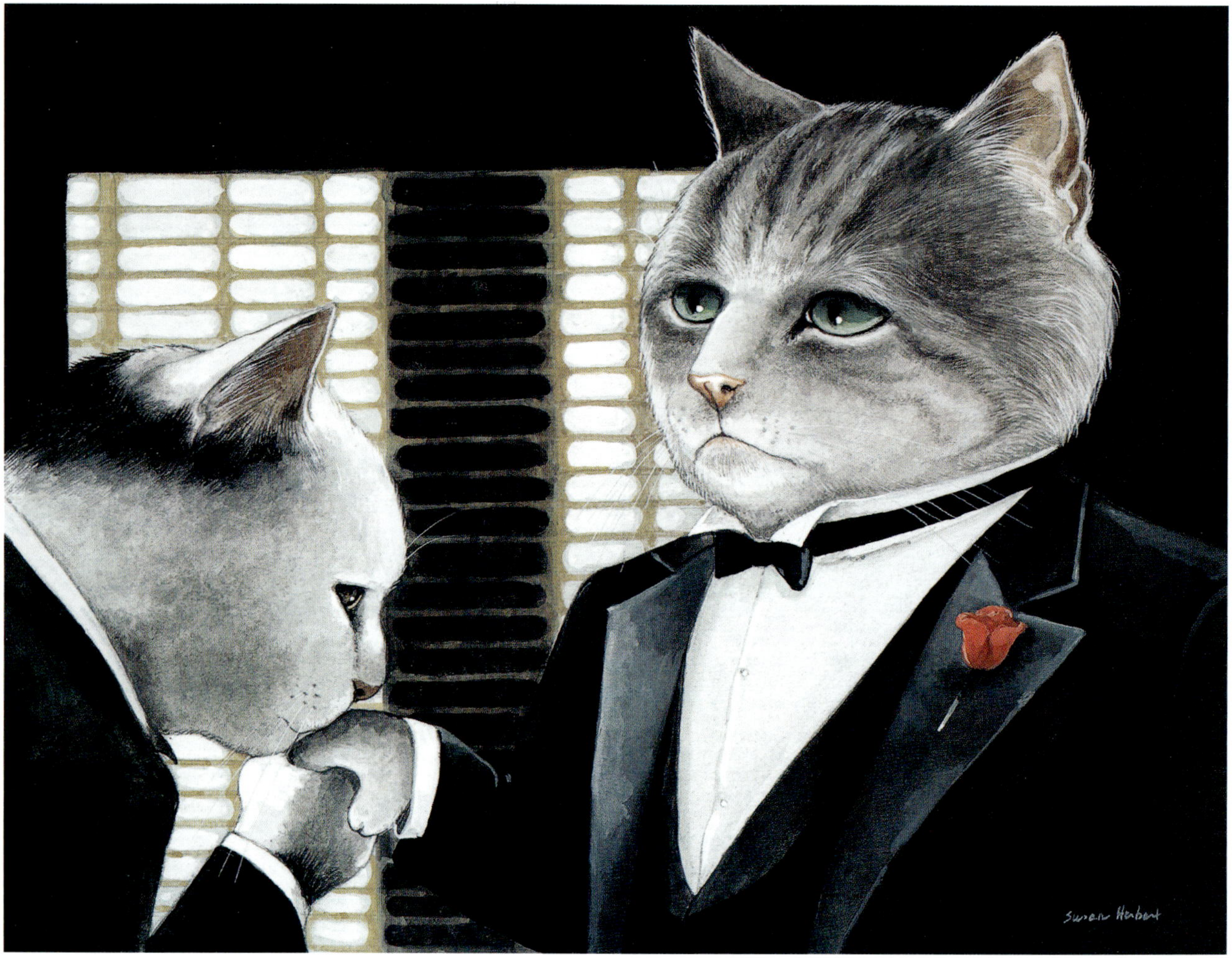

Above THE GODFATHER (1972)

Opposite DOCTOR ZHIVAGO (1965)

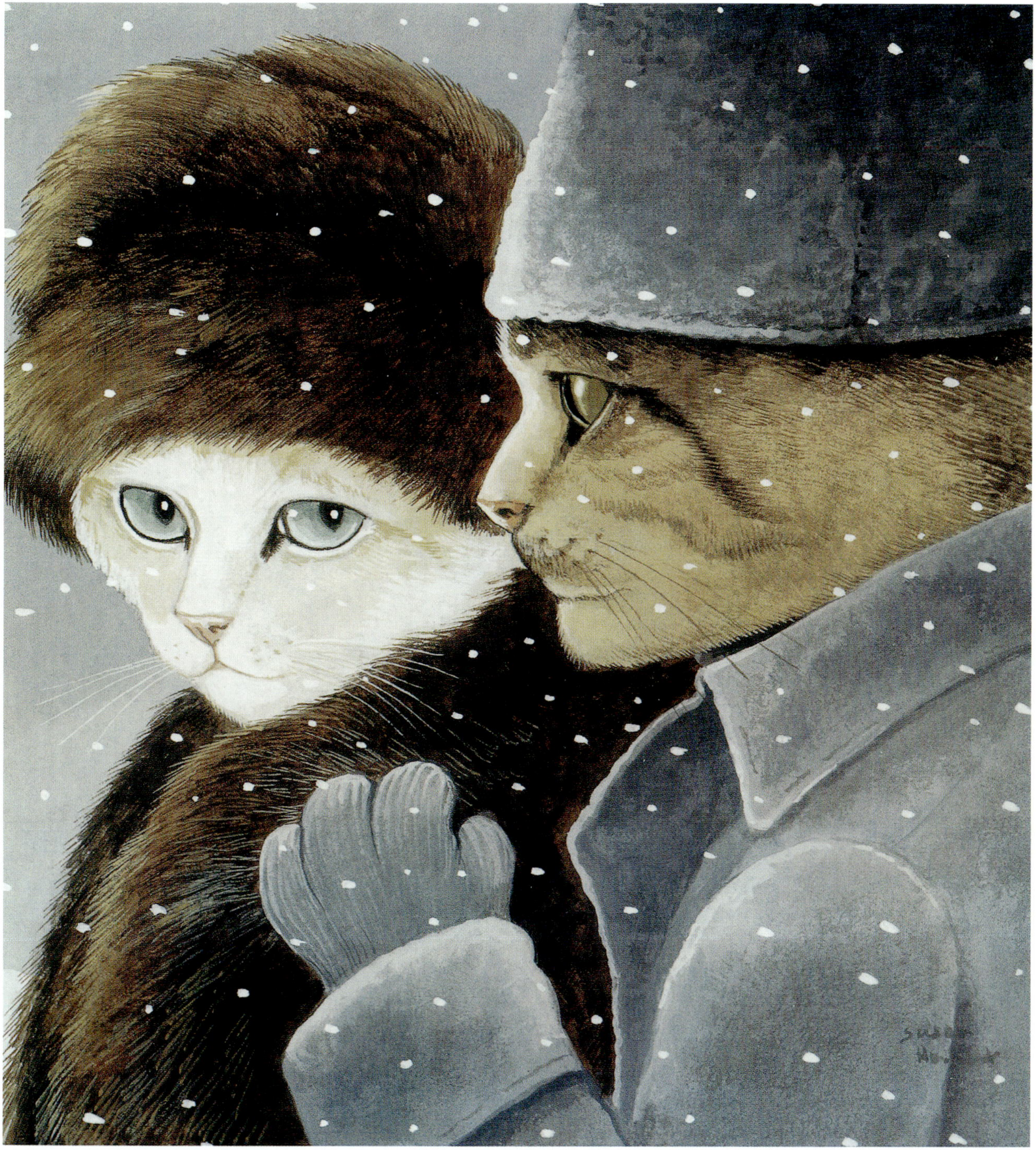

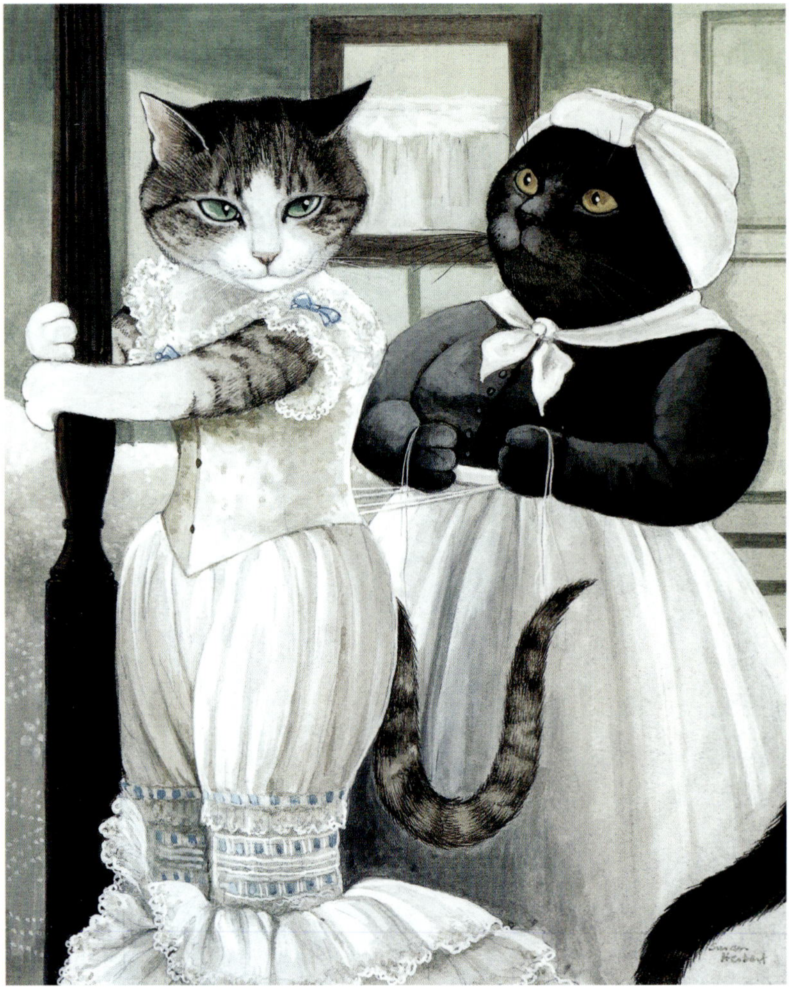

Above and opposite

GONE WITH THE WIND (1939)

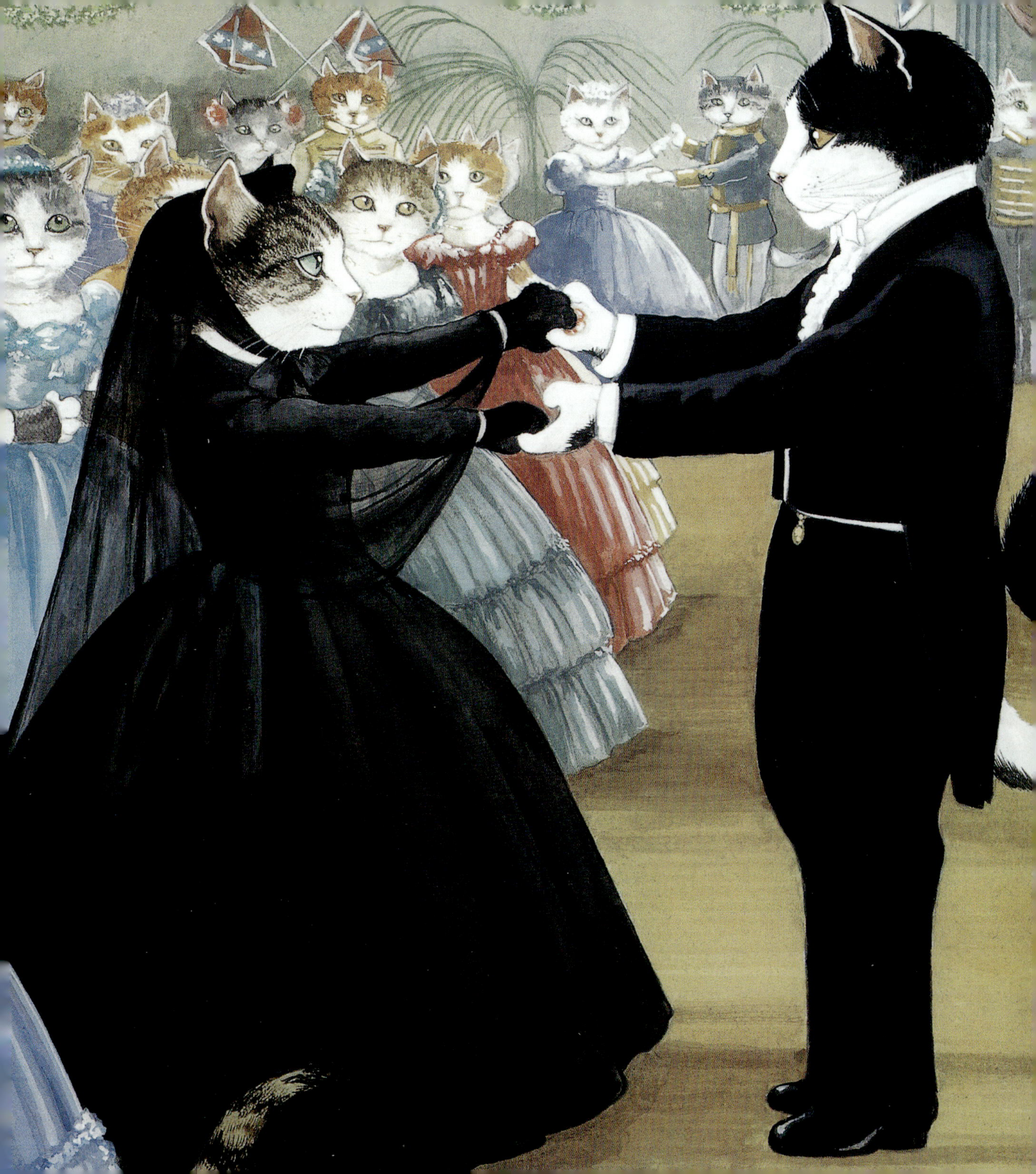

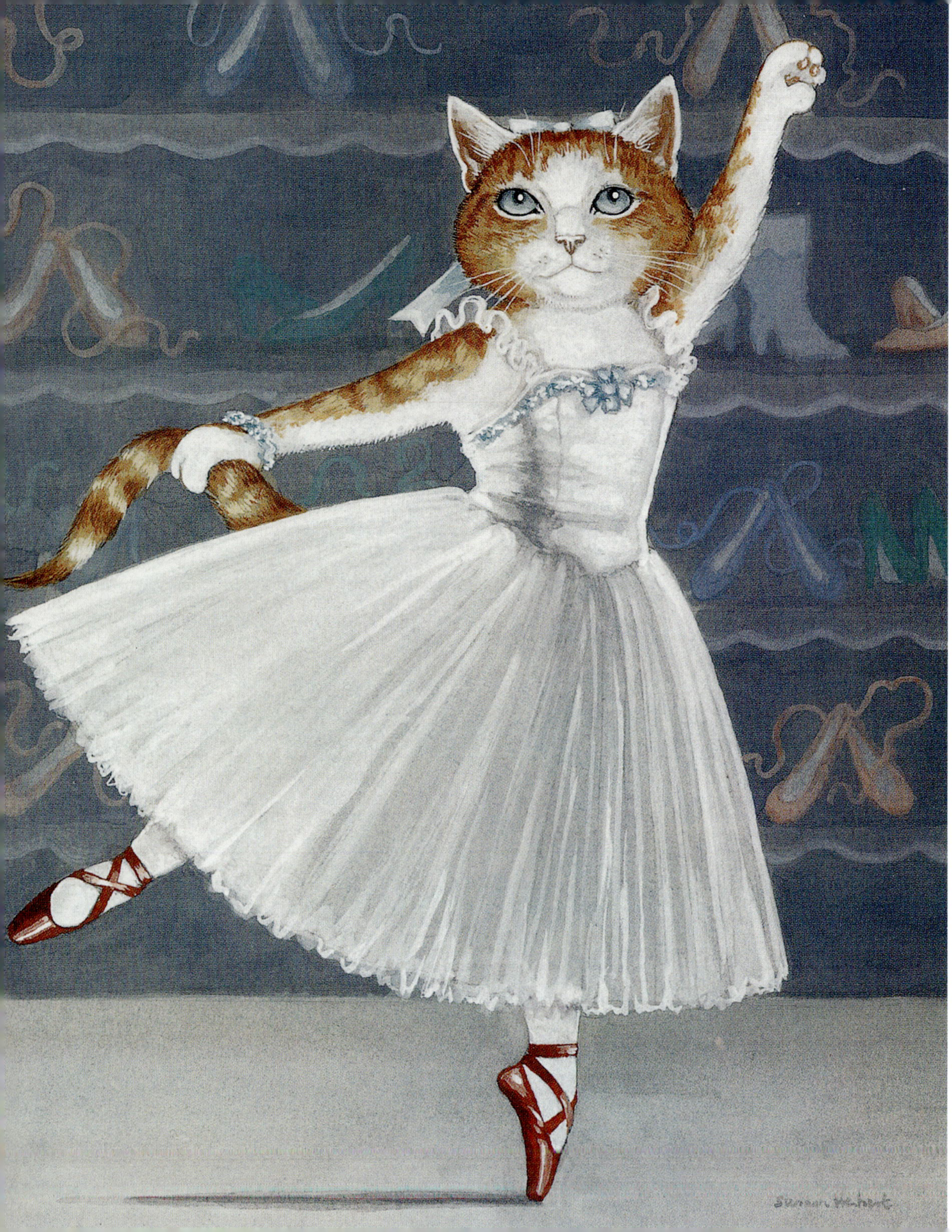

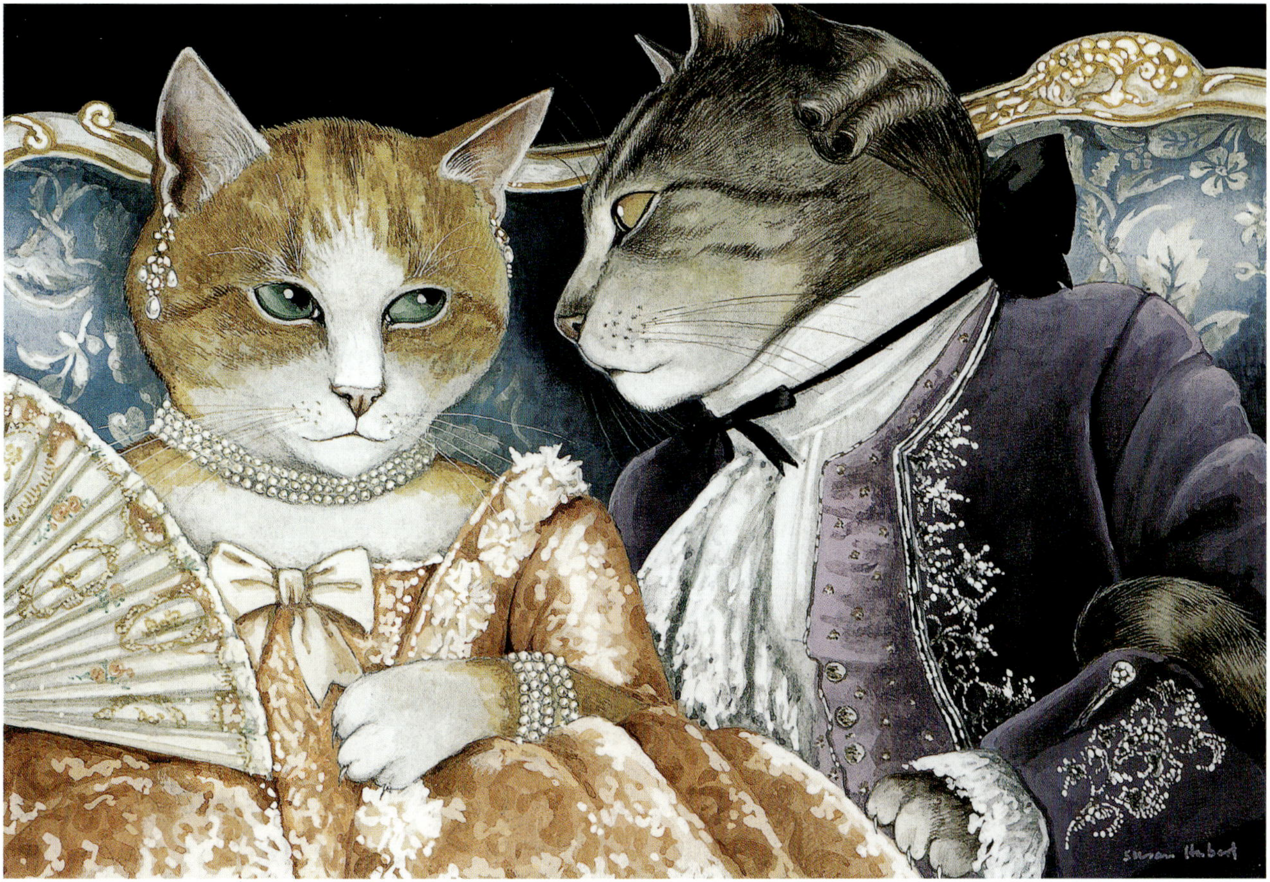

Above DANGEROUS LIAISONS (1988)

Opposite THE RED SHOES (1948)

James Dean in

REBEL WITHOUT A CAUSE (1955)

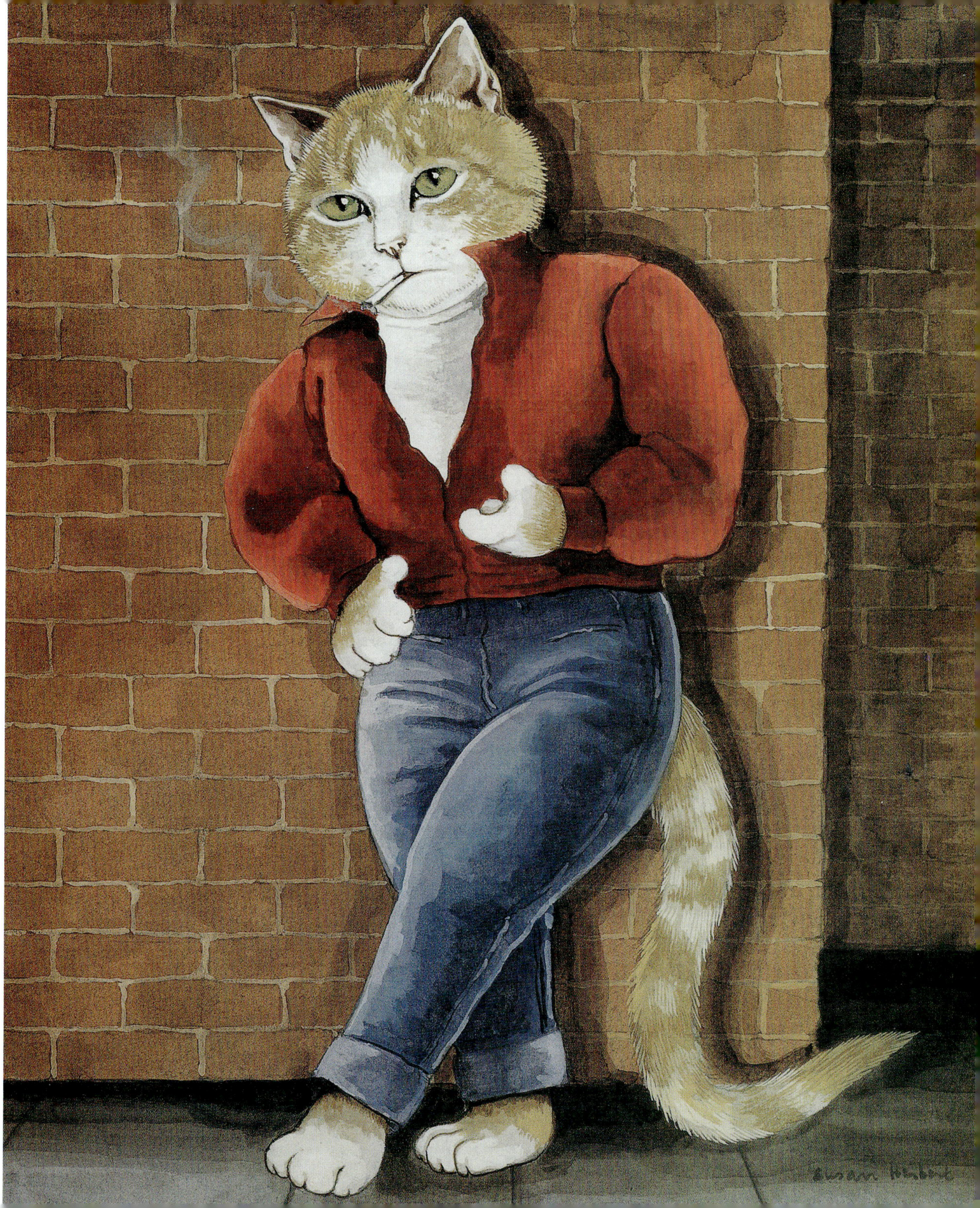

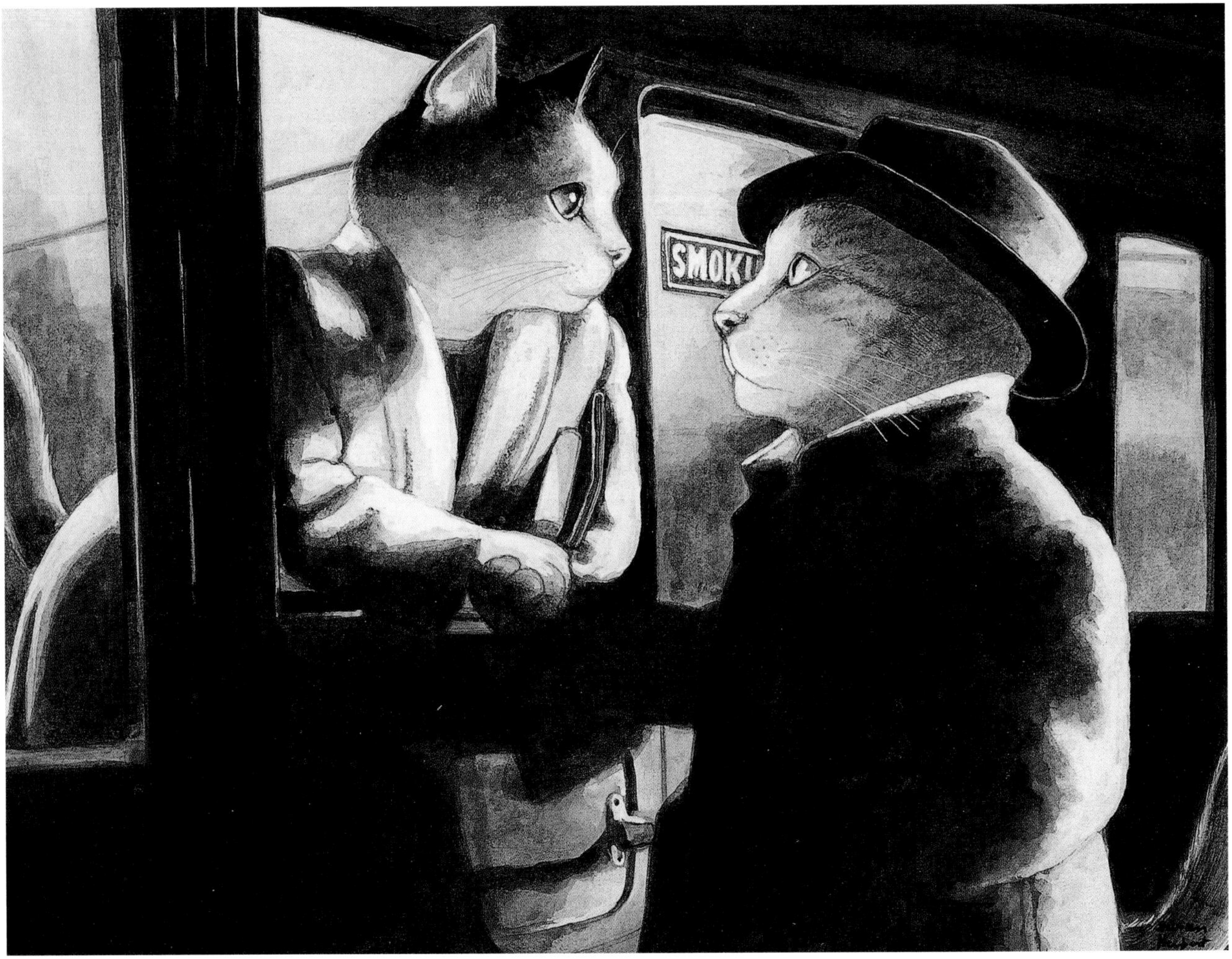

BRIEF ENCOUNTER (1945)

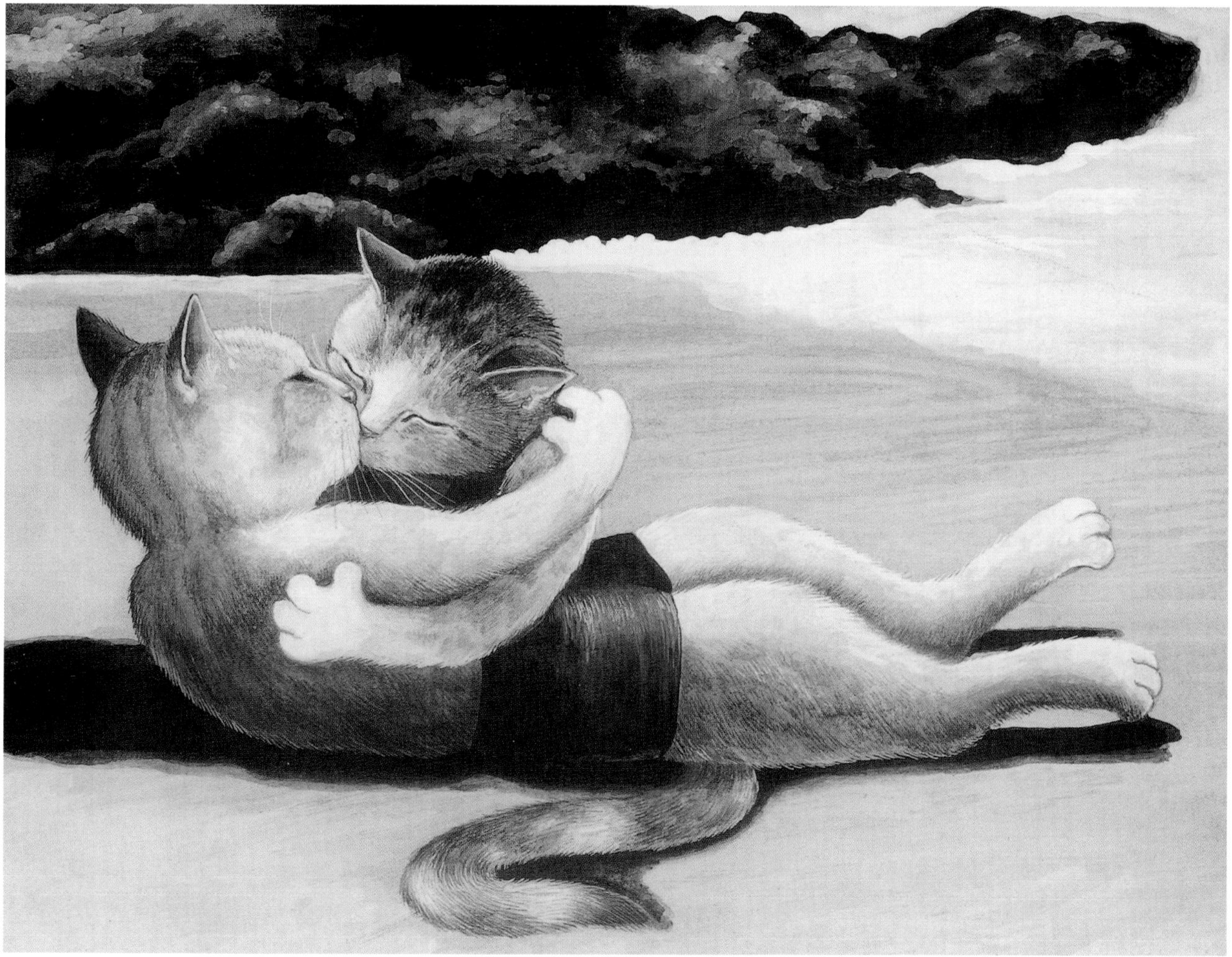

FROM HERE TO ETERNITY (1953)

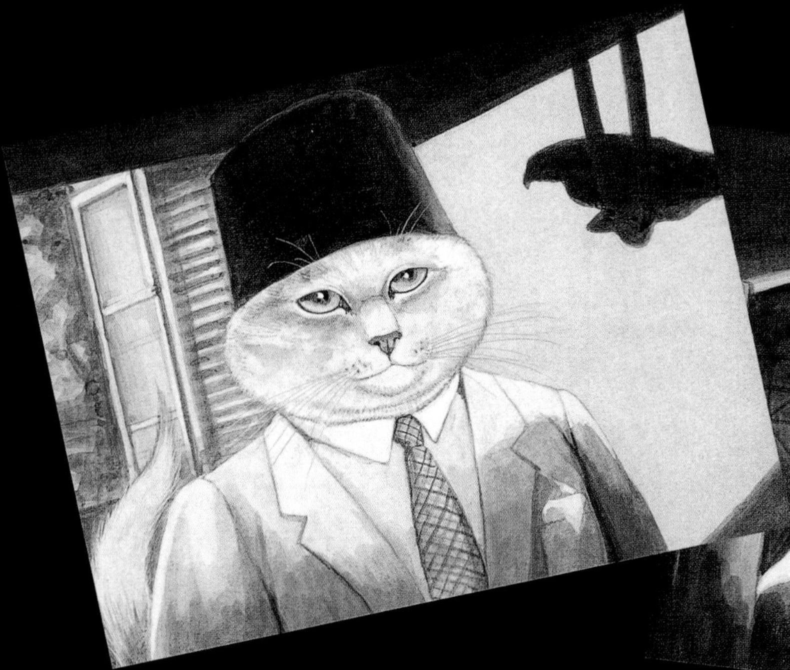
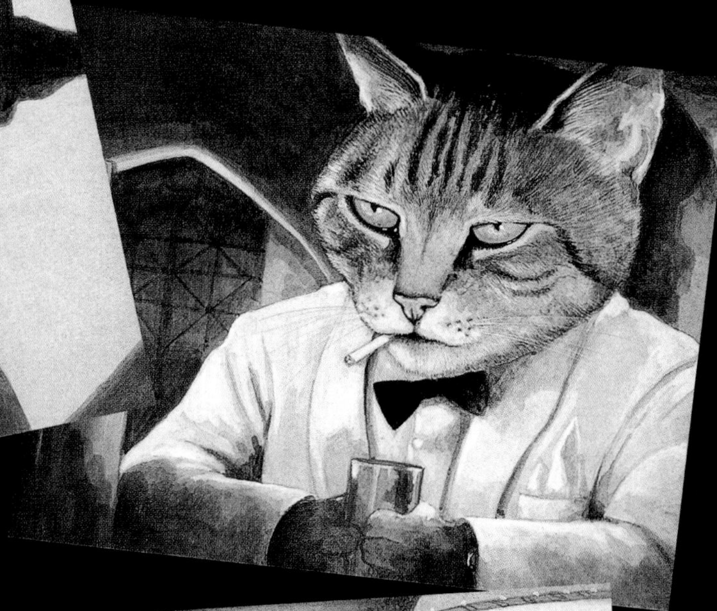
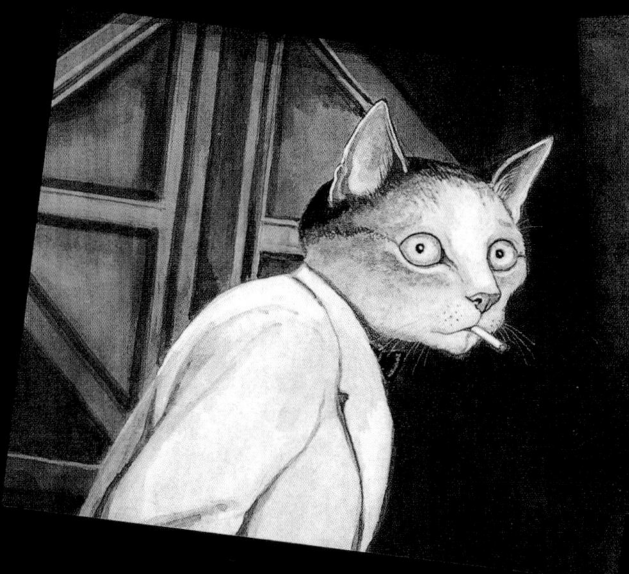
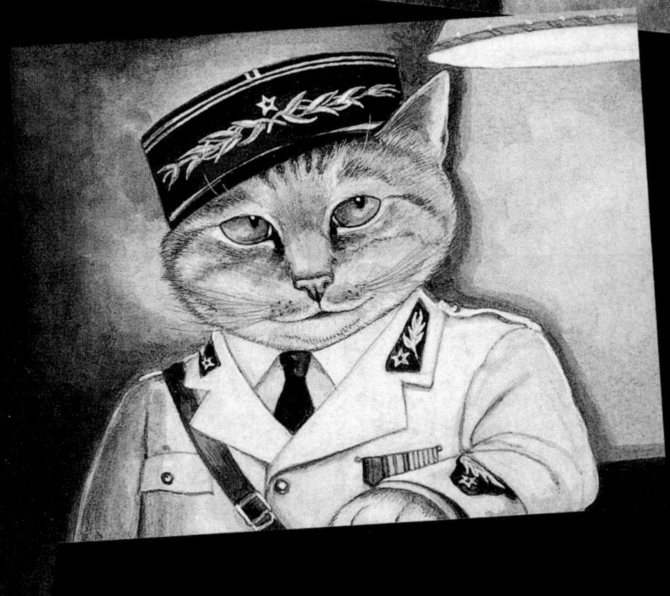

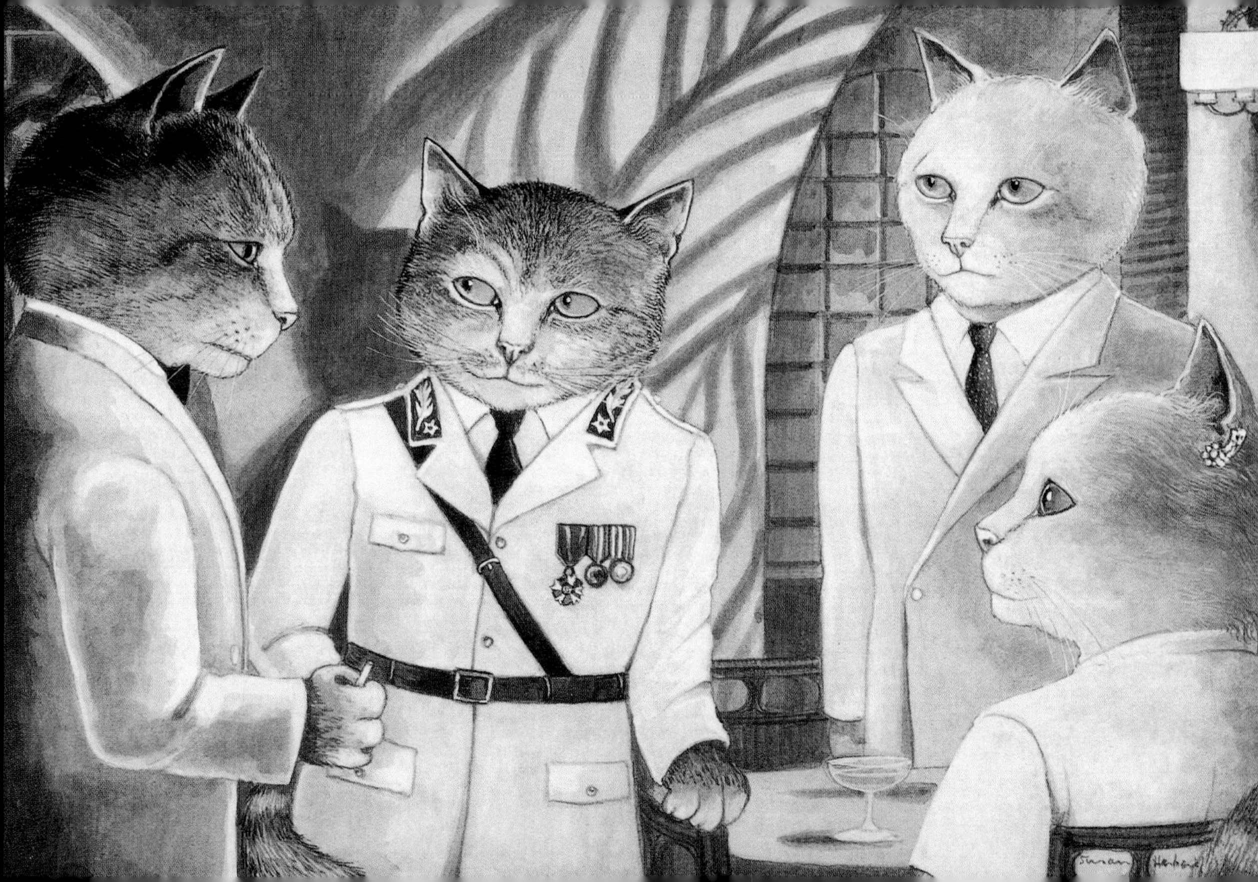
Susan Herbert

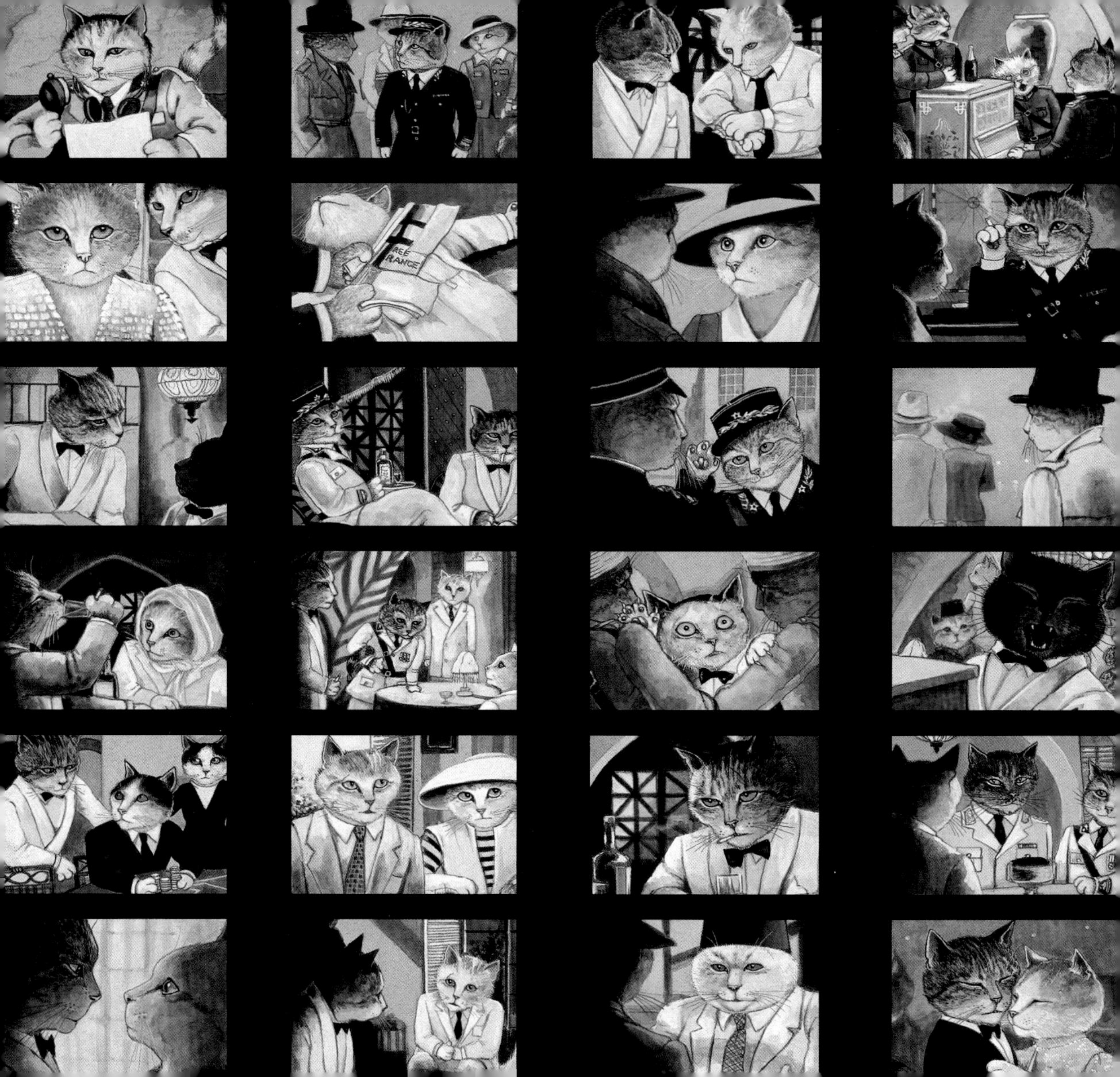

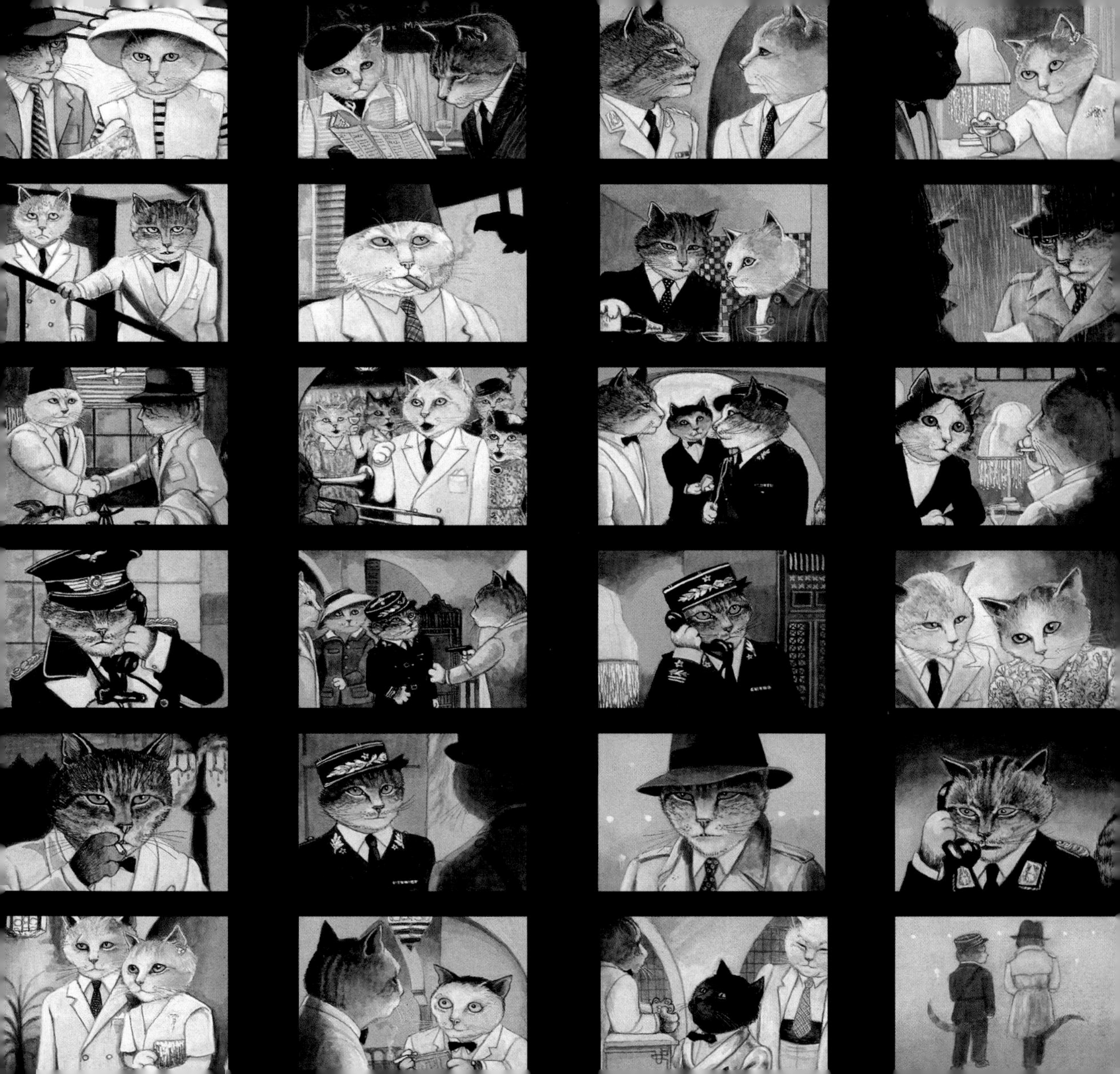

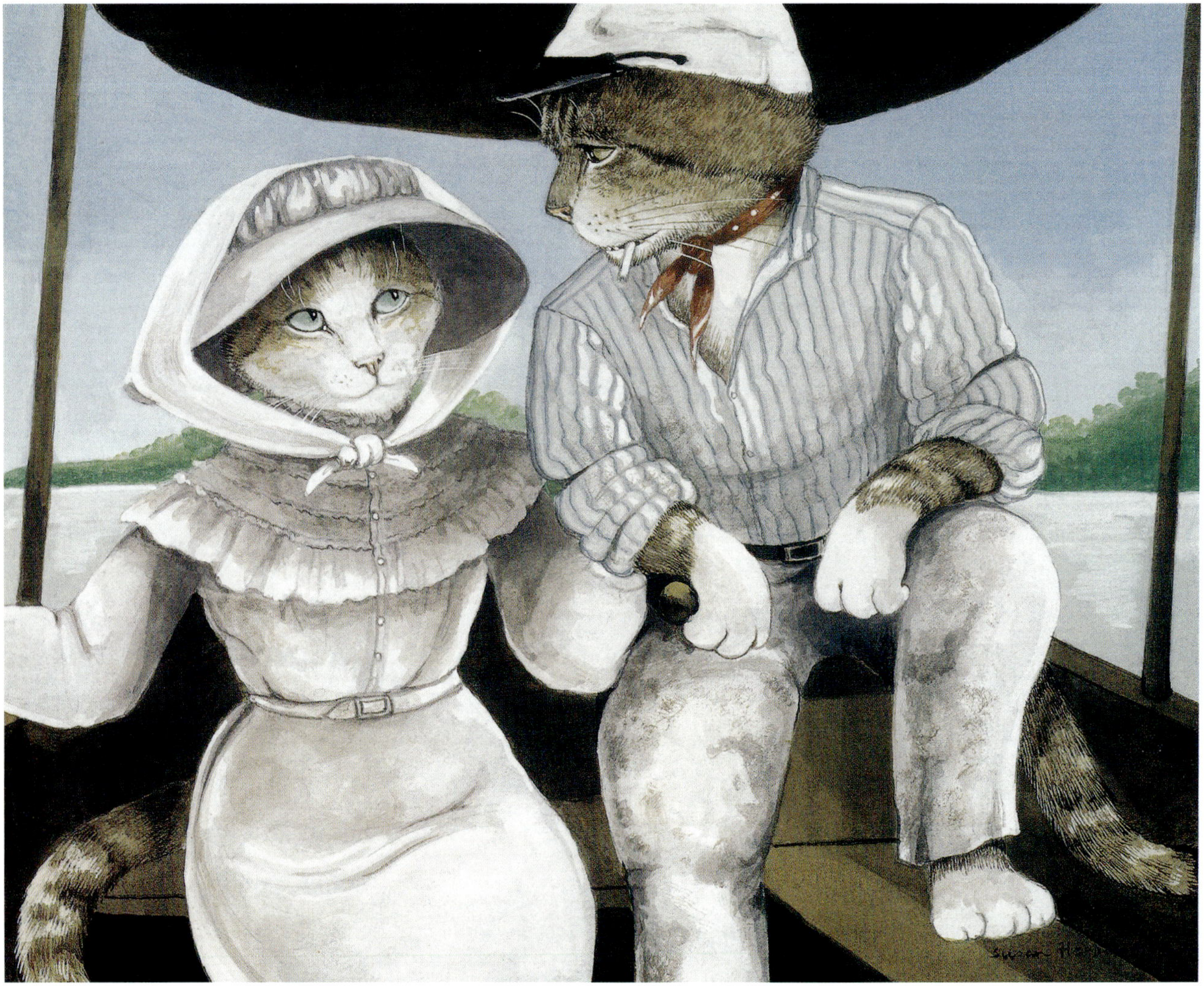

Katharine Hepburn and Humphrey Bogart in

THE AFRICAN QUEEN (1951)

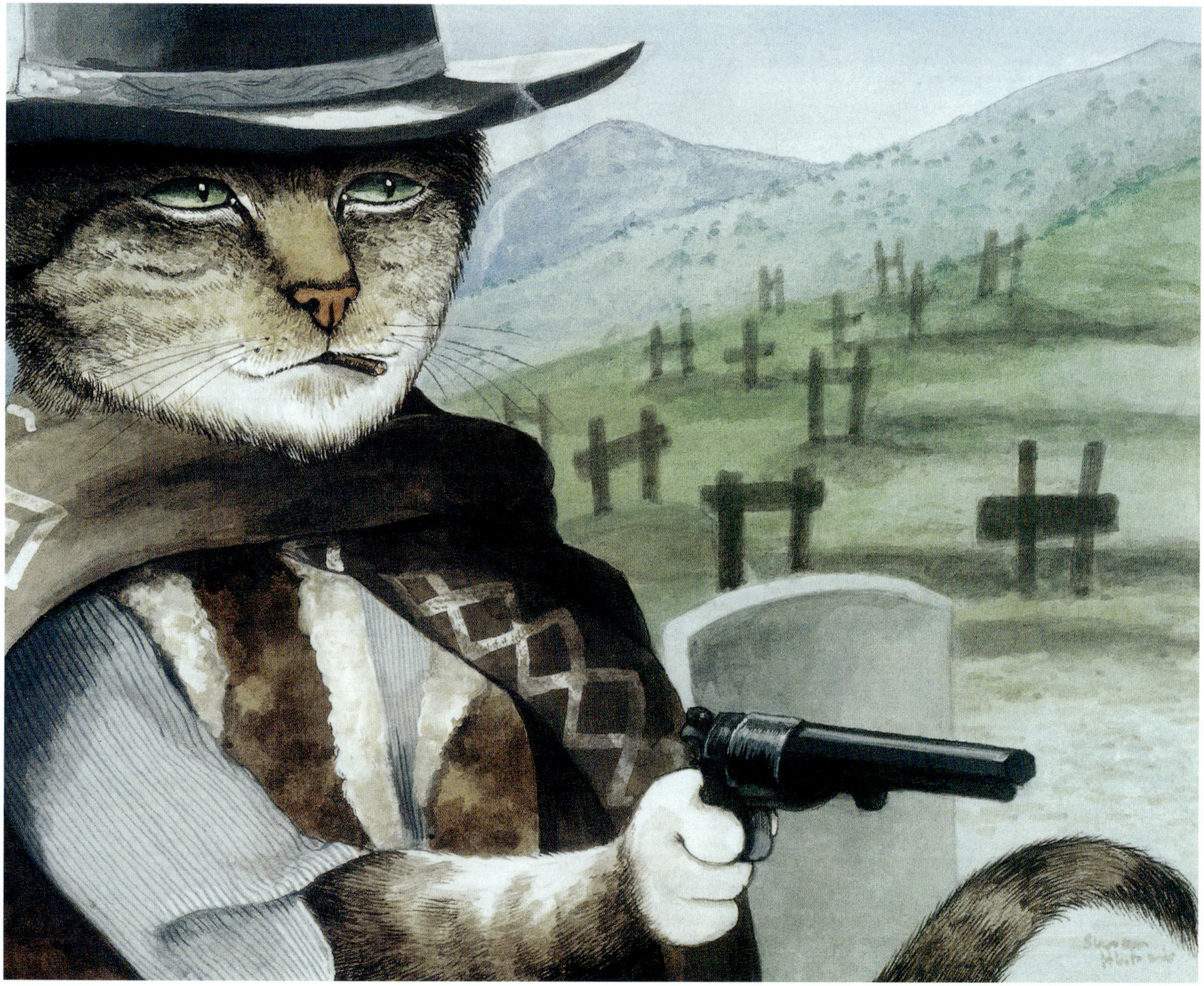

Clint Eastwood in

A FISTFUL OF DOLLARS (1964)

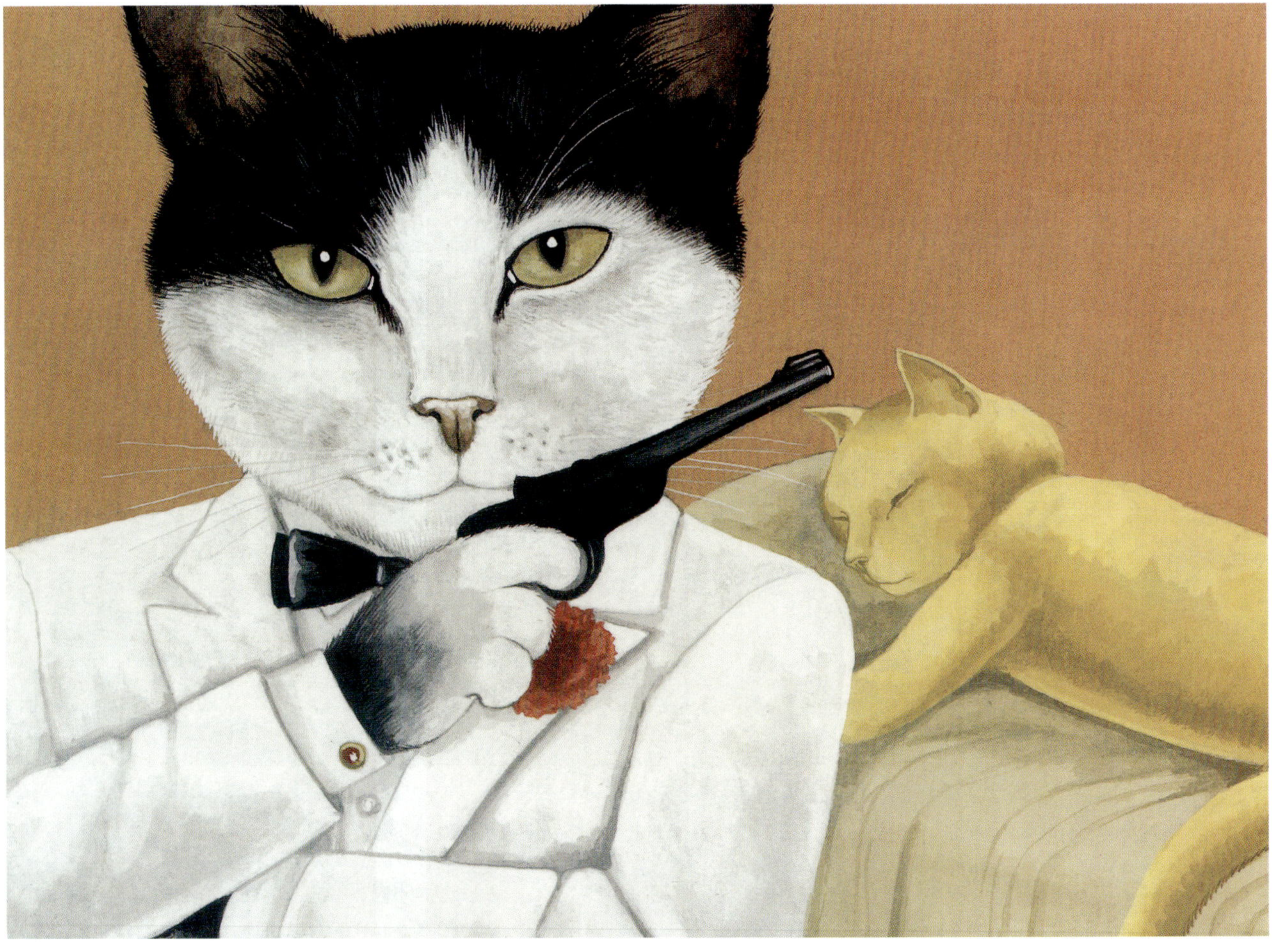

Sean Connery in

GOLDFINGER (1964)

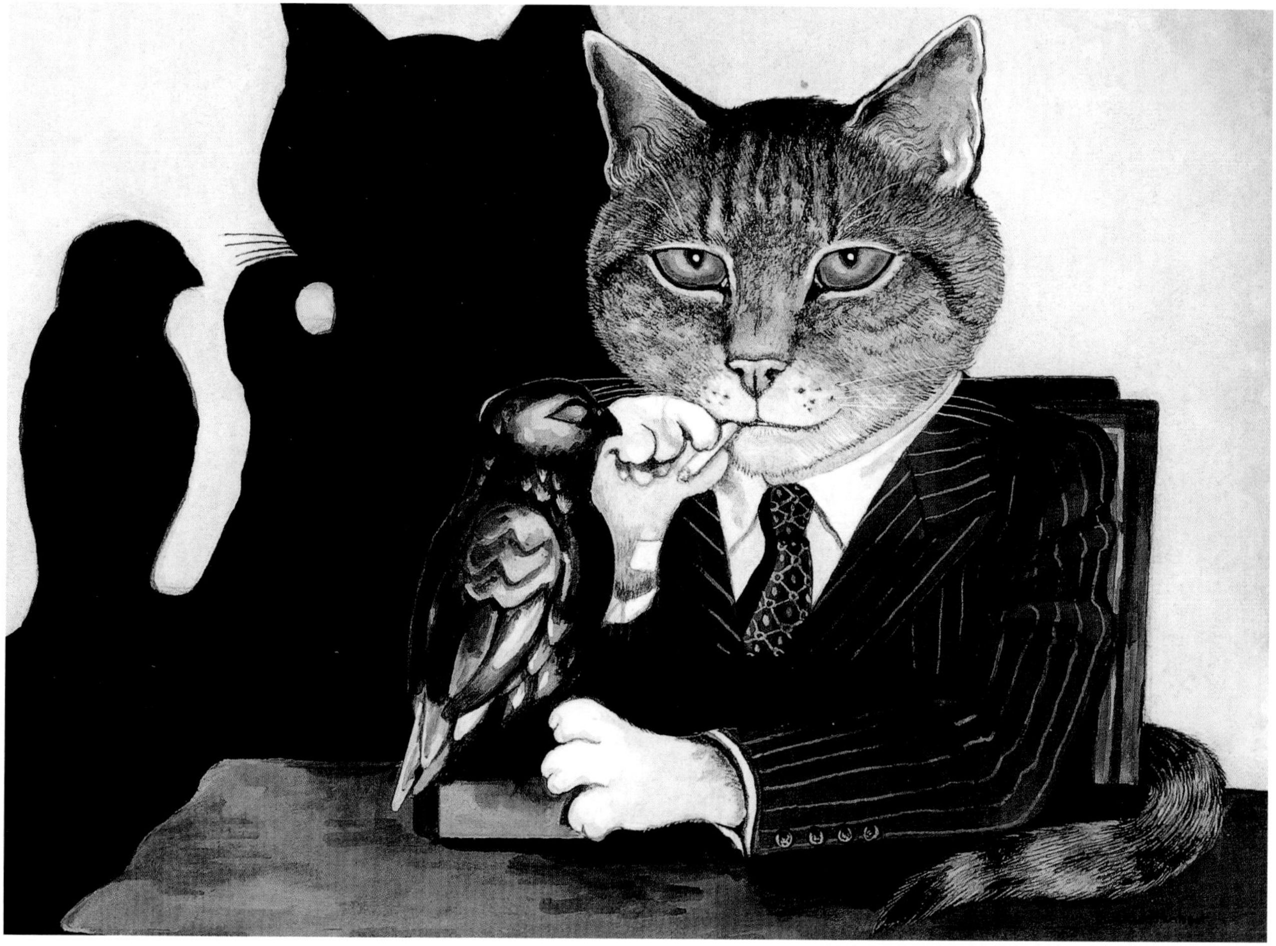

Humphrey Bogart in

THE MALTESE FALCON (1941)

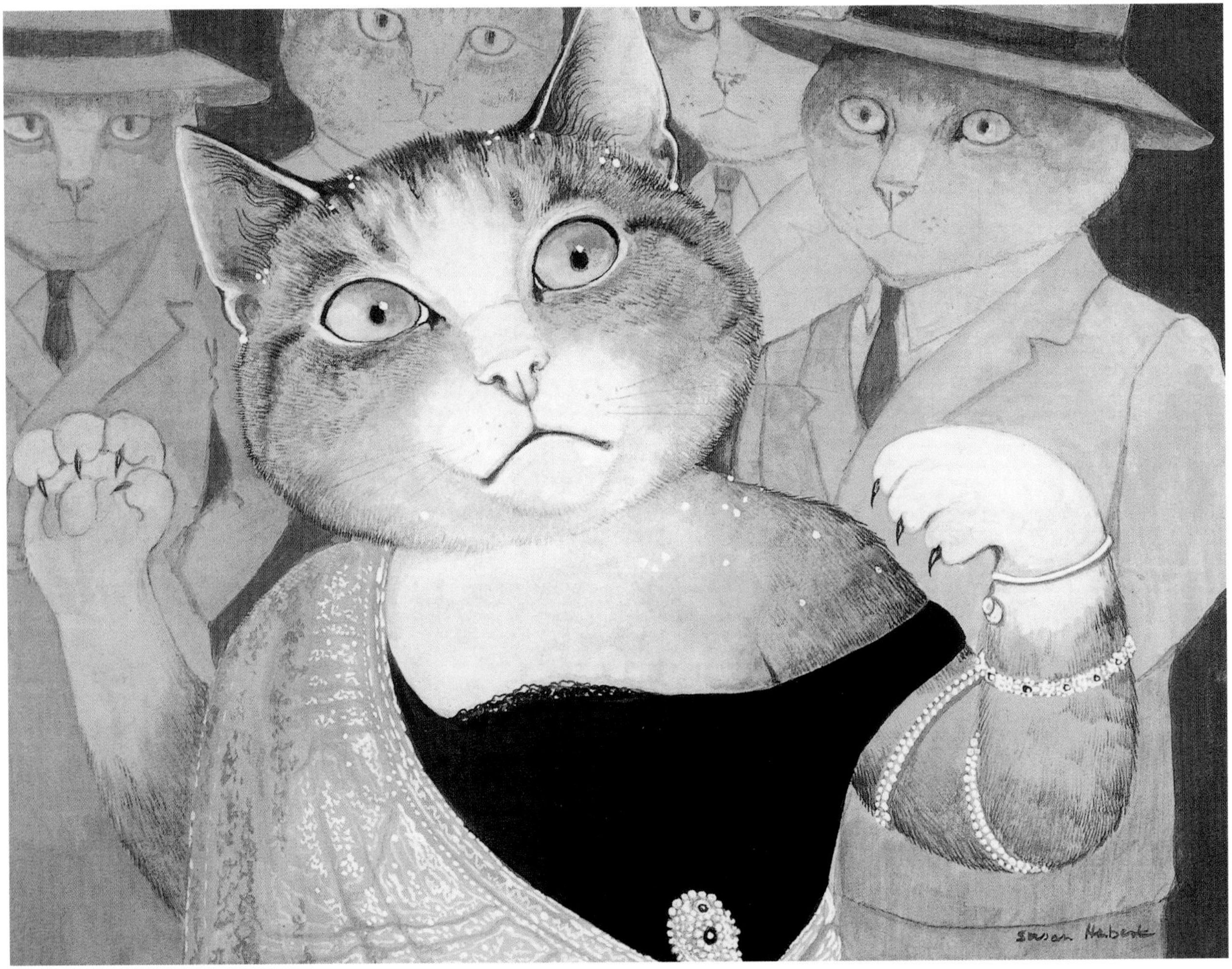

Above SUNSET BOULEVARD (1950)

Opposite THE IMPORTANCE OF BEING EARNEST (1952)

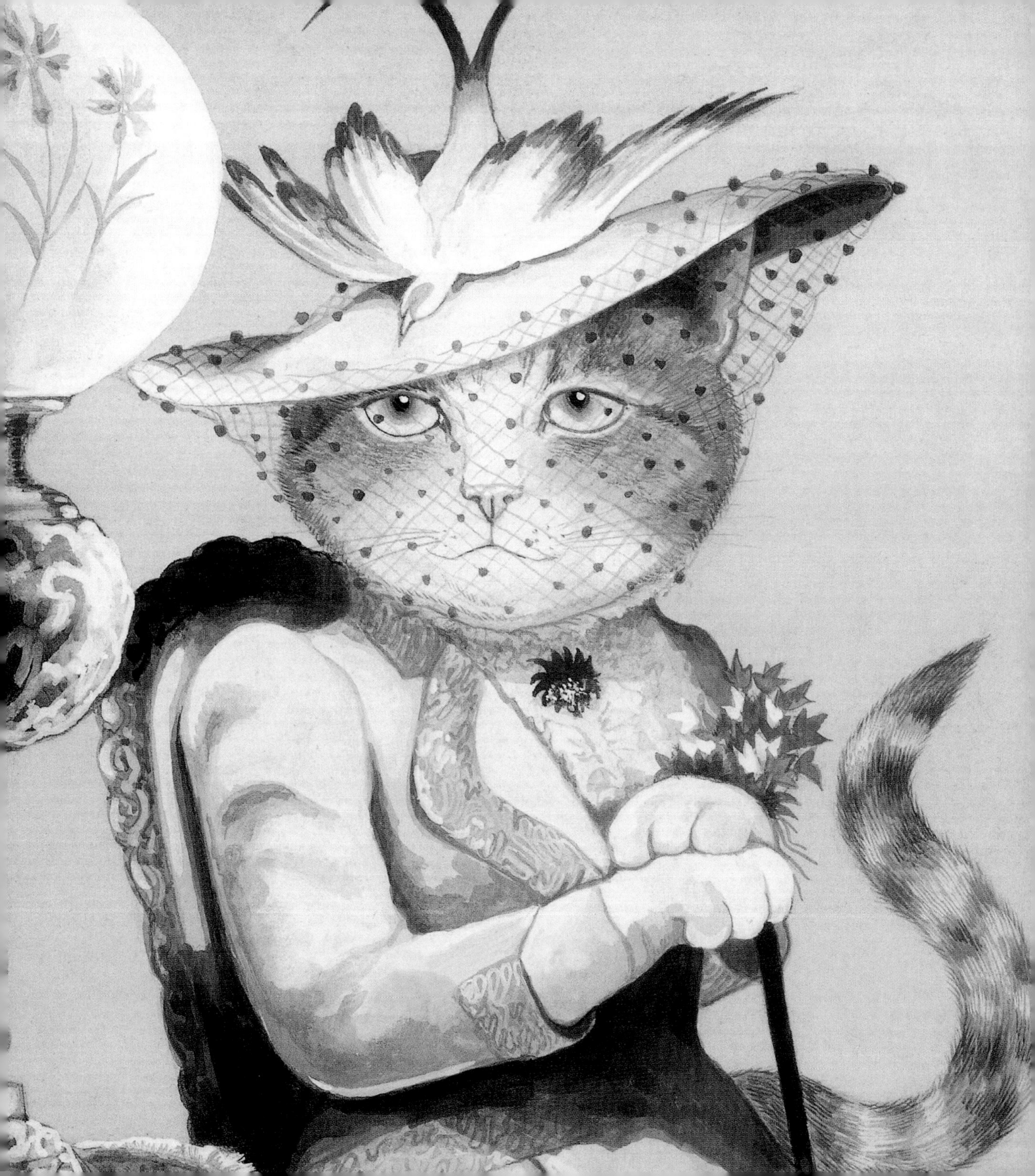

Cary Grant in

NORTH BY NORTHWEST (1959)

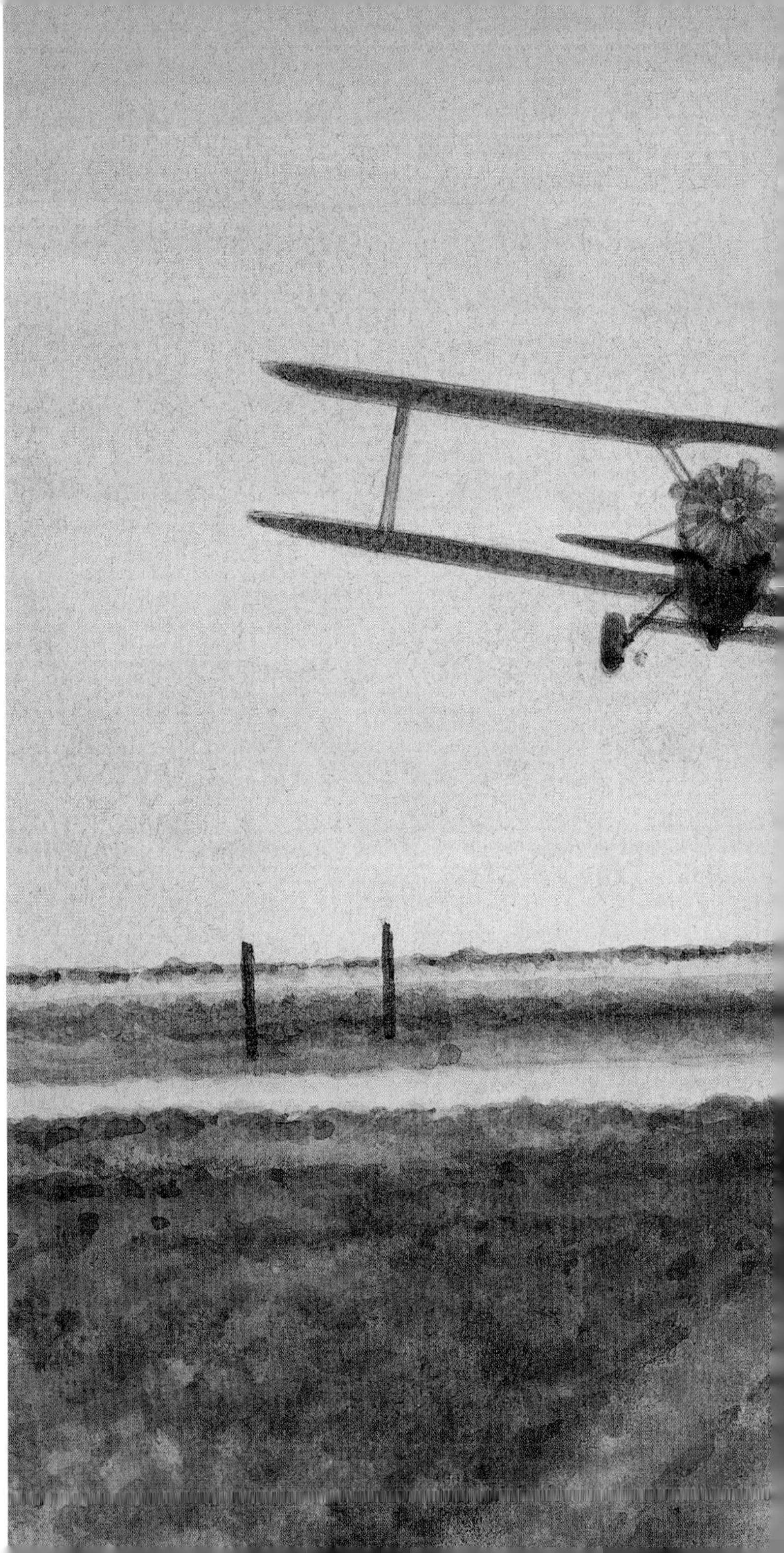

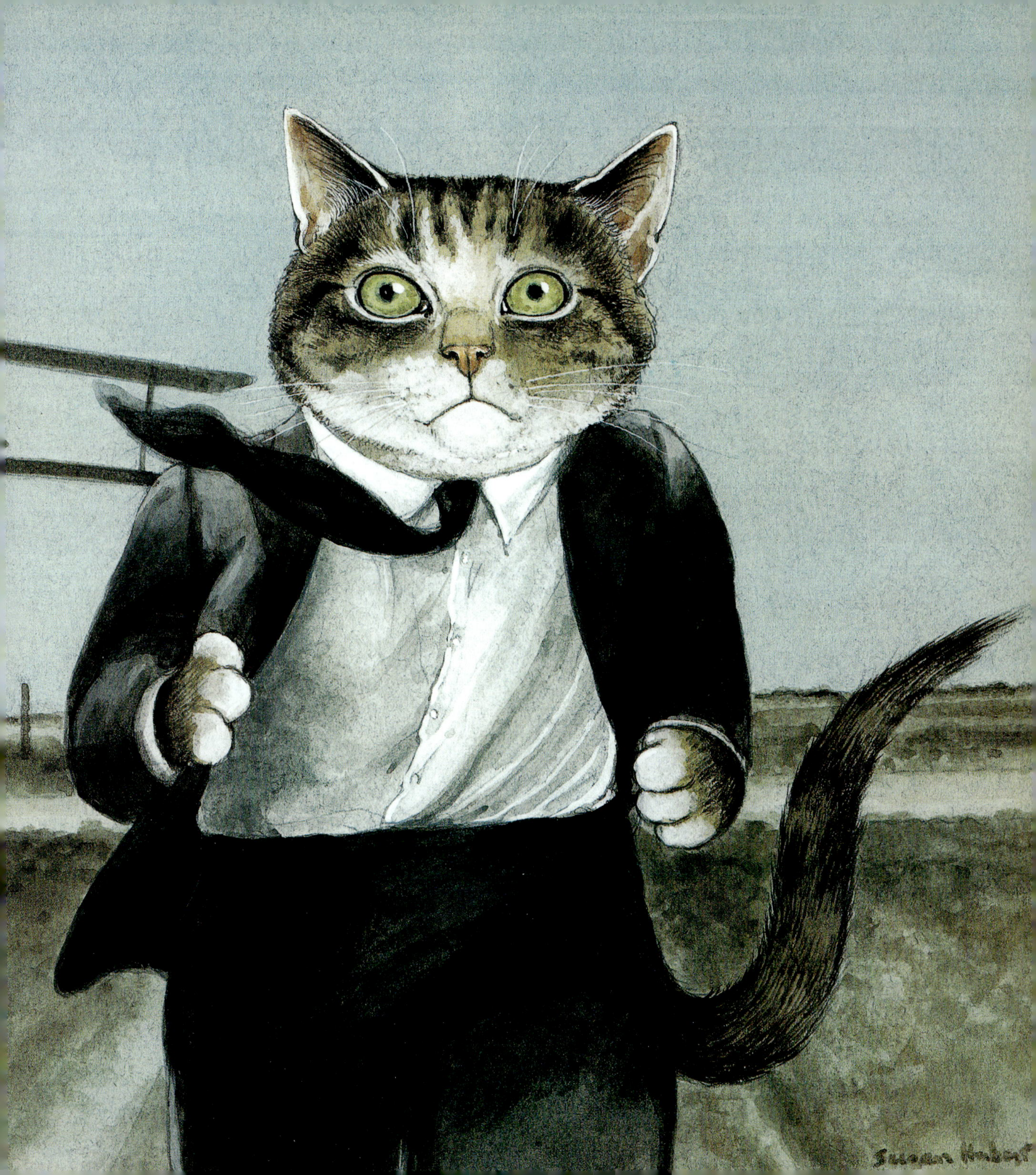

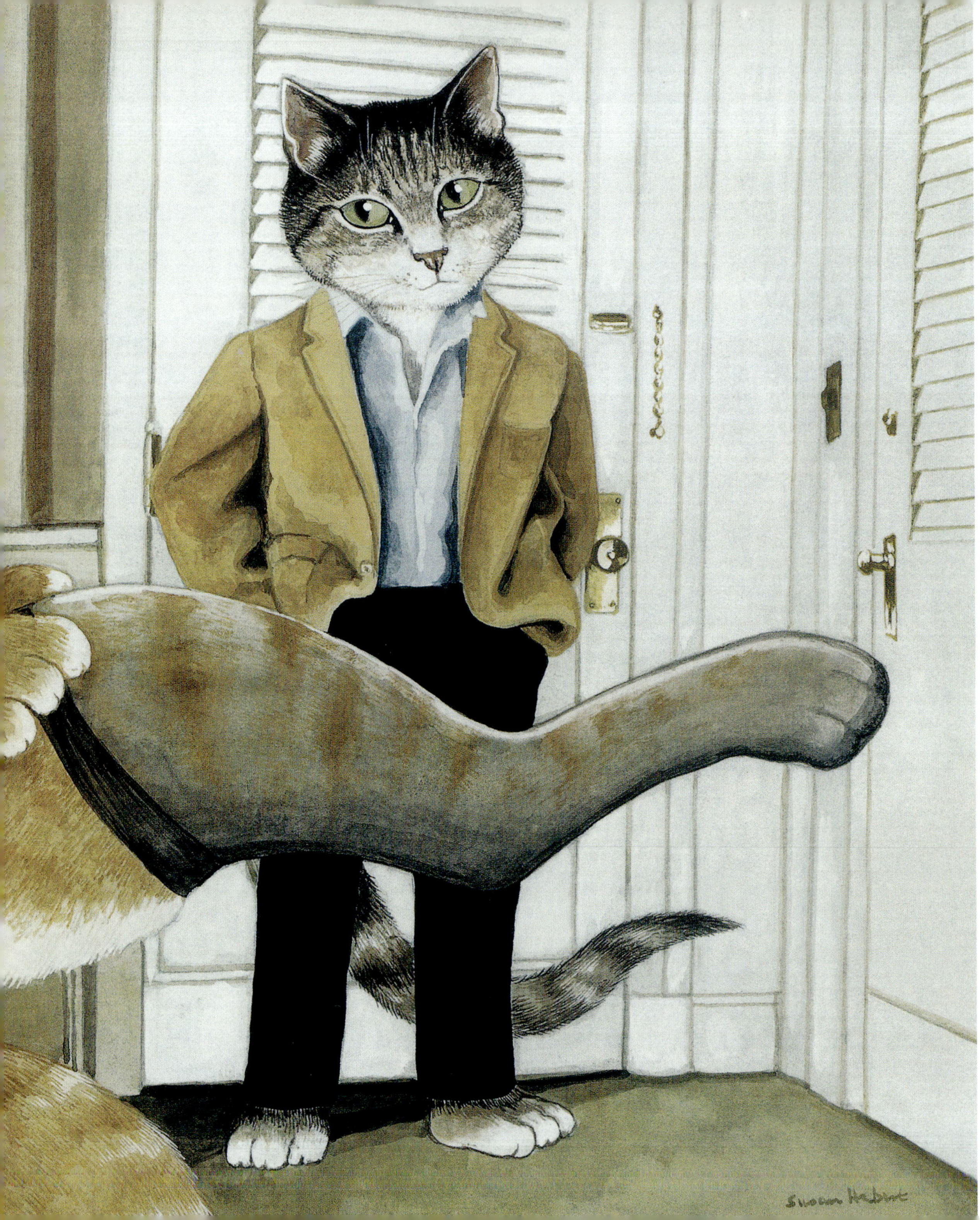

Dustin Hoffman in

THE GRADUATE (1967)

Lew Ayres in

ALL QUIET ON THE WESTERN FRONT (1930)

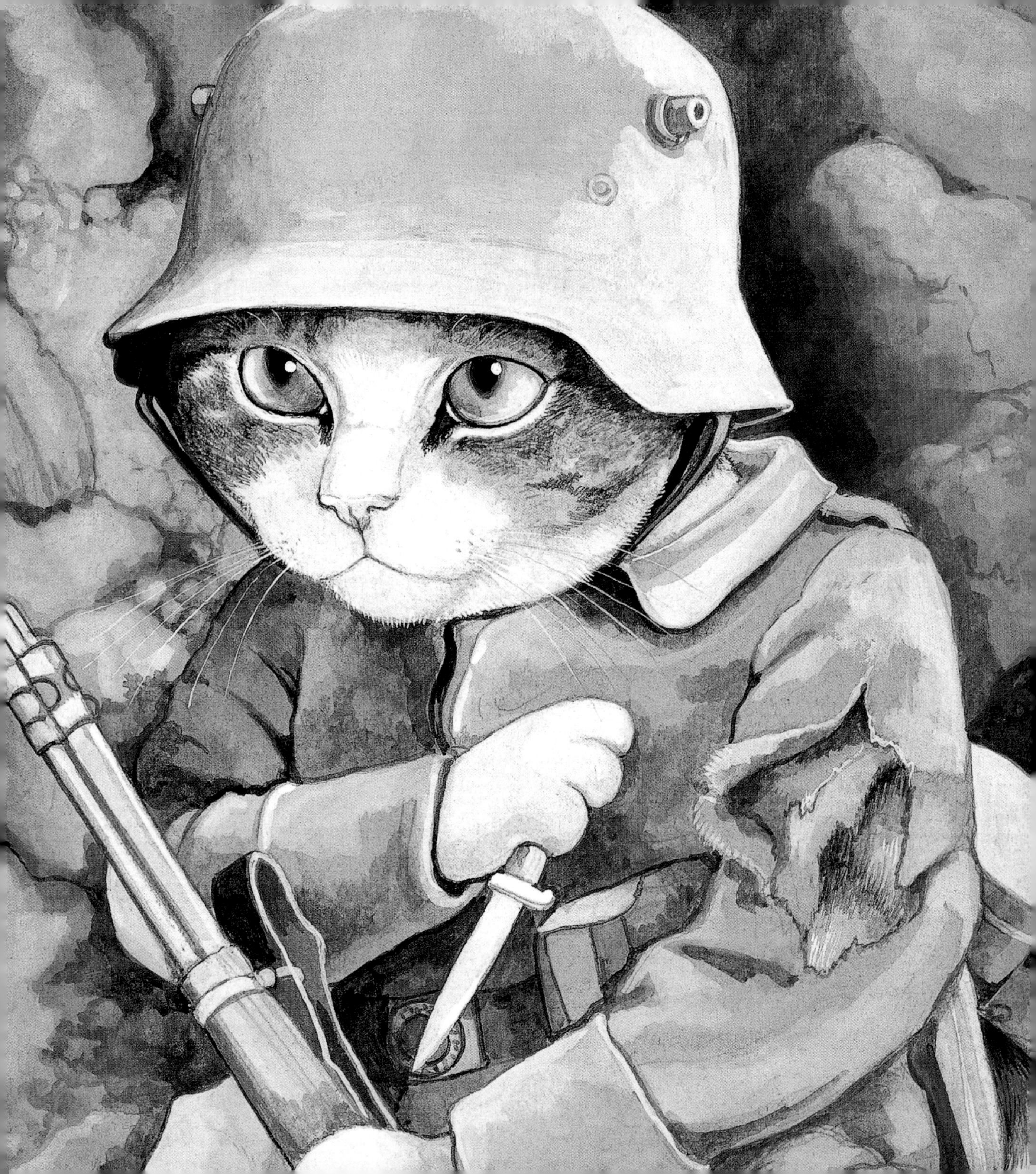

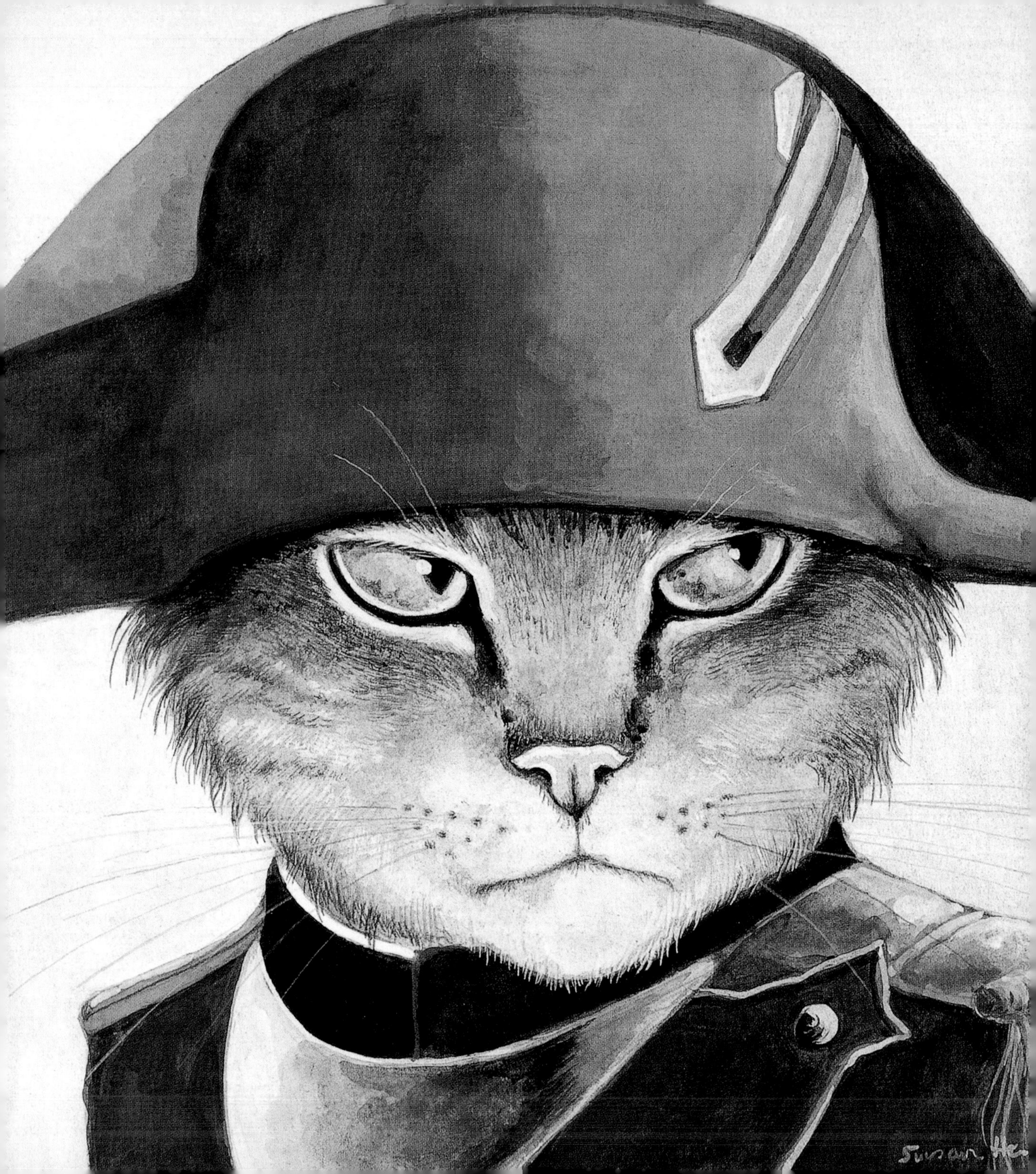

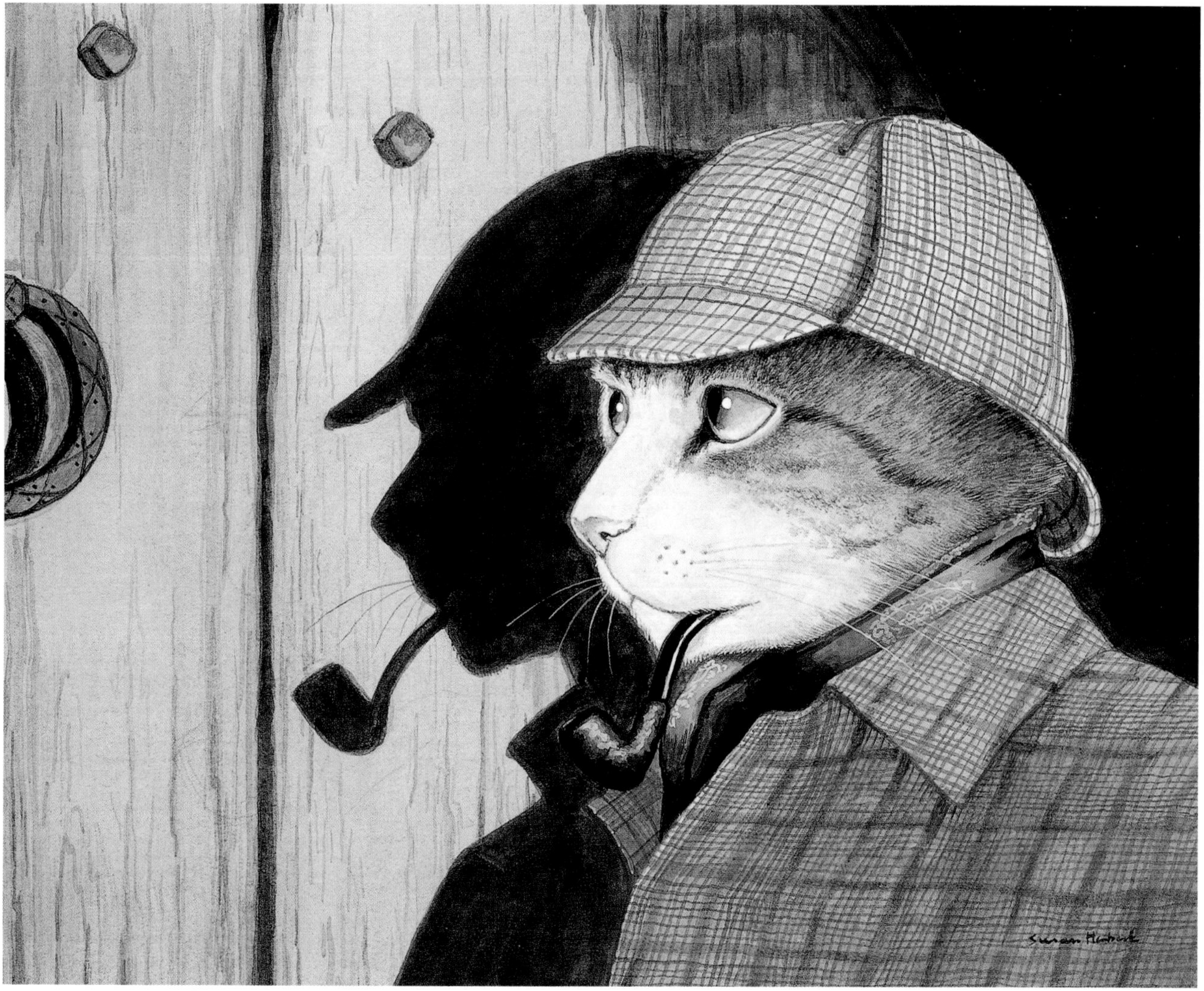

Above THE HOUND OF THE BASKERVILLES (1939)

Opposite NAPOLEON (1927)

Max Schreck in

NOSFERATU (1922)

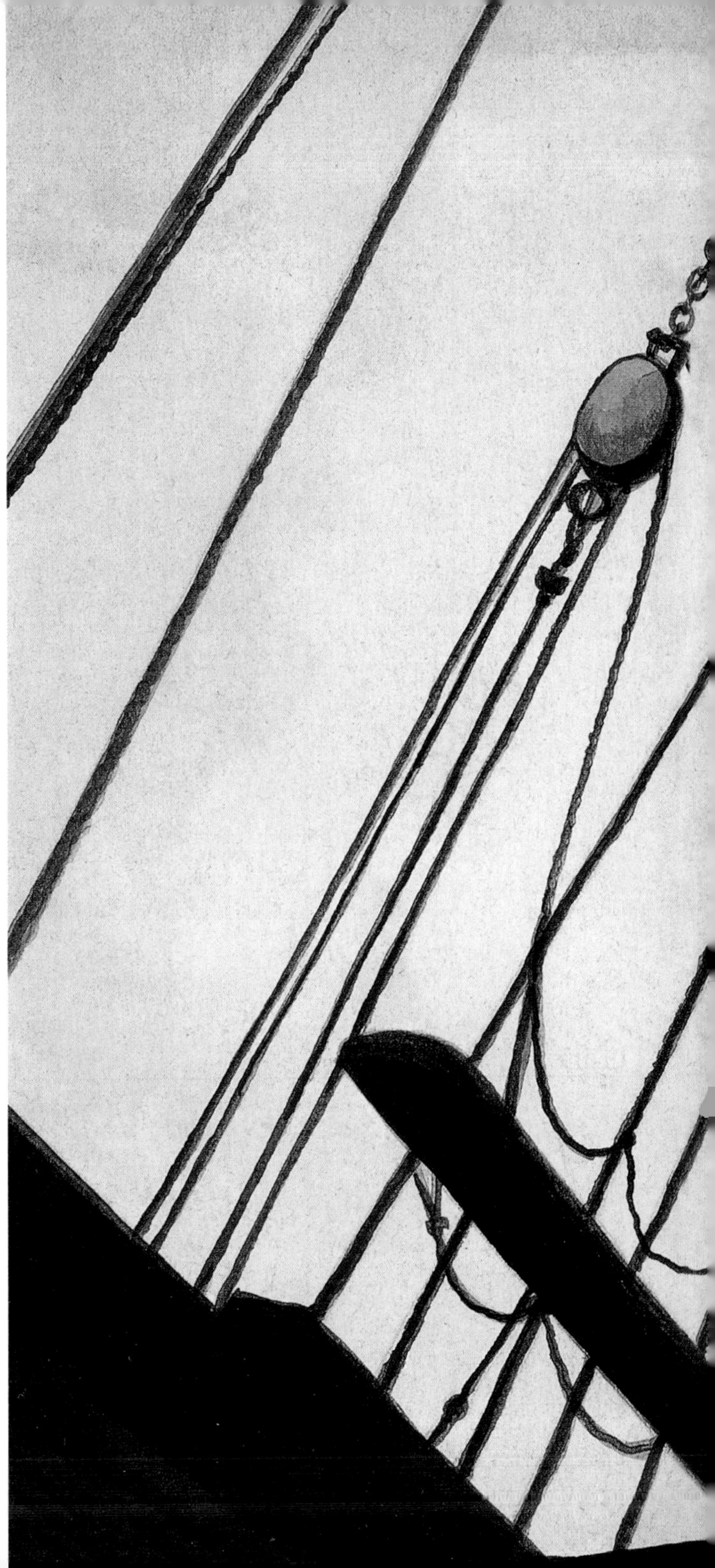

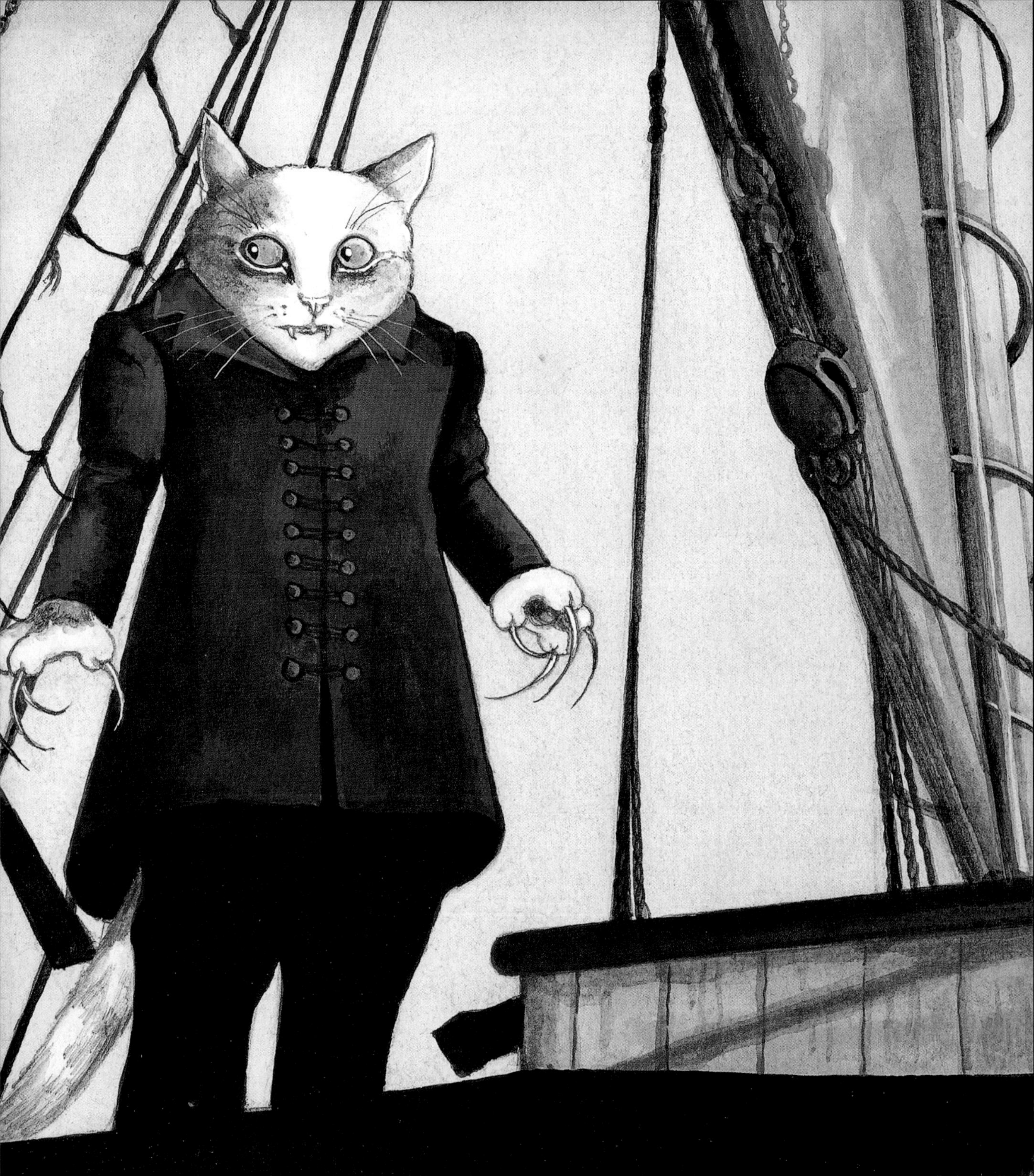

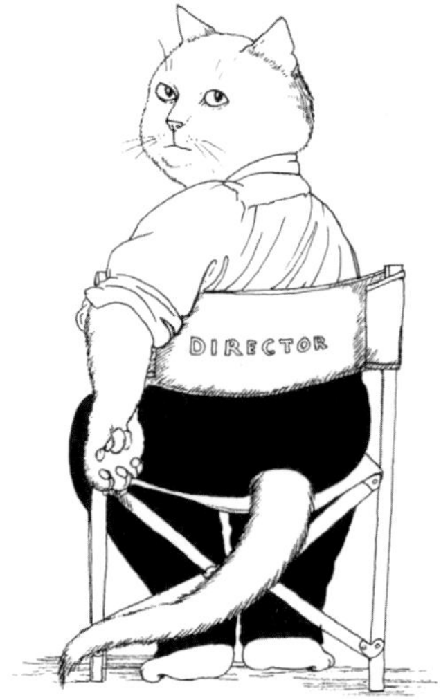

Page 2 HENRI ROUSSEAU, *Self-Portrait* (1890)

Page 4 HAMLET, Act I, Scene II

First published in 2015 in hardcover in the United States of America by Thames & Hudson Inc., 500 Fifth Avenue, New York, New York 10110

thamesandhudsonusa.com

Library of Congress Catalog Card Number 2015932432

ISBN 978-0-500-23936-0

Printed and bound in China by C & C Offset Printing Co. Ltd